The Underground
Railroad in Michigan

To the brave people of Michigan

The Underground Railroad in Michigan

CAROL E. MULL

McFarland & Company, Inc., Publishers
Jefferson, North Carolina, and London

LIBRARY OF CONGRESS CATALOGUING-IN-PUBLICATION DATA

Mull, Carol E., 1952–
The Underground Railroad in Michigan / Carol E. Mull.
p.   cm.
Includes bibliographical references and index.

ISBN 978-0-7864-4638-4
illustrated case binding: 50# alkaline paper ∞

1. Underground Railroad — Michigan.
2. African Americans — Michigan — History —19th century.
3. Fugitive slaves — Michigan — History —19th century.
4. Abolitionists — Michigan — History —19th century.
5. Antislavery movements — Michigan — History —19th century.
6. Michigan — Race relations — History —19th century.
7. Fugitive slaves — United States — History —19th century.
8. Antislavery movements — United States — History — 19th century.
I. Title.
E450.M85   2010   973.7'115 — dc22   2010017191

British Library cataloguing data are available

Illustration from *Narrative of William W. Brown, an American Slave* (1849)

Manufactured in the United States of America

McFarland & Company, Inc., Publishers
Box 611, Jefferson, North Carolina 28640
www.mcfarlandpub.com

Acknowledgments

This book would not have been possible without assistance and support from numerous people and organizations. I began researching the Underground Railroad while working at the Arts of Citizenship Program at the University of Michigan. Involvement in this program fostered an enduring connection with the African American Cultural and Historical Museum of Washtenaw County. The late Willie Edwards was a lovely traveling companion to Buxton, Ontario, and to Chillicothe and Cleveland, Ohio.

Over the past ten years, each research project has increased my understanding of this complex history. Michelle Johnson, Ph.D., past Michigan Freedom Trail Coordinator, and Kidada Williams, Ph.D., were great mentors (projects: "Building Collective Narratives" and "Journey to Freedom Underground Railroad Tours"). I enjoyed my collaborations with the Wild Swan Theater in Ann Arbor. Research on the Underground Railroad in the Flint area received funding from the Ruth Mott Foundation, and CARES of Saline Public Schools supported a study in Washtenaw County. Mary Kerr and Dennis Doyle of the Ann Arbor Area Convention and Visitors Bureau supported several projects. The Rev. Dr. Lottie Jones-Hood and Veta Tucker, A.D., sponsored symposia that brought Underground Railroad scholars together. Students and staff at the Adult Learners Institute of Chelsea offered wonderful encouragement. Authors Karolyn Smardz Frost and Owen Muelder inspired me to seek publication for my work.

I was privileged to earn appointments to the Michigan Freedom Trail Commission by the Honorable John Engler and Jennifer Granholm, former and current governors of the state of Michigan. It has been an honor to work with many dedicated colleagues at the Freedom Trail Commission for the past eight years.

I am grateful to the many friends who have sent articles and documents; Sally Andrews, Nancy Kanniainen, Edwina Morgan, Martha Mull, Janice Webster and many others. I especially want to acknowledge fellow historic preservationists Grace Shackman, Susan Wineberg, Marnie Paulus, Sue Kosky, Patrick McCauley, Ed Rice, Sally Bund, Gladys Saborio, Julie Truettner, and the Eastern Michigan University Historic Preservation Program.

My research could not have been accomplished without the resources and permissions of the University of Michigan Libraries, especially the Bentley Historical Library and the William L. Clements Library. I received invaluable assistance from Karen Jania at the Bentley Historical Library and George Livingston at the Willard Library in Battle Creek. The Rare Books Department of the Boston Public Library helped me locate William Lloyd Garrison's letters from Michigan.

The staff at the Ypsilanti Historical Museum and Fletcher White Archives generously accommodated my research needs. The Burton Historical Collection of the Detroit Public

Library, the Friends Historical Library of Swarthmore College, and the Wilbur H. Siebert Collection of the Ohio Historical Society house rich resources. Additional Michigan libraries whose resources were instrumental include the Ann Arbor District Library, Eastern Michigan University Library, and the public libraries in Ypsilanti, Saline, Milan, Brooklyn, and Manchester. Dr. Charles Lindquist's publications on the Underground Railroad in Lenawee County, Michigan, were also very helpful.

I am especially grateful to all those who shared their personal knowledge and resources: Betty Heap Anderson sent information about her ancestor, Amasa Gillet; Doug Watkins and Laura Watkins-Koelewijn shared records of the Royal Watkins family: descendants of W. W. Harwood, Elizabeth Katz and Janice Harwood, offered family stories; James Smith Benton, descendant of Eli Benton; Marshall D. Hier, descendant of Nancy Beckley Felch, donated Guy Beckley's hymnbook to the African American Museum of Washtenaw County; Dr. Henry Wright of the University of Michigan let me assist in an archaeological dig at the Harwood House; Kel Keller gave me a tour of his Hurd-Nutting house and has been a constant champion; Linda Williams Bowie sent valuable links about the early Arays; Patricia Whitsett, Karmen Brown and all the Aray descendants shared old photographs; Emily Salvette copied original deeds of the Aray family; Jack Kenny photographed the Perry House and uncovered the hiding space; Glenn Curtis invited me to view a very interesting drain or tunnel in his cellar in Belleville; Cathy Horste, John Snyder and Shel Michaels, Rob Roy, Ed Wall, Jerry Hayes, Wayne Clements, John Schaub, the Steinbergs, and Peg Canham also provided valuable information; Justin Blumberg helped with the appendix.

Several online resources were very useful, especially the University of North Carolina's *Documenting the American South*; Cornell University's Samuel J. May Anti-Slavery Collection; the State of Michigan's History, Arts and Libraries website; and the University of Kentucky Libraries. Marsha Todd Stewart is connected to Mecosta's Old Settlers website.

Special thanks to Kjirsten Blander for her editorial assistance. Her skills and talents were critically important and much appreciated.

Most of all, my family has my undying gratitude. Emily and Chris Trentacosta helped me through roadblocks and captions; Patrick Mull and Aerien Kloske created some of the sketches, Hillary Mull provided valuable proofreading, Aron Boros edited and finessed illustrations. My husband Bob, who very generously did everything so that I could research and write full-time for six months, has my love as always.

Table of Contents

Acknowledgments   v

Preface   1

Glossary   5

PART I: SLAVERY, SETTLEMENT, AND THE UNDERGROUND RAILROAD

One.   Underground Railroad Beginnings   7

Two.   Michigan as a Destination and Gateway   16

Three.   Obtaining Freedom in Michigan   27

Four.   Disturbing Influences: Abolitionists   35

Five.   Stations in the Wilderness: A Working System of Assistance   46

Six.   An Interstate Network of Escape   55

Seven.   Persuasion and Politics   69

Eight.   The Port Huron–Pontiac–Detroit Network   76

Nine.   Men of Oppression   83

Ten.   Fractures in the Cause   92

PART II: NEW BEGINNINGS TO END SLAVERY

Eleven.   Southern Men on Northern Soil   105

Twelve.   Trials and Tribulations   116

Thirteen. 1850 Fugitive Slave Act   122

Fourteen. Two Days to Midnight   129

Fifteen.   Colonization of Canada   139

Sixteen.   The Year of John Brown   153

Conclusion   163

Appendix 1: Formerly Enslaved People, Post–Civil War   171

Appendix 2: Underground Railroad Participants   175

Appendix 3: Michigan Underground Railroad Historic Sites   179

Chapter Notes   181

Bibliography   197

Index   205

Preface

In the decades before the Civil War, Michigan played a vital role in the national effort to end slavery. Some antislavery activists expressed their opposition to slavery by helping men and women escape to freedom via the Underground Railroad. From the decades of settlement through the Civil War, Michigan was home to a highly complex and adaptable network of operators assisting freedom seekers. The Underground Railroad is a subject worthy of fresh examination and reevaluation as our nation struggles to understand the complexities of its heritage.

Michigan abolitionists made a deliberate and sustained effort to end slavery. Abolition activity occurred over decades, changing with population shifts, state boundaries, new legislation, and agricultural demands. By the time Michigan achieved statehood in 1837, a rudimentary network for helping people escape from slavery was in working order; however, the published literature rarely provides more than a cursory view of the Underground Railroad in Michigan.[1]

The Underground Railroad remains one of the most significant movements of civil disobedience in our nation's history. While documented accounts of self-emancipation from enslavement are truly compelling, the Underground Railroad is most often presented through fictionalized, mythological stories of escapes. Generalizations about tunnels and quilts engage our attention. Placing the focus on rare objects of popular interest obscures the verifiable history of people and events.[2] It is easy to view the history of slavery in broad brushstrokes of recognizable patterns. But easy isn't honest. Among the hundreds of narratives and biographies cited in this book, not a single one includes any mention of a quilt or lawn jockey, referenced by recent writers as used to guide freedom seekers.[3]

Professor Wilbur Siebert's seminal work, *From Slavery to Freedom* (1898), remains an invaluable source of antislavery activism, recollections, and historical context. Yet, the author admitted his work was inherently flawed by the dearth of first-hand accounts by freedom seekers. A half-century later, Larry Gara criticized histories such as Siebert's that exaggerated northern aide and repeated undocumented legends of nationwide networks of escape. In *The Liberty Line,* Gara questioned the validity of "aged abolitionist" the Rev. H. H. Northrop's testimony, recounted decades after the time of activity, for its lack of objectivity and specific information.[4]

Using its broadest definition, the Underground Railroad included people who may have only once provided a meal or information to forward former slaves to safe places. That one meal may have saved a person from starvation, just as directions to a safe house may have led to a network of stations.

Since 1999, several books have been published that include a broader picture of free-

1

dom seeking in the Midwest. Author Fergus Bordewich pinpoints Detroit as "the most active gateway to Canada."[5] Karolyn Smardz Frost's *I've Got a Home in Glory Land* provides an exhaustively researched story of the Blackburn kidnapping and escape in Detroit. More often, however, one is likely to find only a brief nod to Michigan in recent publications. A guidebook for traveling to 300 North American Underground Railroad sites describes only six places in Michigan.[6]

This book is a documented history of the Underground Railroad in Michigan. It includes an in-depth study of how the antislavery movement intersected with the activity of helping people out of slavery. Intensive research and analysis of archival records, census data, newspapers, and interviews provide a comprehensive understanding of the Underground Railroad in Michigan.

Gateway to Freedom

Families from New York and New England settled much of Southeast Michigan and generally carried with them religious, social, and political beliefs supporting racial tolerance. Free blacks in Detroit gained a national reputation for adroitly transporting freedom seekers beyond the reach of slave catchers. What is less known is that the area southwest of the city is where public discourse and an organized system of helping freedom seekers intersected the national antislavery movement.

Michigan was geographically situated for its significant role as a destination for refugees from bondage and as a gateway to Canada. Of the Northern states offering the promise of safety, Michigan is unique. Michigan's Lower Peninsula is surrounded by three of the Great Lakes: Erie, Huron, and Michigan. Miles of waterways and ports provided an alternative means of escape into Michigan from Ohio, Indiana, Illinois, and Wisconsin. Michigan's eastern cities offered freedom seekers economic opportunities while they were near Canada should sudden flight become necessary. Southwestern Michigan Quaker settlements furnished protection and the opportunity to live independently.

Washtenaw County, in the southeast section of the state, became a hub for men and women opposed to slavery. Their voices aroused public sympathy for the inhumanity of slavery and the injustice of race-based freedoms. Their protests were not always welcomed. Yet, at this place a group of men and women gathered together to form a state antislavery society, publish an antislavery newspaper, and begin a campaign of public persuasion.

Slavery, Settlement and the Underground Railroad

Part I of this book provides the national and regional context for examining Michigan's unique role during the most active decades of verifiable escapes from bondage. Stories of escapes preceding each chapter relate to the way Michigan's citizens responded to slavery on their own soil. From the time of settlement in Michigan, individuals expressed opposition to slavery. White and black communities were involved in several early escapes and remained so as the Underground Railroad took shape in the 1830s. At the same time, some men opposed to slavery put their energy into creating change through a political process, while others preached to the goodness of man. In the 1840s, at least one interstate Underground Railroad system was deliberately established, while others evolved. Blacks in Michigan organized conventions in response to continued oppression but still faced kidnappings and enslavement.

Part II explores the incidents leading to the passage of the 1850 Fugitive Slave Act and its impact on the Underground Railroad network, freedom seekers, and the effort to end slavery. Accounts of escape and settlement provide an understanding of the workings of the Underground Railroad in the Midwest from the 1850s until the start of the Civil War. Diligent research presents a cadre of helpers beyond the Quaker settlements, from rural farms to free black communities and into the halls of justice.

Finally, the conclusion examines the motivations of people engaged in an unpopular and costly struggle to end slavery. It explores the decision to risk life and sacrifice personal relationships in order to break the shackles that bound a person in slavery. The conclusion offers a consideration of whether there existed religious, social or political commonalities among the diverse group of Underground Railroad helpers. This book informs the reader about the significant role of Michigan's citizens in the national effort to end slavery.

Author's Note

The larger purpose in revealing stories of Underground Railroad participants is to connect our past to our present and future. Our ancestors debated issues and defied unjust laws. Powerless citizens spoke out for equal representation and opportunities. Still, issues of racial disparity and discrimination persist in challenging us. Emancipation did not come about by happenstance but by the efforts of men and women seeking true democracy and free enterprise. The lessons of history, the factual stories of our forbears' missteps and forward strides empower us to face our current social and political issues.

This book is not the final chapter but a starting place for people and communities to discover local documents and stories in Michigan. I spent four years exhaustively researching Underground Railroad history connected to Washtenaw County and have shared my

SOUTHERN MICHIGAN COUNTIES

Counties of the southern portion of the lower peninsula of Michigan, as divided in the 20th century.

findings in lectures, classes, and presentations. Subsequent research for this book revealed accounts and biographies describing Underground Railroad activity in the settled areas of the state — at the time, predominantly, the southern portion of the Lower Peninsula.

It is very likely there were pockets of activity and maroon settlements all along Michigan's coastline and in the Upper Peninsula. I hope I have provided the names, links, and resources for others to take up intensive research across the entire State of Michigan. I look forward to the discovery of this history.

For historical accuracy it is necessary to use the factual names of organizations and actual words in quoted passages. Black men and women of the antebellum period often chose "colored" in reference to their schools and organizations. Other words used in quotes and titles might be offensive today. They are included as part of the verifiable record. As the author, I regret any offense taken from the use of these terms.

Glossary

Underground Railroad scholars realize many words used in the past do not accurately reflect our history. For instance, "fugitive" was used to describe someone escaping from slavery, although this person was not breaking the laws in the Northern states that outlawed slavery. The term "freedom seeker" more accurately describes the self-emancipator.

Slaveholders referred to slavery as an "institution" in order to dehumanize withholding the rights of men, women, and children. From the 1800s, the Underground Railroad often used terms similar to those used by railroaders: agents, conductors, track, rails, etc. This led to some confusion, especially after locomotive and railcars were utilized during escapes.

Abolitionist: a person who advocated for the end of slavery, ranging from a gradual process (a gradualist) to the radical who wanted an immediate end with equal rights for blacks (an immediate emancipationist).

Agent: someone who provided assistance to freedom seekers. This person may or may not have been an opponent of slavery. An agent may have provided food, clothing, transportation or shelter.

Colonization: a movement to take people out of slavery in America to freedom in Africa.

Conductor: someone who led freedom seekers from place to place. Early Underground Railroad terms related to jobs on railroads. See Agent.

Free black: a person of African descent who was not enslaved. Some free blacks were never enslaved; others were manumitted (provided legal freedom from slavery).

Freedom seeker: a person who escapes the institution of slavery by flight. This flight was not always north and was usually unaided until reaching a Northern state. *Escapee, runaway*, and *fugitive* were terms used in the 1800s.

Fugitive: used to describe someone who escaped from slavery. This negative term was used to imply that this person broke the law, even in free states where slaveholding was forbidden.

Maroon colony: an isolated community settled by freedom seekers.

Master: the male (Mistress for female) owner, recognized by law, of a person held in slavery during the antebellum period.

Self-emancipated: not legally freed from enslavement by an owner or the legal system, but by one's own determination.

Slave hunter: also known as a slave catcher or bounty hunter, this person sought freedom seekers for reward money. Free blacks were sometimes kidnapped and sold.

Slave patroller: a person who rode in Southern areas looking for any black person without a pass (a written note of permission to travel without supervision).

Stock: faith or belief in the abolitionist cause. Stockholders donated food, money, or clothing.

Underground Railroad: broadly used to refer to the means by which those escaping, and those helping them, effected their flight. Though the term was coined in the 1830s, today it encompasses all manner of flight from an earlier time until slavery ended. Many of the enslaved escaped without help.

Chapter One

Underground Railroad Beginnings

Escape of Saby, Isom, and Nancy

Saby did not fully rejoice in the birth of her child. That privilege belonged to another race of people whose babes would not be snatched from their mother's breast and sold away. Saby and Isom, her chosen husband, held no legal rights to their daughter, Nancy. Nancy, by birthright, was the property of Saby's Master, who might sell any of his commodities at a moment's notice.

One night in 1829, Saby and Isom carried Nancy across the Ohio River from Kentucky to the state of Indiana. On the northern shore, they left behind the fetters that bound them to the whims and punishing of a master. Forty miles through the wilderness lay the town of Brookville, nestled in a valley between two forks of the Whitewater River. Naturally carved cliffs surrounded the dell, creating an illusion of protection. When Saby and her loved ones met other black Americans, they found a place to call home.

Unexpectedly, Saby was kidnapped and taken south. Somehow, "certain" men soon rescued her. Back in Brookville, the black settlers considered their situation in Indiana, especially the proslavery sentiment of the majority of their neighbors and the proximity of enemies south of the Ohio River. Saby and Isom, and nearly a dozen other self-freed people, decided to pack their possessions for Canada.

Their journey to freedom could only be accomplished with a guide. Sprinkled throughout the Northwest Territory were Quakers who had moved north, mostly from North Carolina, under persecution for emancipating their enslaved. Quakers were a minority in southern Indiana where Chesapeake Valley immigrants (from Maryland, Delaware and Virginia) considered slavery an accepted institution.

Frederic Hoover, described as "an earnest advocate of the abolition of slavery," led the freedom seekers and recorded the journey. The Quaker farmer guided the group from Brookville to Richmond, Indiana.

After stopping in Richmond, Hoover directed them north to the outskirts of Fort Wayne, Indiana. The fledgling town contained fort blockades and palisades and a small village. Hoover's group was afraid to move forward and entreated the Quakers escorting them to appeal to the townspeople to let them continue north unmolested. On October 10, 1829, a "strange and motley company" of blacks and whites passed through the streets of Fort Wayne, Indiana.

The group camped on the banks of the Maumee River where songs of praise for their deliverance resounded in the wilderness. Next, they trekked east into Defiance, Ohio, where Edward Howard and the Ottawa Indians of the Maumee Valley were early friends to people on the road to freedom.[1]

The freedom seekers entered the Territory of Michigan at the town of Monroe (French-town), an early French trading post. Prominent men in the village held antislavery convictions, including Colonel Oliver Johnson, judge of the Probate Court. An organizer of the First Presbyterian Church of Monroe (1820), the Rev. John Monteith was known for helping enslaved people escape.

Saby and friends encountered no obstacles in Michigan. They reached Detroit, and then passed safely to Canada. Thousands followed similar paths to Detroit, the city called "Midnight," gateway to Canada. Saby and Isom's journey was one of the first recorded interstate escapes on the Underground Railroad.[2]

SABY ESCAPE

.... Saby Escape Route

As early as the 1820s, Quakers led men and women escaping slavery across state lines. Saby, Isom, and Nancy crossed to Canada at Detroit in 1829 (sketch by Aerien Kloske, 2009).

Underground Railroad Beginnings

The origin of the Underground Railroad will remain forever unknown. Though fraught with difficulty, men and women escaped from slavery during the earliest years of settlement in America. In the 1600s, running away occurred with sufficient frequency to prompt passage of Colonial Acts allowing for the legal return of those owing labor or service. At the same time, some people sought to end slavery in America. From New York to Tennessee, some men and women emancipated their own slaves and formed manumission societies to encourage others to do likewise.

A person escaping slavery might find food and shelter at the door of a stranger, but more often at an enslaved person's cabin. Eventually aid became organized in some places, though it was often a spontaneous response to an unanticipated occurrence. By the 1700s, the refugee from bondage found places of safety among religious groups, maroon colonies of formerly enslaved people, and urban areas with free black populations. After the Revolutionary War, though loosely organized, small networks of people actively helped the freedom seeker travel to these places. This was the beginning of the Underground Railroad.

Slavery Described

Where slavery existed, there were enslaved people who resisted it. In the decades before slavery was legally recognized, blacks and whites worked equally as indentured servants in colonial America. After a certain number of years, their service was completed and they were free to purchase their own land. In 1640, two African servants in Virginia ran away and were punished with a lifetime of servitude. Gradually, the pressing need for agricultural labor led landowners to view African enslavement as a solution.

Samuel Gorton, president of the Providence Plantation in Rhode Island, wrote in 1651 that the same rules should apply to English and African servants. Few supported his view. Massachusetts was the first colony to legally recognize slavery, but Virginia would follow suit with a law that children born of enslaved mothers would be enslaved. Gradually, slavery evolved from labor performed over definite periods of time to a lifelong, inheritable condition inflicted on people of African descent.[3]

Most Europeans chose to immigrate to America, some willing to spend years in servitude to pay their passage. Men, women, and children of Africa were kidnapped, forced aboard slave ships, and, if they survived, sold into a lifetime of work with no promise of freedom in America. The slave owner controlled the most intimate aspects of a human life, from sexual relations and marriage to work and survival. In response to oppression and abuse, some of the enslaved resisted through large- and small-scale rebellions, from work slowdowns to poisonings, arsons, and murders. The response to an infraction was spelled out in state slave codes.

Blacks outnumbered whites in the Carolinas during the early 1700s and were subjected to harsh slave codes, statutes regulating the behavior of owner and human property. During the Stono Rebellion near Charleston in 1739, nearly 100 enslaved men and women killed over a dozen white people. The rebellion was thereafter used as an argument to impose new restrictions. Northern colonies were not immune from violence. Both free and enslaved blacks populated cities up and down the eastern seaboard, agitating for rights and creating rebellions.[4]

Numerous scholarly works reference the scope of laws intended to limit the activities of those in bondage and allow for their legal punishment. William Goodell described how slaveholders meted out punishment so severe that it was necessary to distinguish what was considered cruel. For instance, in South Carolina in 1740, cruelty included severing limbs, castration, and cutting out a tongue, crimes which resulted in only a possible fine for the slave owner.[5]

There was no condition of race in the 1776 Declaration of Independence phrase "all men are created equal." However, stakeholders in the South ensured through legislation that men, women, and children bound by slavery, and free people of color, would not be treated equally. As plantation owners increased their dependence on labor-intensive crops, they needed larger numbers of slaves to work those crops. With the demand for wearisome manual labor came the threat of resistance and rebellion. The system of slavery became even more entrenched as large plantation owners pressed for laws to regulate their unpaid work force, which in turn incited greater resistance.

With little prospect of being granted freedom, some enslaved men and women attempted escape. Before slavery was abolished in northern states, running away more often involved a temporary relocation to a neighboring plantation, an urban area with a free black population, or a remote and unsettled region. Though enslaved people might learn by word of mouth that they could run away to swamps in Florida or unsettled regions in the west, severe beatings and lynching served as strong deterrents. In addition, the decision to sever family connections by leaving permanently often seemed less desirable than an uncertain future of slavery.

Slavery in the Colonies

Most colonists generally ignored the oppressed pleas of those in bondage on American soil until the decades before the Revolutionary War. Slavery was prohibited in Vermont from its inception in 1777, but other states were reluctant to recognize the liberty of blacks. In 1779, three enslaved people in Fairfield County filed a petition to the state of Connecticut for the abolition of slavery. The petitioners wrote that while their skin was a different color, they perceived in themselves faculties equal to those they were obliged to serve. The petition was rejected.[6]

Amid the rallying chants for freedom from British rule rang the false echo of men and women denied rights in American households. At least one abolitionist society was formed as early as 1775: The Pennsylvania Society for Promoting the Abolition of Slavery, the Relief of Free Negroes Unlawfully Held in Bondage, and for Improving the Condition of the African Race. Legislation was introduced in both northern and southern states to abolish slavery, but there would be no widespread movement to manumit [free from servitude] slaves until after the Revolutionary War in 1783.[7]

After America won its independence from Britain, it struggled for basic needs amid a post-war economic depression. Nevertheless, states revised or created new constitutions. Pennsylvania abolished slavery and most New England states legislated slavery's gradual end, but the legal lifetime enslavement of black Americans in southern states continued.

During the summer of 1787, the Continental Congress endeavored to establish provisions for a unified government, but the issue of slavery blocked every action toward unification. Southern plantation owners relied on an unpaid workforce, believing it critical to their economic prosperity. Total emancipation was not a popular idea in America. Who could answer how more than a half-million newly freed slaves would find work in a nation where 80 percent of householders were farmers?[8]

In the midst of creating a national government, Continental Congress delegates passed legislation opening up new land. The Northwest Ordinance of July 13, 1787, included the provision that prohibited enslaving humans in what would become Ohio, Michigan, Indiana, Illinois, and Wisconsin. That the federal government established a free territory during this tumultuous time is remarkable. Perhaps southern delegates, hearing of this untamed wilderness, foresaw no threat to the institution of slavery since the ordinance included another provision allowing for the lawful claim of any person owing labor or service.[9]

Convention delegates thwarted the move toward equality in America when they signed the U.S. Constitution on September 17, 1787. In order to form a Union, a "Great Compromise" allowed for the recognition of slavery as an institution in the South and included a promise not to interfere with the slave trade for twenty years.[10]

In New York, free blacks were able to vote after 1777 if they qualified as property owners. However, in 1785, a new statute restricted blacks from voting. Progress toward racial equality reversed itself with racial prejudice.

Men and women, captured after running away, were often punished and sent to auction houses to be sold. The Old Slave Mart, a surviving slave trading center, originally included a jail, kitchen and morgue. Currently, the Mart is a museum interpreting the system of selling two million people during the antebellum period (2007 author photograph, 6 Chalmers Street, Charleston, South Carolina).

Legislation prompted some northerners to push for laws leading to a total abolition of slavery and equal rights for all citizens. In Philadelphia, the Free African Society (1787), founded by James Dexter, Richard Allen, and Absalom Jones, was the first black mutual aid association. Antislavery societies were formed in Rhode Island and Connecticut in 1789 and 1790. South Carolina prohibited importing slaves in 1787 and tobacco production declined. The decreased need for a large agricultural work force led some to believe that a gradual extinction of slavery was a possibility.[11]

The invention of the cotton gin and the purchase of Louisiana changed the course of events in the South. Cotton became the dominant crop and southerners needed more slaves and a means of keeping them in the fields from sunup to sundown. Southern politicians pressed for a national law to retrieve "property," referring to self-freed people. The individual state laws of Virginia and North Carolina were insufficient to stem the trickling of disappearances among the slave population. Demand for a fugitive law exposed the problem of permanent escapes and belied dubious claims that the enslaved were contented living without rights and freedom.

The 1793 Fugitive Slave Law granted a slaveholder the right to seize a freedom seeker and prove before the local authority that the person was a fugitive from labor. In addition, the law included a fine of $500 for anyone obstructing the claimant and it infringed on the freedom from slavery in the Northwest Territory.[12]

The Fugitive Slave Law had the effect of spurring various antislavery groups to consolidate their efforts. Representatives from several northern states and Virginia met at a convention in Philadelphia in 1798 with the goals to educate blacks and to protest importing Africans into slavery. Theodore Foster of Providence, Rhode Island, served as chairman. Foster's sons followed his example after migrating to Michigan where they were leaders in the abolition movement and part of the Underground Railroad.[13]

Opposition to the Fugitive Slave Law occurred in slave and non-slave territory. Antislavery societies formed in southern states, as well as in the North. The issue of slavery was extremely divisive, leading to the fracture of social, political, and religious organizations. One of the first groups to split over slavery was the Religious Society of Friends (Quakers). The predominantly Quaker Pennsylvania Abolition Society promoted abolition from the time of its founding in 1784, and some members of the group chose an active role in resisting slavery by aiding escaping slaves.

The Rev. Charles Osborn, called by some the founder of the abolitionist movement, moved to Tennessee in 1803 where he began agitating for the end of slavery. A national form of resistance among Quakers involved moving with slaves they owned (or purchased in order to free) from the South to the North where the enslaved were then freed. Many Quakers settled in Indiana and Ohio between 1806 and 1819.[14] Osborn and the Swain brothers founded the Tennessee Manumission Society in 1815 and then oversaw its quick growth into branches with 500 members. Osborn moved north, like many active abolitionists, where he created a safe haven for hundreds of self-emancipated men and women.[15]

Another abolitionist in Tennessee was forced to leave the state after expressing his deepening antislavery views. The Reverend Rankin found himself welcomed to preach in Carlisle, Kentucky. In Kentucky, as early as 1807, churches withdrew from their parent organizations over slavery and formed Emancipation Baptist Churches. Soon members formed the Kentucky Abolition Society. Rankin started a school to educate the enslaved, but the students were repeatedly mobbed and beaten. The Reverend Rankin moved his family across the Ohio River to Ripley, Ohio. From his new home, Rankin wrote letters to his slaveholding brother that would be reprinted in 1825 as *Rankin's Letters on Slavery.*[16]

In 1810, at least five southern states counted the enslaved in the 100,000s and passed increasingly stringent laws forcing black Americans into a lifetime of bondage. In the north, New Jersey and New York each held over 10,000 people in slavery and Pennsylvania, nearly 800. Northern states continued to profit from slave importation by manufacturing goods out of products grown in the south, especially textiles from cotton.[17]

Slavery and Resistance in the Northwest Territory

In February 1788, Arthur St. Clair was appointed the first governor of the Northwest Territory. He spoke frequently against the extension of slavery, as in this speech delivered in Cincinnati:

> Let them say what they will about Republicans, a man who is willing to entail slavery upon any part of God's creation is no friend to the rational happiness of any, and had he the power, would as readily enslave his neighbors as the poor black that has been torn from his country and friends.[18]

The early history of slavery and freedom in the place that would become Michigan is revealed through the life of a girl called Lisette.

Elizabeth (Lisette) Denison was born into slavery around 1787 in the British-ruled "Indiana Territory." William Tucker purchased Lisette's parents, Peter and Hannah Denison, during the 1780s in Detroit where slavery had long been practiced in the area. From 1610 to 1763, both Native Americans and the French who governed the trading posts in the Great Lakes area enslaved people.

The Denisons might have expected William Tucker to be sympathetic to the plight of those held in lifetime bondage. In Virginia in 1754, Chippewa Indians attacked and killed Tucker's father and then kidnapped William and his brother. Held captive in the Michigan Territory, William was given his freedom at the age of 18. His brother did not survive.[19]

Apparently, Tucker had no qualms about holding people against their will because he did not grant the Denisons their freedom after the passage of the Northwest Ordinance of 1787, which forbade slavery in the Northwest Territory. The Denisons and other enslaved blacks in Detroit remained bound by the British who controlled the region. In 1795, the Jay Treaty established protection of property, including human property, before the British agreed to surrender the territory to the United States in 1796.

Baby Lisette, born to an enslaved mother, was Tucker's legal property; even if she had been born on the Canadian side of the Detroit River, she would have faced a life of slavery. The Canadian Parliament directed by law that no one could be enslaved after 1792, and those in bondage would be free at age 25.[20]

In 1805, Congress declared Michigan a territory and Detroit the territorial seat. As a result of his service as interpreter for the Native Americans in negotiating land sales, William Tucker was awarded hundreds of acres along the Clinton River at Anchor Bay, Lake St. Clair, north of Detroit.[21] Tucker moved the Denison family to his large farm, but he soon died. The Denisons may have been promised freedom, but Tucker's will manumitted Peter and Hannah, not their children. The only hope for Lisette and her siblings was to challenge the slave law in the courts.

In 1806, Detroit attorney Elijah Brush leased Lisette's parents from Catherine Tucker,

William's widow. The following year, Brush brought a case before the Michigan Supreme Court on behalf of Elizabeth (Lisette) Denison and her brothers. The case was presented to Augustus B. Woodward, an abolitionist, appointed by fellow Virginian Thomas Jefferson as Chief Justice of the Michigan Territory.

Judge Woodward did not grant Lisette immediate freedom but did establish gradual emancipation rules that granted freedom to children of slaves. A month after the Denison decision, in October 1807, Woodward's ruling in another case assured that slavery ended in the Michigan Territory. Several French families moved with their slaves from Michigan to Canada after the British surrendered the Michigan Territory. Some of these enslaved people returned to Michigan and claimed their freedom under American laws.

On this basis, two "slaveholders" petitioned the territorial court to have nine slaves who moved to Michigan restored to them in Canada. Judge Woodward ruled that no law allowed for this recovery of "property," that every "man coming into this Territory is by law of the land a freeman."

Lisette freed herself by moving to Upper Canada (the southern portion of Ontario) where Canadian courts, in retaliation for Woodward's ruling, refused to return American slaves.[22] Within a decade, Lisette crossed back to Detroit, was gainfully employed, and purchased land in Pontiac. Lisette married Scipio Forth in 1827. The Tucker homestead in Harrison Township remained in the family into the 19th century. An ordinary brick façade hides the pioneer log house and conceals its association with a landmark territorial slavery case.[23]

The black population in Michigan increased very slowly over the next twenty years. The 1810 census showed that of the 4,618 people in Michigan, 144 blacks resided predominantly in the southeast counties. Blacks established a community in Detroit with an opportunity for education. One of the first organizations in the frontier town was the Sunday School Association, formed in 1818, to promote reading and Christian ideals for all races. In 1819, of 150 students, 22 were of color (which may have included native Americans, among the black students). The school reported great success in spite of limited resources and books. The following year there were 19 scholars of color among 160 students. Eventually, the interracial school was transferred to the Presbyterians.[24]

Since Canada began phasing out slavery in 1793, men and women crossed over the border with regularity. Some black veterans of the War of 1812 returned from Canada to spread the word about a haven to escape slavery. Americans fled in numbers sufficient to prompt Secretary of State Henry Clay to press the British government to surrender formerly enslaved Americans in 1826. Articles about Clay's unsuccessful requests appeared in the nation's first African-American newspaper, *Freedom's Journal.*[25]

Wayne County was not the only early place of refuge in Michigan. In the southeast corner of the state, Monroe was an early French trading post and settlement. It was the place where Saby and Isom passed through on their way to Canada. In 1827, Virginians Price and Allen rode into town with a black man seized from the town of Waterloo. When brought before Colonel Peter P. Ferry, Justice of the Peace, the Virginians were prevented from taking their "fugitive," but also ordered to jail. Col. Ferry kept the Virginians behind bars for months until the next court session where they produced "questionable" documents, and were sent home properly dissuaded from setting foot in Monroe in the future.[26]

On April 13, 1827, the Michigan Territorial government enacted "An Act to Regulate Blacks and Mulattoes, and to Punish the Kidnapping of Such Persons." The separate discriminatory laws for black citizens, enacted in many states, were known as Black Codes. In

Michigan, the law required black citizens to register with county sheriffs, pay a $500 bond guaranteeing good behavior. The law was generally ignored and amended in 1828 to allow evictions from the state for non-compliance. It appears not to have been obeyed in Michigan.[27] However, enforcement of the Black Codes in Ohio stimulated an exodus of many free and self-freed blacks to Canada West, where the Wilberforce Settlement was established.

Though Detroit claimed fewer than 2,000 residents in the late 1820s, there were many willing to prevent the re-capture of a self-freed person. In mid–December 1828, Ezekiel K. Hudnell of Kentucky proved his right to possess four self-emancipated men before Michigan's Wayne County Court. Hudnell was issued a certificate by Justice of the Peace John McDonnell allowing him to return two men, Daniel and Ben, to Kentucky. For an unknown reason, Hudnell's attorney suggested the Territorial Governor Lewis Cass confirm the certificate.

In Cass' absence, Secretary of the Territory James Witherell received the papers but did not immediately sign them. The Kentuckians waited for the certificate as Sheriff Thomas Sheldon noted a "large number of runaway slaves" gathering. Fearing an armed rescue of Daniel and Ben, the Kentucky entourage hastened about 15 miles downriver where they could get passage south. During the night, while the Kentucky slave hunters played cards, Ben and Daniel escaped to a nearby island. It is likely the men took off from Wyandotte, made their way to Grosse Isle and crossed by skiff to Amherstburg, Ontario, Canada.

On January 6, 1829, in the Commonwealth of Kentucky, Harrisons County, Ezekiel Hudnell filed an affidavit against James Witherell. Though it is not known whether he intentionally or neglectfully failed to sign the certificate, Witherell's delay did allow for Daniel and Ben to be rescued. It also cost him his job, as President Andrew Jackson did not re-appoint Witherell in 1830.[28]

Chapter Two

Michigan as a Destination and Gateway

Escape of William Davis and Mr. Granger

Solon Goodell wondered why strange wagons, brought from Adrian, Michigan, were left in the family's barn. His father, Jotham, would enter the barn to find at times an old, covered lynchpin wagon. Shrouded by canvas and hidden by hay, two or three people lay waiting for discovery by friend or foe. Near the end of a terrifying escape to freedom, every minute must have seemed an intolerable age of fear and uncertainty.

The Goodell farm, in Washtenaw County, lay on the south side of the State Road to Detroit, later known as Geddes Road. Goodell purchased his land in 1826 and moved from Jefferson County, New York. The area was amenable for farming with the flowing waters of the Huron and lower Rouge Rivers for irrigation, and a road to carry produce to market—and humans to freedom. Jotham Goodell usually put the freedom seekers in the grain crib where they were unlikely to be discovered.

When the time for safe passage arrived, Goodell secreted them under his produce and drove his wagon east toward Lake Erie. Only a few miles along Geddes Road, they crossed from Washtenaw into Wayne County. It was an eight mile journey on Michigan Avenue to Inkster where Henry Ruff Road lay east of Merriman. Goodell usually drove the wagon to "Rough's Hotel" where the self-emancipated men and women were transferred under Goodell's watchful eye onto transport bound for Trenton, Michigan. From there they were ferried across the river to Canada.

If Goodell were away from home, the travelers might have been left at the farm of a neighbor. Two pioneers in Superior Township, Ira Camp and Joseph Fowler, helped from their homes on Geddes Road.[1] Camp came from New York with his wife and two children in 1826, raised two additional children, and remained on the farm 39 years. Camp served as Justice of the Peace in 1837 and was known as an "honorable and hard-working man."[2]

To the east, Goodell's nearest neighbor was Walter Watson in Canton Township, Wayne County, Michigan.

Solon described his father not as a church-going man, but an enthusiastic abolitionist. Solon remembered the names of two who stayed at his family's farm. William Davis and Mr. Granger went on to Canada and returned to Superior Township before the Civil War. William Davis, in turn, helped Henry Smith escape and settle nearby in York Township, Washtenaw County.[3]

Michigan, by its geographical site, was poised to be a destination and gateway to freedom. If a different sort of people settled the state it would not have become a critical axis of the Underground Railroad and the movement to end slavery. From the 1820s through the 1830s, there were three groups of men and women who shaped the antislavery movement and fostered the development of an Underground Railroad network in Michigan: antislavery town founders from New England, Quakers and missionaries, and black Americans. Members of these groups were a small minority of the population, but significant in their influence and humanity. This chapter will explore Michigan's place in North America, the town founders and religious leaders, and will examine one county as an example of early settlement and abolitionism in southeast Michigan.

Geography and boundaries were critical to American slavery. With water and free states on its perimeter, Michigan experienced few forays by slave hunters who were rarely, if ever, successful. While the Mason-Dixon line was the delineator between slave and free states, the Canadian border, and a foreign government, marked the crossing to permanent freedom. Southern politicians pressed, to no avail, for an extradition treaty with Great Britain for returning freedom seekers.

Pioneer Settlement and Abolition

The role of the earliest pioneers in organizing racially tolerant communities may be specific to Michigan. Many antislavery-minded New Englanders were Michigan's first permanent settlers. Others migrated further west after participating in antislavery disputes in Ohio. There is strong evidence from an intensive study of Washtenaw County, that antislavery town founders influenced future immigration and expanded the network of safe passage for freedom seekers.

"Midnight" was the code name for Detroit, the most important gateway to Canada on the Underground Railroad. This 1852 sketch shows the view from the shore of freedom in Sandwich, Ontario, Canada (Bentley Historical Library, University of Michigan: Bentley Image Bank, BL004050).

Though most of Michigan's first land patentees were agricultural colonists emigrating from New York, many were native New Englanders. Heavy rains, flooding, and crop-damaging weather throughout New England in the years following 1810 caused an exodus to newly opened land in western New York, and many left family farms where land could no longer be divided among successive generations. Massachusetts, Connecticut, New Jersey, and other states gave up their children to New York.

Unfortunately, the immigrants from New England experienced similar poor weather conditions and crop failures in New York. Perhaps the harshness of life led some to embrace the new theology of the Second Great Awakening. Evangelist Charles Grandison Finney proclaimed in a series of revivals that both self-improvement and choosing the path to salvation would create a perfect world for the Second Coming of Christ. Most Americans did not participate in the Second Great Awakening, but the movement extended across Genesee County, New York, throughout the 1820s. The Genesee area would be forever known as the "Burned over District," for the evangelized masses who swept across the region.

Finney preached many reforms, for he believed all aspects of society must be orderly and right. Drunkenness, illiteracy, and slavery were issues of immediate concern and the movement to reform these social evils ignited and inflamed the North. These new ideas appealed to moralistic New Englanders who carried their religious fever and reform impulse with them as they moved to the western wilderness.[4]

The Finney disciples of upstate New York created a singular path of migration west. They hugged the southern shore of Lake Erie on an overland trail across northern Ohio, Michigan, Indiana, and Illinois. The New Englanders settled the northern regions of the Midwest states.

The stream of settlers into the southern portions of Ohio, Indiana, and Illinois trekked westward from the Chesapeake Valley/Pennsylvania region on land routes. Many left the shores of Maryland and Delaware, crossed over the Appalachian Mountains, and settled the fertile flatlands of the Midwest. Except for some people moving north because of their opposition to slavery, the pioneers of southern Ohio, Indiana and Illinois were different from their northern neighbors. The regions' distinctions became apparent as people escaping slavery journeyed north.

Cultural geographers like Pierce Lewis characterized Pennsylvania's settlers as religiously tolerant people who valued both individual freedoms and the opportunity to make money. These ideas contrasted with the Puritan's notions of conformity and community building. Lewis observed that the upper Great Lakes states became a "vast Yankee preserve" but not the southern parts of Ohio, Indiana, and Illinois.[5]

The opening of the Erie Canal in 1825 allowed a tide of immigration into Michigan. Most immigrants from New York and Ohio arrived in the port of Detroit. In 1818, the *Walk-in-the-Water* was the first steamboat on Lake Erie to arrive from Buffalo, New York. The Erie Canal provided an easy migration path to New Englanders through New York. New Englanders and their descendants were estimated to account for two-thirds of Michigan's population before it became a state in 1837.[6]

The area's first settlers surveyed the wilderness in search of a worthy home. An early settler described the process with a necessary dose of humor.

> The emigrants who, in the old days, first left Detroit, took a rough road westward, that led to a rude settlement in the woods. Beyond this they found a mere indistinct wagon track that led to a log cabin among the trees; from the cabin they followed a foot-path that led to a log barn, and from that a squirrel track that went up a tree.[7]

Locating a good site, the pioneers rushed to land offices in Detroit and Monroe, Michigan, to stake their claims. The town founders, early ministers, and African-Americans who came to Michigan in the 1820s and 1830s influenced the settlement of those who would follow—a story told repeatedly in county histories. Pioneers came alone, as a single or nucleated family, and sometimes with an entire church congregation. In 1824 a Quaker enticed a group from New York to settle the town of Tecumseh in Lenawee County. The following year, Darius Comstock of Niagara County, New York, purchased a tract of land in the River Raisin Valley midway between Tecumseh and Adrian. His son, Addison J. Comstock, purchased four hundred eighty acres of government land in 1825 and laid out the village of Adrian, a town that was to become a major stop in the Underground Railroad network.

Settlers solicited preachers, attempting to gather together an assembly to support a minister and finance church-building. In Detroit, the Rev. John Monteith formed the first nondenominational Protestant Society in 1818. A year later, a Presbyterian church was built at the corner of Larned Street and Woodward Avenue. The Reverend Monteith, an Underground Railroad agent, also helped found a church in Monroe, where Saby and Isom passed through.

Most early colonists purchased cheap land west of Detroit in western Wayne and Oakland Counties creating towns reminiscent of the places they left behind in New York. Some families sold their cleared and cultivated plots at a profit so they could start the process over again farther west on bigger parcels. Erastus Hussey, well-known leader of the abolitionist movement and Underground Railroad in Battle Creek, Michigan, first bought land on the outskirts of Detroit in 1824. Born in Cayuga County, New York, in 1800, Hussey became a resident of Plymouth, Michigan, in 1826 and took an active part in community affairs as highway commissioner, school inspector, and assessor. Like many others, Hussey sold out and moved farther west, once again becoming an early townsperson. An existing Native American pathway known as the Great Sauk Trail was a vital road for European Americans settling southeastern, and later, southwestern Michigan and Illinois. Linking Detroit and Chicago, in 1830 it was called the Chicago Military Road and later the Chicago Turnpike. A parallel road north of this led to Battle Creek. Hussey remained in Battle Creek where he became a successful merchant and helped over 1,000 freedom seekers.[8]

In 1826, Glode D. Chubb was the first to purchase land in Nankin (later Plymouth, Wayne County, Michigan). Marcus Swift arrived from Palmyra, New York, in 1825, settling on 160-acres in what would become Garden City, where he founded a church made up of abolitionists.

Additionally, some of Michigan's foreign-born citizens were strong abolitionists. General John E. Schwarz served as adjutant general of the territorial militia in 1831 and also held distinguished political positions. In 1852, he moved to western Wayne County where he platted the village of Schwarzburg. Here the Austrian-born military leader retired, but he discovered a new use for his skills as an Underground Railroad agent. Researcher Dr. Siebert wrote the name "Schwarz" in large letters on a map of the Michigan Underground Railroad network. This town on the Middle Rouge River near Nankin Mills was eventually absorbed by Livonia.[9]

One couple who arrived in Detroit in 1835, William and Caroline Kirkland, moved to Livingston County, Michigan, in 1837, for the purpose of creating a frontier town. The adventure failed when the nation experienced a financial crisis at that time. However, antislavery men benefited from William Kirkland's help writing their society's founding papers.

From their town of Pinckney, Caroline Kirkland wrote, *A New Home—Who'll Follow?*, a popular literary success. Jacob Merritt Howard moved to Detroit in 1832, was admitted to the bar, and commenced practicing law the following year. He rose from Detroit city attorney to the State House of Representatives and continued to have a stellar political career. Secretly, he was an Underground Railroad operator.[10] Zachariah Chandler, Josiah Begole, and other early politicians were known to be sympathetic to the antislavery cause.

On the western side of the state, the experience of early pioneers influencing future settlement may have occurred to a greater degree. After all, the pioneers were cut off from cities by poor roads and were more dependent on each other for survival. Of the early settlers, William Baldwin Jenkins was the second pioneer in all of Cass County. After surveying the Pokagon Prairie, he returned in 1825 as a generous host to home-seekers. Jenkins was born into an antislavery family that moved to Ohio to avoid slavery. When he was appointed Justice of the Peace, his territory included everything west of Lenawee County.

Jenkins was one of many early pioneers who swayed future settlement through influential political and judicial positions. As a State constitutional delegate and associate judge, Jenkins' opinions helped shape Michigan's legal system.[11]

Religious Settlements and Circuit Preachers

The Methodist Episcopal Church sent circuit riders to Michigan as early as 1810. The reverends Elijah Pilcher and Henry Colclazer rode through thickets and swamps to offer prayer and assistance to settlers establishing congregations. The Presbyterian and Congregational churches developed a joint plan to provide the religious needs of their members in the Western lands. Seminaries, such as the Auburn Theological Seminary in New York, trained young men in both religious matters and survival. The Baptist church sent the Rev. Henry Tripp, who had spent eight years as a missionary in Jamaica before leaving his native England for America. He immediately headed west to the picturesque region that would be known as Michigan's Irish Hills. At the northern tip of Lenawee County, hugging Jackson and Washtenaw Counties, the Reverend Tripp established the Adrian-Tecumseh Underground Railroad network. The Reverend Tripp "cherished strong convictions upon the question of African slavery, to which he was bitterly opposed."[12]

The Methodist Episcopal Church discouraged abolitionism and radical agitation in deference to the slaveholders in its southern churches; nonetheless, the first preachers sent to the Michigan Territory were antislavery reformers with the passion of youth. Only two years after his graduation from Ohio University in Athens, the Rev. Elijah Pilcher, aged 22, was assigned to preach in the Detroit Circuit of the Church. In 1830, the Circuit included Wayne, Oakland, St. Clair, Huron, Monroe, Washtenaw and St. Joseph Counties, essentially the entire settled area of the Michigan Territory. Pilcher traveled alone on foot or horseback through the wilderness. Scattered settlers were rounded up into small assemblies where Pilcher preached in their cabins or houses. The only meetinghouse lay west of Plymouth in a place called Cooper's Corners. The Reverend Pilcher preached, lectured, and wrote about the need to overthrow slavery. His influence on the early settlers of Southeast Michigan can be measured by the antislavery activity and tolerance in his wake.[13]

In Western Michigan, the Rev. Luther Humphrey labored on Beardsley's Prairie in Cass and Berrien Counties after the Presbyterian Church of New England sent him as a missionary around 1830. Humphrey settled in Lawrence, founded by antislavery pioneer Ann

Arbor's John Allen, in Van Buren Township. Humphrey, like his cousin John Brown of Harpers Ferry fame, believed in the humanity of all people. He may have seemed eccentric, but his congregants must have admired how he upheld his principles.

> His prejudice against slavery was of the most ultra character, and he would neither eat nor wear anything made *by* slave labor, and to obviate the necessity of eating sugar from this source, he annually raised a quantity *of* corn from which he expressed the juice and boiled down to a molasses, which answered the purpose of sweetening.[14]

The Rev. Henry Horatio Northrop wrote that the earliest circuit preachers of the Presbyterian and Congregational churches in Michigan were also involved in the Underground Railroad. While the area was sparsely populated with scatterings of farmsteads and small hamlets, the Reverend Northrop began preaching in Washtenaw County in 1838. Northrop wrote of his Underground Railroad participation while ministering in the Presbyterian Church, and he recalled the names of fellow preachers who helped self-freed men and women: the reverends John P. Cleaveland, Ira M. Weed, John G. Kanouse, Charles G. Clark, and Louis Mills, and Mr. Chester Gurney.[15]

The ministers were in regular contact with each other at the annual conferences of their churches, through correspondence, and attendance at antislavery society meetings. Presbyterian ministers Northrop, Weed, Kanouse, and Clarke were highly respected pastors in Washtenaw County. In directing freedom seekers, Northrop could easily recommend his church brethren across the state. As the young ministers helped found Presbyterian and Congregational churches, they directed their congregations to live by their tenets of Christianity, including the brotherhood of all mankind.

The participation of Quakers in the Underground Railroad is documented, though sometimes misrepresented. As in other religious bodies, the Religious Society of Friends included conservatives who thought social reforms of little consequence, progressives who endorsed antislavery measures, and radicals who lobbied for adoption of new doctrines. During the Colonial Period, many Quakers were slaveholders, and they were among the first religious group to oppose slavery in principle and promote the manumission of slaves.

Quaker Elias Hicks embraced new doctrines that caused a split among Quakers from 1827. His followers, called Hicksites, and another progressive faction known as Evangelical Quakers, were in the front ranks of the Underground Railroad agency. Both Hicksite and Evangelical Quakers migrated to the Michigan Territory.[16]

In studying early pioneers and the Underground Railroad, it is clear that the Quakers had a distinct advantage in helping escaping slaves. Simply put, the Protestants organized many small local churches with preachers connecting distant congregations. The Society of Friends organization involved local, regional, and national Meetings with members traveling great distances to gather together. The Quaker system thereby facilitated Underground Railroad networking.

The Society of Friends is structured in levels, the first being the individual congregation or Meeting. An example is the Hicksite Nankin Meeting, organized in Plymouth Township, Wayne County, Michigan. One or more Meetings together formed the Monthly Meeting. Though nearly 100-miles apart, the Hicksites of Battle Creek (Milton Preparative Meeting), became part of the Plymouth Monthly Meeting. Therefore, the Hussey and Merritt families of Battle Creek regularly traveled from the middle of Michigan to Nankin, to meet with the Powers, Laphams, Glaziers and Waltons. At least one representative from each of these families participated in the Underground Railroad in Michigan.[17]

The men and women attending the Quarterly Meetings learned the roads and distances to Quaker Friends further afield. In 1834, Hicksite Quakers set up the Genesee Yearly Meeting, which encompassed Quarterly Meetings of New York State, Upper Canada, and Michigan. Though the distance to Yearly Meetings in Indiana and Ohio was much shorter, Michigan Quakers' attachment to New York reflected their social and familial associations, and their path of emigration.[18]

West of Detroit, Evangelical and Hicksite Quakers in Southeast Michigan created a network of Underground Railroad stations in the Raisin River Valley around Adrian in Lenawee County. There, the Chandler, Smith, Haviland, and Comstock families founded the first congregation of Quakers in Michigan in 1831 and erected a Meeting House in 1835. The Raisin Valley Friends Meeting House was simple, befitting the tenets of the faith: separate entrances for men and women led to a sanctuary with a movable partition. Daniel Smith served as the first leader. His daughter, Laura Smith Haviland, became one of the most prominent equal rights activists and Underground Railroad operators in the nation who later left the Quaker fold over the issue of slavery to join the Wesleyan Methodist Church. The Reverend Swift founded the Wesleyan Methodist Church in the Midwest. From the start, the church refused membership to slaveholders and promoted the end of slavery.

Later migrants decided whether to settle among these pioneers, live by their established governments, attend their churches, or to move on to another village that better suited their political, religious, and social ideals. Some of the earliest settlers, carrying a hatred of slavery to the new frontier, planted seeds of resistance in the Underground Railroad network.

Washtenaw County: A Microcosm of Antislavery Settlement

A close examination of Washtenaw County reveals how the initial settlers and succeeding generations created pockets of abolitionism and safety for freedom seekers. Washtenaw lies west of Wayne County in the second tier of counties north of the southern border. First purchasers grabbed the choicest parcels of land on the Huron or Raisin Rivers and settled in the early 1820s. Antislavery men founded many of Washtenaw County's earliest towns: Ann Arbor, Ypsilanti, Dexter, Scio, and Geddesburg. As leaders of their growing communities, John Allen, William Harwood, Judge Samuel Dexter, the Foster brothers, and John Geddes shaped their communities.

Men like John Allen and Samuel Dexter envisioned great wealth and prosperity in the burgeoning villages they created. Unlike most settlers who were agriculturalists, Allen and Dexter were land speculators and community builders. Both returned to the Northeast to recruit millwrights, blacksmiths, and other skilled men. Both opposed slavery.

Ann Arbor was the most successful of the towns Allen founded. It became not only the county seat, but also Michigan's center of the antislavery movement. Hailing from Virginia, where he held people in slavery as late as 1820, John Allen revealed an opposition to the institution in a letter penned shortly after settling in his northern home, dated February 20, 1825.

> Oh how great a curse are we delivered from, the thoughts of which at all times constrains me to bless and praise the disposer of all events, for his thus delivering us, by a strong hand, from a land of oppression and Tyrany [sic], and placing us in a land of liberty and peace, where the sweat, the groans, and blood, of the Afflicted Sons and Daughters of Affrica [sic], shall never rise in Judgment to condemn us.[19]

John Allen brought his wife, parents, children, and brother to the remote settlement. He promoted "Annarbour" as a community of families with the finest respectability, though at least one visitor in 1825 was surprised to find only eight rough houses.[20] While there are no records to indicate Allen was involved in the Underground Railroad, his opposition to slavery was important in shaping the future of the town he co-founded. On one of his trips to New York, Allen met Loren Mills in Buffalo and persuaded him to move to Ann Arbor. Two Mills brothers headed west to see John Allen's town and found it lived up to his description. Loren's father, Asa, moved with most of his fourteen children in 1826. At least ten members of the Mills family married and had families of their own in the Ann Arbor area: "all were proficient singers; all were pioneers; all were pledged to total abstinence, all were abolitionists, and all became Republicans."[21]

William Webb Harwood, son of white Massachusetts's pioneers, co-founded Ypsilanti and then helped it prosper. From its earliest days, a small black population contributed to the town's progress. Within a decade Harwood purchased a 1,000 acre property in the countryside. There he befriended his neighbor, Asher Aray, a black man, and cooperated with Aray to help people to freedom. Ypsilanti and the urban area surrounding it attracted numerous blacks from an early period.

Samuel William Dexter journeyed from New York to Michigan in 1824 where he found delight in the prairies, oak openings (savannahs between mature trees), and clear streams. His motivation for going west was primarily emotional: to escape lingering melancholy after the deaths of his wife, Amelia, and second son in 1822. However, his innate business instincts led him to observe how easily the rolling land could be traversed to convey produce to markets. Dexter purchased property along the Huron River where he envisioned a village with prosperous mills sustaining the growing population. He then traveled on horseback with Saline Village founder, Orange Risdon, surveying eastern Michigan and speculating on land for future town development. Samuel Dexter, politician, reformer, and abolitionist, became one of the most influential and esteemed men in the region.

Before Dexter returned to New York later the same year, he established the village of Dexter, named for his father and namesake, a Massachusetts Congressman, Senator, and Secretary of Treasury and War. As pioneers arrived over the next few years, Dexter Township was parceled into smaller townships including Webster and Scio. In 1825, Dexter's new wife, his first wife's brothers, and friends accompanied him to Washtenaw County. Dexter persuaded abolitionist brothers Sylvanus, Nathaniel, and Sylvester Noble to settle in the new frontier, where some of them had stations on the Underground Railroad network. In 1826, Harvard-educated Samuel Dexter was appointed Chief Justice of Washtenaw County in the Territory of Michigan. Judge Dexter's first house, on the Huron River and close to the railroad line laid in the late 1830s, was open to everyone arriving in the region.[22]

Dexter may have known the Fosters of Rhode Island through his father's political appointments. Somehow, Dexter managed to persuade several of the highly educated and cultivated Foster brothers to move to the wild frontier.[23] Theodore Raeljeph Foster offered sanctuary for those escaping on the Underground Railroad in Scio, the town he established between Dexter and Ann Arbor. Though little-known outside Washtenaw County, Theodore Foster was a driving force in organizing a statewide antislavery society, publishing an antislavery newspaper and promoting the cause of abolitionism through civil and political means.

Theodore's brother Samuel and Samuel's sons helped freedom seekers in the Dexter area. Theodore Foster spent his adult years as one of the unsung leaders of the antislavery movement in the Midwest. The discovery of a black man hidden in his home damaged Foster's standing in a community and state which was lukewarm to the issue of abolition in the 1840s.[24]

John Geddes traveled by steamship across Lake Erie to Detroit in 1824, purchased land, and returned to Pennsylvania on foot. The next year he traveled by wagon with his brother and founded a place called Geddesburg, halfway between Ann Arbor and Ypsilanti. Geddes was active in the community by serving as Township Supervisor, Justice of the Peace, and State Representative.[25]

Nutting's Corner in Lodi did not grow into a village, but, like many forgotten places, was a small hamlet. Capt. John Lowry purchased land in the wild plains and timbered area of Lodi Township, and then returned to New York for his family and a few relatives. The party traveled across Lake Erie on the schooner *Lady of the Lake*, reaching Detroit in two weeks. It took about three days to reach Ann Arbor. Weary travelers and goods piled into a horse-drawn lumber wagon, and the men used poles to guide the load through the mud and muck.[26] Few men dared to publicly promote an unpopular antislavery sentiment as Lowry did when he erected a huge wooden sign that welcomed freedom seekers. Fellow abolitionists and Underground Railroad workers Timothy Hunt, Selleck Wood, Eli Benton, and the Reverend Weed surrounded his farm, located six miles south of Ann Arbor. An anti-abolitionist would need to possess great fortitude and will to settle close to ultra-radical Capt. John Lowry.

Some Washtenaw County town founders were also religious leaders. Job Gorton founded a Quaker community in the southeast quadrant of Ypsilanti Township for the Gortons, Bennetts, Moores and Derbyshires. These families provided aid to former slaves and both men and women accepted positions in the re-organized antislavery society in the 1850s. Job and David Gorton were descended from Samuel Gorton who arrived in Boston in 1636. The brothers, born in Connecticut, moved to New Hampshire and New York, and were among the earliest settlers in Ypsilanti Township in 1824. "Uncle Job" and his wife Eliza Comstock Gorton opened their home to so many it became known as the "Friend's Hotel." The Hicksite Quaker Gorton clan formed the Ypsilanti Friends Church, members of the Adrian Monthly Meeting.[27] Job Gorton traveled to Adrian for services and to help Laura Smith Haviland transport freedom seekers, according to one report. The families were connected by the marriage of David Gorton's son to Martha Haviland in 1835.[28]

Another pioneer family, Prince and Esther McCloud Bennett, II, helped found the Ypsilanti Friends Church. Prince Bennett, II, brought his wife and seven children from Otsego County, New York, to Ypsilanti in 1831. The family stayed at the home of fellow Quaker Job Gorton until moving to their farm on Tuttle Hill Road in the vicinity of Paint Creek, in Augusta Township. Bennett purchased a substantial parcel of 320 acres and built the first frame house in the township. This house was a station on the Underground Railroad.[29]

Esther McCloud Bennett was a formidable woman. According to her family, on an occasion when the entire family was to go out, she insisted upon remaining at home to protect freedom seekers hiding beneath her house. Neighbors had informed the Bennett family of approaching slave hunters, and any hope of moving the freedom seekers was deemed too risky as spies could be watching from the woods nearby at that very moment. The family must provide protection while betraying neither concern, nor fear. Mr. Bennett took the children, as planned, to a picnic.

Mrs. Bennett rocked calmly on the porch as the posse rode toward her house on Tuttle Hill Road. The strangers inquired whether any slaves had passed her way. She replied honestly that she had seen none that day. They asked if she might come off her porch to perhaps accompany them to dinner. The busy mother declined the kind invitation and continued knitting. As Esther McCloud Bennett would not be moved, the slave catchers departed without discovering the trap door, shielded by a rug, under Mrs. Bennett's rocking chair. True to her faith, Mrs. Bennett did not see any slaves *that* day.[30]

In June 1830, at the age of 26, Ira Mason Weed came to Ypsilanti with a commission from the Home Missionary Society. "When I came to Ypsilanti, the leading men, with but few exceptions, were infidels." This was the opinion of the young Vermonter assigned to preach in the wilderness town of Ypsilanti. Weed was well-educated, having graduated university and studied law before answering the call to minister.[31] The Ypsilanti Presbyterian Church, organized in 1829, grew quickly under his leadership. Weed's pastorship was described as doing much "toward moulding the moral and religious character of the people" and it extended into Salem, Stoney Creek, and Lodi, where he helped organize churches. The Ypsilanti Church was integrated under the pastorship of the Reverend Weed. Catherine Aray, wife of Asher Aray, was a member.[32]

An early Quaker family, headed by Richard Bunker Glazier and Anna Hutchings Glazier, settled east of Ann Arbor in 1833. They were members of a community of Nantucket Friends including the Hussey, Walton, and Lapham families. Giles Stebbins wrote a reminiscence of the important antislavery leaders he knew and dedicated a section to Richard Glazier. At a young age, Richard worked as a shipbuilder, but contracted lung fever (pneumonia) and moved to Ann Arbor, Michigan, to farm. The one-and-a-half story cabin built on land above the Huron River between two roads leading to Detroit accommodated Richard, Anna and their four children: Robert Barclay, Elizabeth C., Mary, and Richard, Jr. A surviving frame house was built on the foundation of the original cabin.

Robert Barclay Glasier, who chose the traditional spelling for his name, was 16 when he moved to Ann Arbor with his parents. Robert believed his Quaker oaths superior to the laws of man. When ordered to drill with the militia, Glasier refused and was jailed until his fine was paid "by act of imprisonment." Then, he broke the law by transporting freedom seekers from Ann Arbor to Farmington, Michigan. Glasier was considered one of the best "conductors" on the "road," whose activities brought him into a circle of prominent abolitionists, including William Lloyd Garrison.[33]

As early as the 1820s, settlement was underway in the township of Saline. In 1831, the Rev. John George Kanouse and eleven others met in Newark, New York, "for the purpose of constituting a church in Michigan Territory." They settled in Saline in July that same year. Born in 1800 in Rockaway, New Jersey, John Kanouse was 19 when he joined his brother, the Rev. Peter Kanouse, as a missionary to the Choctaw Indians. After two years, John returned to Rockaway and then moved to Newark, New York, to study law. Deciding that law was not his field, he became an ordained minister. When the antislavery group from Newark went west, they arranged for the Rev. John Kanouse to go with them.[34]

The group organized as the Presbyterian Church of Saline landed in the area in 1831. They met in private houses, schoolhouses, and in the meetinghouses of other denominations until 1842 when a frame church was erected. The Reverend Kanouse served as its first pastor eventually ministering to both the Lodi and Saline Presbyterian Churches at the same time.[35] The Reverend Kanouse was politically active as a delegate to the Whig convention from 1838 to 1845. On December 13, 1838, a letter in the *Ann Arbor State Journal* criticized him for his political sermons. He remained convinced a life of Christian duty was supreme to the law of man, as a sermon shows: "God has a moral government extending to all moral beings — government administered through the medium of law — a law embracing precepts directing what should be done."[36]

Charles Grandison Clark was born April 8, 1796, in Preston, Connecticut. After attending Amherst College and the Auburn Theological Seminary, he was ordained in the Presbyterian Church in 1829. The same year he chose to serve in Michigan on behalf of the Home Missionary Society. He arrived in Washtenaw County, organized the Presbyterian Church in Dexter, and struggled to form churches in the small communities of Unadilla and Plainfield. Except for a brief time in Lodi, Clark ministered at Webster Church from 1834 until 1858.[37]

The Reverend Clark stated publicly that as minister of the First Presbyterian Church of Webster, he would not serve the Lord's Supper to a slaveholder. Church member Benjamin Reed challenged Clark on this "unchristian" stance by refusing to attend church. Perhaps Reed was unaware that the congregants had passed an "Article of Practice" condemning slavery as a sin and barring slaveholders from the church. Early officers of the church included abolitionists Jacob Doremus, Munnis Kenny, and Theodore Foster. Benjamin Reed was excommunicated from the church in July 1841.[38]

One might assume from the accounts of early settlers, that the majority were opposed to slavery. However, antislavery activists were a minority until the years preceding the Civil War. This book records several instances of violence and many of public censure against those opposed to slavery and abolitionists.

One man in Michigan who hated abolitionism and defended slavery held prominent positions in society from which to influence the lives of all citizens. A man who knew Judge Abner Pratt of Marshall, Calhoun County, personally and professionally wrote that Pratt "always went armed to battle it [abolitionism] on every occasion. Nothing daunted him in this controversy. If circumstances were in his way so much the worse for circumstances."[39]

When Judge Pratt became a Regent at the University of Michigan, he attempted to silence antislavery discussion among faculty and acted in a manner that led to the resignation of antislavery Professors Whedon and Agnew.[40]

Life was challenging for the newcomers, squeezed into small log cabins, traveling long distances for food and supplies and facing the scourge of ague (malaria). However, they made time for celebrations. When they founded the Masonic Lodge in 1826, the villagers held a "ball" in John Allen's double log house. From Detroit, lantern-lit lumber wagons rolled in the darkness to the cabin carrying General Cass, Judge Witherell, General Larned, and General Schwarz, among others. The Mills Brothers Band played while the merry guests ate turkey and venison and danced late into the night. The occasion was for entertainment, but the Detroit judges and generals met citizens they knew would support their progressive actions and decisions. There would be many dark nights over the next decades where some of these same men and women met in hushed whispers while conducting the serious business of helping people out of slavery.[41]

Chapter Three

Obtaining Freedom in Michigan

Escapes of John Brooks and Isabella Baumfree

John Wesley Brooks was born in Maryland, the son of Fanny (Williams) and Louis Brooks. Under the New York Gradual Abolition Law of 1799, John Brooks was bound in slavery until he reached the age of 28. In his early years, John and his family worked long days for the benefit of Richard Jones. Jones controlled every aspect of their lives, including the sanctity of their marriage, and ties of mother, father, and children.

Louis Brooks was helpless to intervene when his wife, son John, and two daughters were sold and taken hundreds of miles north to New York. The fate of Louis Brooks is unknown. The others became the property of Phineas P. Bates of Ontario County in western New York. John Brooks surrendered 28 years of his life, as he was legally obliged to do by virtue of his race and birth. In 1826, Bates refused to sign the manumission paper and held him illegally.

John Brooks wanted the freedom to which he was entitled under the Gradual Abolition Law, and he took control of his own destiny. Although Bates was an Assemblyman in Canandaigua, he attempted to circumvent the law. Brooks sought legal counsel from John C. Spencer, renowned lawyer and member of the Manumission Society. With Spencer's legal expertise, Brooks gained his freedom at the age of 30. Brooks remained in New York working for Spencer for a year and then, in 1828, left for the Michigan Territory.[1]

Like Brooks, Isabella Baumfree was born into slavery in New York, sold repeatedly, whipped and humiliated until she reached maturity. Promised her freedom in 1826, Baumfree discovered she'd been deceived, and then emancipated herself. She changed her name to Sojourner Truth in 1843 and began a 40-year sojourn around the nation preaching the truth of God and the injustices of humankind. Brooks and Sojourner Truth were enslaved in New England decades after a free Northwest Territory was established. They both fought for racial equality throughout their lives and later claimed Michigan as home.

John Wesley Brooks settled in Michigan, despite its racially discriminatory laws. Though legally free, Brooks' citizenship was shackled by the 1827 law to "Regulate Blacks and Mulattoes." Memories of the Revolutionary War remained in the minds of many Americans, and the desire for a unified nation remained foremost in political debates. Blacks in Michigan struggled during the first decade of statehood to assert their rights and freedoms.

In 1830, of the nearly 13 million people in the United States, two-million were enslaved by race. Acts of rebellion occurred, and David Walker's *An Appeal in Four Articles* (1830) truly frightened white people as it revealed the loathing of many enslaved toward their oppressors: "You may do your best to keep us in wretchedness and misery, to enrich you and your children, but God will deliver us from under you. And wo, wo, [*sic*] will be to you if we have to obtain our freedom by fighting."[2]

Nat Turner, enslaved in Southampton County, Virginia, experienced prophetic visions of battles. When he led a bloody rebellion in 1831, the nation was forced to examine the "peculiar institution." Southern reactions impacted the North; for instance, the Commonwealth of Virginia passed several laws that severely restricted free African-Americans, including enforcement of an earlier law requiring freed slaves to leave the state. In 1831 Tennessee declared it unlawful "for any free person of color, whether he be born free, or emancipated agreeably to the laws in force, either now or at any time in any state within the United States to remove himself to this state and remain there more than 20 days."[3] Men and women agitating for the end of slavery were forced to weigh the consequences of their activity on free black men and women in the South. In that year, the legislation was not widely enforced and there were many friends of enslaved people residing in Tennessee.

In the states of the Northwest Territory, citizens clashed over slavery and indentured servitude through the 1840s. Illinois and Indiana held people in slavery in opposition of the Northwest Ordinance. Even when 331 "slaves" were enumerated in Illinois, just over 3,500 free blacks chose to settle among them in 1840.

Michigan remained far behind its neighboring states in gaining population. In 1830, 261 free and enslaved blacks lived in the state. However, enslaved heads of household were listed in Brown, Crawford, and Chippewa Counties, not part of the future state of Michigan but included in the Territory. As witnessed in the account of Saby and Isom, blacks attempted to build communities in the Northwest Territory. Along the Mississippi River, escaping slaves boarded steamboats to carry them eventually to Michigan and Canada. Some remained in Alton, Illinois, although at times, slave hunters captured and re-enslaved the settlers.[4] It was in Alton in 1837 that white abolitionist Elijah Lovejoy faced anti-abolitionists who shot and killed him, and then burned his *Alton Observer* printing office.[5] Southern Illinois and Indiana were dangerous places for abolitionists during the antebellum period.

Ohio's Western Reserve was a stronghold of abolition, but an early Virginia Reserve in the southern region of the state attracted proslavery settlers. In 1829, white citizens in Cincinnati enacted laws to remove the free people of color from the city. While the black citizens looked for a place of refuge, a mob moved in with three nights of rioting. Sir James Colebrook, governor of Upper Canada, invited the destitute blacks to move to the British Colony where "we royalists do not know men by their color." A large number removed to Canada and formed the Wilberforce Settlement.[6]

Michigan's first constitution became law with statehood in 1837. It upheld the territorial law banning slavery, and allowed only white citizens to vote. Petitions sent to legislators over the next decade failed to gain enfranchisement for black citizens. The state's constitution excluded blacks from jury duty and military service. Another statute forbade blacks and whites to marry in the state.[7]

That some settlers in Michigan espoused radical antislavery sentiment and agitation did not mean that abolitionism was widely supported. Blacks in Michigan were a very small minority in 1830 and they faced varying degrees of segregation in churches and schools. Most lived in Wayne County: 74 in the city of Detroit and 28 in other areas. The rest of the recorded "free colored persons" were scattered across the settled regions. Scipio Denison (Lisette's brother) and Robert Thomas were heads of families in Oakland County, Henry Sanders was alone in St. Clair, and the Stephen Smith family lived in Monroe. Only Jacob

Auray (Aray) is listed in Washtenaw County. One of the families listed in Wayne County was the Forth family, the married name of Lisette Denison, who returned to Michigan without having gained her freedom legally.

Lucie and Thornton Blackburn

On July 3, 1831, Rutha (Lucie) and Thornton Blackburn ran away from their enslavers in Louisville, Kentucky, after Lucie learned she was to be sold. They crossed the Ohio River by steamboat, made their way north, and settled in Detroit.[8] Two years passed before their former owner tracked them to Detroit and had them jailed until he could win legal approval to take them South. The black community viewed the arrest as a kidnapping and was determined to circumvent the legal process.

Caroline French, wife of George French, and Tabitha Lightfoot, wife of Madison J. Lightfoot, free black women, visited Mrs. Blackburn in jail where Mrs. French exchanged clothes and identities with her friend. In disguise, Lucie Blackburn walked out of jail with Mrs. Lightfoot and was taken to Canada. Caroline French was arrested and threatened with being forced into slavery instead of Mrs. Blackburn. When Thornton Blackburn was taken from jail in shackles, a riot broke out during which Sheriff Wilson was wounded. Detroit

The Blackburns lived in Detroit for two years before they were arrested and jailed in 1833. Their rescue was the first of many by Michigan citizens (author photograph, Louisville, Kentucky, 2007).

mayor Chapin dispatched a letter to Secretary of War Lewis Cass, who happened to be visiting, to direct a company of U. S. troops from Fort Gratiot to be stationed in the city until "tranquility is restored." The letter, dated July 25, 1833, stated that the recent excesses and "particularly the repeated attempts to fire the town [start fires], have so far excited the apprehensions of our citizens for their property and lives." Night sentinels arrested all suspicious persons, including Mayor Chapin who was not recognized and was placed in jail. While blacks were banished from Detroit because of the rioting, most crossed the river to Canada temporarily and then returned and settled into racially mixed Detroit neighborhoods.[9]

This case indicates that enough black Americans residing in Detroit were willing and capable of staging an act of resistance that resulted in the permanent freedom of people self-freed from slavery. Though the Blackburns were pursued and jailed, the Canadian government refused to extradite them. Slavery was legally abolished in Canada when the British Emancipation Act went into effect on August 1, 1834.

The Frenchs and Lightfoots, who aided the Blackburns, were members of a group that established the Second Baptist Church in Detroit because of discriminatory segregation at Detroit's First Baptist Church. In 1836, the group met at a hall on Fort Street. The Rev. William Charles Monroe, a black minister, was installed as the first pastor of Second Baptist, serving between 1836 and 1846. In 1839, the church sponsored the city's first school for black children, with Monroe as teacher. In addition to some of the founders helping the Blackburns escape, the church has a long passed down tradition of helping people escape slavery.

Soon after, the black population of Detroit was large enough to sustain another church. The Colored Methodist Society met in 1839 and was granted permission to use the Old Military Hall. The Bethel African Methodist Episcopal Church was organized in 1841, providing assistance to its members and the community.[10]

Black Pioneers in Michigan's Underground Railroad

With its churches and ministers, the Detroit area attracted a number of blacks who publicly challenged discriminatory laws and secretly worked on the Underground Railroad. William Lambert, born free and educated in New Jersey, moved to Detroit in 1838. He helped organize the first State Convention of Colored Citizens and was elected its Chairman in 1843. Lambert was among the leaders who established a school, library, and social society for blacks in Detroit. When interviewed after the Civil War, Lambert described in detail the workings of the Underground Railroad in Michigan. Lambert declared that he helped thousands in Detroit before seeing them carried across the Detroit River to Canada. He was a conspicuous figure in the 1858 meeting where John Brown and a few trusted men planned the events leading to the raid at Harpers Ferry.[11]

Another key person in the Underground Railroad's first phase was George DeBaptiste. Born in 1815 into a wealthy, free black family from Fredericksburg, Virginia, and trained as a barber, DeBaptiste spent a brief time working on river steamboats. That experience prepared him for Underground Railroad work in Madison, Indiana. It is a telling fact that DeBaptiste chose to move to a city overlooking the Ohio River and its southern shore of slavery's stranglehold in order to engage in a secret activity.

DeBaptiste often waited in the solitary darkness on the bank of the Ohio, alert to the sound of oars striking the water. He would emerge from the grasses to meet and guide freedom seekers ten to twelve miles to a local farmer's house. DeBaptiste sometimes walked twenty miles during the night, and in the morning appeared rested and ready for a day's work barbering. Levi Coffin wrote of DeBaptiste concealing a man named Jim and many others in Indiana and afterwards in Michigan.[12]

Except for a time from 1837 to 1841, DeBaptiste helped on the Underground Railroad until Emancipation. He took off several years to serve as William Henry Harrison's valet. Harrison met DeBaptiste and hired him during his Presidential campaign. DeBaptiste followed Harrison to the White House as his steward, but with Harrison's sudden death, DeBaptiste returned to Madison, Indiana, and carried on his Underground Railroad work. In 1846 when riots in Indiana and a bounty on his head made it unsafe to remain, DeBaptiste moved to the far end of his network: Detroit. He became a leader of the Michigan Underground Railroad network.[13]

Beyond Detroit, only a few black families settled in the Michigan Territory. One such family, with a Colonial heritage, arrived in Washtenaw County in 1827. The Arays came to Michigan as a family group when Jacob Aray purchased 160 acres in Pittsfield Township.

Jacob was descended from Aree van Guinea and his wife Jora, living in New York in 1705. Aree was born in Africa, where he may have been kidnapped or sold into servitude. From the early 1700s, Aree and Jora were free blacks, accepted on equal footing with whites in the Lutheran Church in the New Netherlands Dutch settlement of New York. In 1705, the "daughter of Are [*sic*] of Guinea, a negro, and his wife Jora," was baptized. In 1708, on

Public lecturing against slavery was sometimes dangerous but often effective. Wendell Phillips, pictured here, lectured in Michigan in 1860 (*Gleason's Pictorial* [1851], American Memory, Library of Congress).

an Easter Sunday, church members witnessed the baptism of an enslaved "Carolina Indian." The slave had to swear he would remain in servitude, before his "owner" would permit the baptism.[14]

In 1714, the Arays, as they were later known, moved to the Raritan Valley in New Jersey. The existing Zion Lutheran Church claims the first Lutheran service in North America was held on August 1, 1714, in the home of the Arays in Oldwick, New Jersey. During the service three children were baptized, including a black girl named Jora Day, who was sponsored by Jora Aray. A decade later, when German Lutherans were unable to solicit funds from New Yorkers to rebuild the church, church members in New Jersey, including Aree van Guinea, Jr. and Adam Arey donated money. The Zion Evangelical Lutheran Church continues to offer worship in Oldwick, New Jersey.[15]

Descendant Jacob Aray resided in Somerset County, New Jersey, from 1796 to at least 1805. He married Berthena West and they had four children before moving to New York.[16] The reason for the move is unknown. James Aray fought in the Revolutionary War and may have qualified for a land grant. Also, many blacks found work on the construction of the Erie Canal. Another possible reason was New York's voting privileges for free blacks. But by 1838, New York imposed a property qualification for black suffrage, joining the states of Maryland, Tennessee, North Carolina, and Pennsylvania in disenfranchising free blacks.[17]

It appears that some black and white New Jersey German Lutherans, Aray, Depue, Larzelere and later, Day, purchased land as a group in Washtenaw County, Michigan.[18] After several years in Indiana, Silas Randall Day and his wife Sarah moved near Ann Arbor and then south of Asher Aray in 1839 and rented a farm from Jacob Aray. Asher Aray deeded land from his father in 1829. Asher and Catherine Watts Aray purchased land on the Territorial Road near Rev. John Brooks. It is not known when the Arays first opened their house as a station on the Underground Railroad, but it was verified as part of an interstate network by the 1850s.[19]

Another black pioneer helped on the Underground Railroad from the northeast corner of Washtenaw and into Jackson County. Where the River Raisin courses through the scenic village of Manchester, a family arrived from New Jersey. Henry (Harry) and Jane Ockrow were born in New York, moved to New Jersey, Connecticut, New York, then finally Michigan. Jane Ockrow claimed royal Nubian (Egyptian) African descent.[20]

Befriended by a few progressive citizens, this black family remained in the community throughout their lives. Initially, the Ockrows lived in a cabin on George Barker's property, and later bought a small farm just south of the village where they raised their children. The Ockrows had close ties to the Watkins family and provided warning in the dramatic pursuit of John White by Kentucky slave hunters.[21]

On the western side of the state, initially blacks were "accidental settlers" who arrived without a plan to purchase land. "In 1836 a fugitive slave named Lawson came to Calvin Township with a Quaker preacher named Way." Lawson was the first known black settler in Cass County, but one of many when the area became a refuge for blacks in the mid 1840s.[22]

Canadian Settlements 1830s

French settlers founded Windsor, across the river from Detroit, in the mid 1700s. Black Loyalists and freedom seekers settled in the town and just south, in a community called Sandwich. Two other places of refuge east of Michigan were Amherstburg (also known as Fort Malden) to the south, and Sarnia at the St. Clair River opposite Port Huron. Crossings from Wyandotte, Gibraltar, and Trenton were more easily accomplished because of the numerous islands in the Detroit River. At least one person wrote to Dr. Siebert that the Canadian militia no longer needed the Block House on Bois Blanc Island after 1838, and it sheltered freedom seekers from that date. Both Sandwich and Amherstburg had sufficient settlers to establish black churches in the 1830s. First Baptist Amherstburg was a mission for those newly arrived as well as a house of worship.[23]

Anthony Binga, a self-freed man, described in an interview with Dr. Wilbur Siebert how he came to that church to minister and operate an Underground Railroad mission. When he was about 20 years old, Binga lived in bondage on the General Taylor farm in Newport, Campbell County, Kentucky. Binga said he and his family were "well treated" but Binga always wanted to be free.

One day, his brother found a pocketbook with $500 on the road. He told Horace Hawkins, one of their group of friends, who arranged their escape. Their acquaintance James Williams, across the river in Cincinnati, bought a team of horses, a wagon, weapons, and a jug of whiskey. The group got a pass to attend a camp meeting but, instead, met a ferryman who took them in his boat across the Ohio River to the wagon. Binga described the group as follows: "My father had 2 boys, one girl and a wife, and there were two other,

The most dangerous part of an escape was in the South. Henry Bibb attempted to escape several times before making it to Michigan (W.W.B. [1849] *Narrative of William W. Brown, an American Slave. Written by Himself.* www.docsouth.unc.edu).

cousins — Horace Hawkins and his sister, and another one by the name of Wash Burgess — making 15 in the gang." It was late September and the roads allowed for fast travel. The first night, they covered 50 miles heading northeast to Springfield, Ohio, and then to Columbus. When the horses gave out, they paid a Quaker $10 to supply a new wagon to get them to Sandusky, Ohio.

The journey was accomplished in only three days and nights. Next, they boarded the steamboat *Michigan* where Captain Willibur said, "Hello, I wish all Kentucky was aboard." The boat took them to Toledo where it ran aground and they transferred to the *Phoebus* for the final leg to Amherstburg, Ontario. They witnessed others rejoicing as they landed on free soil. Soon after, Binga began preaching and helping the increasing numbers of newcomers.[24] At one time, Lisette Denison sold some property and invested in the purchase of a steamboat called the *Michigan*.

With Detroit the primary gateway to Canada and freedom, most people stayed in towns in that region: Windsor, Amherstburg, Sandwich, Chatham, Sarnia, Dresden, and Buxton. The Rev. Hiram Wilson School was located in St. Catherine's, Ontario, northeast of Niagara Falls, where freedom seekers moved to settlements along Lake Ontario. Blacks migrated to the area with Loyalists before the War of 1812, and especially after the Fugitive Slave Law of 1850.[25]

One manner by which the settlements grew was by successful freedom seekers returning to the South to bring out their loved ones. Dr. Samuel G. Howe, a worker in Canadian missions, said that by the 1850s, as many as 500 people a year "went secretly back to their old homes and brought away their wives and children at much peril and cost."[26] Josiah Henson was among the earliest to make the journey back. Born enslaved, Henson escaped to Canada with his wife and two children in 1830.

On behalf of James Lightfoot, Henson walked 400 miles to rescue Lightfoot's relatives near Maysville, Kentucky.

> The immigration from the United States was incessant, and some, I am not unwilling to admit, were brought hither with my knowledge and connivance. I was glad to help such of my old friends as had the spirit to make the attempt to free themselves; and I made more than one trip, about this time, to Maryland and Kentucky, with the expectation, in which I was not disappointed, that some might be enabled to follow in my footsteps.[27]

Henson could not rescue the Lightfoots on the first attempt, but did bring out about thirty people from Bourbon County, Kentucky, who had been waiting for an experienced escort. They crossed to Cincinnati, then to the Quakers in Richmond, Indiana, and, after two weeks, to Toledo, Ohio. The following year, Henson returned for the Lightfoots and, though pursued, got them on Canadian soil. "And when they reached the shore they danced and wept for joy, and kissed the earth on which they first stepped, no longer the *Slave,* but the *Free.*"[28]

It is not known whether Madison J. Lightfoot of Detroit was related to the Lightfoots rescued by Henson. Henson is generally known for laying the groundwork for the Dawn settlement in Canada. With the aid of missionary Hiram Wilson from the American Anti-Slavery Society, Henson called black Canadians to a Convention in June 1838. Wilson proposed the establishment of a manual labor school. At the 300-acre settlement Wilson created an opportunity for those who fled slavery with nothing but ragged clothes and worn shoes, to become educated and industrious citizens.[29]

Chapter Four

Disturbing Influences: Abolitionists

Escape Henry Bibb, 1837

Henry began running away after being separated from his mother, Milldred Jackson, back in Shelby County, Kentucky. A married man and father of a daughter, his desire for freedom overwhelmed him.

In the words of Henry Bibb:

On the twenty-fifth of December 1837, my long anticipated time had arrived when I was to put into operation my former resolution, which was to bolt for Liberty or consent to die a Slave. I acted upon the former, although I confess it to be one of the most self-denying acts of my whole life, to take leave of an affectionate wife, who stood before me on my departure with dear little Frances in her arms, and with tears of sorrow in her eyes as she bid me a long farewell. It required all the moral courage that I was master of to suppress my feeling while taking leave of my little family.

...I was struggling against a thousand obstacles which had clustered around my mind to bind my wounded spirit still in the dark prison of mental degradation. My strong attachments to friends and relatives, with all the love of home and birth-place which is so natural among the human family, twined about my heart and were hard to break away from. And withal, the fear of being pursued with guns and blood-hounds, and of being killed, or captured and taken to the extreme South, to linger out my days in hopeless bondage on some cotton or sugar plantation, all combined to deter me. But I had counted the cost, and was fully prepared to make the sacrifice. The time for fulfilling my pledge was then at hand. I must forsake friends and neighbors, wife and child, or consent to live and die a slave.

By the permission of my keeper, I started out to work for myself on Christmas. I went to the Ohio River, which was but a short distance from Bedford. My excuse for wanting to go there was to get work. High wages were offered for hands to work in a slaughter-house. But in place of my going to work there, according to promise, when I arrived at the river I managed to find a conveyance to cross over into a free state.[1]

Protests against slavery in the 1830s and 1840s were a cacophony of discordant voices. In general, most Americans disliked slavery in their democratic nation, but were indifferent or opposed to ending it. Antislavery activists ranged from those opposed to the expansion of slavery to rabid abolitionists willing to fight and rend the Union to end the enslavement of humans.

Nationally, abolitionists who agreed on the principle of ending slavery were at odds over the methods to do so. Some men and women believed public suasion would gradually influence slaveholders to voluntarily free their slaves. Active abolitionists encouraged the physical removal of people from enslavement, seeking improved methods to make the journey less haphazard and dangerous for men like Henry Bibb.

Early 1830s reformers had little hope in attacking slavery through political institutions. President Andrew Jackson enslaved many people who worked on his Tennessee farm, The Hermitage. His slave-owning practices were not too offensive to constituents of the Democratic Party, who elected him for a second term in 1832. His hand picked successor, Martin Van Buren, maintained Democratic dominance and the practice of condoning slavery.[2]

Slavery spread across the South and continued to exist in northern states with gradual emancipation laws. As late as 1840, Connecticut and Pennsylvania each had over 50 slaves. New Jersey enslaved 674 people and was the last of the Northern states to legislate gradual, but complete, emancipation.[3]

Theodore Weld's Crusade

In 1825, Theodore Weld heard the Second Great Awakening religious revivalist, Charles G. Finney, preach in Utica, New York. Weld joined the "Holy Band" of Finney disciples. Other disciples included Lewis and Arthur Tappan, wealthy merchants who strongly opposed slavery and could afford to fund activities supporting their views. The Tappan brothers opened a free church in New York and invited revivalist Finney to become pastor. The Tappans asked Weld to join them in Utica, but he felt unprepared to preach against slavery without having observed it firsthand so the Tappans financed Weld's tour of Ohio and the southern border states.

As he traveled and lectured, Weld began to persuade men and women to become disciples of Finney. In Kentucky, Weld met James G. Birney. Birney, elected one of Madison, Kentucky's representatives in its first state legislature, "had been honored with positions of trust and confidence by her people, who had both respect and regard for him." Weld convinced Birney that slavery was an evil that needed to be eradicated. Birney's conversion from slaveholding to abolition bore witness to the possibility of persuading slaveholders to end slavery.

In Birney, Weld and the Tappans gained an abolitionist who would rise to the top of the political movement to end slavery. At first Birney embraced the Colonization Movement as a means of granting freedom to enslaved people in America. The American Colonization Society, organized in 1817, funded transporting blacks to Africa in order to further emancipation. Birney's attempts to promote Colonization in the South were largely unsuccessful, and many of the people who elected him felt betrayed. After Birney moved north, a southern history reported, "with the going of Birney, the last of the disturbing influences was removed."[4]

Another Finney convert, William Lloyd Garrison, was hired in 1828 by Benjamin Lundy to assist in publishing the *Genius of Universal Emancipation*, but Garrison's writing for this antislavery newspaper was far too incendiary for Lundy and the local citizenry. Garrison returned to Boston just as the Tappans, Weld, and a few others decided to create a new society dedicated to antislavery reforms. Weld declined to head the organization, and the Tappans let the plan for the society stall. Garrison, however, saw no reason to wait for the Tappans as every day men, women, and children suffered the cruelties of an institution he deemed sinful.

And so, Garrison created his own newspaper, issuing the first number of *The Libera-*

tor on January 1, 1831. The radical tone of *The Liberator* caused a stir because it labeled slaveholding a crime and called for its immediate abolition. When the Nat Turner Rebellion of August 1831 escalated Southern fears of slave uprisings, some states outlawed *The Liberator* and thereby propelled Garrison to leadership in the antislavery movement.

Massachusetts' abolitionist Samuel J. May recalled that David Walker's 1830 appeal, Garrison's publication of the *Liberator*, and the Turner rebellion escalated proslavery sentiment. May defined the period as the "Reign of Terror" and wrote that "editors of most of the newspapers, religious as well as secular, and of some of the graver periodicals, nearly all of the popular orators, and very many of the ministers of religion, spoke and wrote against the doctrine of the Abolitionists." May said church leaders justified slavery as a political institution, and statesmen declared it firmly grounded in the Constitution. In 1834, May lectured over a month in New England where he experienced "strong expressions of hostility" to abolition.[5]

In the meantime, the Tappans and Weld sought a more discreet course of action, applying financial backing to a school in Cincinnati, Ohio, called Lane Theological Seminary. Lane Seminary was one of several schools founded by New Englanders in Ohio. Connecticut citizens poured into the Western Reserve area of northern Ohio in the early 1800s because the Reserve included the Firelands, a land area given to the Yankees or their descendants in compensation for property losses in British Revolutionary War raids. Missionaries sent to Ohio's Huron and Erie Counties as early as 1800 began work to establish educational institutions.

After years of setbacks, the Western Reserve College opened in 1827 in Hudson, Ohio. During the academic year of 1832-3 discussion of slavery at home and lecturing on the subject abroad seems to have been the chief occupation of some of the students. In 1832, Professor Elizur Wright's articles against colonization and in favor of abolition in the *Observer and Telegraph*, published at Hudson, Ohio, aroused a great deal of opposition.[6]

Weld was aware of a strong proslavery sentiment in southern Ohio when he recommended Lane Seminary to the Tappans. The wealthy New York Tappan brothers funded construction of new buildings in 1829. Lyman Beecher arrived to take on the presidency, with his daughter Harriet (future author of *Uncle Tom's Cabin*). Weld enrolled as a student and was soon class president. He gradually fulfilled the promise to Detroit abolitionist and friend Charles Stuart and the Tappans to persuade his classmates to examine the issue of slavery. Weld's plan for Lane to become a center of antislavery activity came about as students in 1832 provided lectures, Bible classes, and, later, a school to the black population.

Meanwhile, the Tappan brothers had finally organized an antislavery society. Meeting in Philadelphia in December 1833, Lewis Tappan was named President of the American Anti-Slavery Society, Weld did not attend, and William Lloyd Garrison garnered nearly all the attention. For decades, Weld shrank from the spotlight, while Garrison gloried in it. Leading the immediate emancipationist New England Anti-Slavery Society in Boston, Garrison appeared to be the spokesperson for this new society, as well. Garrison pressed hard for the American Anti-Slavery Society to challenge religious leaders and end all discussions with southerners. Weld and James G. Birney knew antislavery men and women could be found in the South and ought to be encouraged and supported. After all, Birney was a southerner who was persuaded to change his views and consulted with Weld, the Tappan brothers and other prominent antislavery activists.

Weld decided to hold a public debate about immediate abolition at Lane in February

One hundred

IOO DOLLARS
REWARD.

——⊙⊙⊙⊙⊙——

RANAWAY from the subscriber, on Thursday, 7th May, 1857, Negro man **LUKE**, commonly called

LUKE WILLIAMS,

very black, about **25** years old, five feet high, prominent projecting forehead; has a slight scar over one of his eyes; speaks quickly when spoken to; has a thin suit of whiskers and mustache; clothing not remembered, as he has various kinds. His father lives in Philadelphia, and he has a sister belonging to Mr. William S. Gittings, formerly of Anne Arundel County, who now resides in Baltimore City. He has also relatives at Mr. Clement Hilleary's, near Bladensburg. I purchased him of Richard C. Bowie, Esq., formerly of this county.

I will give **FIFTY DOLLARS REWARD** if taken in the State of Maryland or District of Columbia, and **ONE HUNDRED DOLLARS** if taken in any Free State. He must be brought home to me, or secured in Jail, so I can get him again.

ZACHARIAH BERRY, (of W.)

Near the Brick Church,

Forest of Prince George's County, Md.
May 7th, 1857.

PRINTED AT THE OFFICE OF THE "MARLBORO' GAZETTE."

Reward posters described men and women who escaped from slavery, such as Luke Williams (Broadsides, William L. Clements Library, University of Michigan).

1834. Interested citizens joined Lane students in the evenings. Of the Lane Seminary students, 30 of the 40 were over the age of 26, were college graduates, and were mostly from upstate New York and New England. At least five were from the South and one was from Guinea.[7] One of the attendees was John Rankin, who secretly ran an Underground Railroad station in his house above the banks of the river in Ripley, Ohio.

After nine nights, the debate participants voted for an immediate end to slavery, and after 18, to end support for colonization. Those who endorsed expatriating slaves to freedom were persuaded by others that colonization was impractical and morally wrong. This conclusion had profound implications for, in abandoning colonization, the debaters faced head-on the issue of race prejudice. If emancipated slaves were to remain in America, then how could they be denied the privileges and liberties of all free citizens?[8]

According to the Lane Trustees, the debates soiled the reputation of the college as a place unified in its disdain of slavery and welcome to scholars of any denomination or color. The Rev. Asa Mahan, a member of the Lane board of trustees, supported free expression about slavery and was forced out along with Weld by the rest of the board. Mahan became Oberlin College president on the condition that students of color were accepted. Over 50 "Lane Rebels" walked out with Weld and many enrolled at Oberlin.

President Mahan served Oberlin and later carried his experience and sentiments to Michigan.[9] Weld signed on as a full-time lecturing agent of the American Anti-Slavery Society with a plan to abolitionize the North.

Weld's Seventy

With help from Henry B. Stanton, a young journalist and former Lane student, Weld began recruiting men and women for the Lane Agency Scheme. Based on Finney's revivals, Weld and his recruits would deliver abolition talks in towns and villages. Weld experimented and his efforts were described as follows, "He had learned his methods from Finney, and his tactics were to speak for two hours or more, night after night, until he brought conviction to his listeners."[10] Those newly reformed citizens would create local abolition societies. Eventually, state antislavery societies would exert the necessary power to force national political and legislative change. Michigan was part of that scheme.

Six former Lane students accepted antislavery agencies and were in the field in Ohio, Western Pennsylvania, and New York throughout 1835. The Rev. John Cross was sent to Pennsylvania as an agent. Gerrit Smith and Lewis Tappan helped found the New York Anti-Slavery Society in Utica, western New York, the same year. The move to Utica solidified the connection between reformers in upstate New York, Ohio and Michigan.[11]

With positive results of his early scheme, in late fall, 1836, Weld prepared to train up to 70 agents, including Sarah and Angelina Grimké and a Miss Wheelwright, who would talk to the ladies at a convention in New York. The acolytes were sequestered for weeks with intensive daily sessions from nine o'clock to one, from three to five, and from seven to nine. William L. Garrison, who came down from Boston, thought the meetings were among the most important antislavery meetings ever held."[12]

The lecturing work of Weld's recruits, sometimes referred to as the "Seventy," was a successful enterprise in that it achieved much more than the stated goal. Through the training sessions, agents and church missionaries formed links of trust and communication. These were bonds of friendship and shared sentiment that would be of extreme importance in the agency of the Underground Railroad. Weld stayed for two weeks with John Rankin in Ripley, Ohio. At the end of the visit, the Reverend Rankin decided to become an agent, lecturing and writing. In addition, he and his sons continued guiding hundreds of freedom seekers through southern Ohio to places throughout the Midwest, including Michigan and Canada by way of Weld's Agents and other friends.[13]

Weld's Agents in Michigan were critical in creating antislavery societies, producing a regional newspaper, and providing leadership in the national antislavery party, the Liberty Party. An early Weld recruit, the Rev. Guy Beckley, from Andover Theological Seminary, honed his skills as a lecturing agent in Vermont. After moving to Ann Arbor, Michigan, in 1839, he dedicated himself to the antislavery movement. He served on the Executive Committee of the Michigan State Anti-Slavery Society from 1840 through 1844, and, in 1845, was elected one of its vice presidents. During this same period he lectured in over 30 towns in eleven Michigan counties. In a pleasant manner, the Reverend Beckley attacked slavery by every means, locally and nationally. He greatly influenced the Liberty Party, the Wesleyan Methodist Church, the state and local antislavery societies, and he publicly promoted helping freedom seekers.[14]

Giles B. Stebbins was appointed as a Weld agent to the West and went to Palmyra, Lenawee County, Michigan, where his brother, Francis R. Stebbins, joined him in 1837. Francis contributed articles to New York's *Emancipator* and other newspapers while moving between Michigan, Vermont, and New York. He settled permanently in Adrian, Michigan, in 1841. In 1846, Giles married Catherine A. Fish, an early antislavery and women's rights activist. His travels back and forth to New York helped with early communication between national organizations and the Midwest. Stebbins wrote of visits with Michigan friends and Underground Railroad workers, Richard Glazier and John Zimmerman.[15]

After leaving Lane and training with Weld in early 1836, Augustus Wattles accepted a commission to aid free black Americans west of the Allegheny Mountains. He traveled internationally to identify ideal locations for black settlements. Early settlements in Brown County, Ohio, failed because of poor soil conditions, while a settlement of 300 in Stark County, Ohio successfully engaged in farming. Wattles traveled to Upper Canada to report on ten to fifteen thousand men and women of African descent living in the area north of Lake Erie.[16]

John S. Cowles and George Whipple, chosen by Weld as lecturing agents for Michigan, bore the greatest antipathy from the public. In late June 1836, Wattles, Cowles, and Whipple went to Michigan to help establish the state's antislavery society. The men met another of Weld's Seventy, Hiram Wilson, who sought financial support for his work in Canada. His mission as an agent of the American Anti-Slavery Society was to promote the education and welfare of blacks in settlements in Upper Canada. Weld agent Charles Stuart advocated internationally against slavery. When not in Britain, Stuart resided in Detroit.

The Rev. John Monteith, early minister in Detroit and Monroe, left the Michigan Territory on a trip to New York where he met Charles Grandison Finney, the evangelist of the Second Great Awakening. Monteith became a serious reformer and moved to Ohio where he joined up with Theodore Weld's band. At first, Monteith helped self-emancipators get to the southern shore of Lake Erie in Ohio, where they boarded boats crossing to Canada. Monteith Hall (1835), his home in Elyria, Ohio, was a station in the Oberlin Underground Railroad network. Monteith returned to Monroe, Michigan, in 1845 as an experienced Underground Railroad operator.[17]

Other Weld agents served as agents in Union City, St. Clair, and Alamo Township, north of Kalamazoo. These men carried the lessons from the Lane Debates north and west.[18]

The Rev. Asa Mahan, former member of the Lane Seminary board of directors, served as president of Oberlin College until 1850, and then followed the path of many former students by moving to Michigan. Former Oberlin student, the Rev. Paul Shepherd, returned from Kansas as Mahan assumed the Adrian College presidency in Michigan. After studying at Oberlin, Shepherd moved for a short time to Allegan County in southwest Michigan to help with a colony and mission of Ottawa and Pottawatomie Indians. The Reverend Shepherd settled in Lenawee County over a sixteen year period where he was "fearless in expressing his opposition to slavery." A letter he penned, revealed in a later chapter, describes Shepherd's intimate experiences with John Brown's army while living in Kansas in the late 1850s.[19]

John Brown and many of his relatives made their mark in Michigan. The Owen Brown family, one of the most important Connecticut families, moved to Ohio. Devout evangelical Calvinists, the Browns abhorred race-based enslavement and espoused the uncommon belief that blacks were equal to whites. The Browns' homes in Hudson, Ohio, were stations on the Underground Railroad. During the War of 1812, Owen Brown and his son John transported cattle and horses to General William Hull in Detroit. Young John was disgusted to witness a lodge owner beating his enslaved boy whom John had befriended. In later years, John Brown referred to this event in Detroit as the time of his commitment to abolitionism. In 1816, John went east to study for the ministry but soon exhausted his meager funds. For a while he operated a tannery and Underground Railroad station in Ohio, and, a decade later, moved to the wilderness of Randolph, Pennsylvania. He returned to Michigan in 1858 with eleven blacks liberated in his national war against slavery.[20]

Owen Brown continued to protest slavery and helped found the Western Reserve Anti-Slavery Society in 1833. Florella Brown, an Oberlin graduate and a half-sister of John, married Samuel Lyle Adair. Adair briefly attended the Western Reserve College and graduated from the Theological Seminary of Oberlin College in 1841. For the next thirteen years, the Adairs served a series of Congregational churches in Ohio and Michigan. In the early 1840s, the Adairs lived in Dundee, Monroe County, Michigan. In 1854, under the auspices of the American Missionary Association, they organized the Osawatomie Congregational Church in Kansas. The Adair's Dundee cabin served as a frequent refuge for John Brown after his arrival in the Territory in the fall of 1855.[21]

Several graduates of Oberlin left Ohio to teach at Olivet College in Michigan. John J. Shipherd, Oberlin founder, formed Olivet in the Michigan wilderness in 1844 and invited two Weld agents, Amos Dresser and Enoch N. Bartlett, to teach. Oberlin supplied teachers for another progressive school founded by Laura Haviland in Adrian, Lenawee County, Michigan. In advance of the western migration of Weld's agents, two pious young women in Adrian had begun a campaign of radical abolitionism.[22]

Michigan Antislavery Societies

In Adrian, Elizabeth Margaret Chandler established the Logan Female Anti-Slavery Society in October 1832. Nationally and in Michigan, women were at the forefront of creating groups opposed to slavery. Chandler's society preceded the Female Anti-Slavery Society in Philadelphia (Lucretia Coffin Mott, first President, 1833) and the Michigan statewide organization. Elizabeth Chandler arrived in Michigan in 1831 with radical views and connections to prominent abolitionists. Chandler moved with her brother Thomas from Philadelphia to the Quaker community, founded as Logan (later Adrian) in Lenawee County.

At the age of eighteen, her antislavery poem "The Slave Ship" resulted in Benjamin Lundy hiring Chandler as a co-editor of his periodical, the *Genius of Universal Emancipation*. She called for immediate emancipation for slaves and total integration of blacks into American society. This position contrasted with the platform of the only national antislavery society. Chandler continued her writings and correspondence with Lundy and other leaders of the antislavery movement from Michigan. Like Laura Haviland, who joined the Logan group, Chandler embraced Hicksite Quakerism. Sadly, her young life was cut short when she died of fever on November 2, 1834, just two years after founding the Logan Society.[23]

Laura Haviland fully concurred with Chandler's ideology of integration and race equality. Like Chandler, Haviland's Quaker upbringing allowed freedom of expression outside the traditional domestic sphere for women. However, her social activism against slavery brought complaint from members of the Quaker Meeting. Rather than submit, Laura Haviland convinced her parents and a dozen others to withdraw from the Society in 1839. They joined the Wesleyan Methodist Church, the religious group endorsing active abolitionism.[24]

Dedicated to ending both slavery and race and gender discrimination, the Havilands suffered deprivations, and every risk of life was matched by satisfaction in rescuing people from slavery. Laura Smith, born December 20, 1808, in Kitley, Ontario, moved with her family to western New York where she met and married fellow Quaker, Charles Haviland. The Haviland and Smith families migrated to Lenawee County, Michigan, from 1829 to 1833. As the new settlers of Michigan organized themselves locally and regionally in political bodies, they also joined forces over social and moral issues like temperance and slavery.

Attending meetings required a sacrifice of time and expense, but the men formed four antislavery societies in Michigan as auxiliaries to the national organization in 1836. The secretaries were William E. Prier of Farmington, George W. Wisner of Oakland County (50 members), Theodore Foster of Webster and Scio in Washtenaw County (20 members), and Darius Comstock of Lenawee County. Eurotas P. Hastings was the only delegate listed from Michigan at the May 10, 1836, American Anti-Slavery Society meeting in New York. However, Theodore Foster recorded that he attended the meeting as well.[25] Of the 527 national antislavery societies quite a few were "female" and very few were "colored." Within six months of the national gathering, new local societies met in Detroit and Niles, Berrien County.[26]

Michigan was not yet a state when 313 citizens signed the printed call for a "Convention of the friends of immediate abolition," dated September 5, 1836. Persons who believed slavery was the "darkest stain on the page of our country's history" were invited to appoint delegates to attend the convention. On November 10, 1836, delegates and attendees gathered at the Ann Arbor First Presbyterian Church, where the Rev. John Beach was pastor, for an "Anti-Slavery State Convention." Beach was known throughout southeast Michigan where he founded numerous churches and would soon organize the area's Presbyterian churches into the Washtenaw Presbytery.[27]

Over two days, the men established the Michigan State Anti-Slavery Society, an auxiliary to the American Anti-Slavery Society; adopted fourteen resolutions denouncing slavery; elected officers; and decided to secure a press.[28] The first business of the Convention was the appointment of Darius Comstock of Lenawee County as chair and J. C. Burnell of Detroit as secretary. A Committee of Arrangements included three men from Wayne, one from Oakland, and one from Washtenaw Counties. Delegates were listed from Lenawee, Livingston, and St. Joseph Counties also. Individuals from Kalamazoo, Monroe, Allegan, Branch, and St. Clair Counties, and four men from Ohio attended. Two of the Ohio men were agents from Weld's Seventy, John Cowles and George Whipple, who had been lecturing in the area.[29]

Most resolutions dealt with the inhumanity and denial of rights concerned with the institution of slavery. After the declarations of the American Anti-Slavery Society were read aloud, convention members decided to draft a constitution immediately for their state organization. William Kirkland led a committee of three to draft a preamble and constitution. Kirkland met Weld and roomed with him at Hamilton College, though he was not one of Weld's Seventy.[30] Apparently, the committee argued and amended throughout the night for the final work was approved at 9:00 A.M. the following day. The goal of the Michigan State Anti-Slavery Society was the "entire abolition of slavery in the United States of America."

The meeting continued to the next day. A vice president was elected from each of eleven counties. Establishing a newspaper was a priority, and it was resolved that women across the state should form Ladies Anti-Slavery Societies. The Report of the Proceedings of the Convention illustrates the principles and convictions of these Michigan men. They chose the cause of abolition. There is no record that colonization was discussed. Everyone assembled was expected to encourage membership in the Society, petition Congress to end the slave trade and slavery, work to extend the vote to all male citizens, and help educate all blacks in Michigan.

The resolution to reject violence supported the constitution of the American Anti-Slavery Society and the non-militant Quakers who helped organize the Michigan meeting. Darius Comstock, Nathan Power, and Elizabeth Chandler's brother Thomas Chandler, as members of the Society of Friends, were bound by an oath of nonviolence. Their means to end slavery would be primarily by influencing the understanding and heart of the slaveholder and secondarily by new legislation. Article Two of the Society Constitution stated that the aim "shall be to convince all our fellow-citizens by argument addressed to their understanding and consciences."[31]

The radical abolitionists at the convention must have been sorely disappointed by the carefully wrought resolutions. For instance, a declaration of the Anti-Slavery Convention in Philadelphia stated that, according to the Bible, every American citizen holding a human in bondage was a "man-stealer."

The Michigan Society declared, "slaveholding is deeply injurious to the temporal as well as spiritual interests of the master, and that he would find it expedient to do right and restore his bondman to that freedom which, by the gift of Heaven, is the rightful inheritance of every human being."

Though the Michigan Society declarations seemed weak and cloaked in religious terms, the delegates themselves acted with resolve to physically assist people escaping from slavery. Of the eleven vice presidents and the executive committee, nearly everyone became involved in the Underground Railroad. It is interesting to note the absence of any known black Americans of Michigan among the delegates. Laura Haviland's father and brother, Daniel and Harvey Smith, attended. Laura would not take up the call to start a ladies society. She and Charles were busy preparing to open the Raisin Institute, an integrated, coeducational school.

Sylvanus Cole, one of the few attendees from Ohio, attended the founding Society meeting and bravely set out on a Michigan lecture tour. On a Sabbath day in February 1837, Professor Cole procured a church in Pontiac for his talk. A correspondent witnessed the "wildest scenes of riot and outrage." Pistols, dirks, and sword canes were drawn. Before the sheriff arrived, the crowd demolished the church windows.[32]

Lewis Hill walked away from enslavement in Augusta, Georgia, with the North Star as his guide. It took six months for him to reach Michigan (author photograph, Kingsley Plantation, Florida, 2007).

The Rev. John Cowles publicized his plan for a debate in Ann Arbor. The *Michigan Argus* of Feb. 2, 1837, provided an inhospitable welcome by stating that while other places had been excited and divided on the topic of abolition, the editors hoped their "community would remain exempt from its vexations." Later, the editors were impressed by the Reverend Cowles' honesty but taken aback by his statement that he had a political viewpoint and that if abolitionism dissolved the union, so be it. The editors asked the citizens of Michigan whether they were ready to see the bricks of government reduced to chips.[33]

Cities and counties soon formed new auxiliary antislavery organizations. On April 26, 1837, the Detroit Anti-Slavery Society was organized with Shubael Conant as president; Charles Henry Stewart, secretary; and George F. Porter, treasurer. These men remained a powerful force in the state antislavery society and the Liberty party for years. Stewart, Detroit lawyer, Irishman, and "fiery orator" was a close friend of Underground Railroad operator Seymour Treadwell.

The First Annual Michigan State Anti-Slavery Society meeting was held in June 1837. Most of the Executive Committee remained in place for another year, with the exception Thomas Chandler. A vice president from Macomb County was added in order to represent a cross-section of organized counties. The Rev. Oren C. Thompson, Lane Seminary graduate of St. Clair, was nominated a vice president. Darius Comstock welcomed his nephew Edwin to the Adrian valley where he remained a dedicated abolitionist. Within the bounds of his Quaker faith, Edwin Comstock supported with money and argument "the cause of the oppressed."[34]

Two resolutions were passed at the first annual meeting, both recognizing the black Americans in their midst. The first resolution dealt with encouraging and aiding "the colored people to seek agricultural employment" and the other to affirm that freed men appreciated liberty. A committee was appointed to compile a list of names of men who would circulate petitions. These men were culled from Wayne, Lenawee, Oakland, and Washtenaw Counties. Perhaps the difficulty of traveling to the more remote areas of the Lower Peninsula led to a decision to conserve their limited funds.

Most importantly, the members clarified their ultimate goal was "freeing our beloved country from the great sin of slavery," which "cannot be fully accomplished until *slavery* is *absolutely* and *universally abolished*."[35]

By December of that year, Henry Bibb was on his journey to freedom, a story recounted at the opening of this chapter. Bibb was given permission to work in the slaughterhouses along the Ohio River over the Christmas holidays. Instead of work, Bibb "found a conveyance to cross over into a free state." He successfully traveled by boat to Cincinnati where Underground Railroad operators helped him further north. He stayed in Perrysburg, Ohio, for a time, but would not remain without his wife and child. In his attempt to rescue Malinda and his daughter Frances, Bibb was captured and sent to Kentucky. Again he escaped, returned to rescue his family, was captured again, and sold to Louisiana. Finally, he returned north to live in Michigan and work with some of Weld's rebels in the fight against slavery's hold.[36]

Chapter Five

Stations in the Wilderness:
A Working System of Assistance

Escape of Lewis Hill, 1838

For months he journeyed on foot, under cover of darkness, supplied with food from the "Negro quarters." The man enslaved as Joseph Mallory left Augusta, Georgia, in March 1838, with a little money and the knowledge to follow the North Star. He reached and crossed the Ohio River as the season changed to fall. On landing in a place where slavery was prohibited by law, Mallory chose a new name for himself: Lewis Hill.

Friends in the Quaker settlements helped Hill through Indiana. The majority of citizens in the southern tier of the state brokered no resistance to the forays of slave hunters. While traveling in Indiana, Hill was attacked by several ruffians who stole his clothes and nearly captured him. Crossing from Grant County, Indiana, to Cass County, Michigan, Lewis Hill found refuge in the home of Josiah Osborn, a Quaker. Osborn sent the weary traveler to Dr. Nathan Thomas in Schoolcraft, Kalamazoo County, Michigan.

Dr. Thomas wrote, "He spent the night in my office. I advised him to go no further as I thought he could safely remain here. But he expressed a determination not to stop short of Canada. I replenished his clothing added to his purse and sent him on his way rejoicing."

Lewis Hill set out on an early October morning after breakfasting with Elder William Taylor. Hill carried a letter with the names of trusted friends in Kalamazoo, Calhoun, and Jackson Counties. In Jackson, Lewis Hill stayed with William Sullivan and then was sent to Amasa Gillet's farm in Sharon Township, Washtenaw County.

By this time, nourishing berries clung shriveled and dried on vines, and once plentiful walnuts lay shrouded by a skin of hard frost. Lewis Hill, in fear for his life, had trekked on foot for seven months through five states. He likely walked along the Brooklyn-Sharon Valley Road into western Washtenaw County. There the tamarack swamps filled the shadows of towering white and burr oaks. Beyond the short hills lay the plains of the Sharon Valley and home of Amasa Gillet.

Lewis Hill remained with Amasa Gillet over the winter. In the spring, the man enslaved as Joseph Mallory crossed the Detroit River to Canada to begin a life of freedom as Lewis Hill. As others soon followed in his footsteps, this method of directing freedom seekers to places of refuge was established in Michigan and became known as the Underground Railroad.[1]

The majority of the early freedom seekers relied on their own ingenuity, and they traveled on foot. By the early 1830s, it was possible to follow established roads from Indiana and Illinois through the state of Michigan. Michigan achieved statehood on January 26, 1837. Since 1833, the stagecoach running from Chicago to Detroit completed the journey in five days, weather permitting.

Just as there were scatterings of Underground Railroad helpers, there were places where slave hunters lurked and found support in the community. Without directions to safe houses, a person escaping slavery's tyranny suffered a long and dangerous journey. A successful escape from the Deep South (the lower Mississippi valley east to South Carolina) to Michigan was less common than those from Kentucky, Missouri, and other mid–American states.

An early history of Alabama describes the patrol system:

> throughout the entire South, where slavery existed, a more or less competent and comprehensive patrol system was maintained. No slave was permitted off the premises of the master, and only in rare instances out of his slave quarters, without a special permit. Free negroes were scarce, and usually well known. Hence, we see the matter of capturing a fugitive slave resolved itself into the simple office on the part of the patrol to take up any negro seen upon the highway, day or night, unattended by some person in authority. Nor was it an easy matter for a run-away to travel across country; since, in doing so he almost invariably came in contact with some slave overseer, or owner, to whom he was unknown; whereupon he was promptly arrested.[2]

Hill's Freedom Trail

Lewis Hill first connected with the Underground Railroad in the Quaker settlements in northern Indiana. He was forwarded to a series of white Underground Railroad agents, beginning with Josiah Osborn, son of Quaker minister, Charles W. Osborn, of the Tennessee Manumission Society. The Osborns were among North Carolina Quakers who emancipated slaves and sent them to colonies in the northern states.[3]

The Manumission Society's petitions and demand for immediate emancipation caused problems for members, and many chose to move north. Charles Osborn was "disowned" from monthly and yearly meetings of the Society of Friends for supporting the abolitionist cause.[4] The Reverend Osborn located first in Mount Pleasant, Ohio, in 1816, where he taught school and published *The Philanthropist,* the first antislavery periodical in the United States (Benjamin Lundy later published his newspaper from the same place). One of his pupils was Dr. Nathan Thomas, who helped Lewis Hill's escape in the preceding vignette. Osborn was one of the most prominent abolitionists in the movement. William Lloyd Garrison in 1847 said, "Charles Osborn is the father of all us Abolitionists."[5]

In 1819, Osborn relocated to Economy, Wayne County, Indiana, a two-day walk to Cass County, Michigan. Osborn and Mendenhall Roads honor early founders of the city northwest of Cincinnati. The Reverend Osborn provided the link in a chain of stations from the south at Levi Coffin's place in Wayne County, Indiana; his children's homes in Cass County; and on to Nathan Thomas in Schoolcraft, Michigan.

The Pokagon Prairie in Western Michigan attracted settlers in the 1820s who congregated near the site of the Carey Mission. As mentioned earlier, William Baldwin Jenkins offered hospitality and lessons on slavery to the newcomers in Cass County. One of the settlers in Calvin Township in the 1830s was Josiah Osborn, son of the Reverend Osborn from his first marriage. Josiah's sons, Jefferson and Leander, and other family members created a nucleus of Underground Railroad activity with protected settlements, shelter, and transportation for freedom seekers. In the early days, The Rev. Charles Osborn was part of the network in northern Indiana, but from 1842 to 1847 he participated with his sons and daughters and their husbands when he resided opposite his daughter Mrs. James E. Bonine in Vandalia, Penn Township, Cass County.

Levi Coffin sent a woman from Indiana to western Michigan around 1836. "Aunt Rachel" arrived at Coffin's home in Indiana after enduring years of emotional and physical distress. Her husband was the first sold away from the family. After she was sold away from her children, Rachel ran away and was caught. She managed a successful escape though burdened by shackles. After months recovering at the Coffin's home in Indiana, Rachel was forwarded to Michigan.

Coffin described using a disguise popular among Quaker conductors. Aunt Rachel was dressed in Quaker garb, including gloves and a large bonnet. "She presented the appearance of a sedate and comely Quaker woman." Rachel joined a committee appointed to visit Young's Prairie, Cass County, Michigan. She remained at the Friends' settlement several days, and was then sent on the mail coach to Detroit." Underground Railroad workers helped Rachel cross to Windsor. When Coffin visited her in 1844, she had married a man named Keys.[6] Rachel's story is one of many that demonstrate how the Meeting organization of Quakers greatly facilitated Underground Railroad work.

Josiah Osborn forwarded Lewis Hill to Dr. Nathan Thomas, who was acquainted with the Osborn family in Mount Pleasant, Ohio. Thomas attended the Reverend Osborn's school and later moved to Schoolcraft, when only a few dozen settlers could support his medical practice. A distant 15 miles south of Kalamazoo, Thomas opened an office in the hotel. From his earliest days as a bachelor, freedom seekers came to him for help and protection.

Growing up in a Quaker household in Mount Pleasant, Ohio, brought the issue of slavery to his doorstep. Thomas wrote, "At an early day my attention was drawn to the enormity of American Slavery, as an institution at war with free government and the rights of man and from 1837 I acted with the antislavery element of the country until slavery was finally overthrown by the great rebellion."[7]

Lewis Hill was not the first freedom seeker to find shelter with Dr. Thomas. In the winter of 1836, George Layne found his way from Kentucky to Schoolcraft, where he attempted to settle in the community and was employed by William and Delemore Duncan. In Dr. Thomas' words "He did not remain long before the manhunter was close on his track but being informed of his approach by vigilant friends barely in time to elude his grasp, the pursuer soon became discouraged, abandoned pursuit and left the Prairie. After an absence of a few days Layne returned and ever after remained in security."[8]

As described in the vignette preceding this chapter, in 1838 Lewis Hill stayed with Thomas in his two room office and residence at Center and Eliza Streets. The distinctive basilica-style Greek Revival house and Underground Railroad station was easily described and recognized. Dr. Thomas' brother Jesse had joined him in the medical practice and, from 1838 to 1840, Stephen B. Thayer studied under them. In the morning, Lewis Hill was afraid to enter the hotel where Dr. Thomas ate his meals. From his office door, Dr. Thomas pointed out the residence of antislavery man William Taylor, and sent Hill there for breakfast.

Lewis Hill walked to unnamed helpers in Kalamazoo and Calhoun Counties, and then to William Sullivan's place in Jackson County. Dr. Thomas was not personally acquainted with Sullivan, but would meet him and station agent Amasa Gillet at an antislavery convention in Jackson the next year in February 1839.[9]

The Rev. William Sullivan was a familiar figure to the frontier pioneers of southeast Michigan as a minister of the Methodist Episcopal Church. He rode to distant hamlets and towns offering services in any agreeable abode. From 1832 until settling in Jackson in 1837, Sullivan served the circuits of Ann Arbor, Mt. Clemens, Sandusky, Dexter, and Clinton.

When his brother Nicholas accepted an invitation to publish a newspaper in Jackson, William joined him in the endeavor. The Sullivan brothers had moved from Virginia to Ohio as children because of their father's opposition to slavery. Shortly after his arrival, the Reverend Sullivan took up the call to promote the antislavery agenda to the one thousand Jackson citizens. In 1838, he proceeded to deliver a lecture on American slavery until a mob put a stop to his discourse. With public sentiment against him, the Reverend Sullivan decided a newspaper might be a better medium to disseminate the cause of emancipation, but establishing a printing operation was a daunting task, and he and his brother printed only four numbers of the *American Freeman*. It would be up to Theodore Foster and the Rev. Guy Beckley to publish an antislavery newspaper in the region.

From the Reverend Sullivan's, Lewis Hill went to Amasa Gillet's farm. As an early Michigan pioneer, Amasa Gillet was able to purchase uncultivated land in a picturesque setting where glacial moraines formed short hills rising above the River Raisin. Here Gillet purchased a tract in an oak opening in 1831. He returned to Ontario, New York, then, with his wife, Esther Dunn, and six children, migrated to Michigan in 1833. His grandson, James Robison, wrote that Amasa used heavy hewn oak timbers to dam the river and build a saw mill in the hamlet of Sharon Hollow. He later built a gristmill as he accumulated a thousand acres.[10]

Lewis Hill spent the winter with Amasa Gillet in Sharon Township, Washtenaw County, Michigan, in 1838. Hill moved to Canada the following spring (photograph of Sharon Mills, Sharon Township, Michigan, by Robert Mull, 2009).

Amasa Gillet was affiliated with the Methodist Episcopal Church and his three sons "distinguished themselves in the ministry." When Gillet became frustrated with the Church's tolerance of slaveholding, he helped found the Michigan Wesleyan Anti-Slavery Society and served as its first president in 1841.[11]

The *Signal of Liberty* reported on antislavery petitions sent to the U. S. Senate. The first petition requested that free states be released from any obligation to support slavery by a federal constitutional amendment. Amasa Gillet and 51 others of Washtenaw County, Michigan, signed this and two other petitions. Another called for the repeal of all laws "authorizing the holding or transporting of slaves coastwise from one State to another in vessels of the United States."

Like tens of thousands of petitions to legislators, Gillet's petitions were ignored. Southern legislators managed to pass a series of rules that postponed action on all petitions relating to slavery. Finally, the United States Congress instituted a "Gag Rule," temporarily silencing congressional discussion of abolitionist petitions from 1836 to 1844.

The resolutions infuriated many northerners who viewed the legislation as suppression of free speech. In addition, some postal carriers diverted antislavery tracts and newspapers. These actions contributed to a growing rift between the North and South.[12]

Gillet apparently chose not to participate in the state antislavery society; however, he did attend an antislavery conference in Putnam, Ohio, in June 1839. There, he met an acquaintance of Lewis Hill who had stayed with Gillet on his journey to freedom in Canada.

David Bristol, Hill's acquaintance, experienced a briefer though equally terrifying journey because he traveled by stagecoach through the slave states with a forged pass. Though Canada was his original destination, Bristol remained in Ohio. He was happy to hear his friend from Augusta, Georgia, was as free as himself. Nathan Thomas recorded in his diary that David Bristol changed his name to Anthony Philips.[13] There is no record of others who passed through Sharon Hollow on their journey to freedom.

Early Stations and Callers

A few places in Michigan were known to harbor freedom seekers in the 1830s. The Raisin Institute opened in 1837, as Laura Haviland wrote in her autobiography *A Woman's Life-Work*. The school was open to any student "of good moral character" of any religion or race. P. P. Roots served as principal for the first three years and was followed by John Patchin who had attended Oberlin College several years after the Lane Debates. Patchin's description of his parents' concern about Oberlin reveals the prevailing anti-abolition views of most Americans:

> Abolition was as yet quite unpopular and Oberlin was decidedly abolition. The popular sentiment was that the negro was an inferior race and should be kept in his proper place. Oberlin recognized the negro as equal to the white man and admitted him on the same terms with the white to all privileges of the institution.[14]

Patchin taught at the Raisin Institute and then returned to Oberlin to continue his studies. After graduation, he settled on property next to the Raisin Institute. By this time, the Rev. Jeremiah Dolbeare had purchased the school. Over the next three years, Patchin brought in students from 50 to 100 miles away, and he mentioned the visits of unwelcome southerners.

In addition to accepting black students, like James Martin, the Havilands leased land to Elsie and Willis Hamilton, a self-freed couple.

Baptist Deacon John Bayliss of Jones-borough, Tennessee, emancipated Willis, but Willis' wife Elsie belonged to a neighboring planter who wanted to sell her to a southern drover. Willis convinced Dr. John P. Chester to purchase Elsie. Part of the bargain required Willis to work for Chester, but with the idea that he would earn money to buy Elsie himself. After several months, Elsie learned that Chester planned to sell both Elsie and Willis to a trader bound for the New Orleans market. The Hamiltons turned to Deacon Bayliss for help.

Elsie was hidden while they devised a plan. Willis' free papers included the names of a group of slaves being emancipated. Two of those listed were brother and sister, Jane and Bill Willis. The Hamiltons assumed those names and began the long walk from Tennessee to Canada.

As Bill and Jane, the pair walked to Indiana, where they stayed with a Quaker family named Shugart. The Hamiltons chose to travel with assistance to Canada. Willis was disappointed with opportunities in Canada and on condition they live near a Quaker family, Elsie agreed to move to the Haviland's property near Adrian, Michigan. They settled there and were three years into buying a property, when Elsie was met by a southerner and she determined they must move away. Over the next six years, the family of four lived near Adrian, then Ypsilanti. When they moved to Monroe, the couple contacted Deacon Bayliss about their daughters in Tennessee. Bayliss responded that the girls were still on the same farm and cautioned them to keep their whereabouts from Dr. Chester.

The Hamiltons returned to the Raisin Institute just after Charles Haviland's death in 1845. Once again, the Hamiltons corresponded with Bayliss and received a letter saying he could deliver their daughters if Willis would meet him. Laura Haviland convinced Willis it was a trick because she knew of slave owners bribing postal workers to intercept letters from the North. Laura Haviland took black student James Martin instead of Willis Hamilton to the rendezvous in Toledo.

Haviland's suspicions were confirmed when she met up with Chester and the Hamilton's daughters were nowhere to be seen. As predicted, Chester had a scheme to kidnap Willis but he met his match in Haviland. Before returning to Tennessee empty-handed, John Chester threatened Haviland at gunpoint. A few years later, Chester returned to Michigan prepared to take his "property."[15]

By the time Principal Patchin left around 1844, the Raisin Institute was in a difficult period of transition. The buildings needed to be replaced and money was scarce. Prospective teacher Stephen Decatur Helms wrote to his brother that he had been preaching in Hudson and Wheatland, Michigan, because when he arrived five months earlier at Raisin Institute, he was turned away. In the stampless letter, postmarked Raisin, Michigan, September 7, 1844, Helms wrote "there is a great deal of sickness through the country." As he penned his letter, inviting his brother to join him teaching at the Raisin Institute, Stephen Helms was unaware of the devastation about to come down upon the Haviland family. A contagious skin rash took the lives of Laura's husband, parents, youngest daughter, and Institute Principal Emily Galpin in the spring of 1845. Laura Haviland was left a widow in her mid-thirties with seven children, helping self-freed people create new lives, managing a farm, and running a school.[16]

The Raisin Institute was known as one of the earliest interracial schools in the Midwest, but Helms' letter reveals a larger purpose not clearly outlined by Haviland herself. Helms wrote, "A committee has been formed and an agent appropriated to solicit aide for coloured students & also to get respectable coloured families to come and settle here &

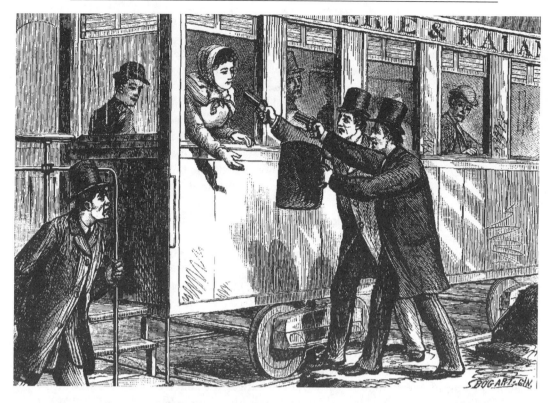

Laura Haviland, held at gunpoint, said, "Man, I fear neither your weapons nor your threats; they are powerless." She risked her life to rescue people held in slavery (L.H. *A Woman's Life-Work* [1889]).

make it their own school — teachers & ministers will soon be wanted at the south and they are now wanted by scores & hundreds in Africa."[17]

The Havilands were not alone among pioneers welcoming self-freed people from the South. East of Adrian, John and Abigail Critchett moved to London Township, Monroe County, Michigan, in the early 1830s. The Critchett's home was midway between Toledo, Ohio, and Ann Arbor, Michigan.

John Critchett was very sympathetic to the heartbreak of kidnapping and separation from family. His father, when out at sea as a young sailor from Connecticut, was taken aboard a British vessel and kept prisoner for two years. John Critchett grew up hearing the story of his father's return to a widowed mother. When John and Abigail Critchett settled in Monroe County, Michigan, they shared their meager supplies with those Americans deprived of their liberty. The Critchett house was a station where self-emancipators would be brought and concealed for a time. When safe, they would be forwarded on the Underground Railroad.[18]

Freedom seekers arrived in the sparsely settled western counties of Michigan in the 1830s. In the spring of 1837, a married couple from Virginia and a man from Alabama stopped at the Oshtemo, Michigan, home of Henry M. Montague on the prairie west of Kalamazoo Village. Montague was a white antislavery man from Hadley, Massachusetts. Only months before moving to Oshtemo, Montague attended the founding meeting of the Michigan State Anti-Slavery Society in Ann Arbor. Montague offered aide to the self-freed travelers in desperate need of food and rest, but, terrified, the men claimed pursuers were "hot on their trail."[19]

After a meal at a neighbor's, Montague drove the freedom seekers to Galesburg and left them with Hugh Morris Shafter, an early Michigan settler from Vermont. "From this time Mr. Montague, so long as need existed, kept an open station of the underground railroad." Henry Montague remained active in the antislavery cause. Dr. Nathan Thomas wrote in his diary, "Montague will lecture in the town of Prairie Ronde the last Wednesday of December at early candle lighting."[20]

Another Underground Railroad station in operation before 1840 was located in Union City, Branch County, Michigan, northeast of LaGrange, Indiana. Giles Stebbins, one of Weld's Seventy and agent of the American Anti-Slavery Society, stopped at Union City on his lecturing tour. Stebbins wrote, "in the pioneer antislavery lecture field, from Maine to Missouri and Delaware, I spent years in cities, towns, and country by-ways, traveled thousands of miles and spoke hundreds of times."[21]

Union City was not easy to reach. Stebbins traveled by the Michigan Southern Railway to Coldwater and then by stagecoach fourteen miles north and across the St. Joseph River. He thought Union City a "pleasant village on a high plateau with beautiful farms and orchards in front of great forest oaks." He met John D. Zimmerman, one of four New Yorkers who came in 1838 with a "force of men" to create a village on a 200-acre tract. Zimmerman and founders Israel and Richard Clarke, were members of the Michigan State Anti-Slavery Society.[22]

After dinner that evening, Stebbins accompanied Zimmerman to an antislavery meeting at the Congregational Church. Over the course of his visit, Stebbins heard his host's story of an attempt to take a man into slavery. Around 1845, a southerner arrived at Zimmerman's blacksmith shop swearing oaths and threats about returning a runaway to his owner. Zimmerman could have felled the man with a single blow from his muscled arms. Instead, with a steady gaze in his blue eyes, the blacksmith calmly suggested the men confer with a lawyer.

After their peaceful meeting in a law office, Zimmerman welcomed the slave hunter to his home for the night with these words, "I have another guest at my house. He shall treat you well and I expect you to treat him well. He is the man you claim as a slave."

The following morning, the slave hunter sat at breakfast opposite Andrew Smith, the self-freed man who escaped by substituting his name in the free papers of

Susan Hussey, a courageous young woman, single-handedly cared for up to two dozen freedom seekers at once when her parents were away from their home in Battle Creek, Michigan (Willard Library, Battle Creek, Michigan).

his father. Though his father was free, Smith was born into slavery by his mother's status as a slave. Andrew Smith was able to get away with help from a neighbor, who was later forced to pay the value of the "human property" loss.

From the time he escaped from the Pedee River area of North Carolina in 1839, Smith had been working in Zimmerman's blacksmith shop. For several days, the slave hunter and his quarry sat at the table, listening to John Zimmerman's views. And one morning, Andrew Smith was gone. In a fury, the southerner left empty handed but with a new awareness of a different view of human equality. Andrew Smith was back home in a few days and lived safely for a long time in Michigan.[23] Zimmerman remained an active abolitionist, supporting the causes in Michigan that might let his neighbor, Mr. Smith, remain at home when southerners came calling.

Chapter Six

An Interstate Network of Escape

Escape of Old Agnes

"Old Agnes was not easily forgotten.... Without a guide, save the north star, she had pushed her way northward, alone, by night, four hundred miles toward freedom." Her steps were slow and painful, ailments of the aged and abused. Her hair was white. Across her face, a deep groove from the strap of a water cask was one of her visible scars. Susan Hussey befriended Old Agnes in Battle Creek, Michigan, and later spoke of witnessing the worst sight of man's inhumanity.

"'Old Agnes' had been the joint property of two white men—men too poor to own more than a half-interest each in a slave—and these exalted proprietors of human 'property' had taken turns in maltreating her. Her back and lower limbs were a network of bone-deep scars." When the old woman reached Hussey's home she soon requested a knife "with which to perform upon her festering wounds some rude surgery."

The wounds were inflicted by her "masters," who thought a beating would quicken the pace of the elderly woman. They used a sled-stake, one of the slender posts used to hold the load on a wagon. They beat her until she could no longer walk. As soon as she recovered, Old Agnes started on her journey to freedom.[1]

One of the most widely circulated depictions of the Underground Railroad shows a train heading into a tunnel above the title "Liberty Line." The advertisement appeared in *The Western Citizen* of Chicago, Illinois, on July 13, 1844, with a description stating the fare: "SEATS FREE, irrespective of color," and "For seats apply at any of the trap doors, or to the conductor of the train," and signed by "J. Cross, Proprietor."[2] Of Weld's Seventy, one of the least known yet most important was the Rev. John Cross. As he traveled from New York to Pennsylvania and then through Michigan to Illinois, Cross put Weld's ideas into action by creating an interstate Underground Railroad network. Untold thousands were carried from Missouri across Illinois, Indiana, and Michigan, to the Detroit gateway to Canada over the next decades.

In 1840, three years after statehood, Michigan was very sparsely populated. Only three counties had over 20,000 inhabitants: Wayne, Oakland, and Washtenaw, all in the southeast quadrant. The "free colored" population in the entire state was around 700, with nearly 300 in Wayne County and the rest living predominantly in Washtenaw, Oakland, Monroe and Berrien Counties. The high proportion of blacks in Monroe was very likely a carry-over from the original French settlement. In Washtenaw, the Aray and Silas Day families made up about a quarter of the black population, while nearly a dozen single men boarded near the home of John Lowry and worked on the railroad. Berrien County had a growing settlement of families emancipated and protected by local Quakers. Across the state, only one in 300 citizens was a black American. The Rev. John Cross learned where black settlements might offer aid to freedom seekers, as well as where known antislavery men lived in Michigan.[3]

John Cross, born in Massachusetts in 1797, was raised in New York where he trained for the ministry at the Oneida Institute. In 1836, the Reverend Cross was chosen by Theodore Weld as one of the Seventy and assigned to lecture for the cause in Pennsylvania. One of Cross' earliest activities was a lecture in Wilkes-Barre, Pennsylvania. Because he was barred from lecturing on the topic of slavery in public places, the Reverend Cross began his lecture in a private home. When the place was mobbed, the rabble-rousers demanded Cross be turned over to them. His friends kept him locked in a side room while the men broke the host's gate and trampled his fence and shrubbery. Undeterred, Cross continued to lecture, organized the Wayne County Anti-Slavery Society in northeastern Pennsylvania and participated in meetings and debates. By the time he returned to New York, the Reverend Cross was acquainted with many abolitionists and a system of helping enslaved people through Pennsylvania.[4]

In 1839, the Reverend Cross moved to Illinois and traveled between Illinois and Pennsylvania setting up an interstate freedom trail.[5] After a connection of several years with Amity College, Cross entered the ministry of the Congregational Church. He was described as a "strenuous antislavery advocate" who propagated his views, actively enforced them, and helped many escape north from slavery.[6]

The Rev. John Cross Testimonies

The testimonies of numerous Underground Railroad workers incontrovertibly substantiate the establishment of an interstate network by the Reverend Cross. The Rev. Wolcott B. Williams penned his reminiscences about the early settlement of northwest Indiana where he transported freedom seekers from his father's home 18 miles to the next station. The Reverend Cross met antislavery sympathizers when lecturing in Indiana, Illinois and Michigan and established stations "bout twelve or twenty miles apart, from Missouri to Detroit." His father's house was a station set up by the Reverend Cross.[7]

On March 17, 1840, Pamela S. Brown married Dr. Nathan Macy Thomas, who had provided help to Lewis Hill on his escape in 1838. She moved into Dr. Thomas' residence and Underground Railroad station in Schoolcraft, Michigan, after he enlarged it with side wings. Together, Nathan and Pamela Thomas and their daughter cared for as many as 1,500 people who stopped on their way to freedom.

Pamela Thomas wrote of her first experiences meeting men and women who had been enslaved, and their stories persuaded her to take on the expense and work of the Underground Railroad. The first freedom seeker who came to her door was an elderly woman who walked alone from Missouri. During the start of her journey, she was helped by enslaved people and, as she continued, by Quakers. Thomas said, "This woman was an eloquent talker. She told me of what some women had to endure from cruel and licentious masters. From that time I felt it was my duty to do the little I could for those attempting to escape from bondage."

Mrs. Thomas remembered when the Reverend Cross asked that their existing station become part of a larger network. "About the year 1843 a Mr. Cross stopped with us. He was arranging for safe and speedy conveyance for fugitives from slavery to Canada. This was 'the Underground Railroad.' Our home was to be a station."

The Reverend Cross told them to expect cargoes from Zachariah Shugart in Cass County. Dr. Nathan Thomas should see them safely to Erastus Hussey in Battle Creek. The first came singly or in pairs, but soon from six to twelve at once. It was hard work and a great expense. Pamela Thomas recalled that, "often after my little ones were asleep and I thought the labor of the day over, Friend Shugart would drive up, with a load of hungry people to be fed and housed for the night."[8] Dr. Nathan Thomas' words echo his wife's, though he was more certain of the year. "In 1842 John Cross of Illinois passed through this state and adopted essentially the same line ... after having fixed the line of the Illinois branch."[9]

Erastus Hussey wrote that a man named John Cross stopped at his house while Hussey was in Detroit, and the man refused to tell Mrs. Hussey his purpose. "After I returned home I received a letter from Cross. He informed me that he was establishing a route from Kentucky and Ohio to Canada, through which freedom seekers could be conducted without molestation, and wanted me to take charge of the station in Battle Creek."[10] Hussey had never heard of the Underground Railroad previously. He learned that Pamela and Nathan Thomas were in charge of the station after Cassopolis where Shugart and Osborn operated. Hussey credited Levi Coffin with the scheme and John Cross with setting up the stations and agents. Erastus Hussey recalled, "It was just four weeks after John Cross had appointed me agent that the first fugitives came. They were two men, William Coleman and Stephen Wood. These men came through under fictitious names and always retained them. This the fugitives frequently did."[11]

While the escaping slaves were at the Hussey homestead, Levi Coffin and Quaker minister John Beard visited. A Quaker mission in Indiana appointed Coffin and Beard "to visit the colored people of Canada and to learn how they were succeeding, and to ascertain what assistance they were in need of."[12] Coleman and Wood were "overcome with joy" when they saw their Quaker friends. Coffin's account confirms that he was part of the Indiana-Michigan Underground Railroad network. Coffin wrote they left Indiana September 9, 1844, and traveled throughout the lower Great Lake State for a month, until landing in Detroit.[13]

Coffin and Beard made regular trips from Indiana to Michigan and Canada, often delivering supplies to black settlements. In Detroit, the men "spent the afternoon visiting the colored schools and various families of fugitives, many of whom remembered us, having stopped at our houses on their way from slavery to freedom."[14]

Several stations existed between Bat-

Erastus Hussey helped Nancy Stevens and about one thousand others on their journey to freedom through Battle Creek, Michigan (*History of Calhoun County* [1877], Bentley Historical Library, University of Michigan).

tle Creek and Concord, two villages in Jackson County, Michigan. Concord was the next station, in an easterly direction, established by the Reverend Cross. Concord lay southeast of Albion, close to Spring Arbor on the road to Jackson. Judge Melville McGee wrote, "As early as 1838, a road had been surveyed, stations established and the Road put in full operation. It was afterwards known as the 'Underground Railroad' and carried passengers only." He described it as running all day and night. The people running it delivered passengers in good condition at their own expense. McGee wrote, "I well remember the man who surveyed the route and established a station at my father's house. His name was the Reverend Cross, residing at some place in Indiana."[15]

Melville McGee was four years old in 1832 when his parents moved to Concord. At the time, Concord Township held two families. Two years later, the David Smalley family arrived and, finding only five houses, they crowded into the McGee's cabin. Smalley "was a strong antislavery and temperance man, and a member of the Baptist church. His house was at one time a refuge or station on the 'underground railway.'" Two sons later moved to Jackson where both were elected in different years to the position of County sheriff.[16]

Melville recalled that his older brothers helped his father, Thomas McGee, transport freedom seekers. One evening they conveyed six strong "stalwart" men to the next station.[17] He does not provide a date, but it is very likely they were the same men described in the *Signal of Liberty* in May 1841. Editors Beckley and Foster wrote of an increasing number of people escaping from involuntary servitude to Michigan.

> A few days since we had the rare pleasure in connection with many of our friends in this place, of bestowing our hospitalities upon six of our brethren, who tarried with us some sixteen hours to refresh themselves on their journey to a "land of freedom."[18]

The editors described the six young men as gentlemanly and temperate, with intelligence superior to many white persons. The men departed for Canada before the newspaper went to print. Beckley and Foster acknowledged acting in defiance of the law, yet they rejoiced in doing what was morally right. The article ended with a plea to all Michiganians to provide safe passage through the state by ensuring that if taken by slave catchers, those escaping to Canada would have a fair trial by jury.[19]

A Network, Not a Line

Though slave escapes occurred in every direction, many historians refer to primary "routes" from the south to the north. "Routes" expresses something linear and defined. William J. Switala, in his published books on the Underground Railroad, condenses the network into three major systems of escape: western, central, and eastern. It appears that Michigan was the only state involved in two of those systems. No matter how broadly or refined the escape routes to Canada are mapped, a convergence of travelers from western and central states occurs in southeast Michigan.[20]

In Michigan, several Underground Railroad agents attempted to correct the notion of routes in their later writings. Erastus Hussey of Battle Creek wrote that there were not defined routes, but a "zigzag" of paths to safe places. Men and women used the terms "lines" and "branches" as a general way to describe the networks of people and places that made up the Underground Railroad. Dr. Nathan Thomas of Schoolcraft distinguished the "Indiana" and "Illinois" lines by their points of origin and wrote that they merged in Cass County to form a main line through Schoolcraft and Battle Creek to Detroit.

Thomas' daughter Ella wrote that the trails for the "transportation of fugitives were never straight."

Siebert wrote, "In truth, the underground paths in these regions formed a great and intricate network, and it was in no small measure because the lines forming the meshes of this great system converged and branched again at so many stations that it was almost an impossibility for slave-hunters to trace their negroes through even a single county without finding themselves on the wrong trail."[21]

The Rev. Henry Northrop, from Ann Arbor, White Pigeon, and later Flint, Michigan, wrote about freedom seekers, "Hardly any two went over the same road and very little was known about the way lest the pursuers might follow." He recalled a specific incident that occurred in May 1841, while he labored in White Pigeon. An unnamed Quaker arrived with a freedom seeker who was closely pursued. The Reverend Northrop must have considered sending him by stage or rail because he mentions a lack of money. As stated earlier, at times Underground Railroad agents were hampered by their own lack of provisions, and this was one more reason to have several agents cooperating within a short distance of each other.

However, Northrop's horse and buggy were quickly readied and they made haste to Chester Gurney's place in Centreville. The men dined together before Gurney set off for the next station twelve miles distant. The Reverend Northrop recalled the man had sent his family ahead, and the family was united after he crossed the Detroit River to Canada.[22] Erastus Hussey said, "In the larger places we had more than one man, so that if one chanced to be out of town the other man would be found." When Quakers attended meetings or antislavery men traveled to conventions, they sometimes left their wives and daughters in charge. At times, the absence of the Quakers was a hardship for freedom seekers, as described in the next vignette.[23]

Modes and Means of Travel

Theodore Foster, coeditor of the *Signal of Liberty*, wrote a general account of how refugees from bondage reached safety in his unpublished manuscript *Refugees of Canada*. His account dispels any notion that the freedom seeker was met with open arms and guided through the northern states. Foster said self-emancipators left in all seasons, traveling by night, hiding in the swamps and thickets by day. The North Star was their guide since they dare not ask the way. "Public sentiment was every where favorable to their masters; the great mass of the northern population regarded their appearance with suspicion and dislike."[24]

Every mode of transportation was utilized. The actual railroad was described in print as a convenient means of emancipation in 1840. The newspaper *Colored American* revealed how a week's journey on foot was reduced to a few days, and the passenger arrived safely ahead of any pursuers. The article referred to a man who left Baltimore after a whipping on a Friday, attended Sunday services at a stop, and continued his travels in order to reach Canada by Wednesday.[25]

Erastus Hussey said, "I usually drove the fugitives through to Marshall (Michigan) myself, in the night, but often got some one to go with me. Isaac Mott, then a boy, worked for me, and used to frequently take the slaves through. Sometimes others went. I used my own horse and buggy."[26]

Melville McGee wrote,

In the early dusk of the evening when objects began to look hazy and indistinct have I seen the horse team silently harnessed and hitched to the lumber wagon and driven to the door, then the poor, hunted fugitives from slavery would come guiltily out of the house, where they had been carefully concealed during the day, and take their places in the wagon, with an older brother in the driver's seat, and a scarcely audible earnest "God speed" and a moment after they would be on their way to the next station in Jackson and to a land of freedom in Canada.[27]

Several accounts of escape refer to the need to borrow horses or wagons from neighbors. A story passed down — but not documented — concerns a harrowing passage from Manchester, Michigan, to Ann Arbor. Captain George J. Barker borrowed the grey horses of Daniel A. Mills and the wagon of Francis Baldwin in order to transport several refugees from bondage. The freedom seekers were well hidden in the wagon on the journey to Canada. Suddenly, on Ann Arbor's Main Street, the kingbolt on the wagon broke. The refugees were thrown to the street in full view of passersby and travelers. Reportedly, no one revealed the criminal act of transporting human property, and they reached British soil and freedom.[28]

Captain Barker may have been heading to Jacob Volland's saddle and harness shop south of Ann Arbor's courthouse square. Volland was a member of the Friends of Human Progress, radical reformers who espoused peace and equal rights without regard to race or gender.[29]

William Lambert described operations in Detroit. Agents met at a lodge on Jefferson Avenue where secret meetings were held. They often hid people in the house of J. C. Reynolds, a black worker on the Michigan Central Railway, moving them in the dark one by one. They were fed and provided clothing. "Our boats were concealed under the docks, and before daylight we would have everyone over. We never lost a man by capture at this point, so careful were we, and we took over as high as 1,600 in one year."[30]

As mentioned in an earlier chapter, David Bristol — the self-freed acquaintance of Lewis Hill — traveled by stagecoach through the slave states with a forged pass. It was not uncommon for self-emancipators to copy a free pass substituting the name. George DeBaptiste possessed a certificate dated January 22, 1835, registered in the office of Hustings in the City of Richmond, Virginia: "No. 606 George DeBaptiste, a mulatto boy, about five feet seven and a half inches high, and about twenty years of age, who was born free...." DeBaptiste said he used his certificate 33 times to help others escape.[31]

Sarah and Erastus Hussey's house in Battle Creek, Michigan, was a station in a network of stops linking Illinois and Indiana to Canada (*History of Calhoun County* [1877], Bentley Historical Library, University of Michigan).

Quakers often dressed women and men in Quaker bonnets to conceal the faces of freedom seekers. Underground Railroad conductors Laura Haviland and the Levi Coffins refer to many instances of disguising people in Quaker garb and sending them out in groups that were attending meetings. Girls dressed as boys, boys dressed as women, and in every garment contrary to one's actual identity. A woman known only as the mother of John Harris escaped from Memphis, Tennessee, with three other enslaved women dressed as men. They stowed themselves among cotton bales on a boat to Ohio.[32]

On free soil, the freedom seeker sometimes chose a name, or was given one by an Underground worker. Isabella Baumfree became Sojourner Truth and Joseph Mallory became Lewis Hill. Levi Coffin and Laura Haviland in their autobiographies, mention assigning new names. Willis and Elsie Hamilton became Bill and Jane Willis.

Hiding Places

Accounts throughout this book describe the variety of hiding places used, from crannies in rocks to swamps and woods to barns or other outbuildings. Some Underground Railroad helpers invited people into their houses, hiding them when necessary. George and Milly McCoy kept people in the barn, out of sight of their children. William Harwood had a hiding space in his cellar that would have hidden freedom seekers from the farm laborers who shared his house near Saline, Michigan.

Erastus Hussey wrote, "Stations were established every fifteen or sixteen miles. The slaves were secreted in the woods, barns and cellars during the daytime and carried through in the night. All traveling was done in the dark." He further explained that after the Civil War, people said his house was built with secret hiding places in the cellar. "This was not strictly true. I will guarantee, however, that if any slaves were secreted there that they were never captured."

In the Depot Town area of Ypsilanti, tunnels ran beneath the railroad crossing. When the Michigan Central Railroad expanded their lines around 1860, the Thompson Block was built on the opposite side of the tracks. Tunnels beneath the Thompson Block were known to connect to a network of basement openings in commercial buildings on Cross Street. The passageways were constructed of stone and brick, and were large enough for an average man to walk upright. The tunnels of Depot Town were constructed for the purpose of providing water drainage, and as a means of safely moving supplies without crossing the busy rail lines.[33]

By oral tradition, freedom seekers hid in the tunnels during the day, then exited to the Huron River at night where a boat carried them to the next station. Some people may have known that Leonard Chase's Underground Railroad station lay behind the Thompson Block.[34] The existing tunnels may have provided a hiding place for freedom seekers by day and a passageway to the river at night, though they were not constructed for that purpose.[35]

Glode Chubb was reported to have tunnels leading to the Rouge River behind his Wayne County house. It is more likely that freedom seekers were encouraged to slip down the steep slope in back of his property where natural rock croppings offered cover.

The 1830s house of William Perry in Ann Arbor was documented by the Historic American Buildings Survey in the 1930s as having a secret hiding space for slaves. Between the walls of a large fireplace is a massive brick chimney with ample space for several people to hide. Most early chimneys were built with extra wall space for fire protection; however, this is unique. In the wall behind the fireplace, a closet conceals a cupboard. The cupboard, when removed from the wall, opens to the chimney. Perry does not appear to have been a participant in the Underground Railroad, however, it seems that he was not the original builder of the house. Later residents of the house believe Josiah Beckley, brother of Guy Beckley, built this house before constructing his second home on the same road.

Josiah Beckley's second home was constructed with a solid brick wall separating part of the basement, with no visible access. Josiah Beckley helped fund publication of the *Signal*, but no verification of his participation on the Underground Railroad has been found.[36]

The greatest burdens fell to the freedom seeker, but Underground Railroad agents described some of the difficulties in providing assistance. Often, it was a hardship to provide food and supplies, especially when money was scarce. In the early days of settlement, survival was precarious and sharing scarce food was an act of great benevolence for many. It can be assumed that the females in the household, even when not specified, gave meals, clothing, and medical care. When Erastus Hussey's wife was sick, he rounded up the food and left it for the formerly enslaved to cook for themselves. The following pages of this book reveal that many women took risks, as did the friends of Mrs. Blackburn in rescuing her from jail, and their contributions were essential for safe escapes to freedom.

Susan Hussey remembered another remarkable woman's escape from slavery. She was spoken of as the "Beautiful Girl" after her brief stop at the Hussey's station in Battle Creek. Few would forget seeing a woman escaping from slavery who appeared white, yet was terrified for her life. In defiance of his white family's slaveholding and the laws of Kentucky, Wright Maudlin guided the girl to freedom.

They stayed only a few hours at the Hussey's because slave hunters were close behind. Though exhausted and frightened, the pair could not afford to rest. Maudlin and the girl did don disguises: he dressed as a farmer and she as an old woman, perhaps his mother or wife. Maudlin knew the route and houses where they could stop when they needed to get off the road. He drove the entire distance and just as they neared Detroit, four horsemen galloped toward them. Maudlin calmed the hysterical girl. The riders believed the poor couple in a carriage were common land prospectors and rode on.

When they reached Detroit, Maudlin observed the secret signal by a man walking along Woodward Avenue, who drew out a white handkerchief and wiped his forehead. Maudlin followed him to a boathouse on the water, where a skiff with two rowers waited for the cargo. The "Beautiful Girl" was on her way to freedom in Canada when the horsemen galloped up to the boathouse.[37]

Wright Maudlin (Modlin, Mandlin) is portrayed as a hero in rescuing the "Beautiful Girl" and indeed risked his life in carrying her to freedom. Some time later, Nathan Thomas wrote to Jordan Osborn to learn what he knew of Maudlin. Though not a Quaker, Maudlin knew a great deal about the operations of secretly transporting freedom seekers between Indiana and Michigan.

Osborn replied that Maudlin moved from Indiana to Williamsburg, Michigan, in the 1840s, but had lived in Kentucky before that time. Maudlin had both a good farm and a bad reputation. Though married, he ran off with a neighbor's wife, and lived in Cass County, Indiana. While there, he worked for a planter who refused to pay him. Maudlin swore vengeance and acted on it by running off with the man's slaves. He helped other enslaved people escape and was forced to move north when he came under suspicion. Eventually, the woman he ran away with left him, and his first wife died or divorced him. He married again and lived in Michigan until his death in 1866.[38]

Very likely, Dr. Nathan Thomas and other highly moral men did not approve of Maudlin's behavior and motivations; nonetheless, more than one enslaved family would be very grateful for Maudlin's aide in the 1840s.

Cross-State Network

Dr. Nathan Thomas and Erastus Hussey described a network that included both of their family's stations. Many of the names each man provided are redundant. Thomas in School-craft, southwest of Hussey, listed more Underground Railroad workers in Cass County. Hussey included the names of many who may have participated infrequently. Neither man could state the names of more than a few agents in the southeast counties of Michigan. Dr. Thomas stated that with the "secrecy with which everything was conducted" he knew only of the western lines. The names of conductors known to Thomas and Hussey are listed in this chapter, with some additional recollections described by historian Charles DeLand. The places and people cited in documented escapes are described throughout the book.[39]

From the southwestern corner of Michigan, Ebenezer McIlvain of Niles was the Circuit Commissioner of Berrien County. He played an instrumental role in an attempted kidnapping in 1847, referred to as the "Cass County Raid." People were transported from McIlvain's by W. S. Elliot. The Nathan Thomas papers include a cryptic letter from Elliot, dated December 13, 1841. "P.S. The fugitive spoken of in the *Signal* [*Signal of Liberty*] of the first inst [instance] passed through my hands I carried him 20 miles on his way to the grateful shadow of Queen Victoria's throne." Elliot was the Secretary of the Niles antislavery society in 1837. Lorenzo P. Alexander carried people from Niles to Cass County, as well as to Flowerfield in St. Joseph County and Schoolcraft in Kalamazoo County.[40]

In Cass County, Charles Osborn was literally father to many abolitionists and Underground Railroad operators. Charles Osborn bore seven children by his first wife and nine by his second. Many of them were located in Cass County in 1837 where freedom seekers found their way to safety at his children's and grandchildren's homes (Josiah, Jefferson, Ellison, and Parker Osborn). His daughters and sons-in-law, Isaac A. Bonine and Joel East, operated stations in Penn Township. Samuel Bonine, a member of the Bonine clan, and Joel East served as ministers.[41] The Osborns and others, however, did not always forward the self-emancipated men and women. Over the decades, they oversaw large settlements of free and escaped black Americans and helped protect them when Kentuckians attacked in 1847. Accounts in a later chapter describe the settlements and escapes. Other agents included Zachariah Shugart, William Jones of Calvin Township, Henry Shepherd, Wright Maudlin, Thompson Nicholson, Ishmael Lee, and William Wheeler.[42]

Dr. Thomas wrote, "Zachariah Shugart of Cass Co. was one of the most efficient agents." Shugart was born in North Carolina in 1805 and then moved to Wayne County, Indiana, where he married Susanna Harris in 1827. The couple lived in Penn Township until 1853 when they traveled further west to Farma County, Iowa. Shugart had a station and transported freedom seekers. Henry Shephard, one of the few black conductors, regularly transported freedom seekers from Cass County to the city of Schoolcraft.

Though Zachariah Ellyson was expelled from the Quaker Meeting for marrying a non–Quaker, he continued to view slavery as a terrible evil and "when the Underground Railroad was formed, he opened his home as one of its stations."[43] The network branched at times in an easterly direction through St. Joseph County where Friend C. Bird may have lived. Little else is known about him. The agents described by Hussey and Thomas were on a path established by the Reverend Cross generally crossing Michigan in the second tier of counties.[44]

Agents in Kalamazoo County, besides Dr. Nathan Thomas, Pamela Thomas and Susan Thomas, included William Wheeler and his wife in Flowerfield, near Schoolcraft. Their house was a sanctuary in the aftermath of the Cass County Raid. Other Kalamazoo agents were Delamore Duncan, William Woodruff, and Rufus Royes (Roys, Royce). Royce moved to Vicksburg, in Kalamazoo County at an early date. He left his birthplace of New Haven, Connecticut, to settle in Brady Township in 1837.

The next station was Schoolcraft in Kalamazoo County, in the charge of Dr. Nathan Thomas. Thomas did not include the names of every participant, omitting his own brother Joseph, who lived with his family in Schoolcraft Township from 1841 until his death, from his list of operators. A Kalamazoo biographer wrote that Joseph S. Thomas was "a strong abolitionist throughout his manhood, and for years was an active and effective worker in the 'Underground Railroad.'"[45] One would expect Nathan Thomas, organizer of the network of escape in the Schoolcraft area, to know whether his own brother participated.

Then came Climax, with the station outside the village run by William Gardner. Little is known about Joel and William Gardner, although Nathan Thomas said Joel Gardner's place was a station. Erastus Hussey mentioned many agents in the Battle Creek area, but it was his own family that was often awakened by the familiar sound of murmuring voices outside their home. Erastus, Sarah, and daughter Susan, were known all the way down in Kentucky for helping runaways. On one occasion, mournful whisperings brought Susan to the aid of twenty-six men and four women. Susan, a poised young woman of unusual courage, invited the group into the house though her parents were away. She stood nobly and spoke encouraging words of comfort to those oppressed by slavery. They boiled cauldrons of coffee and ate all the food they and some neighbors could supply. She gave them a note for Jabez Fitch in Marshall, the next stop on their long journey.

Erastus Hussey said that, early on, only four antislavery white men were in Battle Creek: Silas Dodge, Abel Densmore, Henry Willis, Theron H. Chadwick, and a black man named Samuel Strauther. A few of these men moved on, but many others replaced them. Later antislavery workers were Dr. S. B. Thayer and Henry J. Cushman, an "earnest worker," Dr. Charley Cowles, Dr. E. A. Atlee, and Atlee's son-in-law, Samuel S. Nichols.

Dr. S. B. Thayer moved to Battle Creek after completing medical training under Drs. Nathan and Jesse Thomas. He would have also gained experience helping and guiding freedom seekers under the tutelage of those men. In 1841, he served as an agent for the *Signal of Liberty* newspaper at Climax in Kalamazoo County.

Henry Willis, upon the deaths of his parents, was bound out as generally happened with orphaned children without family. He remained with the Quaker family that reared him in Pennsylvania until adulthood. While in his thirties, Willis chose to settle in Michigan with his wife Phoebe, sister of Abigail and Lydia Mott. He would be remembered as one of the pioneers "who were the leaders in spirit, thought and action in the formative period of the state's history."[46]

Joseph and Phoebe Merritt were Hicksite Quakers who moved with their extended family to Michigan in 1836. The antislavery pioneers helped build their Quaker settlement into a prosperous village called Battle Creek. Joseph Merritt was a worker in the new settlement. He owned a farm within the corporation where his son Charles then resided. Besides the improvement of his farm, he did much for the advancement of the interest of the village and city. He was noted for his hospitality and liberality. "Stranger and alien, bond and free, ever received a warm welcome to his fireside and table. The public lecturer found his house a home, and the poor fugitive fleeing from bondage received his marked attention. He was a warm advocate of emancipation and will long be remembered by those who received his sympathy and help."[47]

East of Battle Creek in Calhoun County, was the Marshall home of Jabez S. Fitch, a nominee on the antislavery ticket for Governor. After Fitch's death, Charles T. Gorham moved into his house and helped on the Underground Railroad. Nathan Thomas remembered that George Ingersoll oversaw a station. Thomas was acquainted with William Sullivan, to whom he sent Lewis Hill. The other agents in Marshall, involved in the kidnapping case of Marshall citizens by Southern men, are described in a later chapter.

After Marshall, Erastus Hussey and Nathan Thomas could name very few agents in the network. Hussey listed Edwin Johnson in Albion, and Lonson Wilcox and Norman Allen in Jackson. As historian Wilbur Siebert explained, the Underground Railroad network meshed into intersecting lines and branches. Neither Hussey nor Thomas was familiar with at least one of the branches, established by the Rev. John Cross around Jackson, Michigan.

Historian Charles Victor DeLand described the Jackson area Underground Railroad, as he knew it from his childhood. His father, William R. DeLand, among the first settlers in Jackson, was highly regarded and elected to positions of county justice of the peace and judge. As the Quaker families of Isaac and Uriah Mott, George and William Hoag, and Samuel and Edward Upton arrived in the Jackson area, they sought out Charles DeLand's mother because she was descended from the Hooker Friends.[48] The DeLands traveled by ox team to visit the Quaker families in Parma and the families developed a strong friendship. Before long, William DeLand's house was added to the network of stations on the Underground Railroad. Charles DeLand described the workings:

> The Quakers were all strong antislavery people, and it was through the influence of those Friends that father's house, on the old Clinton road, in Blackman township, became a regular relay station on the "underground railroad" of those days.... Many a weary night's ride fell to my lot, along the new and rough roads, across Leoni and Waterloo, to aid these poor fugitive slaves on their way to freedom.[49]

The Motts left Parma to join a Quaker colony in Wisconsin around 1844 but the Hoags and Uptons remained on their farms for many years. Charles DeLand wrote that he carried freedom seekers from his parents' house north to Stockbridge, Ingham County, Michigan, or east to Grass Lake in Jackson County.

Erastus Hussey's knowledge of the Underground Railroad from Parma to its terminus was as follows: Townsend E. Gidley in Parma; Henry Francisco in Francisco; Samuel W. Dexter in Dexter; Theodore Foster in Scio; Guy Beckley in Ann Arbor; John Geddes in Geddesburg; he forgot the names of agents in Ypsilanti, Plymouth and Schwarzburg; Horace Hallock, Silas M. Holmes and Samuel Zug in Detroit.[50]

Historian Charles DeLand described the other agents in Jackson. From the time of his settlement in 1838, Lonson Wilcox was a noted citizen of Jackson where he operated a shoe store for over thirty years. He served for twenty-five years as a deacon in the Congregational church. Wilcox "was a pronounced temperance and antislavery man, and was prominent in all work to forward his moral and political ideas."[51] Norman Allen was among the earliest settlers in Jackson arriving from Vergennes, Vermont, in 1831. He settled on a farm three miles east of the village, and opened a public tavern, afterwards known as the McArthur tavern. After moving to the city, Allen opened a store where he sold Rowland's tonic mixtures. In 1841, he was elected Jackson County Commissioner on the Democratic ticket. In the elections of 1842, 1844 and 1846, Allen ran for various offices on the "Abolitionist" ticket representing the Liberty Party, and never won office.[52] Across the state of Michigan, abolitionists were a minority in every sphere of life in the 1840s. In 1854, Norman Allen was narrowly defeated when he ran as a Republican. The tide of freedom was rolling in.

A man named Stephen Allen settled in Madison Township, near Adrian, and shared an interest in helping end slavery. Stephen Allen was acquainted with Gerrit Smith, William Lloyd Garrison, and other prominent men from his hometown in New York, and while in Michigan, from 1842 through 1845, was active in antislavery politics.[53] Abijah and Abel Fitch were not listed in the Liberty Party.[54]

Henry Francisco lived near Seymour Treadwell in Leoni, in a place called Francisco. No details of his Underground Railroad efforts are known. Treadwell purchased a farm in Leoni, east of the city of Jackson. Treadwell's daughter wrote, "Mr. Treadwell did not allow farming to interfere with his antislavery work. His fine new barn, still standing in Leoni, was a station of the Underground Rail Road, and he continued his lectures, which from the first had been an important part of his work."[55]

Erastus Hussey said, "At Dexter we had Samuel W. Dexter and his sons." However, Dexter had only one son of age to assist. Local stories include references to hiding places and trap doors in the porches of Judge Dexter's home, Gordon Hall. Dexter contracted to have a country mansion designed and built by Calvin T. Fillmore, brother of future U. S. President Millard Fillmore. The Fillmore and Millard families were linked to Dexter by marriage and a disdain of slavery. The stately house called Gordon Hall (1843), situated atop a hill in Webster and Scio Townships, afforded extensive views in all directions and, according to at least one account, was a station on the Underground Railroad with at least six avenues of escape. The 1934 Historic American Buildings Survey shows architectural drawings of the first floor and basement where a vent on the south porch led to a crawl space. Crawling under the porch, a person could see a window opening into a long, squat room. The hidden room could not be seen nor reached from the main section of the basement. From 1843 until the drawings were sketched, there were no doors or windows visible from the main basement, and the only way in was from under the side porch.[56]

Judge Dexter was likely an Underground Railroad agent, though the reference by Hussey is almost identical to a description of Samuel W. Foster, who had sons to help. After Judge Dexter's death in January 1863, the citizens of Dexter held a meeting to honor him. The resolutions passed on this occasion, included recognition of Judge Dexter's honesty and benevolence. "His hand and purse were ever open to relieve the wants of the poor, and suffering of the distressed, and to support and foster religious, benevolent and educational interests in our community."[57] A Washtenaw County history described Dexter as a man of firm convictions; a man that no person or public body could convince to compromise on the moral issues of anti–Masonry, antislavery, and pro-temperance.

Judge Samuel Dexter persuaded the Fosters to move to Michigan. Samuel Foster was born into a family where dedication to public service was a privilege and duty. His father, Theodore Foster (1752–1828), served in numerous political positions, including Senator from Rhode Island. Dwight Foster, Samuel's uncle, was elected to the U. S. Senate from Massachusetts to fill the vacancy left by Samuel Dexter (father of Judge Samuel W. Dexter who founded his namesake town in Michigan). Dwight and Theodore were born in Brookfield, Worcester County, Massachusetts, and educated at Brown University (then

Top: Nathan and Pamela Thomas offered their home as a station on the Underground Railroad benefitting over one thousand self-emancipators in Schoolcraft, Kalamazoo County, Michigan (author photograph, Schoolcraft, Michigan, 2002). *Bottom:* The Rev. Guy Beckley and Theodore Foster published the antislavery newspaper, *Signal of Liberty* in Ann Arbor from 1841 to 1847. It was printed in this building block on Broadway St., Ann Arbor, Michigan (Chapin, L. E. [1835–1840], Bentley Historical Library, University of Michigan: Bentley Image Bank, BL000936).

Rhode Island College). Theodore Foster and his wife, Esther Bowen Millard, would see several of their children leave Foster, Rhode Island, for Michigan Territory.[58] Descendants of the Millard (Millerd) family, including siblings of President Millard Fillmore, and the Foster family settled in the Dexter area.

The first of Senator Theodore Foster's children to migrate to Michigan was Samuel, persuaded to do so by Judge Dexter, who needed a miller at his gristmill in Webster Township. After a few years, Samuel Foster laid out the village of Scio and erected his own mill. Sometime later, he relocated again to a hamlet called Foster's Station.[59] Samuel Foster and his sons operated an Underground Railroad station in Dexter, west of another Underground station overseen by Theodore Foster in Scio. The brothers' work hiding and conducting refugees from bondage on their journey was known to a few of their friends.[60]

From the time of his settlement until he left Michigan in 1850, Samuel W. Foster was an active resister of slavery. He was among the men who met in Ann Arbor in 1836 at the founding of the Michigan State Anti-Slavery Society and one of seven, including his brother, who called for antislavery men across Washtenaw County to form an organization. He was a member of the Executive Committee of the Washtenaw County Anti-Slavery Society in 1838.[61] In 1841 and 1845, Foster was listed in the *Signal of Liberty* as a candidate for representative to the legislature. He lost the bid for Surveyor on the 1844 Liberty Party ticket. Samuel Foster supported the Liberty Party in the 1840s, yet he did not appear at the meetings of the State Anti-Slavery Society during the same decade.[62]

It is apparent that Washtenaw County was too far removed for Thomas and Hussey to have intimate knowledge of the Underground Railroad on the eastern side of the state. Hussey knew of John Geddes' involvement because Geddes' uncle, Albert H. Geddes, lived in Battle Creek. Erastus Hussey knew of at least two branches leaving Ann Arbor—one conveying people to Ypsilanti, and another more northerly to Plymouth, along the River Rouge to Swartzburg, then to Detroit.[63]

Hussey and Thomas were familiar with the men prominent in the antislavery societies but could not provide a single name for Ypsilanti, one of the most active areas on the Railroad. Those agents are discussed in a later chapter.

From the descriptions given, it is apparent that the men and women on this network were not a homogeneous group. The Cross network included many Quakers, members of other Christian churches, and some not affiliated with a church, like Nathan Thomas and Wright Maudlin. Many participants were farmers, as were most early settlers in Michigan. But the white agents included doctors (Thayer, N. Thomas, Cowles), merchants (Hussey, T. Foster, S. Nichols), ministers (Beckley, Foote), judges (J. Fitch, S. Dexter), and journalists (Sullivan). Most were literate, in an age of limited educational opportunities. Black agents (Strauther) participated in this and other branches in Michigan. The networks on the freedom trail in Michigan, though sometimes organized by a distinct group, mirrored the diversity described in the Cross network.

Chapter Seven

Persuasion and Politics

Escape of Caroline Quarrls

In 1842 Caroline Quarrls slipped away from her mistress in St. Louis and boarded a steamboat to Alton, Illinois. A black man she met upon disembarking warned that the place would offer her no refuge. The stranger then put Caroline on a stagecoach to Wisconsin where she stayed at the home of a black barber named Titball. After a week, word arrived that those sent to capture her had discovered her whereabouts. Some white lawyers intervened and Caroline was taken by wagon to Samuel Dougherty's house, north of Pewaukee, Wisconsin.

From Wisconsin, Caroline traveled with helpers south to Naperville, Illinois, then east to LaPorte, Indiana. Because there were many close calls with the slave hunters, several abolitionists decided Caroline must be escorted to Canada. Lyman Goodnow of Wisconsin accepted the charge. Caroline wanted to be free and had thought about "the North.'" When her slaveholder/father, Robert Prior Quarrls, died, Caroline became the property of Mr. and Mrs. Charles R. Hall. The Halls had lived in Kentucky before Mr. Hall became a merchant in St. Louis. Caroline decided to run away after Mrs. Hall cut off her long and beautiful hair.

At the start of their journey, Caroline lay concealed and Goodnow drove the wagon at night. After a stop at Deacon Fowler's, a white antislavery man, Caroline was given clothing, gloves, and a thick veil. She had her own jewelry, money, and a bundle of clothing thrown from a window in advance of her escape. From this point, she sat in the wagon seat and the pair traveled by day. Caroline was readily perceived as white, with her light skin and fashionable attire. Before the Lockport-area, a man named Freeman directed Goodnow to the Underground Railroad network. Goodnow drove across Michigan on a long and harrowing journey. Many Quaker men were away from home and their wives provided a meal and directions, but not a place of rest. Goodnow feared being overtaken but needed to provide rest for the horses.

Finally, after many days on the road, they arrived at a place of known safety, the home of the Rev. Guy Beckley. His stately brick house on Pontiac Trail sat above the Huron River on the opposite shore of the city of Ann Arbor, only forty miles to their final stop at Ambler's, a place near the Detroit River. Many members of the Beckley family lived in the area called Lower Town and were strongly antislavery. It had taken three weeks to reach Detroit. At Ambler's, the travelers enjoyed a final meal before crossing to Canada. Goodnow left Caroline with the Reverend Haskell at the mission in Sandwich, safely in the Queen's Dominion.[1]

Theodore Weld's Seventy lectured across the Great Lakes States, introducing the topic of slavery and arguing for its abolition in the early 1840s. It seemed that every few months a new organization was formed to reach another segment of the populace. The *Signal of Liberty, The Colored American,* and other newspapers carried accounts of escapes, ongoing threats, and assistance in the free states. When antislavery agitators considered adding a political platform to the movement, some Michigan men privately maneuvered toward that purpose. And, in another arena of resistance, the Underground Railroad, stations were generally located in the homes of leaders of the antislavery movement in Michigan.

The Anti-Slavery Platform

At the time the Michigan State Anti-Slavery Society was established in Ann Arbor, some of the organizers convinced Seymour Boughton Treadwell to "come to Michigan as editor and lecturer for the Society." Treadwell published "American Liberties and American Slavery" in 1838, establishing himself as one of the nation's prominent opponents of slavery. After visiting Michigan, Treadwell moved to the Jackson area and quickly rose to the leadership of the antislavery society.

Charles Henry Stewart of Detroit wrote in a letter to Treadwell (Aug 11, 1845), "you are the State Committee, the heart and the Head. All of us are the hand and feet." Nathan Thomas believed Treadwell was one of the most important antislavery organizers in Michigan. Like Guy Beckley and James Birney, Treadwell spent much of his time on the lecture circuit in Michigan. And, as with most of the antislavery leadership in Michigan, Treadwell participated in the Underground Railroad.

Treadwell was among the few men who believed a third political party was expedient to bringing about an end of slavery. At least one historian wrote, "Up to the time of the Birney nomination none of the leading men in the State [Michigan] had favored a third party; but in the spring of 1840 the current began to set that way, and S. B. Treadwell, of the *Michigan Freeman,* gradually came to approve the "Liberty" nomination."[2] The historian's statement was based on a published statement in newspaper accounts. In private, Treadwell corresponded with New York political antislavery men and was supported by Michigan abolitionists Guy Beckley and Arthur Porter. A few Michigan men, though separated by distance, participated fully in the creation and development of the Liberty Party.[3]

Abolitionists who believed slavery should be a national party platform issue met in New York in 1840 to form a third party: the Liberty Party. William Lloyd Garrison opposed the action, believing abolition could not be achieved through the political process. In fact, many Liberty Party supporters did not disagree with him. However, they saw the opportunity to give voice to the antislavery issue in the political arena, as well as the chance to influence legislators to block the extension of slavery and interstate slave trade. Entering the political arena caused a separation in the antislavery ranks away from the Garrisonians and a power shift to the west.

In January, a call went out for a national convention to be held April 1, at Albany, New York to decide whether to nominate a presidential candidate. Gerrit Smith, New York reformer, wrote to Seymour Treadwell on March 24, 1840, expressing concern about abolition ministers opposed to independent political action. A month later the Reverend Beckley was on his way to Utica, upstate New York, and New York City to meet with prominent leaders in the cause.

Before his departure, Beckley met with Arthur Porter in Detroit to discuss holding a Michigan convention. Without the opinions of Charles Stuart and William Goodell, they decided to wait. Porter wrote to Treadwell, "I have just had the pleasure of a conference with our mutual friend the Reverend Mr. Beckley and friends. Want to call a conference, but no word from leaders."[4]

Beckley attended the New York convention. "In spite of a very inclement season delegates from six States were present. After a full discussion the convention decided to make the nominations. In the selection of candidates no one was mentioned for the presidency except James G. Birney. He was unanimously nominated." His supporters, primarily in the New England states, opposed political action. Nonetheless, the Liberty Party was formed.[5]

William Harrison won the 1840 election on the Whig ticket. He narrowly bested his Democratic opponent though both got over one million votes. Birney, running as president for the Liberty Party, got nearly 7,000 votes. Though he had been raised on a plantation with slavery, Harrison lived in Ohio at the time of the election. However, any hope of federal legislation to limit slavery was lost with the untimely death of President Harrison one month after his inauguration. Vice President and Virginian John Tyler, chosen to provide Southern support in the election, became president. Tyler defended the institution of slavery.

James Birney, Liberty Party presidential candidate, moved to Bay City, Michigan, in 1841. Across the Northwest, men gradually came around to support a national political party. The antislavery men of Michigan created the first Liberty Party ticket in the Northwest. "There is no doubt that at this time Michigan abolitionists were much better organized and more united in sentiment than those of any other Northwestern State; but we shall see that this superiority was held for a few years only, and that after 1844 antislavery political sentiment in that State rapidly lost its coherence."[6]

Liberty men poured energy and money into ending slavery through a political process denied to men of color and to all women. Several prominent black men participated in meetings of the Michigan State Anti-Slavery Society in the early 1840s. Robert Banks, a clothier, joined the Rev. Monroe and Madison Lightfoot from Detroit. Brothers James and Asher Aray, the Rev. Brooks, formerly enslaved in New York, and Ockrow traveled from Washtenaw County to the 1841 meeting. The 1843 and 1844 meetings held in Ann Arbor and Jackson included Monroe, Lightfoot, Lambert, and Aray.[7]

The black men in Michigan had no success in gaining suffrage although many were property owners, literate, and may have voted previously in other states. The Michigan State Anti-Slavery Society leaders were preoccupied with publishing, lecturing, and creating new societies in order to increase their number. The antislavery men and women were a minority and an irritant to many of their neighbors.

It appears that most of Guy Beckley's income working in his brother's dry goods store was spent publishing the *Signal of Liberty* newspaper. Beckley and coeditor Theodore Foster printed the first issue April 28, 1841. Beckley wrote to Dr. Nathan Thomas in 1841 that in order to undertake publication of the paper, he had invested $100 and was "poor." He begged for support in order that the paper could be published, "till [*sic*] slavery shall cease." Through the *Signal of Liberty,* the Reverend Beckley publicly declared that he kept his door open to travelers on the Underground Railroad, including Caroline Quarrls, Robert Coxe, George Lewis, and others.[8]

Fortunately, within ten years of settling in the budding Lower Town of Ann Arbor, Guy's brother Josiah Beckley was a person of wealth and property. He made several land purchases and, in the spring of 1836, opened a mercantile shop in Ann Arbor's Huron Block on the east side of Broadway Street. The *Signal of Liberty* was published above the store.[9]

One of the earliest escapes described in the newspaper concerned a man escaping from the lead mines of Missouri in 1841. The man defied his enslaver by leaving his workplace to visit the wife he'd not seen in a month. Another man who committed the same "infraction," was whipped to death. The self-emancipator articulated his reasoning for leaving slavery, "Life and death are before me — if I can make my escape all is well; if not, I am a dead man."[10]

After Beckley and Foster helped six men escape in 1841, some citizens of the Ann Arbor area accused the editors of being transgressors of the law and "worse than horse thieves." Beckley and Foster defended themselves by denying they broke any laws of their state or country. They obeyed a higher ruling found in the Bible. The editors clearly delineated their reasons for printing the newspaper, "This paper was established to promote the abolition of slavery, and to that purpose it will be devoted."[11]

A brief article submitted by "M.H.C." (Martin Cowles) provided the name of one of the eight who stopped on his way to Canada. George Lewis, when asked if he wished to take vengeance on the man who enslaved him, replied, "Oh no, I would not injure a hair of his head if I had the power. He has a wife and four children, and they love him and think a great deal of him, and it would not be right for me to injure so many to gratify the revenge of one."[12]

At least one contributor observed increasing public sentiment in favor of liberty from bondage. The writer described the near abduction of a self-emancipated man named Sylvester. Sylvester, born and educated in St. Louis, Missouri, worked as a steward on Mississippi steamboats, and he learned of free states. He left for Detroit. During his residency, an attempt was made to take another self-freed man into custody. When the black community intervened, a white man was threatened with a pistol. Sylvester was convicted of the crime of the threat, sentenced to five years in prison, but was later pardoned by the governor when proven innocent. Somehow, slave hunters in Missouri learned of his pardon and traveled to Jackson, Michigan, to take him. While they attended church, Sylvester stepped out of prison and made haste to Canada. His escape did not deter slave hunters from further incursions into Michigan to take both escaped and free people of color.[13]

Caroline Quarrls was one of several people to stop with the Beckley family in Ann Arbor. The Rev. Guy Beckley's house on Pontiac Trail, north of the Huron River, was nicknamed "the old slave house" for serving as a sanctuary for freedom seekers. Where people were hidden in the house remains a mystery. The two story New England Georgian-style house was constructed using fieldstones and exterior bricks, likely from brother Josiah's brickyard. The 16 inch walls include hollow cavities around the chimneys and lowered ceilings over the second floor closets, though these would have been uncomfortable hiding places for freedom seekers.

In the third floor walls, there are small openings into an attic space. The openings could be hidden by furniture. Underground Railroad operator Levi Coffin hid people by this means in his Fountain City, Indiana home. Oral histories from subsequent owners of the Beckley house include stories of secret chambers in a kitchen wing that was later removed.[14]

The Reverend Beckley may have had alternative hiding places when needed. He and his brother Josiah built a brick schoolhouse nearby. The schoolhouse (still extant) has a trap door in the floor leading to a small room with fieldstone walls. Houses of this period often had cellars for storing foodstuffs, yet this was not a residential building. The schoolhouse on Traver Road is within an easy distance of the Huron River, railroad tracks, and both Beckley brothers' houses.[15]

While there is no documentation that other Beckleys were involved in the Under-

In 1842, Caroline Quarrls escaped from St. Louis and stayed at the Rev. Guy Beckley house in Ann Arbor, Michigan, on her journey to freedom in Canada (author photograph, Ann Arbor, Michigan, 2009).

ground Railroad, multiple sources reveal that many of them participated in the antislavery movement. Guy Beckley's sister Nancy married Sabin Felch in Ann Arbor in 1842. Felch served with Guy on the Executive Committee of the Michigan State Anti-Slavery Society in the 1840s. His shoemaker shop was in Josiah Beckley's Huron Block. Nancy and Sabin raised their five children just down the road at 88 Broadway Street. Josiah's son Luke lived at 85 Broadway and Josiah and Guy's cousin Oramel lived at 75 Broadway.

Another Beckley sibling, Olive, came to Ann Arbor and married Sumner Hicks who became a business partner with Josiah in the store. There is no record of his involvement in politics. Sumner and Olive were busy raising a family at their home on Wall Street, around the corner from the Huron Block.

Distractions from the Cause

Abolitionists accused Garrison of obscuring the goal of abolition by endorsing too many other reforms, including women's suffrage and equal rights. But, the men making the charge found themselves occupied with temperance (abstinence from alcoholic liquors) and religious reforms. In addition to annual statewide meetings of the Michigan State Anti-

Slavery Society, there were also county meetings. Liberty Party Conventions were held regularly at the state and local levels. Guy Beckley and William Sullivan were officers of the Temperance Society. An Anti-Slavery Missionary Society was formed in Ann Arbor in 1842. Sullivan called for a Christian Mission for the colored people of Canada. A Young Men's Liberty Association, organized by Dr. Thayer in Calhoun County, S. M. Holmes of Wayne County, and Dr. J. C. Gallup of Genesee County, oversaw 160 young men pledge to end slavery. In addition to all these groups, Beckley and others actively supported the Wesleyan Methodist Society.[16]

The first group to secede from the Methodist Episcopal Church over slavery was a group of Michigan pastors and laymen. The Rev. Marcus Swift was pastor of a Methodist Church and in charge of the Plymouth Circuit in Wayne County in the 1830s. The Methodist Episcopal Church (M.E.) in 1792 refused to denounce slavery and admitted slaveholders to membership. In the 1830s, the Reverend Swift and his congregants in Michigan agitated, against strong opposition, for the M.E. Church to reform.

According to family papers, the Reverend Swift was persecuted for his antislavery protests. Though he and Samuel Bebbens qualified, both were denied an ordination as Elders at the M. E. Annual Conference because of their active abolitionism. This denial was the incident that led to the formation in Michigan in 1839 of Congregations of the Wesleyan Methodist Church in Plymouth, Manchester, and Wolf Creek.[17]

Angry members of Swift's church in Nankin, Michigan, signed a petition denouncing the M.E. Church. "Believing with the venerable founder of Methodism that slavery is the sum of all villainies: that American slavery is the vilest that ever saw the sun & that this exists to an alarming extent in the M.E. Church ... we withdraw from the church ... our relation as Ministers and Members of the Methodist Episcopal Church is considered by us to be dissolved this 6th day of June, A.D. 1841." Swifts, Osbands, Fullers, and Glode Chubb signed the petition, among others.[18]

The Reverend Swift established congregations of the Wesleyan Methodist Church in Michigan and eight other states. In 1843, the new churches organized into a convention and met in Utica, New York. The Reverend Swift accepted a charge on the Ypsilanti circuit, the year that his house was burned. The following year he preached on the Plymouth circuit. His sons followed the preaching of their father. George Swift lectured against slavery and "was ostracized by society."[19]

The Rev. William Sullivan, early publisher of the *American Freeman* of Jackson, left the M.E. ministry, attended the Utica, New York, convention in 1840 and was given a circuit in the Jackson area, serving members in Jackson, Hillsdale, and Lenawee Counties. Five years later, the Reverend Sullivan was asked by the Wesleyan Methodists to help form an educational institution in Leoni. From that location, the Reverend Sullivan lived out his days helping people escape from slavery. The Michigan Union College later moved to Adrian.[20]

Though Guy Beckley was ordained an M. E. minister, he chaired the Ann Arbor District Wesleyan Methodist Conference. Formally charged with slander and falsehood, Beckly published an account of his 1843 trial. Many active abolitionists joined the Wesleyan Methodist Church, including Quaker Laura Haviland and her parents, William Harwood of Pittsfield, Samuel Noble of Ann Arbor, and many other Underground Railroad agents.

Many Wesleyan Methodist Churches were known as Underground Railroad stations. The church in Romulus, Wayne County, Michigan, was built in 1855, with trap doors opening to cellars. The "White Church" was located near the Underground Railroad stations of Gen. Schwarz and Glode Chubb. Harwood built a Wesleyan Church behind his property in Pittsfield Township, a nationally recognized station.[21]

In 1845, the First and Second Wesleyan Society of the Township of Pittsfield met and elected trustees of the First Wesleyan Methodist Society of the same place. The trustees were neighbors, including W. W. Harwood, Ezra Carpenter, and others. Harwood was part of the network of Wesleyan Methodists who helped on the Underground Railroad.[22] In 1852, reports of the circuits across the state showed the number of members overall was small. Jackson, Plymouth and Grand River/Ionia each had over 150; Flint, 24; Genesee, 45; and Pittsfield, 50. The conference records made no mention of helping people out of slavery for another decade.[23]

In Michigan, the leaders of the antislavery society were abolitionists and Underground Railroad agents. The *Signal of Liberty* newspaper included announcements and annual minutes of the antislavery society and Liberty Party meetings and articles from national antislavery newspapers. The men serving as president and vice president in the Michigan State Anti-Slavery Society in the 1840s were also Underground Railroad agents, with few exceptions. The exceptions, such as John King of Genesee County, G. L. Crane of Lenawee, and C. S. Youngs of Branch County were very likely involved in helping self-emancipators, but their participation cannot be documented.

In 1844, for instance, Seymour Treadwell was president of the antislavery society, with Vice Presidents Nathan Thomas, Erastus Hussey, Chester Gurney, Martin Cowles, Roswell Rexford, Charles Cowlam, William Canfield and Arthur Porter. The executive committee was Guy Beckley, Theodore Foster, Sabin Felch, S. D. Noble and C. J. Garland. Antislavery men in Michigan essentially advertised their political and societal views in the newspaper.[24]

Over the next few years, citizens in Michigan agreed in principle to ending slavery but were less understanding when self-emancipators were found in the homes of their neighbors.

Chapter Eight

The Port Huron–Pontiac–
Detroit Network

Escape of Malinda Robinson Paris

"Born free" did not guarantee liberty to people of color in antebellum United States. Malinda Robinson's mother, a free black American from Maryland, fought to provide as much security as possible for her children. In 1829, when Malinda was five, the courts declared the children free. Their father remained enslaved in Paris, Kentucky. Sometime before 1840, the Robinsons sacrificed the happiness of the family for liberty. Mr. Robinson insisted his wife take their nine children north rather than risk their being stolen into slavery. One night, the family walked nine miles from their home to a designated place. Malinda and her brothers and sisters knelt to pray with their parents. Together they sang a parting hymn and then watched the husband and father turn back to a life of bondage. The children and mother hurried to a safe place.

Terre Haute, Indiana became their new home, where Mrs. Robinson worked as a tailoress and the children had various jobs. Malinda, a young woman of 18, met and married William Paris (born around 1812 in Virginia). Though freeborn, Paris was kidnapped three times before his 1842 wedding. The first two times he was held six months and the final time, a year before finally escaping.

Malinda and William moved to Vincennes, Indiana, where they worked as cooks in a hotel. After a short time, the man who last enslaved Paris came after him with bloodhounds and, with the help of the Underground Railroad, the young man escaped. Malinda soon joined her husband in Chatham, Ontario, where their first child, Jane, was born. While many blacks headed to Canada, the Paris family moved to Detroit around 1845. There they met General S. B. Brown who offered Paris a job as cook in his St. Clair hotel. The Paris family remained safely in St. Clair, though Malinda never saw her father after they separated in Kentucky.[1]

Michigan offered distance from slave states, proximity to Canada, and myriad waterways for travel. Many accounts suffice to designate the waterways as important freedom trails. And these same records, hint at a much larger story than is known today. Historian Wilbur Siebert learned the names of at least six boats on Lake Erie carrying passengers to freedom in Detroit. The names of those hidden below deck did not appear on a manifest. Some of those who disembarked in Detroit and crossed by ferry to Canada told their stories, while most are recorded as numbers in a growing Canadian population.[2]

From the southwestern shore of Lake Michigan, freedom seekers left Wisconsin and Illinois ports, voyaged up through the Straits of Mackinac into Lake Huron and into ports

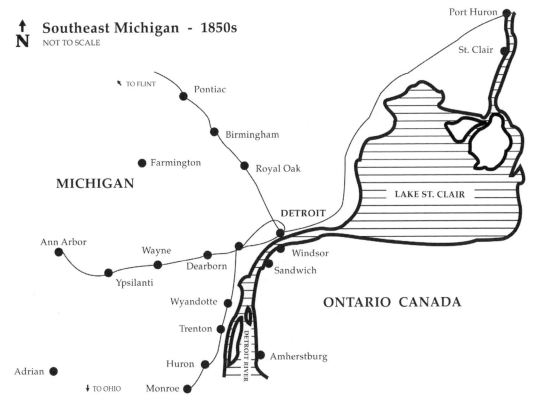

Lake vessels carried freedom seekers to ports along the Detroit River en route to Canada (Lang and Laing [1859], Library of Congress Geography and Map Division: g4071p, rr001230).

such as Bay City in the Saginaw Bay and Port Huron at the opening of the St. Clair River, on a 500 mile trip around the Lower Peninsula of Michigan.

From the same western ports, a person might land on the west coast of Michigan in New Buffalo or St. Joseph in Berrien County. Berrien and adjacent Cass County attracted a higher percentage of black Americans than counties settled earlier, with the exception of Wayne County, home of Detroit. Philo Carpenter of Chicago claimed to have steered at least 200 people to vessels bound for Canada.[3]

On Lake Erie, every type of watercraft was used to carry people to freedom across or down the lake. Burgeoning migration meant many schooners and steamers plied the waters, offering opportunities to stow away or board in disguise. Some boats were known as abolitionist boats for the captains or crewmembers that regularly offered impartial service. Captain T. J. Titus was an experienced pilot of sixteen years when he commanded the *Erie* on its final voyage. Between Buffalo and Dunkirk, New York, the vessel burst into flames, nearly taking the life of Capt. Titus. In the account of the disaster, Capt. Titus nearly drowned but for the aid of his steward, James, a black American who was ready to forfeit his life for the Captain's. Of the *Erie's* passengers, 170 died.

From this time forward, Capt. Titus participated in the Underground Railroad. On one occasion, he picked up two extra sailors at the first stop out of Buffalo. The sailors, called George and Clara, were in disguise on what they hoped was the final seagoing leg of their escape. The siblings left the house of Major Curtis when they learned Clara was to be sold south. The young pair went southeast from the Frankfort, Kentucky, area to outwit notorious slave catcher Bill Shea. As Major Curtis' "body servant," George traveled extensively, knew the roads and had contacts in nearby slave quarters. George led Clara to the Appalachian Mountains and, over several weeks, they worked their way northeast to cross the Ohio River from Parkersburg, West Virginia.

Underground Railroad operators protected the siblings in Oberlin, Ohio, while Major Curtis sent spies to every major port. Finally, a plan was set in motion to get Clara and George on a vessel to Detroit. Imagine the coincidence that Major Curtis and Shea would board the same side-wheel steamer as George and Clara at the next stop. Curtis and Shea recognized their quarry at once and prevailed upon Capt. Titus to land them in Detroit. The captain devised his own scheme. He stopped the boat in Malden, Ontario, with an urgent need for more wood, and they all watched Clara and George walk to freedom.

The Kentuckians attempted to follow the pair but were soon discouraged by townsfolk who showed a particular disdain of slave hunters. Captain Titus continued to ply Lake Erie, and he was not alone in aiding escapes by water. Many of the vessels on the lakes and rivers employed black American cooks and stewards.[4] One crewman was William Wells Brown, who wrote about the preceding account in an autobiographical narrative. Brown escaped from slavery to permanent freedom in January 1834. For two years he worked on a boat running between Cleveland, Buffalo, and Detroit. Brown's activity became known in the Underground Railroad system, and he was called into regular service. "In the year 1842," he says, "I conveyed, from the first of May to the first of December, sixty-nine fugitives over Lake Erie to Canada."[5]

George DeBaptiste bought the steamer *T. Whitney* around 1850, which, with Capt. Atwood at the helm and DeBaptiste as clerk and manager, ran first to up-river ports and afterward on the Sandusky route to Wallaceburg, Dresden, and Chatham, Ontario. He finally traded the steamer for city real estate.[6]

Crossing the River

At times, Detroit was under surveillance for the self-freed and not a safe place to cross to Canada. Branch networks and spurs carried freedom seekers in other directions to safer crossing points. In the area north of Detroit, the port cities of Mt. Clemens, Marine City, St. Clair, Port Huron, and Fort Gratiot were fed by travelers from friendly towns in Genesee, Oakland, and Macomb Counties.

St. Clair was home to one of the more prominent abolitionists in the state, the Rev. Oren Cook Thompson. The Reverend Thompson arrived in Port Huron in 1834 to minister on behalf of the Presbyterian/Congregational Church that Malinda Paris attended. The Reverend Thompson graduated from Ohio's Western Reserve College and Seminary and moved to Michigan in 1831. After a year in Ann Arbor, he moved to the St. Clair/Port Huron area. In later years, Thompson rose to prominence and participated in the founding of the First Congregational Church at Fort and Wayne Streets in Detroit.[7]

The Reverend Thompson may have had at least one helper in Underground Railroad work in St. Clair, a man named John Clark, one of the earliest settlers of China Township a few miles south of St. Clair. Clark attended the state's first antislavery meeting, held in Ann Arbor, where he was nominated as a vice president (replaced by the Reverend Comstock the following year). Other East China neighbors included John and Martha Walker

Donihoo who reportedly brought the men and women they enslaved in Virginia to Michigan in order to send them across to Canada.[8]

During the time Thompson lived in St. Clair, he operated the St. Clair Academy and participated in helping a family out of slavery. Eber B. Ward, wealthy shipbuilder and owner, was known to employ blacks on his boats and, in order to keep a man employed as a chef from being taken by slave hunters, Ward purchased him. The freed man saved his earnings and entrusted Thompson to go to the South to purchase his family.[9]

The Beacon Tree

In a few rare instances, Underground Railroad station keepers created a means of identifying their location. John Rankin in Ripley, Ohio, built his house atop a steep hill and shone a lantern at night while Capt. John Lowry erected a huge sign on poles. In Macomb County, Michigan, near Utica, the Lerich family planted a "beacon tree" twenty-four miles directly east of Pontiac Courthouse.

By 1835, several interior places surpassed early towns in population and commerce. Pontiac was the largest interior town north of Detroit, connected to that city and Ann Arbor. Increased settlement and traffic opened a new network on the Underground Railroad. Peter and Sarah Lerich planted the Beacon Tree on Spring Hill Farm with help from neighbors John Naramoor, John Waters, and Mr. and Mrs. Fuller. Liberetta Lerich, only five years old, wondered why the men dug up a massive cedar tree to plant atop a hill. It took three yoke of oxen to pull the tree to the site, where it was righted.

Then, the men and women gathered to pray. Liberetta overheard references to "black brethren" and "down-trodden race" and wondered why clippings of the *National Era* newspaper were sprinkled on the roots. Mrs. Narramoor arrived to announce the tree could be seen a mile away. Liberetta believed John Owen organized the network passing instructions for those seeking the Beacon Tree.

In the 1850s, Charles C. Foote visited late at night, so that Liberetta could not see, but heard that some men were in the haymow at the Seymour Finney barn, where slave hunters were sniffing around and guarding the ferry. She then heard her father say he had a place to hold 16 standing up. She peered up to see her father lead the guest to the Beacon Tree. Here he stopped the pump of the well and traced his hand along the tamarack-pole fence to the springhouse door built in the side of the hill. The spring itself was surrounded by a brick wall wide enough to walk on. The small amount of water trickling down the pole masked any trace of human interference as it flowed into the Clinton River.

Friends sent freedom seekers from Mt. Clemens and Port Huron, meaning they traveled from the north and east to escape from slavery. After Mr. Foote departed, Lerich announced he would be taking a load of wheat to Detroit and would return with a load of plaster. Liberetta saw no sign of plaster the following day but noticed her mother baking another batch of bread.

On mornings when her father announced that the pump had run off, Sarah Lerich rose immediately to fill pails with food and pots with coffee. Liberetta's parents tried to keep the children from learning of their activity, especially because neighbor Jay Phillips needed bounty money to pay off his mortgage. Eventually, brother Will discovered several people hiding in the springhouse and Liberetta returned home one day for forgotten schoolbooks to find four black men and two black women at the dining table.

Liberetta believed that those who learned the secret hiding place were encouraged to leave the area. Her brother soon hired out to do surveying in Wisconsin. She and her sister kept silent. Only later in life did she connect names such as Fred Douglass, Sojourner Truth, and Peter Jaxon to those heard in her house. Liberetta Lerich Green told the story when she was 76 years old.[10]

Liberetta's parents, Peter and Sarah Fishbaugh Lerich, born in New Jersey, lived to witness the end of slavery from their home in Michigan. Lerich was a strong temperance man who would not sell his grain to distilleries and championed rights and progress. He first voted for Birney, being one of the first seventy in the United States who cast a ballot for the abolition candidate. Mr. Lerich was a very strong antislavery man and did all he could to further the cause.[11]

Charles C. Foote was one of five children of Dr. Henry K. Foote and his wife Minerva Henderson. Dr. Foote was "a Whig and then a Republican, and always an ardent antislavery man." The family came to Michigan in 1834 and made the village of Milford, in Western Oakland County, their permanent home.[12]

Northwestern Counties

West of St. Clair and north of Oakland County, Lapeer County was settled gradually. In 1830, the Rev. Luther Shaw created a settlement called Belle Arbor in the southeast corner of the county. Though many died of malaria, Amasa Ross, and the Farley and Foster families enjoyed the clear water of the Belle River, sharing their antislavery views for generations.[13] Professor Rufus Nutting left the faculty at Western Reserve College to head the prestigious Romeo Academy in Macomb County, Michigan. His house on Fremont Street was reputedly a shelter for escaping slaves.[14]

Among the earliest settlers in Farmington (formerly called Quakertown), Oakland County, was the Quaker family of Arthur Power. They were soon joined by blacksmith Esek Brown and Dr. Ezekiel Webb. Arthur Power donated land for a meetinghouse on Gill Road where Arthur and his son Nathan opened their home to people escaping slavery. John Thayer, a Methodist, helped Ethan Lapham assist people at Lapham's Corners (later part of Farmington).[15]

Four of the 17 antislavery societies in Michigan were located in Oakland County. Listed by name, secretary, and number of members they were: East Bloomfield, Nathan Stone, 70; Farmington, Nathan Power, 80; Troy, Charles Hastings, 72; and Oakland County, George W. Wisner, 50.[16] George Wisner arrived in Michigan a proclaimed abolitionist from New York, "In January, 1834, Wisner became half-owner of the *Sun,* and he developed into a fiery and facile editorial writer, especially of articles favoring the abolition of slavery."[17] Wisner was a brother of Moses Wisner, the Governor of Michigan from 1858 to 1860. When George Wisner ran unsuccessfully for Congress in the Third District, the *Oakland Gazette* of July 24, 1844, read, "He proclaims himself a whole hog abolitionist opposed to the admission of Texas because he says it is going to make ten new slave states."[18]

Another reported Underground Railroad operator was a nephew of the Wisner brothers, William Merithew. The county history stated he "was antislavery in principle and was interested in the Underground Railroad. Many a negro did he help to send through to Canada to find freedom." His home was in West Bloomfield Township.[19] The Power family was involved in the antislavery society in Michigan where Nathan was elected vice president in various years throughout the 1840s. Nathan Power described some stories of helping freedom seekers after the Civil War. On one occasion Ellen and Aaron Wilson escaped from

Virginia to Farmington in the 1850s. During their escape, bloodhounds tracked and caught them and Aaron was forced to club the man who grabbed him in order to escape. The couple left Michigan for Canada but returned after the war with their three children.[20]

The William Gilmour house in Oakland County is listed with a state marker because it was reportedly an Underground Railroad station. It was situated well for that purpose, on Pontiac Trail between Ann Arbor and Farmington. The frame house features a two story center structure with one and a half story wings, forming a "T" footprint. Reportedly, there are two secret rooms. In a bedroom, an opening behind built-in drawers provides access to a hiding space, and another secret place exists in the rear of a closet.

William Gilmour was an active community member from the time of his settling in 1831, opening his house for town meetings, and serving as justice of the peace in 1842. For ten years, his house was the place of worship for the Congregational/Presbyterians in the area under the ministry of the Rev. Isaac W. Ruggles, a delegate at the Michigan State Anti-Slavery Convention in 1836.[21]

From the interior of Michigan, Genesee County's antislavery men promoted the cause, though linking them to actual escapes remains a challenge. One Underground Railroad agent who moved to Flint was the Rev. Henry H. Northrop, who wrote that he and several other Presbyterian ministers were Underground Railroad agents. Northrop graduated in 1837 from the Presbyterian Auburn Theological Seminary and, after a single year in New York, spent

After Rufus Nutting left Oberlin College in Ohio, he moved into this house in Romeo, Michigan, where he was a known abolitionist (author photograph, Romeo, Michigan, 2009).

his entire ministry in Michigan. He moved with his wife, Maryette Wood, to minister in Dexter (1838–1841) and White Pigeon (1841–1845) followed by calls in Homer, Monroe, and Flint. After 1854, the Reverend Northrop retired to Flint, accepting temporary assignments of ministerial duties.[22]

Lewis Buckingham, the first Sheriff of Genesee County, moved to the River House tavern in Flint in 1836. Buckingham was "intensely antislavery." James G. Birney, Liberty Party presidential candidate, on his way to Saginaw in 1841, stopped to lecture in Flint. The abolitionists asked him to return the following week for another lecture. His letter to the *Signal of Liberty* (Oct. 6, 1841) reported that the courthouse was filled with attentive, intelligent-looking people. The men of Genesee County who were most active participants in antislavery efforts and the Liberty Party were John W. King, John C. Gallup, and A. W. Hart.[23]

Dr. John B. Barnes set up medical practice in Owosso in 1842. The Shiawassee County history described him as a "director of the 'underground railroad.'"[24] Before 1850, Barnes' Underground Railroad experience was very limited. No blacks were recorded as settled in Shiawassee or Saginaw Counties before 1850. The following decade showed the spread of settlement throughout state, including dozens of "people of color" recorded in each of the counties bordering Shiawassee.

Chapter Nine

Men of Oppression

Escape of George and Milly McCoy

George McCoy fell in love with a young woman from a nearby farm. Emillia (Milly) was a fine housekeeper who could sew, knit, and weave. George possessed a horse, saddle, and small savings from working in his father's cigar shop in Louisville, Kentucky. When George and Milly married around 1837 there was but one obstacle to their happiness: Milly was enslaved by the Gaines family who refused to give her up.[1]

Born into slavery in Kentucky, George McCoy was freed at the age of 21 by his father, wealthy Irish-American Henry McCoy. It was not uncommon for city slaveholders to permit the men and women they enslaved to find employment on the bustling docks, in shops, or as domestics. In this manner, many slaves earned money, learned about freedom across the Ohio River, and emancipated themselves. George was free to travel north but had to convince Milly to run away with him, in spite of the fact that her two brothers had been sold for $1500 and $1000. Milly felt she was "treated well" by Mrs. Gaines and her parents remained nearby.

One day, without a word to family, Milly and George fled north toward Canada, along a route planned by George. They journeyed with another man to Cincinnati, where Underground Railroad helpers hid them. Mr. Gaines advertised for Milly and pursuers searched throughout Ohio and up to Detroit. When the threat from slave hunters subsided, the McCoys continued on to Essex County, Ontario.

George and Milly lived in a one story log house in Colchester Township, where George supported his growing family by farming. Their first five children were born between 1839 and 1851 in Canada. Life was hard for early farmers in that area, but George and Milly were blessed with their freedom and the assurance that not one of their children would be taken from them. For a reason unknown, the family moved to Michigan at a time when blacks were fleeing to Canada as never before.[2]

Black leaders, on the periphery in national antislavery organizations, rose up in protest in the 1840s in Michigan. Vigilance groups protected and promoted the rights of blacks in major cities. Newspapers, music, poetry, and literature gave voice to words of justice and equality. Antislavery organizations added a new weapon to their arsenal in the attack on slavery: the formerly enslaved lecturer. Shrouded by secrecy, blacks created an order generally restricted to men of color. Across the nation, known only to members, by various exotic names with the words "mystery" or "orders," the system was a full-blown military plan to remove thousands from enslavement.

Black men who once attended meetings were rarely seen in Michigan State Anti-Slavery Society listings after 1845. However, black men and women did not idly wait for others to serve them equal rights. William Lambert and the reverends Monroe and Brooks led other men in Michigan in forming their own churches, and public and secret organizations.[3]

A call went out for a National Convention of Colored Citizens to meet in Buffalo, New York, August 15, 1843. Apparently, some of the leaders in New England were unhappy with arrangements and so 47 of the 58 delegates who attended came from Ohio, Michigan, Illinois, and upstate New York. The Convention assembled at the Vine Street Church, Buffalo, New York. The Rev. Samuel Davis of Buffalo was elected Chairman Pro Tempere and asked to give the keynote speech. Davis was born Samuel McCarty. He trained at Oberlin College before moving to Buffalo to teach at the African School and minister at the Michigan Street Baptist Church of Buffalo. By the end of the decade, the Reverend Davis brought his experience and associations to Detroit.[4]

Convention attendees included well-known abolitionists Frederick Douglass, Amos Q. Beaman, Charles L. Remond, and H. H. Garnet. Beaman was elected president and Douglass, one of the vice presidents. Convention members voted to officially support the platform of the Liberty Party with only two dissenting votes: from Frederick Douglass and Charles Remond of Massachusetts.

Just two months after the national convention, black men of Michigan assembled for a state convention. They met at the Fort Street Second Baptist Church October 26, 1843. Lambert provided the opening address, a moving petition calling for brotherly affection and unanimity. "Therefore, let us by our upright, correct, and manly stand in defense of our Liberty, prove to our oppressors and the world, that we are deserving of our rights, and are determined to be free." A disturbance occurred when eight men of Detroit asked to be seated without having been elected by the "mass of the people." Elected delegates represented Detroit (12), Jackson (2), Marshall (2), and Washtenaw County (7).[5] Both free and formerly enslaved men elected the Rev. William C. Monroe as president. Henry Bibb called the meeting to order. The men of color cited the Declaration of Independence and the injustice of their oppression. In addition to calling for the right to vote, the convention addressed issues of other legislation and limited employment opportunities for youth.

Some progress was made to improve educational opportunities for black students. The Woodstock Manual Labor Institute opened in Michigan in 1844. Black educator Prior Foster (no relation to Samuel and Theodore Foster), began work founding an institute to serve "colored people and others." Four years later, J. G. Birney, William P. Russell, Prior Foster, Joseph Hewitt, William W. Jackson and Joseph Foster incorporated the school. It was located in Addison in the northwest corner of Lenawee County, serving the educational needs of the community during the antebellum period.[6]

Vigilance Committees

In addition to the antislavery societies and colored conventions, other organizations formed in major cities were Black Vigilance Committees. While the conventions engaged in polemics, the vigilance groups helped prevent the arrest of fugitives, provided financial and legal aid, and fought crime. The "People of Color in Philadelphia" held a convention in 1832. In New York, David Ruggles, Theodore S. Wright, and other black men founded a state Committee of Vigilance in 1835, and soon prepared for a state convention.

The Colored Vigilant Committee of Detroit focused on education and suffrage in its early years. The annual meeting in December, 1842, revealed remarkable progress. Around 60 to 70 members of the group contributed to a fund for the day school, 100 people signed a temperance pledge, and a Young Man's Society, debating Club, library, and two female societies were created. The state code of school laws of 1837 did not define who could attend school, and townships or districts chose to discriminate on the basis of color or race at their discretion. The committee founded a free school with a teacher.

The Vigilance Committee met in the basement of the Second Baptist Church. Mr. French opened the meeting with a prayer. The Rev. William C. Monroe, Chairman and pastor of the church, called for a petition to the Legislature that the colored citizens of the state of Michigan enjoy the right of suffrage. A report about Nelson Hackett, a fugitive from Arkansas, noted that the Committee followed the case very closely but did not interfere. Hackett admitted theft and was extradited from Canada. William Lambert composed an annual report to be delivered at Detroit City Hall on January 10, 1843. He wrote, "the committee have learned that education is the principle means by which an enslaved and degraded people can be elevated; and that our moral, upright and correct deportment will be one of the strongest arguments we can present, in favor of our universal elevation to our civil, religious and political rights."[7]

Some of the men participating in these meetings may have moved to Detroit after acts of violence in other cities forced them out. The states carved from the Northwest Territory offered a degree of safety for freedom seekers, but not the certain protection of Canada. In cities throughout the North, citizens clashed over racial issues and job opportunities, especially as waves of Irish and German immigrants swarmed into states like Michigan.

After a spring 1841 riot in Dayton, Ohio, sixty to seventy black men, women, and children fled a mob and made their way to Detroit. Of those seeking refuge, at least four died and as many others were gravely ill with pleurisy. Dr. Arthur Porter tended to the ill. H. P. Hoag of Detroit was one of the sympathizers who helped the self-emancipators find work. The homes and possessions that the black settlers in Dayton worked to own were burned to ashes and no compensation was given. Some attackers went before a grand jury in Dayton, without being charged. The *Signal of Liberty*, reporting the event, posed the question of how the "colored man" could answer the accusation of being unable to take care of himself when he is attacked, robbed, and left without legal redress.[8]

In Cincinnati, a minor assault occurred when an Underground Railroad agent resisted the capture of a self-freed person discovered at his house. While the agent was in jail in June 1841, a mob attacked his house. In September, trouble broke out between some Kentucky "river men" and local citizens against a number of blacks in a city settlement. Over weeks, violent acts escalated until a cannon was fired on the black neighborhood. The mob destroyed the office of the antislavery newspaper, the *Philanthropist*, wounded 20 to 30 people and damaged their property.[9]

Black Lecturers

Only after Bibb realized he could not be united with Malinda, as described in Chapter Four, did he settle into a life dedicated to resisting slavery. The Michigan State Anti-Slavery Society recruited him to join the lecturing circuit. In the antebellum years, many formerly enslaved toured Northern states sharing their personal experiences in slavery. The intelligence and social graces of black lecturers exposed race-based prejudices as poor justification for enslavement.

Bibb wrote, "The first time that I ever spoke before a public audience, was to give a narration of my own sufferings and adventures, connected with slavery. I commenced in the village of Adrian, State of Michigan, May, 1844." The life of a traveling lecturer in the 1840s was not for the aged and infirm. The men often spoke in houses where people were poor and could not furnish lodging. Bibb carried candles and often rode for miles on log-covered roads to find a place for the night. Yet, despite the discomfort, Bibb pressed on. As he wrote in his narrative,

> the principle part of my time has been faithfully devoted to the cause of freedom — nerved up and encouraged by the sympathy of antislavery friends on the one hand, and prompted by a sense of duty to my enslaved countrymen on the other, especially, when I remembered that slavery had robbed me of my freedom — deprived me of education — banished me from my native State, and robbed me of my family.[10]

A man from Saline, Michigan wrote that he rarely attended antislavery meetings but went to hear Bibb in 1844 out of curiosity. Afterwards the listener felt that Bibb would become one of the "most distinguished men in our country" and that there would be a substantial increase in Liberty votes. Bibb addressed 1,000 to 1,500 people at the Liberty State Convention. The turnout was so large that the assembly moved from the Ann Arbor Courthouse to the public square. Mr. Bibb addressed the annual State Liberty Convention in Marshall with "great effect" according to the *Signal of Liberty* of July 21, 1845. The *Pennsylvania Freeman* reported in February 1847 that Henry Bibb addressed a large crowd on two successive nights in Faneuil Hall, Boston. He was described as a pleasing and fluent speaker whose three hour discourse each night was insufficient.[11]

In the strongly antislavery town of Salem, Washtenaw County, Bibb was invited to speak at the schoolhouse in 1846. The crowd was so great that the lecture moved to a barn that was likewise filled to capacity. Immediately after his talk, the ladies of the town formed a Ladies Anti-Slavery Association to send Bibb money.[12] In Flint, Genesee County, Bibb was invited to lecture in the Courthouse.

In his autobiography *Life of an American Slave* (1845), Frederick Douglass cautioned that the promotion and descriptions of the Underground Railroad might inhibit its success. "I would keep the merciless slaveholder profoundly ignorant of the means of flight adopted by the slave." His words reflect the schism between the Midwestern antislavery faction and the men and women in New England: "I have never approved of the very public manner in which some of our western friends have conducted what they call the underground railroad, but which I think, by their open declarations, has been made most emphatically the upperground railroad."[13]

Some formerly enslaved men and women provided lectures but were not put on a circuit. Lewis Clarke spoke on several occasions in the East about abuses by slaveholders and patrollers. His words were taken down by abolitionist Mrs. Lydia Child and reported in part in the *Signal of Liberty* on January 9, 1843. Clarke referred to the sexual abuse of women by enslavers and patrollers, and Kentucky laws that made complaint impossible. Clarke said his sixteen year old sister had been called to the "master" one night. After crying and complaining, the girl was sold to Louisiana where she soon died. Every new personal story added fuel to the fire of abolitionism. Together they added credence to the belief that abuse was more prevalent than had been supposed. But, to some people, one story was enough to compel them to board the antislavery wagon.

In Detroit, black churches continued to serve as havens for freedom seekers and places of worship. After teaching ended in 1846, the Rev. Samuel H. Davis moved from Buffalo, New York, to Michigan's Second Baptist Church to serve as its pastor from 1848 to 1851. The church had 180 members in 1850 but then changed affiliation. Madison Lightfoot, who contributed to the welfare of Detroit's citizens since the time the Blackburns escaped, accepted a position as pastor of First Baptist Church in Dresden, Ontario, and Davis resigned to teach in Chatham, Ontario. Students moved to St. Matthew's Mission, an Episcopal Church founded in Detroit by the Reverend Monroe and William Lambert, where the Reverend Monroe taught.[14]

Underground Railroad agents offered a degree of security to the formerly enslaved, but the threat of a sudden kidnapping happened with frightful regularity. In 1845, when Samuel Bowles, a free black American in Berrien, Michigan, was arrested as a runaway slave, the *Signal of Liberty* headline read, "Kidnapping a Free Colored Man. Great Outrage." Samuel S. Gunn colluded with the Berrien County sheriff and local justice to help arrest Bowles when he was working as a cook on the steamboat *Algoma*. At trial, Bowles was sworn in as a witness. He stated that he was born a free man near Brownsville, Pennsylvania, and presented a full account of ten years employment as cook or steward on numerous steamboats. The justice of the peace in Niles found no criminal intent, leaving every spectator at the trial in astonishment. An argument followed that if a horse rather than a man were taken, a different legal action might be expected. White abolitionist J. L. Alexander wrote lengthy descriptions of the trial for the *Signal of Liberty*.

Bowles was jailed overnight, handcuffed, and on November 6, 1845, taken by wagon out of the state. Only by the intervention of friends was he rescued in Indiana and brought back to Michigan. John Orr and William P. Reese of Niles rode after Gunn, catching up to him in Door Village, Indiana. Here the tables turned. Bowles applied for warrants of false imprisonment and kidnapping to be issued against his kidnappers. Gunn was taken back to LaPorte, Indiana, where both pro- and antislavery elements voiced complaints.

For some reason, the warrant against Gunn was not served, and Gunn slipped away in the night. It was found that Gunn once lived in Niles but had moved to St. Louis. Samuel Bowles returned to Niles. The black settlements offered safer haven and Michigan's black leaders found the time ripe for a revolutionary organization.[15]

African American Mysteries

When historian Dr. Siebert described and listed the Vigilance Committees across the nation, he included the "League of Gileadites," formed by John Brown of Harpers Ferry fame. The League met in Springfield, Massachusetts, in January 1851. This League was not founded to help people with legal issues or education. Members of the League of Gileadites were supposed to gather implements [weaponry], make no noise, and resist the law for any attack upon the rights of blacks. Black men, women, children, and infirm were invited to sign the pledge. John Brown's rules reflected his grand plan to create an army, "Stand by one another, and by your friends, while a drop of blood remains; and be hanged, if you must, but tell not tales out of school." When the 44 black men and women adopted the Agreement and Rules, they became a branch of the United States League of Gileadites. This was one of several secret organizations formed to resist and end slavery with violence, if needed.[16]

Historians questioned the theory that Vigilance Committees were a "great secret system." But, what about the League of Gileadites? F. B. Sanborn wrote in *Life and Letters of*

The Old Finney Barn in Detroit sheltered many self-emancipators, even as slave hunters rested at nearby Finney's Hotel (*City of Detroit, Michigan,* Bentley Historical Library, University of Michigan).

John Brown, that John Brown had been traveling across the north for four to five years promoting secret organizations. As expected, few records remain. However, there is verifiable evidence that secret societies, in addition to Vigilance Committees, did exist and, in the decade preceding the Civil War, members contributed to escapes on the Underground Railroad and plotted to overthrow slavery.[17]

In separate accounts, William Lambert and George DeBaptiste described a secret organization in Detroit, Booker T. Washington wrote of one in St. Louis, and two of John Brown's men mentioned secret societies in several cities in Ohio. The earliest document mentioning a secret society came from a member of John Brown's army. Richard Realf wrote a letter on May 31, 1858, to "Uncle John" (John Brown). After an important pre-attack meeting of Brown's army, Realf became concerned that some of the men revealed the whereabouts of supplies and details of the mission. "Nor am I better pleased to learn from the same source that a certain Mr Reynolds (colored) who attended our convention, has disclosed its objects to the members of a secret society (colored) called 'The American Mysteries' or some confounded humbug."[18]

The group described by Booker T. Washington was headquartered in St. Louis.

Founded by the Rev. Moses Dickson, it was called the International Order of Twelve of the Knights and Daughters of Tabor. Dickson, born in Cincinnati, Ohio, in 1824, worked the steamboats on the Ohio and Mississippi Rivers for many years. He and eleven men met in 1844 to form the order and decided to spend two years developing a plan of action. After traveling north and south for two years, the group met as planned in 1846. The Knights and Daughters of Tabor, their new name, agreed on a plan to support eleven men organizing local societies in the south, while Dickson remained in St. Louis. They would allow ten years to secretly prepare for their project. The men dispersed among Southern states, except Alabama and Texas, recruiting men and women into the Knights and Daughters of Tabor and stockpiling weapons for a mass assault on the slave system.

William Lambert called the Detroit organization "African-American Mysteries: Order of the Men of Oppression." George DeBaptiste called it "Order of Emigration" and described the highest degree in membership as "Men of

Second Baptist Church in Detroit, Michigan, was known as a resting place for self-emancipators and an important meeting place for Michigan's African American community (Silas Farmer's *History of Detroit,* 1890).

Oppression."[19] The Grand Chapter lodge was located on Jefferson Avenue between Bates and Randolph in Detroit. The Detroit Order included free and self-freed blacks and select white men. Their primary business was transporting freedom seekers as part of an Underground Railroad operation, and funding settlements in Canada.

Lambert said he and others began the organization of a more thorough system of assisting self-emancipators find employment so they might contribute to getting their families out of slavery. Underground Railroad workers were sent into the south and were placed on boats on the Mississippi and Ohio rivers to facilitate rescues. Decades after the Civil War, William Lambert showed a reporter ledgers where names of people who passed to safety and detailed information about the operations of the Order were recorded. Members of the Order hid self-emancipators and rescued men and women in the house of J. C. Reynolds, a worker on the Michigan Central Railway. They were fed, provided clothing, and moved in the dark one by one.[20]

William Lambert's ledgers were rare remnants of recorded Underground Railroad history. Most Underground Railroad agents destroyed lists and notes before the Civil War. In 1886, the sheepskin-bound books and letters from prominent abolitionists were viewed and described by a reporter. Their whereabouts today are unknown.

William Lambert described the elaborate rituals to test men as they earned degrees or rankings within the Order. In the first chapter were three degrees: Captives, Redeemed, Chosen; and a branch called Confidence, used on the Underground Railroad. Agents sent to the South passed the confidence degree after they swore an oath of allegiance. Then, they memorized passwords taught to fugitives. The ritual included the word "Cross" and the reply "over" and many others. In addition, a sign of "pulling the knuckle of the right forefinger over the knuckle of the same finger of the left hand" was expected to be performed in reverse by the Underground Railroad agent. Lambert described rituals with blindfolds and much "frummery" to pass from captive to chosen. There were five degrees beyond Chosen before one could reach "sterling black knight of St. Domingo." Though the test required a challenging study of history and government, Lambert states that 60,000 men took that order. And then they learned the "full intention of the order."[21]

Lambert's descriptions of the rituals and history lessons are described in Moses Dickson's lengthy book *A Manual of the Knights of Tabor, and Daughters of the Tabernacle, Including the Ceremonies of the Order, Constitutions, Installations, Dedications, and Funerals, with Forms, and the Taborian Drill and Tactics.* Dickson's book was written for the men and women of St. Louis and others in the international society.[22]

Curiously, about the time the Orders of Mystery came into existence, Martin Delany founded a newspaper called *The Mystery.* It was in publication from 1843 to 1847 in Pittsburgh, Pennsylvania, and later merged with the *North Star.* The Rev. William Monroe, Robert Banks and George W. Tucker were the agents who handled subscriptions in Detroit.[23] Robert Delany, editor of *the Mystery,* wrote a final message to readers, "We feel loath to leave our 'Mystery' but duty calls and we must obey. To our brethren and oppressed fellow men everywhere we give the assurance that so long as reason serves as the dictator of our will we shall never cease to war against slavery and oppression of every kind and defend the cause of the oppressed."[24] The use of words such as "war" and "defend," intimidated slaveholders whose fear of uprisings and violence tended to bring about harsher treatment. But, the failures of past rebellions taught Delany and other black leaders to channel their impulse for violence into helping with escapes and other measures designed to end slavery.

William Lambert made some seemingly ridiculous claims about the number of people guided to freedom on the Underground Railroad. If he were speaking on behalf of the African American Mysteries and the international Orders, the figures were probably accurate. But, it would take a decade to amass the weapons needed to stage a revolt with tens of thousands of men. Lambert, Dickson and others were not quite prepared. In the 1850s, the Orders awaited the word of Moses Dickson to attack from within the South and the North. In the meantime, the Underground Railroad in Detroit ran a brisk and efficient enterprise getting self-emancipators across the Detroit River to Canada.

"Midnight"

William Lambert described an interracial group of Underground Railroad operators, including white agents Seymour Finney, Luther Beecher and Glode Chubb in Detroit in the 1840s. Lambert confirmed what others wrote about Seymour Finney's hotel and barn. "Finney's barn used to be filled with them [freedom seekers] some times."[25]

As mentioned earlier in the book, Lambert said his group (Underground Railroad agents or members of the Men of Mysteries) had boats under the docks in Detroit and took to Canada over 1,500 persons a year. Seymour Finney's son said that George Dolarson, a black baker in Detroit, was an agent.[26] The others who helped in the effort were Alanson Sheley, the Rev. Charles C. Foote, and Samuel Zug. Sheley was a Presbyterian minister. Samuel Zug, a furniture dealer, owned land on a peninsula at the mouth of the Rouge River (later known as Zug Island). He participated with Chubb, Silas Holmes, Horace Hallock and other political activists in the Wayne County Liberty Party. In 1845, under the leadership of Marcus Swift, the group voted for the right of suffrage for the colored population. Horace Hallock, a prominent person in the antislavery movement, furnished lodging and meals. The back yard of Horace Hallock's residence extended to the Detroit River and, from that point, freedom seekers were sent across to Canada in a skiff. Hallock was one of several men who contributed to the colonization of Canada by purchasing land that could be leased by formerly enslaved people. The men purchased a tract of land ten miles from Windsor and parceled it into farms of ten to fifteen acres each for self-emancipators, many of whose descendants continued to live in Windsor decades later.[27]

For some self-emancipators, the only goal was Canada, while others found suitable opportunities in Michigan. If the factions of antislavery men and women could unite in their purpose of ending slavery, it might not be necessary for self-emancipators to move to a foreign country.

Chapter Ten

Fractures in the Cause

Escape of Robert Coxe, 1843

"CONDITION OF SLAVES"

We have taken pains to inquire of different fugitives respecting their former condition. Their statements have varied greatly according to the character of their master, and the surrounding circumstances. Some were well fed, clothed and treated, and never beaten. The condition of others was the reverse.

The last who called on us was a young man, age 23, named Robert Coxe, from Frankfort, KY. His master's name was O'Harra (O'Hara), an Irish Catholic, who kept an academy for boys. Robert had twelve brothers and sisters, a part of who were sold down the river. His father was a Baptist minister.—He had shown his back to Robert, where the whip had cut it up when he was young. Think of that, ye pro slavery Baptists! That is the way some of your ministers are educated at the South.

Robert had often seen his aged mother and four sisters hauled up to the whipping post, and flogged. Upon asking if they were stripped, he said it was considered no whipping at all unless they were stripped to the skin. Their treatment was so bad, that they were all forced to run away, and then whipped for that. His sisters had been severely flogged for looking into the books that lay around the house and trying to read them. The mistress usually kept a rawhide beside her on the sofa, so that she could punish the girls without the trouble of getting up.

Robert was overworked. He often had to work hard Sundays and holidays. He and his master had a falling out about work, and O'Harra (O'Hara) thought Robert must be whipped. Robert was of a different opinion, and by the help of his brother, broke away from the whipping post, and fled for a land of liberty, followed by two men & a bloodhound, which was kept in the family on purpose to hunt fugitives.

When he arrived at the Ohio, he followed Gerrit Smith's advice without having ever read it, and "took?" the boat from one side of the river and left it on the other.

Where is the man, unless it be the Rev. Editor of the New York Observer, who will not acknowledge he did right? Robert and his brother traveled three weeks without entering a house, led by that unfailing guide, the North Star. Robert had learned a little Geography by looking at the map with his master's son. They came into Adrian in the daytime, and were kindly accosted by a broad brimmed gentleman, who saw their necessities relieved. Robert is a Methodist, and is determined to get an education at Hiram Wilson's Institute in Canada."

From the Signal of Liberty, May 22, 1843

A journey of weeks shrank to days after "railroad mania" took hold and tracks linked states, cities and small towns. Pioneers rolled west, immigrants filling cities to overflowing until 17 million called the United States home. The terrible irony was that foreigners could purchase land as soon as their pocketbooks allowed, while the country's nearly two and a half million enslaved blacks could not expect to own a speck of the soil on which they were born or toiled, and in 1844, the nation elected a president who replaced servants with slaves in the White House.[1] Free blacks were denied suffrage and after years of involvement in the Michigan State Anti-Slavery Society were passed over in elections of officers.

Robert Coxe may have followed newly lain tracks on the journey north. He left the academy of Keen O'Hara in Danville, Kentucky, with geographical knowledge from viewing a map. Attempting to read while in the home of the headmaster of a respected classical school was one of the reasons Robert and his sisters received whippings. Robert and his brother took a boat to cross the Ohio River, did not enter a single residence on the 350 mile journey, and did not make contact with the Underground Railroad until Adrian, Michigan. A man familiar with the Adrian network, Norman Geddes, described the places freedom seekers like Robert Coxe stayed on a freedom trail in Michigan.

Southeast Michigan Network

Judge Norman Geddes was a man of high integrity and sympathetic interest in all. He came with his family to Lenawee County in 1835, remaining there all his years except while studying law. He was intimate with a network of the Underground Railroad from the Ohio River to Sandusky, and Toledo, Adrian, Tecumseh, Ypsilanti, and Detroit. As in earlier years, the connections avoided Monroe County where some strong Democrats made it a risky link to Canada.[2]

The network described by Norman Geddes branched off from the Wesleyan Methodist Network. This line came from the stations in the East across northern Ohio, and, instead of linking to Ohio ports, continued west to Adrian. From there, it branched north to Tecumseh. Judge Geddes wrote that Warren Gilbert once had 40 armed men at his place in Rome. Deacon James B. Wells of Clinton was the final stop in Lenawee County. Once in Washtenaw County, the branches zigzagged, "where Moses Bartlett['s] house was a station; thence north to John Lowy's (Lowry's) on Lodi Plains in Washtenaw County then north easterly to Farmington." Judge Geddes specifically described the Bartlett place as 27 miles northeast of Adrian. He added that there was a "colored man east of Saline on the Chicago turnpike." Like many others on the Chicago Turnpike, Asher and Catherine Aray were part of more than one network and worked with Capt. Lowry and the others, in the area. Unfortunately, Judge Geddes added no other names.[3]

From Adrian, freedom seekers were taken to the house of Reuben L. Hall, later of Ypsilanti. Hall's sons remembered "the arrival of dusky passengers at their house, whence they were forwarded to the Quaker settlement in this township [Ypsilanti] and thence to Detroit or Trenton." Further reflecting on the need for multiple routes to freedom, the article mentioned that when slave catchers were on the lookout in Detroit, freedom seekers were sent back to Plymouth and Ypsilanti and sent along the Trenton and Grosse Ile route.[4]

Moses and Pebses Bartlett resided on Burmeister Road. Their daughter Mary was united in marriage to Sylvanus Hull, with whom she had much in common. Apparently, Mary Bartlett and Sylvanus Hull were raised in homes where slavery's refugees found food, shelter and guidance to the next safe haven. John Wesley Hull, son of Mary and Sylvanus, said, "My father's house was a station on what was called the underground railway. Sometimes we had as many as 27 negroes in the house at one time. All the women would help prepare the food, and the men would do their share also, so they were no great trouble, except for getting the food to feed so many. I can still remember how good the food tasted that some of the old colored cooks used to prepare."

Hull was in his mid-eighties when interviewed, but his memory of the escape was shared by a neighbor, Elizabeth Larzelere. When the large group passed down the road, her father told her not to look so she could later say with honesty she had not seen escaping slaves.[5]

John's parents, Sylvanus Hull and Mary Bartlett Hull, lived on a farm west of the Larzeleres in Saline Township. Hull was an antislavery man, *Signal of Liberty* subscriber, and State Liberty Fund donor.[6]

"Liberty to the Fugitive Captive"

Captain John Lowry and his wife Sylvia defied both public scorn and the law by boldly inviting freedom seekers to their home in Lodi Township, Washtenaw County, Michigan. They erected a large board sign on poles that could be seen from a distance. Antislavery lecturer Giles Stebbins recalled that the daily stage would stop so passengers could read the message. Capt. Lowry enjoyed hearing people chose to travel the Ann Arbor–Saline Road in order to view his sign.

Capt. John Lowry painted a large board sign with, "Welcome to the Fugitive Captive" to mark his Underground Railroad station near Saline, Michigan (photograph courtesy of J.S. Benton.

Above the gate to his yard, high enough for a hay wagon to pass beneath, Lowry's board sign was painted with two figures, one white and the other black, holding a scroll between them. Capt. Lowry's daughter, Mary E., described the sign.

> The figure at the right is a female form, with heavy chain in the left hand, but broken are the links. In her right hand she holds the balances: to the left, and in the act of rising, is the figure of a man of darker hue, and lips so thick and hair like wool, but clad in freeman's gar; while around one wrist is clasped the other end of slavery's chain, with many missing links, and to his sister he looks up for help and perfect freedom, their faces all aglow with triumph, and just below appears this motto: "liberty to the fugitive captive and the oppressed over all the earth, both male and female of all colors."[7]

Mary E. Lowry Foster said this was her father's expression of his desire that slavery and oppression would end. In a family history presentation she gave to the Michigan State Pioneer Society in 1880, Mary Lowry Foster described a family tradition that every child, grandchild, and great-grandchild was presented to family patriarch John Peter Lowry for his annual blessing.[8] Until his 99th year, John Peter Lowry bestowed upon his descendants his personal story of the cruelties that men inflict upon each other. In England in the 1700s, John Peter was a young lad of thirteen away at school. In an instant, his safe and ordered world was shattered. He and twelve classmates were stolen from the school, kidnapped aboard a ship bound for America. John Peter was sold into five years servitude in Pennsylvania as payment for passage. When his service was complete, John Peter remained in Pennsylvania, changed his name to Lowry and married a woman of Dutch descent. The Dutch speaking family grew to include a son Peter, grandson John, and great-granddaughter Mary.

One can imagine John Peter Lowry describing the horror of being forever separated from his family, the days at sea as the distance from home stretched to permanence. A boy once able to attend school full time, suddenly denied his freedom and privileges as he was forced into labor. Is it not at all surprising that his grandson, Captain John Lowry, would be sympathetic to those stolen from their homes, sold into slavery, and forced to work without pay?

John Peter Lowry's grandson, John, was born in Onondaga County, New York, on February 1, 1793. He married Sylvia Wickham in 1821 and the two resolved to secure a home of their own. The Lowrys lived in Ann Arbor a short time and then moved to Lodi Plains, five miles south of the village.

Giles Stebbins recalled that the sign stood for years. He believed that Capt. Lowry "was of a sort not safe to tamper with" and his full barns and broad acres revealed a man of "sturdy will" rather than a madman. The sign was likely protected by the neighbors at Nutting's Corner who supported his cause and helped Lowry transport men and women to safety in Michigan and Canada.[9]

Great-great-grandson, Robert James Lowry of Ann Arbor, was aware of his ancestor's work on the Underground Railroad, but said the family did not speak of the illegal activity. Robert compiled a scrapbook of family photographs and read from the passed-down family Bible. He said Capt. John Lowry's parents joined him in Lodi Township and were buried in the cemetery at Textile Road.[10] Mr. Selleck Wood told Mr. Cheever that "he drove a number of loads of fleeing negro slaves from Mr. Lowry's home to the Detroit river and saw that they were safely carried across to Canada." Selleck Wood recalled that Capt. Lowry traveled to Washington, D.C. to warn President Polk that the nation was in danger unless the slaves were freed.[11]

Several accounts offer verification of Capt. Lowry's involvement in the Underground Railroad. Pamela Noble of Ann Arbor recalled that Capt. Lowry helped transport the Washingtons in 1850 (see Sylvester Noble) and Norman Geddes wrote in 1893 that after Adrian, they traveled north to "John Lowy's [*sic*] on Lodi Plains."

After his wife's death in 1859, Capt. Lowry married Rhoda Comstock and moved to Shiawassee County, Michigan. Upon his death in 1872, Captain Lowry's body was returned to Lodi, where he was buried alongside his first wife and parents. His epitaph is a line from the abolitionist poet John Greenleaf Whittier's *Raphael*, "The tissue of the Life to be we weave with colors all our own and in the field of Destiny we reap as we have sown."

At the intersection of Textile and Ann Arbor–Saline Roads in Saline Township is Nutting's Corner. Captain John Lowry's farm lay at the northwest corner; the Congregational church, parsonage, and homes of Eli Benton and Ira Weed southwest; Nutting Academy southeast; and the farms of the Wood family members just beyond. Nutting relocated to Washtenaw County where he presided over Lodi Academy from 1847 to 1864. Students boarded at private homes for a small fee, and nearly every neighbor was a staunch aboli-tionist. Every place Nutting resided is associated with Underground Railroad activity. Though documentation of his participation has not yet been found, Prof. Nutting influenced many young men and women.[12]

Timothy Hunt, friend and business partner of Capt. John Lowry, was an active abo-litionist. According to Mrs. Hunt, her husband's motto was "Liberty to the fugitive, cap-tive, and oppressed and sympathy for the poor," and his home was forever open to the weary traveler. The reminiscences by Mrs. Timothy Hunt state that Lowry and Hunt traveled and purchased land together.

Though Timothy Hunt was a Baptist, he donated five acres of land at the southwest corner of Saline–Ann Arbor and Textile Roads for the Presbyterian Church and parsonage led by Underground Railroad agent the Rev. John Kanouse. Kanouse eventually ministered to both the Lodi and Saline Presbyterian Churches.[13] Hunt was mentioned in the records of the First Baptist Church of Saline. In 1854 at a covenant meeting, Deacon Timothy Hunt presented a list of resolutions concerning slavery that were subsequently rejected. Hunt stopped attending church meetings and performing his duties.

He must have been an influential man, because soon, his resolution was passed: "Resolved, that we regard American slavery as wicked in the sight of God, and for the sup-porters of this evil, we have no fellowship as a Church of Christ." And the resolution was to be published in the *Christian Herald*. Resolutions such as this, sometimes led to congre-gations separating from the national body of the church that included Southern and slave-holding congregations.[14]

Another known Underground Railroad agent with Lowry was Selleck Wood. "The Woods" of Lodi Township would seem a reference to the hickory, oak, walnut, button-wood, and maples of the heavily timbered area. Instead, it was a nickname for the families of pioneer brothers Abijah and Ira Wood, whose farms formed an extensive colony. By the late 1800s, the Woods were exemplary farmers and achieved an international reputation for fine merino wool breeding.

Abijah Wood's son Selleck came from Ovid, New York, with the family in 1834 and lived on his father's farm for many years. The farm was in close proximity to the Congre-gational church established by the Rev. Ira Weed and under the pastorship of the Reverend Kanouse.[15] More importantly, Selleck Wood was a close neighbor of Capt. Lowry. Accord-ing to an early writer, Noah Cheever, "Mr. Selleck Wood ... told me that when he was a young man he drove a number of fleeing negro slaves from Mr. Lowry's home to the Detroit river and saw that they were safely carried across to Canada."[16]

Brothers Ezra and Zina Lay left New York for Michigan with 25,000 cultivated trees for the establishment of a nursery. They chose a site along Michigan Avenue in Ypsilanti Township and were rewarded with success, primarily in fruit tree production. In 1834, the Lays built the first greenhouse in the area, attracting customers traveling along the old Chicago Road from Detroit. The classic Greek Revival house Ezra built around 1833 has long been linked to the Underground Railroad. One story describes a false floor in the rear section of the house.[17]

Though the name of Ezra Dennison Lay is not found on antislavery lists, the county biography describes him as one of the most influential men in Washtenaw County who served as Supervisor of Ypsilanti Township and "used his influence in every possible way in favor of abolition."[18]

A former neighbor who was aware of the Underground Railroad, Solon Goodell of

Superior Township, wrote that William H. Lay could provide the record of his father's Underground Railroad activity.[19] William, son of Ezra and Malinda (Kinne) Lay, continued the successful operation of the nursery but did not provide a record of his father's activity.

In telling his personal history, self-freed man Robert Coxe mentions his siblings being "sold down the river." The allusion referred to the sale of people to work as slaves in the ever-expanding cotton fields. The explosion of slavery into the South and West after the cotton gin's widespread use changed the institution of slavery. By 1850, three-fourths of all enslaved people in America were agricultural laborers, with over half growing cotton, primarily in the Mississippi Valley states of Alabama, Mississippi, and Louisiana.[20]

After sharing his story with the *Signal of Liberty* editors, Robert Coxe and his brother left for Hiram Wilson's British and American Institute at Dawn, Ontario, Canada.[21] Hiram Wilson described conditions at the Dawn Settlement in an article for the *Signal of Liberty* (March 4, 1844). Wilson and his family and friends had been living at Dawn for two years. The school was located on rich land along the Sydenham River, with black walnut trees and fine soil. Wilson reported that fugitives were frequently arriving, and that prospects looked good. According to Wilson, the entire Canada Mission offered about ten schools, religious services, accommodations, and training. Yet, increased funding was needed for an expansion of land and new buildings at the Dawn school. Wilson announced that Josiah Henson was authorized to solicit funding. The school was plagued by budget shortfalls, especially as more students arrived. There were 70 students by 1845.[22]

Foster and Beckley believed that publication of the personal accounts strengthened the argument that assisting and harboring runaways was a justifiable action for northerners. They hoped to arouse sympathy by letting self-emancipated men and women speak for themselves. How could the hearts of even hardened Democrats not be touched by the story of Robert Coxe, helpless to stop the beatings of his sister and mother, and then grief-stricken as the family was sold off and separated? The Reverend Beckley had no wish to keep his aide of freedom seekers a secret.

Liberty Party Schism

The upcoming election and the western expansionism garnered much attention in 1844. After four years of President Tyler's "southern slavocracy" neither the Whig nor Democratic Party wanted him as a candidate. James Polk, a surprise Democratic nominee, faced Whig Henry Clay instead. Once again James Birney of Kentucky was the Liberty Party nominee in the presidential election of 1844. With the slave status of Texas a central issue, Liberty Party members expressed concern over taking votes from the Whig party. Samuel Foster sent articles to the *Signal of Liberty* supporting the Liberty Party stating the "Whig party are not to be trusted in their pretended love of personal liberty...."[23]

The following month, Samuel Foster dared to attack an inviolable foundation of his country, the United States Constitution. His speech appeared in the newspaper under the provocative heading "The Constitution is Pro-Slavery, and Therefore Ought to be Amended." Foster argued that the privileges granted by the Constitution were contrary to those sanctioning slavery and cited specific articles to address issues of "habeas corpus" and freedoms of religion and speech. He wrote that the provisions allowing slavery were "the conspiracy of a large portion of the people of the United States against the liberties of another portion of the same people." It was his reasoned conclusion that as long as states could legally adopt slavery, the Constitution must be amended. The lengthy ruminations show a writer who possessed legal and historical knowledge and an ability to controvert commonly held beliefs.[24]

The arguments and endorsements may have improved the outcome of the election for Birney who got 62,000 votes, a very small two percent of the popular vote. The percentage helped the Democrats gain a victory. The Democrats passed a joint resolution in Congress, over nearly unanimous Whig opposition, to offer Texas immediate entry as a slave state in March 1845. David Wilmot introduced his famous Proviso barring slavery from any land acquired from Mexico as a result of the war. Wilmot's Proviso set off four years of sectional strife that would not be resolved until passage of the Compromise of 1850.

Facing another four years with a southerner in the White House, Theodore Foster and Guy Beckley in Michigan and men in New York initiated pressure to expand the Liberty Party platform to include issues other than ending slavery. Foster presented the agenda to the Washtenaw County Liberty Party in September 1845. After a "full and animated discussion" the members voted "that the time has now fully come when the Liberty party ought to carry out the principle of Equal Rights in all the legitimate consequences and applications, by taking the right side of all questions, civil, financial or political, that affect the welfare of the community." Convention reports from across the state (Kalamazoo, Cass, Van Buren, Genesee, and St. Joseph Counties, and the districts of Pontiac and Oakland) endorsed a ticket of Birney and Dr. Nathan Thomas, but not the expanded platform. Only the Van Buren convention passed a resolution similar to that of Washtenaw for a broad platform.[25]

At the annual Michigan State Anti-Slavery Society meeting February 4–5, 1846, in Marshall, Executive Committee Treasurer Foster and Vice President Beckley read their proposal for an expanded Liberty Party platform including free trade, judicial reform, and other issues. Their report was referred to a select committee of Chester Gurney, Guy Beckley, Charles Stewart, J. C. Gallup and Seymour Treadwell. It received virtually no support.

On February 5, the officers for the coming year were nominated. Foster was installed as Secretary. And for the first time since 1840, the Reverend Beckley, losing favor over his expansion campaign, was not elected to serve on the Executive Committee. The Select Committee expunged from the report all references to the policies of the Liberty Party. Undaunted, in June, Beckley and Foster printed a circular inserted into the *Signal of Liberty* and sent to all Liberty Party newspapers proposing the Liberty Party endorse issues beyond slavery. The circular was unsigned, but coeditors Foster and Beckley came under attack across the nation. The only consolation was that a similar plan led by William Goodell in New York was gaining ground in northern Ohio.[26]

Theodore Foster wrote to James Birney that after meeting with antislavery leaders in Chicago, he felt the Liberty Party "are determined to be no party at all." The *Signal of Liberty* reported that the American Anti-Slavery Society was too fractured and of waning influence.[27] In the summer when Foster wrote this letter, Birney suffered a stroke. He was forced to withdraw from public speaking, though his letters show he remained active politically.

Foster's assessment of the Liberty Party was correct, though it would take several more years for the majority within the political party to realize they would not bring in new members without expanding the platform. William Lloyd Garrison and Frederick Douglass continued to support moral over political power. Garrison and his supporters began a new lecture tour promoting immediate freedom for the enslaved and consideration of rights for women. Garrisonian female lecturers from New England showed great fortitude lecturing in Pennsylvania. In April 1845, Abby Kelley and other speakers attracted large audiences in Harrisburg, Pennsylvania. They also attracted volleys of eggs, and the *Liberator* of April 25, 1845, reported that the women were threatened with tar and feathers. In Michigan, Henry Bibb spoke without incident. The Democratic newspaper attack on Bibb's lecturing indicated he must have spoken effectively, "a hypocrite by the name of Bibb, a colored man and a rascal ... a scamp, unworthy of belief."[28]

Anti-Abolitionism

In Quincy, Illinois, two students of the Mission Institute and a local villager attempted to convey two people from bondage in Missouri. Plans went awry and the men, surrounded by angry citizens, were committed to jail. James E. Burr, George Thompson, and the villager Alanson Work were sentenced to twelve years of imprisonment. The men were released early, but some Missourians assured no future rescues would be attempted. On a winter night, some people crossed the frozen Mississippi River and set the Institute on fire.[29]

The Illinois Underground Railroad operated throughout the antebellum years with the Rev. John Cross helping some people pass through Knox County. In 1843 Cross, one of Weld's Seventy and the man responsible for creating an Underground Railroad network in the Midwest, was arrested. The Reverend Cross invited a neighbor, Jacob Kightlinger, to the Presbyterian Church where Cross ministered. On their wagon ride home, Kightlinger recalled that Cross bragged about defying the law to help freedom seekers. It is probable that Cross hoped to challenge Illinois' black laws in court.

The following week a group was conveyed to the Reverend Cross's house where Kightlinger, no friend to abolition, found them hiding in a cornfield and made sure that Cross was arrested and indicted. When the deputy sheriff could find no one to bring Cross, Cross delivered and represented himself. The judge threw out the case.

Kightlinger said the next day that Cross swore out a warrant against him, and he was fined $100 by an "abolition squire" [lawyer]. Kightlinger appealed to the circuit court, and that judge threw the case out. Next, Kightlinger took Cross before a grand jury with witnesses, where Cross was indicted on three counts of stealing negroes and Cross was put in jail. The *Signal of Liberty* of May 20, 1844, reported Cross' incarceration for feeding and sheltering freedom seeking children in a state that never allowed legal slavery. If Cross had conducted the same activity in the South, he might have been hanged. Within a month, Cross was removed from prison. An Illinois statute was revised on March 3, 1845, to state "Any person who shall hereafter bring into this State any black or mulatto person, in order to free him or her from slavery, or shall directly or indirectly bring into this State, or aid or assist any person in bringing any such black and mulatto person to settle and reside therein, shall be fined one hundred dollars...." Only when the constitution of 1848 was adopted, was slavery illegal in Illinois.[30]

Another Underground Railroad operator received a barbaric punishment. Jonathan Walker was tried and convicted of slave stealing in 1844. On a voyage from Florida to the Bahamas, his boat was overtaken and discovered to be carrying freedom seekers. The abolitionist poet John Greenleaf Whittier in the poem, "The Branded Hand," immortalized the price paid for Walker's benevolence: Walker was jailed and a hot iron seared the skin of his right palm with the brand "S. S." (Slave Stealer). Fined $600, Walker endured a hellish year in solitary confinement. After his release, Walker lectured for five years, and then moved to Lake Harbor, Muskegon County, Michigan.[31]

About the same time that Walker went to jail, the Rev. Charles T. Torrey was arrested and jailed for "slave-stealing" in Maryland. He helped as many as 400 people escape to freedom before his arrest. His six year sentence began in 1844 and ended when he died of tuberculosis in jail at age 33.[32]

Though perhaps more wary, Underground Railroad agents in Michigan continued to guide people to safety. An Underground Railroad operator in Union City, Branch County, Michigan, provided a detailed account of an unusual escape which was published March 4, 1844. A thirteen year old girl led her young sister and mother on a nine week journey to Michigan. Her mother, though only 36, appeared crippled from a lifetime of hard fieldwork and suffered from a recent beating. The older girl rowed her mother and sister across the Ohio River from Virginia on their "master's" boat and then was met by a friend who carried them 30 miles. Along the way, they were instructed in using the celestial sky as their guide. Unfortunately, the family became lost and wandered about until friends and helpers intervened. The freedom seekers were hidden by day and "in motion" at night. On several occasions, their pursuers overtook them.

At one stop, the women were hidden in a haystack by the barn where the horses of the nine slave hunters rested. The posse stayed in close pursuit, riding one horse to death. By chance, they narrowly missed capturing their quarry by taking a wrong fork in the road. At another place, the slave hunters shot a man in the hand whom they believed helped the family escape.

After five weeks on the road, the trio reached helpers in Centreville, Michigan, north of LaGrange, Indiana, only a few hours ahead of at least two or three men still in pursuit. Within a day's ride of freedom, the escape very nearly failed. Just five miles from Union City, some friends of freedom convinced the slave catchers that the family was put on a train to Detroit and now was beyond their reach. The writer assumed the women were breathing the free air in Canada by the time the article was published.[33]

It is likely the helper in Centreville was Chester Gurney, a faithful writer for the *Signal of Liberty*. From his home, Gurney assisted freedom seekers traveling north from Indiana or east from Cassopolis through Three Rivers. The Reverend Northrop was south of Chester Gurney in White Pigeon and named Gurney as a fellow agent. Gurney forwarded freedom seekers along the old Colon Road to Coldwater where the Chicago-Detroit Turnpike intersected. It was helpful to other Underground Railroad workers, that from 1839 to 1858, Gurney held various influential positions of prosecutor, judge, and circuit court commissioner.

In this period, Michigan abolitionists were not subject to the violence of neighboring states, but individuals suffered from censure by the most important institution in their lives: their church. Ministers opposed to slavery were bound by the tenets of their church and conflicted in answering to a divine power.

In Monroe, Michigan, a minister stated that there was a strong prejudice against ministers participating in political enterprises to end slavery. While he felt it was the duty of Christians to do anything within their power to overthrow slavery, he would not preach the subject within the church.[34] The Reverend Weed was listed among the Washtenaw County delegates at the 1836 founding meeting of the state's antislavery society, but not on antislavery lists in the 1840s.[35] One might surmise that the Reverend Weed experienced a threat from proslavery forces similar to that of others who chose discretion in order to remain at the pulpit.

The plight of ministers using the pulpit to forward the cause of abolitionism is revealed in the sufferings of the Rev. Rufus Budd Bement. Dissension over slavery within Protestant churches was at a critical point after the 1842 publication of James G. Birney's pamphlet, "The American Churches, the Bulwarks of American Slavery." Birney, the Liberty Party presidential nominee, accused the church of propagating slavery. Accepting slave owners within the national body of the church was a ruling most Protestants could accept. But, Birney argued that the church, in refusing to condemn slavery, was helping to spread it.[36]

Though the church did not formally charge the Reverend Bement, his enemies exposed his debt and absences to attend antislavery meetings.

Battle Creek, Dec. 16, 1843

Dr. Nathan M. Thomas

> *My Dear Friend: I received your letter yesterday and hasten to reply. I am on the verge of ruin. I have been so forward in the cause of Antislavery that I have brought upon me the indignation of my Ministerial Brethren and they have stirred up the Layity to the utmost. One would think they had scraped earth and the pit to carry their enmity and I have no doubt it is the intention either to silence me as an antislavery lecturer or to drive me out of the Ministry. I am accused of descending from the pulpit to enter the arena of Politics.*[37]

In fact, the Reverend Bement was called upon regularly to lecture for the Michigan State Anti-Slavery Society and was poorly compensated. A subsequent letter to Dr. Nathan Thomas revealed that the Reverend Bement asked to be dismissed from the Presbytery at the end of January. He ventured into politics, losing as the Liberty Party representative in 1843.[38]

The Reverend Cleaveland, after serving as pastor of the First Presbyterian Church of Detroit, moved to Marshall, Michigan, as President of Marshall College from 1837 to 1841. Furthermore, Cleaveland was elected president of the Michigan State Anti-Slavery Society in 1841. His antislavery discourse irritated Judge Abner Pratt, known anti-abolitionist living in Marshall. Another Michigan judge recalled the time that Pratt tracked down Cleaveland in Battle Creek. Judge Pratt, "in one of his bitter pro-slavery onslaughts, assailed this disturber [the Reverend Cleaveland] of the public peace again. In this fight Pratt gave no quarter."[39]

The Rev. Henry Northrop wrote that the Reverend Cleaveland, like himself, was an agent on the Underground Railroad. While preaching in the Presbyterian Church in White Pigeon, Michigan, Northrop attempted to "create a healthy antislavery sentiment." In the early 1840s his transporting refugees from his town to Centreville or other places of safety on the way to Canada became generally known. Some members of the Presbyterian faithful scorned his message of brotherly love and efforts to help freedom seekers.

"Being Pastor of the Presbyterian Church my helping the fugitives aroused the wrath of the proslavery element in my congregation, when my most prominent influential Deacon came to me and informed me that my helping the runaway slaves would probably result in my removal." The Reverend Northrop delivered a conscience-stirring sermon about the Good Samaritan to prevent his immediate dismissal, but relocated in Homer shortly thereafter.[40]

Perhaps in reaction to the separations within the Congregational faith, a new ecclesiastical body was organized, "The General Association of Congregational Ministers and Churches of Michigan." Minutes from 1842 to 1859 show over 100 antislavery ministers from Presbyterian, Congregational, Baptist, and Wesleyan Methodist churches in Michigan attended annual meetings. The churches sending ministers endorsed this resolution: "That this Association most earnestly reccommend to all the Ministers and Churches connected with it, to exclude from their pulpits those Ministers, and from their communion those members of churches, who persist in sustaining the legal relation of Slaveholder, and also practically treat men as property." While churches split over the issue of slavery, some joined forces over the same issue.[41]

An undated petition to the Presbyterian Church Session of Lodi from members of the Benton and Wood families expresses a desire to break from all slaveholding churches. The words speak of an uncompromising stance against the institution of slavery.

> And, whereas the voluntary enslaving of one part of the human race by another, is a gross violation of the sacred rights of human nature, utterly inconsistent with the laws of God; and utterly irreconcilable with the spirit and principles of the gospel of Christ, we do earnestly and sincerely petition and request, that the said church and session take such action as shall forever bar the slaveholder, and the apologist of slaveholding, from fellowship and communion in said church, nor admit to our pulpit any man that vindicates the system, or sustains the relation of slaveholder, and practically treats men as property.[42]

The church in Lodi had a history of opposition to slavery, but the actions of church member Eli Benton pushed the issue too far for new minister, the Reverend Marsh. In 1853, Benton was summoned to appear before a Session of the Presbyterian Church, charged with Breach of Covenant for refusing to pay to support the preachers. It was standard practice at the time that members sustain the church in proportion to their earnings and were thus permitted to vote on issues. Over the past two years, Eli Benton gave $1 or $2 though he had regularly contributed $20 to $25 in the past.[43]

The church trial lasted through the month of August. Minutes of the Sessions describe witness testimony and Eli Benton's defense. Witnesses were sworn in and reported having conversations with Benton about why he contributed so little to the church. Mr. Benton said he supported the gospel elsewhere but "thought the church did not take the stand on the subject of slavery that they ought" and "that the meetinghouse had been withheld from antislavery lectures." It was stated that Brother F. M. Lansing had applied to use the house for political antislavery lectures and his request was denied.

In mid–August, Seth Smith was called to report on his conversation with Mr. Benton about Benton's not providing his share of wood for the meetinghouse. Apparently, Mr. Benton said that if the Reverend Mr. Sinclair, an employee of the Michigan State Anti-Slavery Society, was permitted to lecture in the meetinghouse, he would provide wood. The trustees initially agreed to the lecture, but the Reverend Marsh, one of the pastors from whom Benton withheld financial support, objected and consent was withdrawn.

John D. Bennett's testimony was especially damaging to Mr. Benton's case. Bennett recalled a conversation in which "Benton said he did not give money because the church did not keep covenant with God over the issue of slavery." Mr. Benton was given the chance to question Bennett and asked whether he used his antislavery sentiments to save money by not supporting the gospel. Bennett's response was "I do not think that Benton's antislavery principles are based upon covetousness; but I do think they prevent his supporting the preaching of the gospel here."

Eli Benton was found guilty of breach of covenant with only Darius S. Wood dissenting.[44] After two decades in Lodi Township, Benton and his wife moved to Ann Arbor, as public censure by one's church was a stigmatizing event. A descendant of Eli Benton stated he was not only involved in helping freedom seekers, but was an early organizer of the Underground Railroad.

On April 23, 1854, the First Presbyterian Church of Lodi dissolved their relationship with the Rev. Justin Marsh "because of opposing views on slavery."[45]

Theodore Foster was another person censured for his antislavery agitation. Upon his arrival in Michigan, Theodore Foster helped in his brother's mill, married Delia Seymour in 1832, and then erected a store and dwelling house at the crossroads of Zeeb and Huron River Drive in Scio in 1835 in Washtenaw County. The building consisted of a front room that served as a store, a living room, a kitchen and sleeping quarters above. Seymour Foster later remembered that every night his father closed the store and then went to the living room where he wrote articles for hours, "always against Slavery...."[46]

Theodore Foster was born into a family of Millards and Fosters that had served the nation for generations. For some reason, Foster left home at the age of 14 by boarding a vessel bound for the East Indies, but deserted the ship in New Orleans. The youngster passed through the slave states of the South on his walk home to Foster, Rhode Island. After three years, and following the deaths of his parents, Theodore joined his older brother Samuel Willis Foster in Dexter, Michigan.[47]

Theodore Foster was of slight build and a little taller than average. He had black eyes, dark hair and a healthy complexion. Foster was not known as a lecturer but wrote prodigiously for the *Signal of Liberty*. Foster organized antislavery societies in Webster and Scio Townships in the 1830s, throughout the 1840s was a member of the Executive Committee of the Michigan State Anti-Slavery Society and was coeditor and publisher of the *Signal of Liberty*.[48]

Not only was Theodore Foster involved in the county and state antislavery societies, he supported the Liberty Party and in 1843 published a notice of a meeting at his house. Foster was an elder of the Presbyterian Church in Webster. Over the years he consistently agitated for the church to take a stand on the issue of slavery.

Foster's house was a popular site for neighborhood children to gather to play, especially when the store served as the village schoolhouse with Foster as the teacher. An outside stairway at the back of the house led to the cellar where merchandise was stored. The dark cellar, with its crates, barrels, and hogsheads (very large casks), was an ideal place for games of hide and seek. Seymour Foster recalled the time some children tipped over a hogshead and were frightened by the sight of a black man squatting there. Of course, it was necessary to tell the children about Theodore Foster's clandestine and illegal activity. Seymour now understood why strangers would knock on the back door at night and his father would ride off for hours. Because he published the *Signal of Liberty*, most of the community supposed Foster was involved in the Underground Railroad, but the hogshead incident confirmed their suspicions.[49]

The incident must have excited some concerned parents in the area. Church members who grew tired of Foster's persistent protests caused him to feel unwelcome. When the situation was unbearable, Foster stopped attending services. Soon, he was ex-communicated.

Abolitionizing Michigan was challenging. Several of Theodore Weld's Seventy moved west, where work was greatly needed. Amos Dresser, Deodat Jeffers and Asa Mahan joined Guy Beckley, Giles Stebbins, Martin Cowles, Oren Thompson, and Charles Stuart in Michigan in the 1840s. William Allen, Jonathan Blanchard, John Miter and S. Lucius Parker moved to Illinois, John and Augustus Wattles located in Indiana. Enoch Bartlett and Sereno Streeter would arrive in Michigan a few years later.

If Theodore Weld had predicted the events of 1847, he might have sent the entire force of Seventy men and women to Michigan. However, the times ahead called for active abolitionists. Words would be no match for pistols and daggers. The black and white Underground Railroad agency in the Lower Peninsula of the Great Lake State would be severely tested.

Chapter Eleven

Southern Men on Northern Soil

Escape of John White, Autumn, 1847

Laura Smith Haviland disguised her suspicion of the stranger at the Raisin Institute. It was common knowledge that she harbored freedom seekers at the interracial school she and her husband founded in Adrian. The gentleman claimed to be associated with the Underground Railroad and expressed knowledge of agents in Ohio and Indiana. Mrs. Haviland immediately became concerned for John White, a former student now working in the area.

By mid-afternoon, Mrs. Haviland received word that her gentleman caller was J. L. Smith, lawyer for Kentuckian slave owner George Brazier. Reportedly, student Nelson Ockrow rode the horse of the local miller Bretherton, to the Watkins' farm to sound the alarm. Kentuckian Brazier learned of John White's whereabouts and frantically tried to gather a party of men to hunt and trap him before nightfall.

The following day, George Brazier led a posse to the Watkins farm at the convergence of Lenawee, Jackson, and Washtenaw Counties. Royal Watkins and his wife, Sally Carpenter, settled the property in 1834 after traveling from Keene, New Hampshire, via the Erie Canal. The southerners approached the rolling hills reminiscent of the Scottish Highlands of Watkins' forbears. They saw a lone man toiling in a field. Brazier instructed the men to guard the perimeter. The posse drew near and grabbed their defenseless quarry.

Instead of the self-emancipated John White, they held a fieldworker with skin the color of their own. Brazier was livid that he'd been set up and proceeded to Royal Watkins' house in hopes of locating John White. Brazier swore angrily that Laura Haviland was responsible for arranging White's escape. Mr. Watkins interrupted Brazier to state that the Kentuckian was mistaken since he had taken White to the depot the previous day. Watkins declared that there were others besides Laura Haviland willing to "save a self-freed slave from being taken back to Southern bondage." He described John White as highly esteemed by all who knew him and claimed that he himself would not allow White to be taken south without doing what he could to prevent it.

In spite of his near capture, White made a fateful decision to attempt to rescue his wife from slavery.[1]

In 1847, America seemed unable to remain still long enough to settle old conflicts. Though the telegraph connected people as far apart as Boston and Chicago, divisions over issues — especially slavery — hampered progress and threatened national unity. In-fighting among antislavery groups and Liberty Party leaders opened a door through which southerners trod on northern freedoms. President Polk witnessed increasing sectional tension

Laura Haviland of Adrian, Michigan, holds shackles and a "knee stiffener" used to prevent and punish escapes (Laura Smith Haviland Papers [1868–1933]. Bentley Historical Library, University of Michigan).

A posse of men attempted to kidnap John White from a field on Royal Watkins' farm in Jackson County (author photograph, Brooklyn, Michigan, 2003).

during his administration. When a bill to abolish the slave trade in the District of Columbia was proposed, slave-holding state legislators wanted to meet separately. President Polk wrote, "The agitation of the slavery question is mischievous and wicked, and proceeds from no patriotic motive by its authors."[2]

From the dawning of the new year and until its close in 1847, Kentucky slave-holders conducted a series of planned assaults in Michigan. Every month brought both hope and dread.

Assaults on Northern Soil

Frustrated over their human property losses, some northern Kentuckians banded together. The group sent Francis Troutman north to Michigan in December 1846. Posing as a student and abolitionist, the young lawyer visited the western counties of Michigan, noting the whereabouts of black settlements. He traveled east to Calhoun County where he found the Crosswhite family living in Marshall. Troutman prepared a warrant and waited for others to join him in January when they would make the arrest.[3]

When he was 45 years old, Adam Crosswhite learned that members of his family were to be sold away from Kentucky, so the six Crosswhites made their escape with help of the Underground Railroad. Believing they were beyond the snare of slavery, in 1843 the Crosswhites settled in a cottage on the Ferguson farm in Marshall, Michigan. Adam Crosswhite, born in Bourbon County, Kentucky, in 1799 to an enslaved woman and her white "master," was given to his white half-sister. Upon marrying slave dealer Ned Stone, the half-sister sold her half-brother Adam Crosswhite to Francis Troutman for $200. At the age of 20, Crosswhite was traded to Frank Giltner, grandfather-in-law of Francis Troutman. Over the next twenty years, Crosswhite married Sarah and they raised a family. Once safely on Michigan soil, Adam and Sarah lived in a home of their own.

On January 26, 1847, in the hours before dawn, Francis Troutman broke down Sarah and Adam Crosswhite's barricaded door to forcibly take the family into slavery. Crosswhite fired a shot to alert neighbors as four Kentuckians and a deputy sheriff rushed inside and took hold of his children. Calvin Hackett, a prominent black man, was the first to arrive at the house. The Kentuckians told Sarah to leave her baby, who had been born on Michigan soil. She refused. A black neighbor, Moses Patterson, rode his horse through town, waking all with his shouts and clanging bell. Sarah would not move from her home, swearing she would die before standing trial. With a crowd of nearly 200 black and white citizens gathered around, Troutman was unable to take the Crosswhites by force.[4]

Kentuckian Francis Troutman threatened those in his way and demanded they give their names. A voice called out, "Charles T. Gorham and write it in capital letters." Next, Oliver Cromwell Comstock, Jr. and Jarvis Hurd added their names. Finally, Charles T. Gorham stepped forward to say that Troutman could not take the Crosswhites because "this is a free country, and these are free persons." The crowd went before Justice Randall Hobart who wrote out two fines, one to Troutman for trespassing and breaking down the Crosswhite's door and another to Crosswhite for firing his gun. Crosswhite was not available to accept the fine, as George Ingersoll had taken the Crosswhites into hiding. With the warrant against Troutman executed, the Kentuckian was held over for trial. Meanwhile, the Crosswhites traveled by train to Detroit and were met by George DeBaptiste who, informed of their expected arrival, saw them on to Canada.

Troutman returned to Kentucky with a $100 fine and no members of the Crosswhite family he sought on behalf of his grandfather. He would return for trial in Michigan in December. Some outraged Kentuckians of Trimble and Carroll Counties gathered together on February 10, 1847, to propose that a committee present a resolution to the Kentucky legislature and the U.S. Congress for imprisonment of abolitionist mobs. The men published their resolutions and a copy made its way to the *Signal of Liberty* office by April. The editors published the entire resolution, mocking the threat from the southerners. If the intent was to ridicule the Kentuckians, it succeeded. The Kentuckian's backlash of abductions and kidnappings throughout the year devastated blacks and whites across the state of Michigan.[5]

Within a month some Kentuckians attempted to outwit the "abolition mob" while waiting for the slow course of political action. Only a brief newspaper account describes the treacherous kidnapping of a Detroit man in February. Two men working in an upholstery shop grabbed a co-worker, bound his hands and feet, and sent him off by sleigh. Upon his arrival in Toledo, an attorney from Kentucky attempted to get a writ to remove the man from the state. Instead, the attorney was charged with assault, battery, kidnapping and was bound over for trial. One of the men was arrested; meanwhile, the abducted man was set free.[6]

On February 3, 1847, the Michigan State Anti-Slavery Society meeting opened in Kalamazoo in a severe and blinding snowstorm. A member from Eaton County attempted to open a discussion about national interests, but the society refused to discuss it at any length and rejected the idea. The Rev. Guy Beckley was called upon to discuss the matter, as he was the person suspected of the "heresy" of suggesting the extension of the Liberty Party platform to include "other interests." The Reverend Beckley described, "with much cheerfulness," that he saw two roads for the Liberty Party. He favored the one that would separate the Liberty Party from all others as a powerful, antislavery party. Though Beckley's arguments were not new, the fact that he brazenly published them in a Liberty newspaper opened the debate within the party.[7]

On March 16, 1847, the Reverend Beckley wrote to his friend James Birney confirming his belief that the Liberty Party should take on all questions of national interest, and furthermore, he would cast his vote for whatever man of any party upheld his antislavery principles. Birney's reply on April 6, expressed his opposition, "In any view I can take of your project, it is calculated at once to break up the Liberty Party. It is therefore, wild and visionary, and one that I was not prepared to expect from the ripe reflection which has heretofore, distinguished you."[8]

Samuel Noble offered a public endorsement of the Beckley/Foster plan. In a lengthy letter to the *Signal of Liberty,* Noble stated his concern that the Liberty Party was no longer gaining membership. Samuel Burrell Noble, an avowed abolitionist, operated a nursery business in Ann Arbor. He was one of the Noble brothers who moved to Michigan at the behest of Judge Samuel Dexter in the 1820s.

Samuel Noble fervently expressed his opposition to slavery, challenging all Liberty Party members to renounce any church organizations that condoned and sustained slavery. Noble reflected that the church was so interwoven and dependent upon slavery for support that all efforts at moral suasion had been unsuccessful. This forced the cause to use the ballot box to effect change. Noble wrote that as long as the Liberty Party refused to adopt a position on any national policies besides slavery, it could not expect to defeat the Whigs and Democrats. As Noble asked, how could they compare the problems of banking and immigration when three million were held in hopeless bondage?[9]

Nationally, the slavery debate was often heated and sometimes violent. Northern legislatures sent petitions to Congress about slavery in newly acquired land in New Mexico and California. The 1847 Missouri Legislature pressured Congress for negotiations to begin between America and Great Britain to address the problem of slaves escaping to Canada. The state of Missouri described their "heavy losses of property" that could not be recovered once on the Canadian shore.[10]

While the debates raged, some Southern slaveholders found it expeditious to slip into northern states to physically abduct humans they claimed as property. On March 5, 1847, the Supreme Court ruled that the federal government had the power to enforce slavery in the *Jones v Van Zandt* case. The case had worked its way up the judicial system since Wharton Jones sought compensation for a person John Van Zandt helped to escape in 1842. At that time, Van Zandt concealed nine people in Hamilton County, Ohio, who had run away from Kentucky. They were all captured and placed in Kentucky jails. Van Zandt was released and refused to pay Jones for the loss of one formerly enslaved person. Van Zandt was forced to compensate Jones by the 1847 ruling.[11]

While the political debates raged, freedom seekers walked and rode to Michigan by pairs and large groups. In late March, a group of 22 enslaved people, including William Casey, George Hamilton (father of John Evans) and Nelson Stephens with his wife and daughter escaped from northern Kentucky. They stayed in Young's Prairie in Cass County, Michigan, joining the growing settlement. Early communities had grown suddenly over the previous few years when free black families in Logan County, Ohio, despaired of the poor lands and followed Quakers west. Harvey Wade, Kinchen Artis, Harrison Ash, and the Byrd family settled on small farms. When Virginia planter Sampson Sanders left $15,000 with his administrators for the purchase of land and the settlement of his liberated slaves in a free state, Calvin Township, Michigan, was selected as the site. The free black Michiganians would come to the aid of their self-freed neighbors at their time of need.[12]

On the eastern side of the state, after years of quiet, in April, Detroit experienced another race-motivated melee. David Dunn in St. Louis, Missouri, learned of Robert Cromwell's whereabouts from a postmark. After his self-emancipation, Cromwell settled first in Indiana, then Flint, Genesee County, Michigan. With money from barbering, Cromwell sought to buy his daughter's freedom. He realized after sending a letter with a false return address that the postmark would lead Dunn to Flint. Cromwell fled to Detroit. Dunn found him.[13]

Dunn enticed Cromwell to enter the Detroit courthouse where he planned to seize him and order a warrant. Cromwell chose not to yield gently and a riot ensued. African and Irish Americans whisked Cromwell to the Detroit River where a skiff carried him to Canada. Dunn was jailed and preferred to remain behind iron bars until judged not guilty. Horace Hallock reported that citizens followed Dunn peacefully to ensure justice by the law. Dunn remained six months in the Detroit jail rather than face the citizenry of Detroit.

There was no doubt that he attempted kidnapping, but it could not be proved that Dunn intended to remove Cromwell from the state. On May 8, 1847, a meeting of the Colored Persons of Detroit passed a resolution to thank the eminent counsel who defended Robert Cromwell. Dunn departed while Cromwell remained beyond his reach in Canada.[14]

Perry Sanford's Story

Perry Sanford described his reasons for escape: "One day the master's son, a talkative youngster, told me that his father had sold us into Mississippi. He was afraid that we were going to run away. I was struck with dismay. The horror of all horrors to the slave was the Mississippi cotton field. It was a living hell."[15]

The fear of the slaveholder was aroused by the escape of 22 people from a neighboring farm in Kenton County, Kentucky (the same group which stopped in Cass County). Perry Sanford was bound to Milton W. Graves in Kenton County after being sold from Greenup to Boone Counties. It was fortunate for Sanford that he learned the news on the Easter Monday holiday when the enslaved had a day off. Sanford worked that day in order to add fifty cents to the $2.00 he had saved. Another of the men used a pass to make arrangements with a white man to cross the Ohio River.

At 10:00 P.M., April 1847, Dave Walker, his mother, Susan Reynolds, Sanford, and nine others walked twelve miles across fields, avoiding roads and tollgates. They were late and the man expecting to meet them in Covington left. By fortune or the Underground Railroad, a skiff found on the Ohio River bank carried them to Cincinnati. In the dawning light, two men, one black and the other white, accosted them as runaway slaves. A moment's terror eased when the men introduced themselves as Underground Railroad agents. They hastily divided the group into pairs, secreting them in cellars of the business blocks. One can imagine, night and day, hearing wagons groan to a stop, shouts and cracks of the whip, and then, a knock on the cellar door. For seven days, the freedom seekers endured their dark seclusion within a stone's throw of the river and their former Kentucky homes.

One night, carriages arrived to carry them to Hamilton, Ohio, Jonesborough, Indiana, and on from one station to another.

> We only traveled nights, and in covered wagons, and would be secreted day times in some
> Quaker's barn or in the woods. Some places we would stay over a night, and in others sev-

eral days. We were one month in reaching Cass County. You see, everything had to be done with great caution, as the slave owners were very often close on the track of the fugitives. At a Quaker store in Newport we were all supplied with clothing.[16]

They had trouble in one town. Instructed to walk to the next station, the group took a wrong turn. They proceeded through the center of town without incident but, on the other side, met two slave owners returning without their quarry. Though the freedom seekers traveled at the direction of some Quakers, each one carried a club and some had pocketknives. They had prepared how to confront anyone who stopped them. The spokesman of the group answered for all that they were headed to Turkey Prairie (Indiana). The horsemen asked to see their pass.

Perry Sanford escaped from slavery to Cass County, Michigan, and then ran from kidnappers in the Kentucky Raid of 1847 (Willard Public Library, Battle Creek, Michigan).

> "The spokesman replied, holding up his big club: 'Here's our pass, and it will make your eyes sore to read it.' They drew up to one side of the road and drove past us. We felt relieved. They halted after they had passed, and turned around, and we were afraid that they were going to shoot at us, but they finally rode off."[17]

After the group arrived at John Shugart's place, the women were hidden in the cellar and the men in the woods. The confrontation with the southerners created excitement and fear of arrest. When it was safe, the group was taken by wagon to Young's Prairie, three miles from Cassopolis, Michigan. Perry Sanford first stayed with John Shugart's brother Zach near Vandalia, and then went to work for Stephen Bogue.

In May 1847, three men, six women, and four children passed through on their way to Canada. A *Signal of Liberty* article asked "Is it not shameful, that men, women and children, born upon the soil, are obliged to flee this boasted land of Liberty, to escape chains and servitude?" The article appeared on a page with another describing a Presidential pardon of two men convicted for "being in the slave trade" by President James Polk, who held slaves on his plantation in Fayette County, Tennessee.[18]

Francis Troutman returned to Michigan in the summer of 1847, and brought an action against numerous defendants in Marshall to recover the value of the rescued slaves, in the United States Circuit Court. The Kentuckians who returned from Michigan without their "property" circulated vicious accounts that received Congressional attention. The Commonwealth of Kentucky, outraged by northerner's conduct, appropriated funds to help prosecute the case. Gerrit Smith came to Michigan to testify, but defense attorneys felt the radical abolitionist might not help the case.[19] This first trial did not have a result. The next trial occurred a year later.

The Kentucky Raid

In the heat of the summer, 20 to 30 heavily armed Kentucky raiders swept across the settlements in the southwest corner of the state in the largest raid on Michigan soil. At least one advance scout noted that the small settlements were scattered over thousands of acres, separated by chains of lakes and creeks but called "Ramptown" locally. The most populated settlements were in Calvin and Porter Townships near the protection of ultra abolitionists. The protection proved insufficient during a surprise attack on the settlements.[20]

In early August 1847, 13 strangers arrived in Battle Creek. They put up at the hotel, introducing themselves as salesmen for an improved washing machine. Their particular interest in black settlers alarmed Quaker Erastus Hussey, who accused them of being slave hunters and ordered them to leave town.[21] The Kentuckians reconnoitered in Bristol, Indiana, east of Elkhart. The men planned to break into squads, ambush several settlements at once, and remove those who had escaped from their Kenton County farms. They brought tobacco wagons to carry back the dozen or so people they expected to capture. John, Joseph, and Milton W. Graves were intent on capturing Perry Sanford.[22]

The first arrests were made at Josiah Osborn's, east of Diamond Lake, where an old man and his two sons were seized, handcuffed, and taken out to the highway; a baby was left behind in the hurried escape. When Baptist preacher the Rev. A. Stevens carried off the baby, the mother rushed out of hiding and into the clutches of her former "master." Apparently, the minister felt no remorse even as he passed the Quaker Birch Lake Meeting House.[23]

Perry Sanford was awakened at about four in the morning by a knock at the cabin he shared with Rube Stephens and the Joe Stanford family. When Perry Sanford asked who was there, they recognized the voice of Jack Graves, brother of Milton Graves. Joe Stanford, his wife, and daughter were captured. Reuben Stevens and Perry Sanford escaped. Perry ran for his life and lost his pursuers in a cornfield. "I alarmed Stephen Bogue and he mounted his horse and ran him to Cassopolis to alarm the people there. Mrs. Bogue secreted me upstairs in their house."[24]

One account states that only Moses Bristow, on the farm of Stephen Bogue, resisted the attack, being "struck down with the butt of a riding whip, cutting his ear and the side of his head severely." But, Perry Sanford remembered that William Casey and his wife also fought bravely to keep the Kentuckians from grabbing their daughter Mary. It took three men to bring Casey down, but he delivered a severe blow to his young "master." Mrs. Casey escaped into a cornfield and fended off her attacker, but both her husband and daughter were loaded in the tobacco wagon.[25]

The alarm spread swiftly from the Bogue and Zach Shugart farms. While the Kentuckians waited at the Osborn's for the other troops, local citizens grabbed guns and clubs. It was too late for the Kentuckians to make a break. Surrounded by armed and enraged people, they were forced to travel to a justice in Cassopolis. Along the way from Vandalia, passing north of Diamond Lake, the procession attracted more followers. Ebenezer McIlvain, circuit commissioner of Berrien County, heard the case.[26]

No doubt the Kentuckians entered the stately Greek Revival courthouse confident that within this hall of justice, their bills of sale would be honored. However, they were unaware of two facts: Firstly, McIlvain hated slavery and secretly helped on the Underground Railroad. And secondly, Cass County extended rare privileges to blacks. While black citizens could not testify in court against whites across the nation, Cass County allowed that right along with the right to bail, to trial by jury, and to file suit in court. Instead of a quick

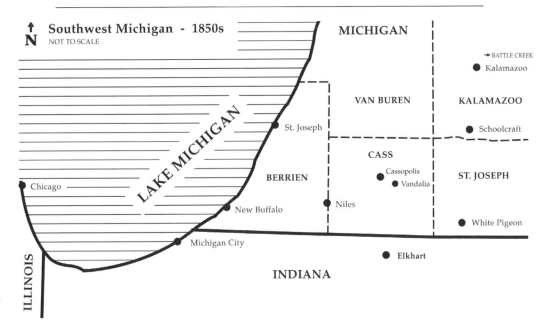

In August 1847, armed men from Kentucky raided the settlements in Southwest Michigan, dragging men, women and children from their beds to take them back into slavery (Lang and Laing [1859], Library of Congress Geography and Map Division: g4071p, rr001230).

judicial decision, there would be a trial. Commissioner McIlvain required the Kentuckians to show just cause why the fugitives should not be released. He then ruled that without a certified copy of the Kentucky statutes offered as evidence showing the legal existence of slavery in that State, the captured men, women, and children must be released. The nine released from custody were taken to the farm of Ishmael Lee.[27]

A courier took off to alert Dr. Nathan and Pamela Thomas to expect a large party in Schoolcraft. Zach Shugart took charge of getting the nine, and any others, ready to leave for Canada. Many who recognized the Kentuckians joined the group headed to Canada. Pamela Thomas hastily put together all her food and what she could borrow from a neighbor, and handed all of this to Shugart and the 50 or so men, women, and children in his care. Mrs. Thomas recalled "they soon arrived, took the provisions without alighting, and passed in safety to Canada." Nathan Thomas noted that two men rode ahead on horseback to give notice at stations of the group needing food; the others rode in wagons. At William Wheeler's house in Flowerfield, they stopped to rest. Erastus Hussey wrote about the same escape. He said the group stopped in Battle Creek. With the help of Abel Densmore, Silas W. Dodge, and Samuel Strauther they got the use of an empty building. Elijah Mott donated sixty pounds of flour and other men bought potatoes and pork. By moonlight, everyone in the city watched the arrival of nine guards escorting the wagons rolling down the street. Erastus Hussey recognized Shugart, "the old Quaker, with his broad-brimmed white hat and mounted upon a fine horse — he always had good horses" leading the group in Battle Creek.

The next morning, the majority of them went on to Canada, but the few who remained became honored and well-known citizens. Not all of the 52 continued to Canada. Perry Sanford, William Casey, Joseph Skipworth, and Thomas Henderson remained in Battle Creek, working for Jeremiah Brown, David Cady, and other farmers.[28]

The Kentuckians later proceeded with legal action against seven Quakers in Michigan who stopped their raid, but the year of raids was not over and more trouble lay ahead. George Brazier vowed he would not return to Kentucky empty-handed. He rode east to Adrian with lawyer Smith and attempted to kidnap John White, as described at the beginning of the chapter.

Brazier returned to Kentucky where he swore out a federal warrant for the arrest of Laura Haviland if White was not returned to him within a year. Brazier wrote several vile letters to Laura Haviland, warning her not to set foot on southern soil where he posted a $3,000 reward for her capture. John White stayed in Canada for one week. Back at work in Michigan, White raised money and borrowed from friends in order to send Laura Haviland south to retrieve his family from slavery. Mrs. Haviland traveled to Cincinnati, where she consulted her friends Levi and Catherine Coffin. The Coffins and the Vigilance Committee devised a plan for her to go to Indiana and then visit Jane White in Kentucky with Mary and Joseph Edgerton, free black friends. Benjamin Stevens, Jane White's father, was grandfather and legal owner of her five children, all kept in slavery.

Slave codes generally forbade any unsupervised contact between visitors and the enslaved and it was extremely risky to enter the lion's den. Somehow, Laura Haviland met with Jane to propose the escape. But Jane refused to leave without two of her children who were away at the time. She was convinced her husband would come for all of them. It proved to be an unfortunate decision, but he did make the attempt.

As soon as possible, John White arranged his family's escape. He waited on the Indiana side of a creek above Rising Sun, Kentucky. Jane and the children were escorted by Solomon, a bondman of Benjamin Stevens who planned to escape with the White family. Jane's hopes to be united with the man who risked his life for her and her children ended abruptly when six men captured the group. A death warrant hanging over his head, John White was held back in despair.

Before she could attempt another escape, Jane died of cholera. Infamous slave hunter Wright Ray of Madison captured John White, who had assumed the name of James Armstrong, in Indiana. Unaware that he held John White in possession, the slave catcher offered to sell "Armstrong" to his northern friends for $400. John wrote to Watkins' son-in-law who dispatched Laura Haviland to rescue White. Within three weeks, she again traveled to the Coffin's house, collected the money and sent an emissary to purchase John. This time, White returned to Canada and reconciled himself to bearing the sorrow of slavery while living as James Armstrong, a free man.[29]

Though unsuccessful in carrying freedom seekers back into enslavement, interstate conflicts contributed to national political pressure. The Adam and Sarah Crosswhite case received national attention and Francis Giltner was outraged. He had sent his son-in-law, Francis Troutman, at great expense to Michigan to recover the Crosswhite family, and the citizens of Michigan defied the law and let them escape. Throughout the winter months, Francis Giltner complained of the financial losses suffered by Kentuckians at the hands of northerners. He was gratified when, on Dec. 20, 1847, a Kentucky Senator submitted a resolution to the Senate in favor of a law to enable citizens of slaveholding states to recover slaves escaped into non-slaveholding states. Before the end of year, several Southern men filed suit against seven residents of Marshall, Michigan: Charles T. Gorham, Dr. Oliver Cromwell Comstock, Jr., and Jarvis Hurd, all white men; and four black men, Charles Bergen, Planter Morse, James Smith, and William Parker.[30]

Michigan abolitionists remained steadfast with great hopes for the future. It had been a difficult year with setbacks, conflicts, and violence, but now the prospect of consolidating the splintered political parties into a powerful force looked good. The raids and attacks seemed to have stopped. After the holiday festivities, when men and women got back to the business of ending slavery, they would be shocked by the sudden death of one of their worthiest men.

Chapter Twelve

Trials and Tribulations

Caroline Hill

    Caroline was born into bondage in 1827 or 1828. She was the "property" of Bill Jones, a plantation owner with many enslaved people working 980 acres in Franklin County, Alabama. Caroline and others enslaved on the Jones' farm had plenty of food, decent clothing, and Fridays and Saturdays free. In the evenings, everyone gathered to dance and sing to the tunes Mr. Jones played on the violin. Caroline remembered her early childhood as generally happy, though she and her family worked hard. From age six to 16, every day Caroline labored in the kitchens and then help plow the cotton and cornfields.

    When she was 19, Caroline decided to run away because her sweetheart from a neighboring plantation was sold. Forced to move 300 miles away to Mississippi, he suggested they run away together. Caroline dressed in her brother's clothes and they took off, hiding by day and traveling on foot by night. Only once did they take a couple of horses to ride five miles and then turn the horses free. The couple found their way by traveling along "the pike." The rocky terrain of the Appalachian foothills in northern Alabama was difficult to traverse. A misstep on the rock cliffs could be fatal.

    At one point where a narrow pass forced them out of hiding, Caroline became tired and the couple rested in a natural gorge. Just then, their pursuers appeared in the bright moonlight on the open road. Caroline and her lover tucked themselves into the hollow where they were hidden by shadow yet overheard every word of their pursuers. The men stopped to discuss whether their quarry would have taken the dirt road or the pike, determining they should turn around and take the dirt road. For some time, Caroline and her sweetheart continued on the pike without fear of imminent capture.

    Three months of arduous travel brought them to a free state. Both Caroline and her lover had worn out their shoes and soldiered on. On the northern shore of the Ohio River, they connected with the Underground Railroad in Cincinnati. Wagons carried them from station to station until they reached Springfield, Ohio, east of Dayton on the National Road. Here, Underground Railroad workers met the freedom seekers with a pass and locked them in a rail car heading north. In an obscure place near Sandusky, Ohio, the train came to a stop and someone hustled them out of the railcar and into the back of a house. A man took them to the attic of his house and his wife brought them dinner.

    Caroline worked for the family while waiting three weeks for a boat. Finally, they completed their journey. A boat took them to Detroit and, from there, to Windsor, Ontario, Canada. The sweethearts moved to Chatham, Ontario, and had two children. The first died in infancy and the second child died at age 20, soon followed by her father. Caroline married a second time and moved to Ypsilanti, Michigan, when her husband became sick. His treatment from a doctor in Ann Arbor failed to save his life and Caroline wanted to return to Canada. However, she had begun purchasing a house on Prospect Hill in Ypsilanti in installments and the owner refused to re-purchase it. Over time, Caroline paid for her house in full.[1]

The issue of slavery anchored every move toward progress in America in the late 1840s. Expansionists applauded a near victory in the Mexican-American War, while many mourned the loss of over 10,000 American lives. Michigan men contributed to the split in the Liberty Party making prospects for change through political means unlikely. And excursions by slaveholders threatened to undermine the Underground Railroad. Abolitionists needed to break down the barriers of race, religion and politics, and quickly.

The Signal Dies Out

The Reverend Beckley was in good spirits though just "a little unwell" when he began a letter to his brother-in-law in Vermont on November 20, 1847. It was a Sabbath day, but Beckley was not required at the pulpit since his dismissal by the church over the slavery issue. The Washtenaw County Liberty Party met in October without him. Beckley must have taken solace in the New York Liberty Party's vote to add other issues to the platform. Events during the previous year must have discouraged Beckley, but he would not worry his family. He wrote, "thought a little about the Polk-devil," and then dwelt on family issues. He expressed contentment in his situation: "Times on the whole are good, business lively & our state prosperous. Religion is at low ebb & politics are not producing the least excitement. Abolitionism is about so so, & all is quiet."

The letter was not mailed for nearly two months. The children had been asked to write their own messages and did so. On January 3, 1848, Abby, Martha, Charles, Sarah, and John wrote that their father, without a struggle or complaint, had passed away. Within a year, his widow Phyla died as well.[2]

The sudden death of the Reverend Beckley cast a pall over the annual Michigan State Anti-Slavery Society meeting in February 1848. The following resolution was passed: "Resolved, That in the death of the Rev. Guy Beckley, this Society feels that a serious loss has been sustained, and a large chasm made in the Anti-Slavery ranks...." After some discussion the following was adopted: "Resolved, That in every National and State code, and in every church code, slaveholding ought to be prohibited as highly criminal." No longer would the churches be exempt from censure for tolerating slaveholders among their congregations.

At a glance, the minutes of the February 1848 meeting give the impression that the men from across the state met in Ann Arbor to conduct business as usual. Delegates from a dozen counties attended, including George DeBaptiste and Horace Hallock from Detroit. The resolutions reveal a discontent that foreshadowed disintegration of the organization. A new national political party composed of Whigs, Democrats, and Liberty men, called the Free Soil Party, opposed the extension of slavery, but not its abolition. The Liberty Party proposed John P. Hale as candidate for President. In the ensuing debate, Hale was described as a "novice of confessed ignorance on antislavery questions."

During the dinner break, Theodore Foster must have announced his intention to end his position as editor and publisher of the *Signal*. A financial report published the previous year revealed the Liberty Fund, the fiduciary reserve supporting lecturers and the newspaper, suffered a staggering debt. The *Signal* was never financially solvent, and frequent requests for payment by cash or in goods were ignored. The newspaper managed to go to press nearly every week but with repeated notices appealing to subscribers (up to 1,800 in 1846) to pay their accounts.

In reflection, Foster believed the newspaper was effective in promoting antislavery reform. Scholarship supports his assessment. John W. Quist studied the *Signal of Liberty* subscription list in order to measure the constituency of abolitionism. Quist found that the "Liberty Party's strong showing in Michigan was probably due to its effective newspaper, the *Signal of Liberty*, published in Ann Arbor from 1841 to 1848."[3]

Theodore Foster felt he "devoted almost seven of the best years" of his life to the publishing effort, and was leaving without regret. He did not abandon the cause, but could not continue the newspaper business without Beckley's support. Many of the old guard were gone, with Birney unable to lecture after a stroke, Dr. Arthur Porter of Detroit and coeditor Guy Beckley deceased, and Foster, worn down.

An early 1848 treaty with Mexico brought in Texas and the Mexican states of New Mexico, Arizona, and northern California. With nearly all the land south of the compromise line, the South claimed it as slave territory.

The Free Soil Party

In June 1848, Liberty League Convention members in Buffalo, New York, nominated Gerrit Smith for president and Charles C. Foote of Michigan for vice president. Seymour Treadwell was appointed chair and Hovey Clarke, secretary. Foote's nomination was not unanimous; Frederick Douglass received a dozen votes and Lucretia Mott a handful. The Liberty League welcomed the ladies and accepted their votes. The outcome of the convention was moot after the Free Soil Party was established.[4] At Jackson, Michigan, on August 16, the Michigan State Liberty Convention met under Thomas McGee's leadership and resolved to form themselves as Free Soil men. On August 25, 1848, the *Michigan Liberty Press* [successor to the *Signal of Liberty*] published proceedings of the Michigan delegation at the Buffalo Convention. One might have expected a dozen or so delegates to travel to New York during the heat of the summer. In fact, the number assembled at Huff's Hotel in Buffalo exceeded 125, representing 15 counties in Michigan. Familiar Underground Railroad names appear on the list: Hussey, Thomas, Francisco, Rexford, and Willis. A state Central Committee was formed to act on behalf of the group until a convention and elections were held. All six members of the committee resided in Ann Arbor.[5] Antislavery men from emerging cities like Grand Rapids in Kent County joined the convention. Erastus Hussey met for the first time the Rev. John Cross, eight years after accepting an Underground Railroad agency in one of Michigan's many networks.[6]

Sabin Felch wrote a letter encouraging antislavery men to stay the course. Published in the *Michigan Liberty Press* on June 30, 1848, Felch's note ended with the postscript "Now is the time for vigorous action, united effort." The *Michigan Liberty Press* was rarely published. Erastus Hussey assumed the editorship of the *Liberty Press,* and faced daunting publishing costs. One year later, on a night in June, the office building on Battle Creek's Main Street was set on fire and all of the printing material was destroyed.[7]

Erastus Hussey need only remind himself of Nancy Stevens' tragic story to innerve himself to continue his activity in spite of public censure. Nancy Stevens told a story of such terrible loss that only a hard-hearted person hearing it would not be distraught. "Master Tom" sold her husband "down the river," and then he brutally killed her son, Joe. Young Joe got up early to bring in the cows. The ground was frozen and Joe's bare feet were bitterly cold. Joe stepped in the place the cows had lain to warm his feet. Master Tom, angered that Joe took so long, found him standing idly.

Nancy saw that the cows were home but Joe had been gone a long time. She looked for him and finally saw, in the distance, what appeared to be a big dog creeping along the lane. Nancy watched for some time wondering what creature moved along so slowly. And then, she realized it was her son. Racing to his side, Nancy found him terribly wounded. Master Tom kicked the boy and the spur on his boot had ripped open Joe's belly.

Nancy carried her son to their cabin, holding the poor child until he bled to death that night. It was a case of murder, unchallenged in the slave system. The irresistible appeal of disclosures such as these kept the managers of the Underground Railroad nerved to action.[8]

On November 7, 1848, Americans voted on the same day in a presidential election. When the Liberty and Free Soil parties merged into the Republican Party, abolitionists were energized. Finally, a political party with an expanded platform offered the hope of a presidential victory. Former President Martin Van Buren ran as president of the Free Soil Party, on a campaign to oppose further expansion of slavery into the western territories. Gerrit Smith kept the Liberty Party alive by running for the presidency with Charles Foote, of Michigan, as vice president. Zachary Taylor barely won election over Lewis Cass. Taylor was a moderate on slavery, and like all Americans, Michigan abolitionists were uncertain how Taylor would handle the controversial issue of slavery expansion in the new territories.

With the election dominating the public sphere, attention was drawn to the second trial of the Crosswhites and citizens of Marshall, Michigan. Since the time of the first trial, an appointed commission took depositions from witnesses and the case was ready to be retried.

The second trial, held in the U.S. District Court in November 1848 allowed Adam Crosswhite to testify. A Detroit newspaper reported, "the Courthouse was literally crammed with people of color, who knew the fugitive was to appear on the stand against the Kentucky slaveholders." Sarah Crosswhite stated in her testimony that when the men broke down the door, she told them "she would not go to trial with them or allow her children to go, for she would die first...." Giltner begged and pleaded and sat down and cried, but Sarah refused to be moved. In November 1848 the court awarded Kentuckian Giltner the value of his loss of property, $1,926 and costs (totaling around $5,000).[9]

To save the defendants "personal inconvenience and embarrassment" a committee was formed to defray the legal costs. Most of the money came from Detroit where Zachariah Chandler headed a subscription paper with his $100. George F. Porter acted as treasurer and Robert Cross, Charles Dickey, J. Wright Gordon, J. Chedsey, and Hovey K. Clarke formed the committee.[10] Not only was Francis Giltner compensated for the value of his human property but also with bill S. No 239 (also known as the "Affidavit of Francis Troutman"), submitted to the Senate of the United States May 3, 1848. Ten thousand copies of the bill were printed.[11]

Live or Die, Sink or Swim

The North Star published the proceedings of a late 1848 mass meeting of the "Colored People of Detroit." The meeting, held in the Colored Methodist Church, was organized in response to the Crosswhite case with Richard Gordon as chairman and William Lambert as secretary. George DeBaptiste was called to the chair, Benjamin F. Dade appointed secretary, M. J. Lightfoot, James Maten and Richard Gordon, vice presidents. William Lambert, Henry Bibb, and Edward J. Cooper were appointed a committee to draft resolutions regarding the decision in the *Giltner v Gorham* [Crosswhite] case. Their words express the extreme agitation felt by men whose security could no longer be guaranteed.

> Resolved, That we hold our liberty dearer than we do our lives, and we will organize and prepare ourselves with the determination, live or die, sink or swim, we will never be taken back into slavery.
>
> Resolved, That we will never voluntarily separate ourselves from the slave population in the country, for they are our fathers and mothers, and sisters and our brothers, their interest is our interest, their wrongs and their sufferings are ours, the injuries inflicted on them are alike inflicted on us; therefore it is our duty to aid and assist them in their attempts to regain their liberty.[12]

In spite of their grievances, black organizers in Michigan committed themselves to fighting slavery, rather than fleeing to Canada or Liberia. The Rev. Calvin Fairbank related that while visiting Detroit in 1849, he discovered several families he had helped from slavery living near the city. He went to see these families, and afterward wrote concerning them: "Living near the Johnsons, and like them contented and comfortable, I found the Stewart and Coleman families, for whom I had also lighted the path of freedom."[13]

The Michigan Legislature approved a resolution on January 13, 1849, in favor of the "prohibition of slavery within any territory of the United States now or hereafter to be acquired." This related to the ongoing controversy over the Wilmot Proviso, which would have prohibited slavery in the Mexico territory. A *Michigan Argus* newspaper submission asked northerners to desist in irritating the South, as it threatened the "stability of our happy Union." The writer felt Americans should reflect on the fact that slavery was a British institution, thrust upon the South, not easily eradicated, and best handled by changing the heart of the slaveholder. The evidence for this approach could be found in the 1840 census record where, because of voluntary emancipation, 215,000 free blacks lived in southern states. The anti-abolition article stated this was the result of voluntary sacrifice by southern slaveholders. The writer offered no accounting of blacks born free or self-emancipated by escape or purchase. Nor does the article mention the nearly two and one half million enslaved blacks.[14]

On the western side of Michigan, the men who failed to recover their former slaves in Cass County filed lawsuits to reclaim their losses. John and Milton Graves and other slaveholders instigated trials and retrials, which over several years, devastated some Michigan families. Pamela Thomas said that although friends donated generously, a few neighbors sold their farms and moved to Oregon but not before another raid took place in Cass County.[15]

On September 27, 1849, John Norris left Lawrenceburg, Indiana, with seven men on a midnight raid. They were after David Powell who ran away from slavery two years previously and had been tracked down in a secluded place eight miles from Cassopolis. The gang forcibly broke into the Powell home. The men drew their pistols and bowie knives, bound Lucy Powell and the children, Lewis, George, and James, with cords. The gang hastily carried them off in covered wagons. Somehow, neighbor and Underground Railroad agent Wright Maudlin learned of the abduction and overtook the wagons near South Bend, Indiana. Maudlin and other neighbors forced the men to go before a judge.[16]

Maudlin swore out a writ. Over the next few days, up to 200 Cass County neighbors arrived in South Bend for the hearing. The Powells were released and safely escorted to Detroit. On Dec. 21, 1849, Norris commenced suit in the United States Circuit Court initially naming Wright Maudlin in the suit, but Maudlin was dropped over his citizenship outside Indiana. Norris won his claim as the alleged owner of the slaves, and the jury assessed the damages at $2,856. Years later, the United States marshal sold a quantity of real estate owned by some of the parties in the suit to satisfy it. Northerners were again drawn into the injustice of slavery in a free state.[17]

The local and regional squabbles were soon eclipsed by national legislation. After years of failing to vote on the Wilmot Proviso, the government passed the Compromise of 1850. This allowed admitting California as a free state and left the issue of slavery up to the citizens of New Mexico and Utah. Part of the Compromise of 1850 included the strengthening of federal enforcement of the Fugitive Slave Act.

Signed into law in September by President Millard Fillmore, who became president after the death of Zachary Taylor, the Fugitive Slave Act of 1850 not only doubled the penalty for aiding runaways, it required everyone — civil authorities and even ordinary citizens — to assist in the retrieval and return of fugitives to their purported owners. The penalty for obstructing the arrest of a fugitive was a fine up to $1,000 and up to six months in jail.

Many citizens in Michigan, and other free states, wondered how the law would affect their black neighbors. The 1850 federal census, taken earlier in the year, showed that of the nearly 400,000 people in Michigan, about 2,600 were listed as people of color. The census race categories were white, black, and mulatto. All people, including native Americans, were listed at the discretion of the census taker.

By county, Wayne, with its major city of Detroit, contained far more blacks than any other place in Michigan (724 "free colored"). Settlements in Cass (389) and Berrien (239) pushed those counties ahead of southeastern counties settled at an earlier date (Washtenaw, 231; Calhoun, 207). It would appear that a small number of "free colored" were scattered in northern counties and the Upper Peninsula. However, only a thorough study would determine whether those identified as "free colored" were African or Indian American.[18]

Overall, the number of black residents in Michigan in 1850 doubled from 1840. The "free colored" increased at a greater rate than the white population so that in 1850, about one in every 160 people in Michigan was African or Indian American. Suddenly, self-emancipators were unsure whether Michigan was safe. Underground Railroad agents who allowed Caroline Hill to stay in their homes considered the risks to their families. And, both free and self-freed people who created homes, befriended neighbors, and joined churches realized all their hard-won possessions and liberties were imperiled.

Chapter Thirteen

1850 Fugitive Slave Act

Kidnapping of the David Gordon Family

The passage of the Fugitive Slave Act of 1850 emboldened slave catchers to travel into free states to take their "property" back south into unpaid, lifelong servitude. As expected, one of the first to return to Michigan in 1850 was Thomas K. Chester on behalf of his father, John P. Chester. Chester visited the law offices of Robert R. Beecher, to ask for a legal paper to remove the fugitives from the state, as he had a posse of thirty men to assist in the actual abduction.

Beecher declined to provide the warrant on the grounds it would ruin his business to aid in the scheme. Chester attempted to persuade him with an offer of $100 in addition to his standard fee, but Beecher replied that all the money in Tennessee would not induce him to help. When asked for the name of an agreeable lawyer, Beecher assured Chester he would be unable to hire anyone in the state of Michigan.

At this point, Chester revealed his desire to avenge Laura Haviland of Adrian for thwarting him in his earlier attempt to take the Hamiltons and swore he would see Haviland imprisoned if she obstructed him. When the lawyer stood firm in his refusal to help, Chester asked that he keep their conversation a secret. Immediately, Beecher sent word through Lenawee County Sheriff Spofford that the Hamiltons were at risk. Word came back that the Hamiltons had been in Canada for two years, but Thomas Chester refused to accept that the family was out of his reach.

Hearing a rumor that the Hamiltons were living in Ypsilanti, a home to many blacks, Chester headed north. Passing himself off as a drover or a peddler, Chester called on the blacks several miles into the countryside. After a month prying and sniffing out his quarry Chester wrote his father back in Jonesborough, Tennessee, that the Hamiltons were living with their four children under the assumed names of Mr. and Mrs. David Gordon.[1]

Chester applied to Hon. Ross Wilkins, U.S. District Court Judge, for a warrant to arrest the family. Judge Wilkins, who had been involved in the Cromwell case, was duty-bound to produce the warrant, but he also informed George DeBaptiste, of the Detroit Underground Railroad. DeBaptiste contacted a friend in Ypsilanti who was unable to locate the Hamilton family, but arranged for Underground Railroad helpers to watch the train depot and follow the Chester posse when they returned to Ypsilanti.

The officers, Chester, and his posse traveled from the Ypsilanti depot to Augusta Township. The men entered the home of David Gordon and immediately secured him in handcuffs. As expected, Gordon was astounded by his arrest and the news that he was Willis Hamilton, a freedom seeker from Tennessee. He pointed to a trunk with his free papers from Virginia, while behind his back, Chester drew a six-shooter and held it to Margaret Gordon's head while she lay sick in bed. Chester ordered Mrs. Gordon to admit her name was Hamilton. Amidst the terrifying screams and threats, David Gordon produced the papers proving him to be a free man and the officer made certain the family was left in safety.

Thomas Chester and his Tennessee cohorts were taken by train to Detroit and the unserved warrant was returned to Judge Wilkins. Chester charged Wilkins as a co-conspirator with the "damned abolitionist" Laura Haviland and, upon returning to Tennessee, campaigned to destroy Wilkins' reputation and impeach the judge.

A decade later, John Chester challenged a man to produce his free papers and was shown the barrel of a six-shooter.[2]

The passage of the Fugitive Slave Act of 1850 spurred the issue of slavery to the forefront in political debates and onto the platforms of the national parties. Drafted by Senator James Mason of Virginia, it was the product of months of contentious debate in the Senate. The claims of loss of slaves by southerners were likely exaggerated, but ranged from 30,000 from North Carolina to 100,000 for the entire South.[3] Counting those among the three million people enslaved from birth until death, that number would seem very small.

Michigan Outrage

Many northerners were outraged by their legal obligation to support a purely Southern institution within their states. Citizens awakening for the first time to the issue of slavery and its consequences were as likely to be converted to abolitionism than to assist in the capture of people escaping slavery. As slaveholders encroached on Michigan soil, men and women witnessed how the southern use of enslaving African Americans trod on the rights of all citizens whether in slave or free states.

At least one newspaper article described the reactions of the Michigan citizenry to the Fugitive Slave Act. "In this as well as other parts of the State, there is one general burst of indignation against the 'Fugitive Slave Law,' ... the rights of citizens cannot be trampled upon with impunity."[4] The same paper reported that in the November 1850 election, the citizenry expressed their anger at the ballot box by voting for the newly united Free Soil and Whig candidates, sending those politicians who voted for the "abominable" slave bill a farewell ticket home.

Samuel Noble wrote from Ann Arbor, Michigan, to the *National Era* in Washington, D. C., "Many of the Fugitives that resided in this village and other parts of the county have left for Canada; others have armed themselves, and are determined to resist any encroachment upon their persons or families to the last extremity."[5]

The Rev. Elijah Pilcher, one of the first preachers in Michigan, was among many to denounce slavery and the Fugitive Slave Act in public addresses and submissions. Retired from circuit preaching, the Reverend Pilcher published *Unconstitutionality of Slavery and the Fugitive Slave Law*, from his home in Ann Arbor.

The Rev. Gustavus Lemuel Foster was rebuked for a sermon condemning the Fugitive Slave Law. Foster, not a close relative of Theodore and Samuel Foster, graduated from Andover Theological Seminary, and was known as a "fearless and eloquent preacher" in Jackson, Michigan. He would not be intimidated nor "change his antislavery opinion or spirit." Whether by force or choice, two years later, Foster transferred to the First Presbyterian Church of Ypsilanti. The congregation there did not object to his political views since they were aligned with those of the Reverend Weed. Foster maintained a successful ministry for a decade, oversaw construction of a new building, and increased membership.[6]

One of the women's antislavery societies in Michigan, organized several years earlier, revived their activities after the passage of the Fugitive Slave Act. Ladies of the Female Anti-Slavery Society of Grand Prairie (Schoolcraft area) "devoted half a day every two weeks to knitting and sewing, while one of the number read such antislavery information as they had obtained." The goods were sent to Amherstburg, Ontario.[7]

Vermont immediately passed a Personal Liberty Law, and several other states followed suit. Michigan was the first state in the Midwest to enact similar legislation, introduced by Erastus Hussey of Battle Creek and others, but not passed until 1855. The legislation forbade justices and judges to recognize the claims of slave owners, to extended the Habeas Corpus Act and the privilege of jury trial to the self-freed. And it punished false testimony.

The Northern states that gained a black population between 1850 and 1860 were Ohio, Michigan, and Illinois, primarily. The three states offered easy travel to Canada and a history of Underground Railroad activity. It is estimated that fifteen- to twenty-thousand blacks moved to Canada, especially Canada West (Ontario). New England states gained very few blacks during this period.[8] Black churches in Buffalo and Rochester, New York, reported large losses of members of around 100 congregants at each church by 1851.[9]

From Indiana, Calvin Fairbank, a Methodist Episcopal minister and graduate of Oberlin, appealed to abolitionist lecturers. He believed that proslavery sentiment was stronger in Indiana than Kentucky "because in Kentucky, many of the people are beginning to see the advantage of freedom over slavery."[10] Within two years, Calvin Fairbank was arrested, convicted, and sent to prison for the second time. From 1852 until his pardon in 1864, Fairbank endured horrific treatment in prison.[11]

New Yorker Lewis Tappan published a pamphlet to warn all Americans that not only was the Act unconstitutional, but that white children could be taken, as well as black children. Tappan directed concerned citizens to note that the word "slave" was not used in the Act, but "fugitives from labor." Any person hired out for service or labor, was therefore subject to possible kidnapping or arrest.[12] The charge was obviously sensational, but effective in stoking the ire of the public.

Victims of the Law

James Hamlet of New York was the first victim of the Fugitive Slave Act of 1850. He was surrendered to Mary Brown's agent and taken to Baltimore in September 1850. In the book, *The Fugitive Slave Law and Its Victims*, Samuel May described several of the first recoveries of self-emancipators in the north. Local abolitionists immediately worked to purchase Hamlet's freedom, the demanded sum of $800 was raised, and Hamlet was brought back to New York with great rejoicing.

In a subsequent case during the first two months of 1851, a woman living in Shawnee-town, Illinois, was released by two Justices of the Peace to a Georgia man. Around January 20, 1851, near Ripley, Ohio, a self-emancipator killed the man trying to take him hostage. The former slave was caught and taken south. In another case, a boy who may have been legally free was kidnapped in Pennsylvania and taken into slavery. In Madison, Indiana, a Kentuckian claimed a man named Mitchum. Mitchum, self-freed 19 years previously, had been living with his wife and children in the intervening years. The case was tried before a justice who agreed that Mitchum was a slave and served him up. Mitchum was taken from his home and family.[13]

William and Ellen Craft had lived in security for years since their famous escape from slavery in disguise as a woman and her doctor, yet an attempt was made to seize them and they left America for England. In Sandusky, Ohio, a large group of freedom seekers were removed from a steamboat ready to depart for Detroit. When taken before the mayor, a man identified as R. Sloane claimed custody and allowed them to board the boat. Shortly thereafter, another man suddenly spoke up as the owner, but the steamer was gliding out of the port with its human cargo. Sloane was later prosecuted and judged to pay the $3,950 value of the slaves.[14]

Levi Coffin wrote of the first case within his court district in Ohio. In August 1853, Washington McQuerry was arrested and tried as a fugitive slave. James Birney traveled from Michigan to aid in the man's defense, but Birney was stymied by the law. McQuerry's "owner" offered to sell him for $1,200, but Coffin was unable to raise the money. McQuerry was taken from the state of Ohio, where slavery was not allowed, into enslavement.[15]

On October 8, 1850, in Detroit, Michigan, Giles Rose was arrested as a fugitive slave. Rose was placed in jail as citizens armed themselves to prevent his removal from the state. The mayor asked General Schwarz to secure the peace. Three volunteer companies prevented bloodshed, while people opposed to slavery raised money to secure Rose's freedom.[16]

A case reported by New York abolitionist Samuel J. May lacks corroborating evidence; nonetheless, May wrote that Markwood and Chester had taken seven men back to slavery, according to the *Huntsville Advocate* newspaper. Perhaps Thomas Chester contrived the story after failing to capture Willis and Elsie Hamilton or kidnap the Gordon family near Ypsilanti.

Self-emancipated men and women in Michigan felt the effects of the Fugitive Slave Law. Perry Sanford said that after the Cass County raid in 1847, families were "in a constant state of alarm," and left for Canada. Sanford stayed in Battle Creek with his family. When the Fugitive Slave Act passed, all of Battle Creek's black population but Sanford and William Casey stayed on. Casey sent his wife and family to Canada.[17]

The attempted kidnapping of the Gordon family in Ypsilanti put Underground Railroad workers on guard. Another sheriff might have arrested not only the Gordons but also Beecher. Robert R. Beecher may have been an esteemed lawyer and elected judge in Adrian, but his constituents would not be able to save him from federal prosecution.[18]

Sumner F. Spofford, as a U. S. Marshall, was able to provide protection to lawyer Beecher, Laura Haviland and other Underground Railroad workers. Spofford grew up in the abolitionist community of Tecumseh, was elected constable in 1841, and for the next twelve years served as sheriff or deputy U. S. Marshall from his home in Adrian.[19]

The 1850 Fugitive Slave Law required citizens to help in the capture of someone who escaped from slavery. U. S. Marshall Spofford and Underground Railroad agents recognized that the law was now firmly against them continuing to operate the Underground Railroad in Michigan.

Several Underground Railroad operators acknowledged that in 1851, slave hunters confidently marched into Michigan to retake their "property." Despite adopting the common names of George and Martha Washington, a couple in Ann Arbor was discovered by their former "master." The Washingtons had been living in a small house on Chapin Street near the home of Sylvester Noble in Ann Arbor, Washtenaw County, Michigan, where they gardened and did other work for the Nobles. The Noble brothers moved to Michigan at the urging of Judge Samuel Dexter and originally lived in the Dexter area. Sylvester Noble purchased land on the western edge of the village of Ann Arbor, where he worked as a carpenter and pattern maker. His house was open to freedom seekers, who were fed and cared for, and sometimes hidden in the cellar.[20]

One evening, after 1850, some of the Noble children were sent to the Washingtons with a basket of food and were surprised by some commotion. A number of people were there, hurrying to help them make a run for Canada that night. By some means, a rumor reached George and Martha that their former "owner" was coming for them.[21]

Sylvester Noble's daughter Pamela recalled that her childhood home was a place of refuge where freedom seekers were "coming constantly." Little was said to the children, but Pamela remembered people would be hidden in their cellar, and her father would take mysterious journeys. She recalled once seeing two men in the back of the wagon and a woman up front with her father. Pamela said her father took the freedom seekers either to or from Captain John Lowry's home in Lodi.[22]

Both Samuel and Sylvester Noble were known antislavery activists, their names appearing in the *Signal of Liberty*. After the Civil War, a county history referred to Noble's abolitionism in his biography, "Sylvester D. Noble ... was very active in the antislavery cause, and his home was many times a station on the underground railroad. He was highly esteemed by all who knew him."[23]

Noble may have been helped by his neighbor, Eber White, an early white settler, active in the community, associated with the Methodist Church and the agricultural society. Like Noble, the county biography described White as a person whose benevolence and love of liberty led him to assist "in helping forward the fugitive slave as he passed through Michigan toward Canada and the North Star."[24]

Underground Railroad Improvements

In response to the attempted kidnappings of Giles Rose, the Gordons, and Washingtons, the interstate network of assistance evolved. Laura Haviland of Adrian, and Roswell Preston of Pittsfield Township, wrote that the routes changed and refugees from bondage were moved quickly out of the state to Canada ahead of the slave hunters.

The network forwarding people from Ohio and then west into Indiana, was shortened by distance and time. Freedom seekers crossing from the Kentucky region were more frequently sent directly north through Ohio to Sandusky and Toledo, or along the Ohio/Indiana border into southern Michigan. Trains from Fort Wayne, Indiana, led to Hillsdale County, Michigan. At Jonesville, a traveler could transfer to the Southern Michigan Railroad whose line included a junction at Adrian and terminated at Monroe. Or from Fort Wayne, a passenger could remain on the train until Jackson where the Central Michigan Railroad intersected and led to Ann Arbor and Detroit. If a person remained on the train, the line carried the traveler to Pontiac, north of Detroit.

Underground Railroad operators in western Michigan noted a decrease in traffic after 1850. Mrs. Pamela Thomas of Schoolcraft noted, "After the passage of the fugitive slave law of 1850, greater precaution was observed, and less passed-on the regular route." From Battle Creek, Erastus Hussey described his assistance after 1855, "We did not assist so many fugitives then, as they went over a shorter route through Ohio, by way of Sandusky, and thence to Malden."[25]

Quaker conductors Levi and Catharine Coffin moved from Indiana to Cincinnati,

Ohio, in 1847 and aided as many as 1,500 escaping self-emancipators from their new home. Fitch Reed, an Underground Railroad conductor in Lenawee County, Michigan, wrote that from 1851 to 1855 many freedom seekers traveled through Lenawee and Washtenaw Counties.[26]

Shall We Submit

Henry Bibb was among many black men who believed that people of his race were no longer safe in the United States. He crossed the Detroit River to Canada. Both individuals and large groups headed to the British Provinces. On January 1, 1851, Henry Bibb printed the first issue of *Voice of the Fugitive* in Sandwich, Ontario, near Windsor. Bibb and his wife Mary Miles saw no future for the African race in the United States and strongly urged others to immigrate to Canada. Though female antislavery societies in Michigan sent clothing and bedding, Bibb believed self-sufficiency could happen only through land ownership. Bibb issued a call to the "Friends of Humanity in Michigan" to attend a convention in Detroit to discuss a scheme of colonization in Canada.

The Refugee Home Society was founded in Detroit on May 21, 1851. Abolitionists and friends in Michigan donated funds to purchase land to aide self-freed people in their journey to independence. The joint stockholders fell far short of their goal of obtaining 50,000 acres, yet served around 150 families over the next several years. In *Voice of the Fugitive*, Bibb implored blacks to unite in this cause. Bibb wrote "shall we submit like dastardly cowards to the kidnapping laws of the whites, and be dragged off into helpless bondage on the one hand, or bow in submission to the American Colonization scheme on the other?"

The Reverend Anthony Binga (Bingey), a black minister, traveled with missionary the Rev. Hiram Wilson who estimated there were 60,000 self-freed people in Canada. Binga knew of many other settlements. About fifty miles away in Dresden, Father Henson had a school and mission but "they had a great deal of trouble there" because the settlers did not all agree with the community rules. New Canaan was a large settlement about ten miles away and a larger settlement was in Colchester. Binga preached in Toronto for three years and said there were not so many settlers there.

Near Niagara Falls, there was Hamilton and St. Catherine's. Binga said he preached at Cuckston (Buxton), where people were doing better than at any other settlement. Most of the settlers had 50 to 100 acres, nice schools, and churches. In 1849, Reverend William King, a white man, founded the Elgin Settlement in Buxton with fifteen formerly enslaved men and women. Six years later there were 300 people living in the community that offered an unrivaled classical education.[27]

Articles appeared in antislavery newspapers reporting the success of the settlements, in hopes of encouraging desperately needed funds for the increasing numbers of emigrants. "S. J." described the Elgin Association, established on 9,000 acres, eight miles from Chatham, which allowed settlers to purchase 50 acre plots, paid in installments. For those unfamiliar with Canada West, the writer offered a description, "The climate is healthy and considerably milder than in New England. The soil is good: producing wheat, Indian corn, Irish and sweet potatoes, oats, tobacco, hemp, peaches, melons, and various other fruits."[28]

The article was intended to aide agents visiting New England cities and towns in getting donations. "The Rev. Charles C. Foote of Michigan is now visiting Boston and vicinity in its behalf ... and brings with him most cordial testimonials from wise and good men of different religious and political views." Laura Haviland moved to Bibb's settlement to teach and accepted donations to the school from her friends in Adrian.[29]

Henry Bibb boasted in November 1851 that the Underground Railroad to Canada was moving faster, with more passengers. "We can run a lot of slaves through almost any of the bordering slave states into Canada within 48 hours and we defy the slave holders and their abettors to beat that if they can."[30] Others noticed a dramatic increase in the number of people moving to Canada. The Reverend Anthony Binga helped to receive fugitives at Amherstburg, Ontario, distributing provisions, caring for the sick, and setting them up with jobs for white farmers. Soon, some were able to lease land and build their own cabins. Binga observed only a few arriving in the 1830s and, later, as many as thirty a day. He said that "after the Fugitive Slave Act took effect by fifties every day — like frogs in Egypt," they arrived.[31]

African Americans who remained in northern states after 1850 included self-emancipators who worked on the Underground Railroad. Louis Washington in Columbus, Ohio, Elijah Anderson in Madison, Indiana, and William Still in Philadelphia employed greater secrecy in continuing to forward self-emancipators to safety.[32]

It is impossible to measure the Fugitive Slave Act's effect on Michigan's population. No census was taken in 1851 or 1852 to show whether a decline occurred after the Fugitive Slave Act was enacted. The *Voice of the Fugitive* reported that from 1851 to 1852, 1,314 freed and 1,018 self-freed black people emigrated to Canada, mostly from Kentucky and Maryland.[33] The *Provincial Freeman* wrote of emigrants arriving at such a record pace, 200 formerly enslaved people landed on freedom's soil between editions of the newspaper.[34]

The 1850 census lists only one person of color in Houghton, in the Upper Peninsula of Michigan, though the copper mines offered good work opportunities. Perhaps the one person was "John Brown, the fugitive slave" who wrote an autobiography. In 1847, Brown fled cruel treatment and enslavement by Thomas J. Stevens in Decatur, Georgia, and, after some problems, landed in Mississippi. He used a forged pass in Illinois and then stayed in a free black community in Terre Haute, Indiana. Quaker Underground Railroad helpers got him to Michigan where he lived in Marshall for a year. After a short time in Detroit, Brown joined some miners in Houghton's Lake Superior copper fields, working as a carpenter for nearly two years. In early 1850, Brown moved to Dawn, Canada West, and then went to England.[35] Capturing John Brown with his constant moves would have been a remarkable feat.

Chapter Fourteen

Two Days to Midnight

Fairfield's Freedom Seekers, 1853

April rains swelled the Ohio River. Normally, the waters swept forward with a steady, noble force but on this night, threatening torrents rushed and heaved. As John Fairfield reached the Kentucky shore and saw the roiling river, he must have felt an overwhelming dread. If they waited, he and his group faced certain capture; however, if the boat capsized, most, if not all, would drown. He must choose.

Fairfield, a white Virginian, had led many people from slave soil to the free state of Ohio. This was likely the largest group he had ever helped. The value of so much "human property" ensured that slave hunters were at their heels. The party of 28 men, women, and an infant, had to race ahead of their pursuers through Kentucky. Fairfield told them what to expect if they were caught, and so they armed themselves with pistols, swords, and whatever they could lay their hands on. They would fight to the death rather than be taken back into slavery.

Fairfield was aware of what his own punishment would be. Most of the escaping enslaved would be returned to slavery, too valuable as free labor to maim or kill. They would be sold off in the Deep South where escape from the grueling fieldwork might be accomplished by an early death. Fairfield had recently been jailed for slave stealing and could reckon on torture and hanging for himself.

And then, there was the weather. The group must have anticipated that the worst of the journey would be behind them when they reached the Ohio River. Instead of its usual quiet, they were met by surrounding echoes of colliding waves. At nightfall, the group crossed in overloaded and leaky boats, paddling against strong currents while being tossed and sprayed by frigid water. When one boat sank, Fairfield attempted to drag it to shore and was barely rescued by the men he was leading to freedom.

The drenched, exhausted travelers found no warm fire nor rest in Cincinnati. With slave hunters upon them, it was necessary to stay hidden outdoors. Fairfield alerted Underground Railroad helpers of his desperate need for immediate assistance. Since passage of the 1850 Fugitive Slave Act, northerners faced harsh punishment for protecting formerly enslaved people from those who claimed them as property. In fact, though many refused, citizens were required by law to assist in the capture of escaped slaves.

The first to offer aide was John Hatfield, African American deacon in the Zion Baptist Church. Next, the Coffins and their friends came forward. Levi Coffin, a Quaker, expressed disapproval of Fairfield's use of violence and lawbreaking, but as on many occasions, Coffin rushed to help the endangered freedom seekers. Black and white workers on the Underground

The house of William Webb Harwood, ally of Asher Aray on the Underground Railroad. Behind the house, Harwood and Aray family members are buried in an early interracial cemetery (author photograph, Saline, Michigan, 2009).

Railroad supplied dry clothes and food, and devised a plan to get the weary travelers across town without arousing suspicion and arrest. By the time the group was given shelter, the infant had died.

It was determined that the safest route was north through several towns in Ohio, then west into Indiana. Having lived in Newport (Fountain City), Indiana, before moving to Ohio in 1847, Levi and Catharine Coffin relied upon trustworthy friends in their former hometown. Three wagons were sent by Underground Railroad "stockholders" to carry the group from station to station. Underground Railroad agent Fitch Reed sheltered them at his house in Cambridge, Michigan, until they departed at sunset in four teams.

Reed drove them through Clinton into Washtenaw County to the Ypsilanti area before daylight. Fairfield's freedom seekers were hidden throughout the day on the farm of Asher and Catherine Aray. The Arays, free blacks, participated on the Underground Railroad with white neighbors, William Harwood and Roswell Preston. Many women toiled in their kitchens to prepare food for the unexpected guests.

While the freedom seekers waited for darkness on Aray's farm, John Coe took the noon train to Detroit to make arrangements to get the group across to Canada. At sunset, Aray led his team and Preston's horses and wagons on the thirty-five mile journey to Detroit. Within hours of reaching the city called "Midnight" the travelers were met in the road. Word had spread about the incredibly large group of freedom seekers and, ten miles from Detroit, sympathizers provided the party with an escort. In the moments before daylight, 200 people gathered to welcome the travelers to freedom.

As the ferryboats pushed off from American soil, the freedom seekers rejoiced in song and fired the weapons they had carried along the way. The Underground Railroad agents who had accompanied them safely through Michigan, crossed the Detroit River and spent the day at the Sandwich Settlement in Windsor, Canada. Henry Bibb, self-emancipated lecturer and journalist, and Laura Haviland, an Underground Railroad agent from Adrian, Michigan, participated in the celebration.

A handbill was circulated announcing the safe arrival of this large group of men and women by the "express train" and asking the "Stockholders of the Underground R.R. Company" to donate farming tools and equipment. The abolitionists spent a day filling three wagons with food and clothing, stayed overnight in the English Barracks, then helped distribute the goods the following day.

The vignette preceding this chapter reveals much about the workings of the Underground Railroad after 1850. It was extremely difficult to escape the southern states. John Fairfield, a southerner, instructed and led the armed group across the river. They "borrowed" the boats to cross. Fairfield went first to an African American person for help and then enlisted the help of Quakers and others. Once in Michigan, the group relied on assistance from agents who were white and black, male and female, Wesleyan Methodist and Quaker. Two dozen people moved successfully through the state in just two days. It had taken decades for the Underground Railroad to reach this degree of efficiency.

Illinois and Indiana passed laws prohibiting the settlement of people of African descent in their states. Citizens said the laws were necessary because of all the freedom seekers and those enticed to run away by abolitionists. "Now the people of Illinois are not slaveholders, and have no liking for slavery, but they have had quite enough of Abolitionism. They have been taxed heavily long enough to support runaway negroes."[1]

Fitch Reed, a Wesleyan Methodist, did not give an opinion about the fact that the men and women had 52 rounds of ammunition, though Levi Coffin expressed strong disapproval of Fairfield's use of violence. Fairfield agreed to rescue relatives held in slavery, then insisted those fleeing arm and defend themselves. Quaker Levi Coffin told Fairfield "we should love our enemies." To this, Fairfield replied, "Love the devil! When I undertake to conduct slaves out of bondage I feel that it is my duty to defend them, even to the last drop of my blood."[2]

William Lambert said that Fairfield once worked with him as part of a gang. Lambert called them McKinseyites, in reference to followers of Mackenzie, who led a rebellion for reform in Canada. According to Lambert, Fairfield and others would go into the south where they took enslaved people, sold them to slave hunters, and then stole them again. The operation originated during the time Lambert lived in New Jersey and associated with the fifty to sixty "McKinseyites" who took willing people out of slavery. "We traveled at night, or if in daytime with peddling wagons. We had at one time more than sixty tin peddling wagons with false bottoms, large enough to hold three men, traveling through the south." The operation was short-lived as many were eventually identified and caught, imprisoned or out of the business.

Lambert believed Fairfield was the best of the group because he was fearless, "a perfect desparado." He was known by all the original Underground Railroad helpers and at least Haviland, Coffin, Reed, and Martha Washington revealed personal accounts of him.

Quaker Levi Coffin objected to Fairfield's weaponry, but Lambert described Fairfield's appearance with apparent admiration and a little pride. Lambert, a successful tailor, created Fairfield's special coat.

Fairfield's overcoat was intentionally loose fitting to conceal a belt holding seven revolvers. The wide openings for the pockets cut high on the garment, actually had no pockets. Lambert described how Fairfield used the coat, "Into the holes he thrust his hands and drew his weapons unperceived and fired with telling effect through the cloth of his coat. I used to make these coats for him, and knew how often they were marked with bullet holes and burnt by exploding powder." Lambert thought Fairfield enjoyed the excitement of going into the south, getting a job as a driver or overseer, and then carrying out a load of people. Lambert said he brought over 1,500 to Detroit.[3]

Wesleyan Methodist Network

Fitch Reed described the workings of the Wesleyan Methodist network decades after the Civil War. Though Reed forgot the names of the workers northwest of Cincinnati, the vignette identifies Levi and Catharine Coffin and John Hatfield. Reed wrote that the freedom trail followed a general path north from Cincinnati, through Indiana to the Wesleyan Methodist settlement in Coldwater, Branch County, Michigan. Dr. Wilbur Siebert wrote that the Wesleyan Methodists included African Americans on an equal standing in their church and, where the denomination was located, "the Road [Underground Railroad] was likely to be found in active operation."[4]

The network Reed described began with known conductors Levi Coffin and Laura Haviland, and linked places of Wesleyan Methodists in Hillsdale County, and then either Cambridge Station or Rome in Lenawee County, and following the Chicago Turnpike into Washtenaw County. After Pittsfield and Ypsilanti, it was a short trip to ports on the Detroit River.

Reed did not remember the names of the Wesleyan Methodists in Coldwater, Branch County. From Coldwater, they may have traveled on the Chicago Turnpike through Quincy, Jonesville, and Moscow before stopping at Wheatland, located near the Lenawee County line in Hillsdale County. Reed knew the regular helpers in Wheatland were Anson Backus, Oliver Streeter, and Mr. Adams.

Anson Backus' service as secretary of the Wesleyan Church and his attendance at some antislavery meetings attest to his opposition to slavery. The only reference of Oliver Streeter relates to his work as a teacher. Mr. Adams remains unidentified and could be any of the Adams family for whom Adams Township and the town of North Adams are named. Fitch Reed seems to be the only person to know of Streeter and Adams in this network. The Wesleyan Methodist Church of Pittsford was formed when two distant groups merged. The first quarterly meeting of the Jefferson Circuit was held in the schoolhouse near the home of Anson Backus on March 6, 1858.

Reed does not list Captain George Bansill who was bestowed with a lengthy biography in the county history. Bansill sailed from England in 1827 and landed eventually in Jefferson County, New York. His work on Lake Ontario steamers led to Captain's rank on the *Phoenix*. He married in 1835 and brought his bride to Moscow Township in Hillsdale County. According to the historical record, Capt. Bansill was an active abolitionist.

> In the old days he was always ready to leave his harvest field, or any other pressing work, to go to the assistance of the fugitive, fleeing from his oppressors, and many a time assisted

the victims of the peculiar institution to make their way safely by the "underground rail-road" to Canada.[5]

South of Wheatland, the Rev. Caleb M. Preston and his son William ministered in a Wesleyan church in Wright Township. Caleb Preston, born in Virginia, moved to Columbiana County, Ohio, as a child and learned from his parents about the sin of slavery. He became an early convert to the Wesleyan Methodist Church in Ohio, accepting an appointment as a circuit preacher of a 200 mile area. Though advised against it, Preston crossed into Virginia to preach. While standing at the pulpit, a dozen men on horseback rode up, entered the church, and carried him off. Several of his friends followed the man-stealers on the way to jail. At the right moment, Preston suddenly turned his horse and galloped away at break-neck speed. After an arduous trek in the darkness, he landed at a friend's house at two in the morning. Preston soon remounted his horse in order to reach Pennsylvania before daylight.

Preston retired from preaching in Ohio, moved to Wright Township in 1854 and once again joined and preached in the Wesleyan Methodist Church. He lived out his days with his wife, Ann Eliza Morris Preston, whose parents were Quaker abolitionists in Beaver County, Pennsylvania. At that place Jonathan and Sophia Morris had a station on the Underground Railroad. It is unimaginable that Caleb and Ann Preston would not have opened their home to men and women escaping slavery in Michigan.[6]

Fitch Reed operated a station a short distance from Wheatland, in Cambridge. He must have relied on other helpers when John Fairfield arrived with over two dozen hungry and tired men and women in 1853. Fairfield's group was hidden until sunset when four teams of horses and wagons departed. It seems that Reed drove one wagon and John Coe another. There was no need to stop at James Wells' station, six miles south of Clinton.

Reed was well known as an ultra-abolitionist in Adrian. He fit the profile of early Michigan settlers — from Canandaigua, New York, white, aged 21. Reed settled near Adrian, built a log shanty to live in and log schools and meeting places. A number of neighbors were as opposed to slavery as he was, and they formed a Wesleyan Society and Church. Reed voted only the Whig party and had Whig literature to read. The Wesleyan Church members felt it was their duty to vote their principles and therefore formed an abolition party, suffering the abuse of neighbors. When Reed was nominated to serve as Justice of the Peace on the Republican ticket, he informed the public that they would be nominating an abolitionist. He was duly elected but voted the Abolitionist ticket during his eight year term.[7]

At least three men helped from Rome, west of Adrian in Lenawee County. John M. Coe, described in the vignette, resided in Rome Township throughout the 1840s and 1850s. He was born in New York in 1803. James H. Parker and his wife settled in Rome in 1834. As antebellum histories rarely record the efforts of women, especially as participants in the Underground Railroad, the recognition of Mrs. Parker is noteworthy. James Parker, the historian wrote, was a consistent abolitionist "and he, with his wife, in the slavery days, helped through several fugitives who came along on the 'underground railroad.'"[8]

Warren Gilbert was another New Yorker who settled in Rome Township (1843). He married Almira Reed two years later and succeeded in farming and raising stock. A 20th century county history stated:

> At a time when it was considered almost a disgrace to be characterized as an abolitionist, a
> champion of woman's rights or an apostle of temperance, Warren Gilbert was a staunch

friend of each cause, and strong by voice and vote to advance every good work. His home was one of the stations of the underground railroad, and many a poor black fugitive has been helped on his way to freedom by his aid.[9]

Reed listed the Rev. Jeremiah Dolbeare as another agent near him in the area south of Brooklyn in the Irish Hills. At the time of the Fairfield rescue, Dolbeare, formerly of the Raisin Institute, was in Canada helping Laura Haviland and Henry Bibb. Dolbeare and others from Adrian provided supplies for Bibb's school. Henry Bibb's wife, Mary Bibb wrote an article for the *Voice of the Fugitive* recognizing the contributions of Dolbeare, Coe, and Cook to the school.[10]

James B. Wells, born in Vermont and raised in Ontario County, New York, came to Michigan in 1835. He cleared mostly wild land until he owned a property of 600 acres in Clinton, northeast Lenawee County. An early Presbyterian, Wells joined the Congregational Church in later life. He held strong convictions and participated in local politics. Apparently, Mr. Wells was a man whose opinion was generally respected. Reed described Wells as a "keeper," presumably his word for station keeper. Reed described Harwood and "Ray" as keepers, also.[11]

Fairfield's group followed the Chicago Turnpike through Manchester, Bridgewater, and Saline into Pittsfield Township, arriving before daylight. Fitch Reed wrote that the group stayed at "Ray's place," referring to the farm of black agents Asher and Catherine Aray. They first passed the farms of Underground helpers Harwood and Preston.

As mentioned in the beginning of this book, William Harwood cofounded Ypsilanti before moving to Pittsfield Township. While it was sometimes a hardship for Underground Railroad operators to feed freedom seekers, Harwood could afford it. The value of his Pittsfield property far exceeded that of most, if not all, of his neighbors in 1850: $30,000. Descendants in the area have conflicting reports concerning his contributions to the Underground Railroad.[12]

A Harwood great-granddaughter, Elizabeth Harwood Katz, said she was taken to the basement and shown a place along the stairs where boards concealed a hiding place and she recalled putting her hand into the space near the east end of the house. Katz also remembered a woodshed that connected to the back of the house as another place where self-emancipators were hidden.[13]

Another family member and current owner of the house, Janice Harwood, said her father told her the house was not used to hide freedom seekers. However, in restoring the original farmhouse in 2006, the area described by Mrs. Katz was partially revealed. Behind the fieldstone wall to the basement, a hollow column with an opening through a crawl space was discovered. One or two people would be able to hide within the column out of sight of the busy household.

William Harwood deeded two acres of his land for a Wesleyan Methodist Church and burial grounds in 1836. Later, the frame church was moved away, but the cemetery remains as the resting place for the Harwood and Aray families.[14]

Between the Harwood and Aray farms, a white couple, Mehitable and Roswell Preston, Jr., helped freedom seekers. Often great effort was made to prevent children from seeing people escaping slavery for fear of endangering everyone with capture, imprisonment, or worse. Children who witnessed the rare sight of a group of armed black men and women were left with indelible impressions. One of the Preston children wrote in a family history that "I well remember the terror I felt when I saw one of those burly negros display his sword-cane with its narrow, keen, glittering blade, which was long enough to pierce entirely through the body of a man."

Between the cellar stairs and a crawl space, a compartment could hold one or two people standing upright. William Harwood's son identified the place to his granddaughter (author photograph, Saline, Michigan, 2006).

Initially, the Preston family from Connecticut located in Freedom Township. Roswell Preston, Jr. built a house near his family in Freedom Township and farmed from 1833 to 1845. In the latter year, he purchased an improved farm in Pittsfield Township adjoining the property of Asher and Catherine Aray. Preston was an "avowed abolitionist." In addition to providing an Underground Railroad station, the Prestons offered their wagon and horses to transport those en route to Canada. The improved roads allowed them to travel thirty-five miles from Pittsfield to Detroit in a single night.[15]

Freedom seekers traveled along Michigan Avenue in Pittsfield Township in greater numbers from 1852 to 1856. When detectives were in pursuit, the Prestons offered sustenance and safe hiding. After 1856, the route of travel was changed to avoid troublesome slave hunters. According to the Preston history, several freedom seekers fled to the farm of Jacob Preston in Freedom Township where they were given food and lodging. Jacob Preston shared his brother Roswell's disdain for slavery.[16]

The Prestons are buried in Waters Road Cemetery, also known colloquially as "the cemetery of the unchurched." According to descendants of the family, there had been a church attached to the cemetery that was destroyed by a suspicious fire and was part of a dispute.[17]

Catherine and Asher Aray lived near a few friendly neighbors where their Underground Railroad activity was either applauded or ignored. Jacob Aray died in 1839, leaving his property to his wife, and his children. Asher Aray's farm steadily increased in value, his children attended school, and his eldest son James, became a barber.

Ypsilanti

Between Aray's farm and the terminal Underground Railroad stops along the Detroit River lay Ypsilanti. For at least a decade, the city had a growing black population and an active network helping freedom seekers. Brown Chapel African Methodist Episcopal Church was organized in 1843, the oldest African-American church in Washtenaw County. Brown's founders, Flora Thompson and formerly-enslaved Sylus Jones initially held meetings in their homes. Thompson's home, where most meetings occurred, stood at Ballard and Cross Streets on the northern side of Ypsilanti.[18]

One station, at the home of Elizabeth and (Andrew) Leonard Chase, operated from the 1840s to 1860. Leonard and his twin brother Charles were born in New York to James and Elizabeth Holright Chase on March 31, 1809. The Chase family can be traced to the 1600s, and one of Chase's ancestors operated an Underground Railroad station in New Hampshire. Elizabeth Swift Chase was sister of Marcus Swift, well-known founder of Wesleyan Methodist Churches in the Midwest.

In 1841, Leonard Chase settled on an Ypsilanti village lot that had been divided and sold to John W. Putman in 1839. His property was located within steps of the Ypsilanti train depot, in the second block after River Street, between Mill and Cross Streets.[19]

By 1850, Leonard Chase was 40 years old, employed as a blacksmith, living with his wife and two daughters and numerous others. The household included Nathan Johnson, aged five, black, born in Michigan; the Albert Loomis family of three from the Sandwich Islands; and Adam Delon (Dellon), a 30 year old black farmer from Virginia. Certainly, this was a peculiar living arrangement for the time.

The fact that Chase, a white man, shared his home with African Americans and that he was an avowed abolitionist was public knowledge. His efforts to help people escape to freedom may or may not have been conducted in secrecy. At least one person later remembered the Chase home. Eunice Morton Lambie Hatch recalled that her grandmother used to carry food for freedom seekers to the home of Leonard Chase.[20] Maria Morton carried her baked goods to the Chase home just a few blocks from her house on River Street.[21]

Born free, Asher Aray sheltered and transported 28 former slaves escaping with John Fairfield in 1853. His farm was located on the Chicago Road in Washtenaw County, Michigan (Aray Family File [undated] Ypsilanti Historical Society, Ypsilanti, Michigan).

Shortly after 1850, a radical abolitionist couple moved to Ypsilanti. The journey of Helen and William McAndrew from Scotland to America in 1849 was fraught with discouragements. The moment they landed in New York, William's chest of tools was stolen, forcing the cabinetmaker and his bookbinder wife to adjust their plans. After a brief time in Perth Amboy, New Jersey, the McAndrews moved south to Baltimore, Maryland. While the location seemed promising, the couple got "themselves into trouble teaching Negroes to read." When neighbors and friends objected to a behavior considered "not respectable," Helen and William saved their money to move on. They traveled along canals and by steamer to Detroit, settling for a short time in Rawsonville and, finally, in Ypsilanti.[22]

In 1853–54, William built an octagon-shaped house for his growing family at 105 South Huron Street. In an era when few women finished high school, Helen McAndrew left husband and young son in the care of an African American housekeeper while she earned a medical degree from Trall Institute in New York. Ypsilantians were at first unimpressed with a female doctor, whose clientele was blacks and poor whites. Eventually, Dr. Helen McAndrew earned the respect and admiration of the community for her water cure and other successful medical treatments.

The McAndrews' son, William McAndrew, Jr., described their lives of modest deter-

Michigan Underground Railroad agents posted this notice in Detroit to announce the safe arrival of Fairfield's group of formerly enslaved men and women. The hand-bill, dated April 19, 1853, requested donations of farming tools for the new settlers in Canada (S.F. *History of Detroit* [1890]. Bentley Historical Library, University of Michigan).

mination for social reforms. Their' beliefs in tolerance, temperance, and women's rights were actively pursued through organizing temperance schools, marching in the streets, and helping refugees from bondage. He described his parents' work in the Underground Railroad:

> The McAndrews were forever in the salvage movements of the day. First it was the abolition of Negro slavery. William McAndrew helped hide the runaway Negroes in barns and drove them in wagons at night, covered with loose hay, to the outskirts of Trenton, where rowboats ferried them to Canada.[23]

Sometime during the 1850s, the Chase family moved to Wayne County, near Elizabeth's brother the Rev. Marcus Swift. Leonard Chase earned his living farming and continued to live in an interracial household. In addition to their married daughter Sophia and Sophia's husband James Chase, there were five unrelated members of the household. Only one is listed as other than white in census records, Matthew Johnson, who appeared previously as Nathan Johnson.[24]

Fitch Reed continued to forward people on the Underground Railroad, but had some challenging times keeping freedom seekers out of view. "The next year 1854 — ten came one night, all women and children. And it was nearly morning no time to get to Clinton Station." After breakfast, the women and children hid in the cellar. As long as they were quiet, they could remain there until dark. Unfortunately, Mrs. Reed had an all-day visitor. Fitch Reed hurried off to the home of Mrs. Daniels, of the Wesleyan Methodist Church, to explain the situation. Mrs. Daniels then called on the ladies and invited them both to her house. The family was not exposed and Reed drove them to the next station at dusk.[25]

Chapter Fifteen

Colonization of Canada

Escape of Martha "Grandma" Washington

Martha "Grandma" Washington told the story of her early life and escape to freedom, a story one would not forget. Martha grew up in Virginia. Her grandmother, Mrs. Pamella Caseway, was enslaved in Maryland until she was given to her owner's daughter as a wedding gift. Mrs. Caseway moved with the new bride to the King plantation in Virginia and was freed at the age of 21. Martha's grandmother remained there where the slaves were "treated kindly."

Martha was born on the plantation around 1812. As a young girl, she lived in the main house working as a "nurse girl." Nurse girls played with the children, fed them in the dining room, and slept with them in the nursery. Martha was responsible for the care of Jane King.

When she was twelve, Martha was gathered up with 25 people, including her aunt and uncle, by Virginian John Fairfield, rescuer of thousands, said Levi Coffin. The freedom seekers traveled through Sandusky, Ohio, to Detroit, Michigan, across to Windsor, and ultimately to Colchester, Ontario. The group was carried in a covered wagon pulled by four horses, moving by night and hiding in the day. Martha said railroad workers helped them along the way. As they hid in the attic at one stop Martha spied through cracks the men pursuing them.

Martha married at 16 and, years later, returned to Michigan to settle in Ypsilanti. She recalled knowing of other freedom seekers fleeing through the region. One self-emancipated man had been on his own a year living on nuts and foods he gathered in the woods and sleeping with cows for warmth. By this time, his clothes were worn out and he was nearly frozen, an Underground Railroad conductor found him, provided him with clothing and sent him to Canada.[1]

Throughout the 1850s, many abolitionists despaired that neither moral suasion nor the ballot box could improve race equality or extinguish slavery. Underground Railroad workers stepped up their efforts to help men and women to freedom. Escapes escalated from Missouri and the Mississippi Valley while the flow continued from the South. Remarkably, some self-freed people moved from Canada to Michigan and helped with the Underground Railroad.

Michigan was at the crossroads. Opinions debated among abolitionists and politicians in the East were expressed by the gun in the Western Territories. William Lloyd Garrison attempted to redirect energy into a new Michigan antislavery society; the Free Soil Party succumbed to a new party. After the Supreme Court's Dred Scott decision eliminated possible compromise regarding slavery, the country was headed toward disunion or war.

Tide of Travel

Major newspapers from New York to Chicago now used the term "Underground Railroad" and described the organized arrangements in places throughout the country conveying a stream of people to Canada. Writers observed the operation and noted that the freedom seekers were armed and had a great deal of assistance. In one case, two women helped a man to freedom. The writer suggested facetiously, that in order to preserve the Union, it might be wise to root the humanity out of the hearts of the masses.[2]

George DeBaptiste said that since the passing of the Fugitive Slave Act, a larger business was never done on the Underground Railroad at Detroit. DeBaptiste announced that eight or nine passengers arrived at the Detroit station a day. "The Underground Railroad and especially the express train is doing a good business just now." On one occasion, 39 came together. "Thus are the plans of the wicked defeated, and the cause of COLONIZATION in Canada progresses."[3]

In 1853, Congress passed a bill creating the Nebraska Territory, soon followed by splitting that land to create the Kansas Territory. Northerners rushed to settle Kansas and clashed with proslavery Missourians. A Chicago paper reported that the Underground Railroad made improvements after the Nebraska bill passed.[4]

The proslavery Detroit newspaper offered a sort of rebuttal in a story reprinted from the *Richmond Enquirer*. The Virginia newspaper claimed that two self-emancipators fled to Ohio two years previously and returned voluntarily to Virginia for want of food and work. The assessment was that, "while they maintain underground routes of transportation, they do not keep good taverns at the end of the road."[5]

Arthur Power from Farmington had visited Windsor, Canada, at that time and found conditions were indeed very poor. By 1853, Bibb and Detroit benefactors contributed to the Refugee Home Society's finances for building improvements and supplies. Laura Haviland continued to teach at the school, as she was doing when Fairfield arrived in 1853. Levi and Catherine Coffin visited Henry and Mary Bibb's settlement in the summer of 1854. The Coffins encountered numerous people they had assisted doing Underground Railroad work and were hard-pressed to remember so many names."[6]

Assessing the number of people who escaped to Michigan and Canada between 1850 and 1860 is difficult. Southerners provided different numbers depending on whether it was advantageous to minimize the problem or attempt to gain new legislation to stanch the bleeding. Generally, southerners described the loss as value of property, rather than numbers of human beings. Historian Siebert's population-based count of slave losses, showed around 1,000 escaped in both 1850 and 1860. The number seems low based on population increases in northern states and Canada.

Some observations can be made based on general population trends. Between 1850 and 1860, the Northern states that gained a black population were primarily Ohio, Michigan, and Illinois — the three states that offered easy travel to Canada and a history of Underground Railroad activity. Estimates of the "fugitive slaves" in Canada ranged from fifteen thousand to a figure of forty thousand reported by the *Provincial Freeman*, a Canadian black newspaper on November 24, 1855.[7]

The same newspaper recognized that the border was very open, especially in Detroit, and people crossed back into America for jobs and rescues. Benjamin Drew introduced the concept of the "fluid border," to describe men like William Lyons, working for two years in Amherstburg, Canada, while his family lived in Detroit, Michigan.[8] It was not uncommon for people to return to America as they headed south to rescue their families, as represented by Henry Bibb and John White. In one case, a sixty year old woman fled to Canada and then went back for her children. She carefully hid until she had gathered up seven children and grandchildren. The family nearly starved on the return journey north until they were discovered by Underground Railroad agents.[9]

While the settlement of blacks in Canada after 1850 was documented, there was a reverse migration to Michigan. For now, some individual accounts must suffice as evidence of a reverse settlement in southeast Michigan after the passage of the 1850 Fugitive Slave Act. A study of the Michigan's 1860 census in the next chapter will help in understanding whether these cases represented a trend.

William Walker was sold to a "humane" gentleman in Missouri but could no longer endure enslavement. He was haunted by the terrible abuse he suffered while in bondage on the Purgoo plantation in Louisiana. Walker planned his escape from Missouri for a year, and early in June 1859, he and John Harris left. They paddled on the Missouri River in their "master's" rowboat for thirty miles before daybreak. After a month's travel, only at night, the men reached St. Louis, Missouri, and then crossed into Illinois. Another week of nightly walking wore the men out. They stopped at a small village where the men worked the summer harvest season, were fed, and paid wages.

After leaving Illinois, the pair traveled by train across Michigan to reach Canada on August 8. In spite of his fear of slavery, Walker chose to return to Detroit where he was employed by abolitionist John J. Bagley. Bagley recommended Walker to James F. Joy, whose farm lay four miles northwest of the city. After two years, Walker purchased ten acres of land. John Harris, his fellow traveler, found his mother and stayed with her in Windsor.[10]

Another person returned to Michigan and settled in the place where he had been sheltered on the Underground Railroad. William Davis was one of the freedom seekers who passed through Jotham Goodell's Underground Railroad station in Superior Township, Washtenaw County. Davis had moved to Canada, but by 1860, was living in his own house near the Goodells with two daughters, Mary Jane and Sarah Jane.[11]

After the 1850 Fugitive Slave Act, the George and Milly McCoy family moved from Ontario to Ypsilanti, Michigan. Initially, the family settled on the farm of Mary Ann and John Starkweather, northwest of the city. A steam railroad track ran along the rugged banks of the Huron River, passing through their land. The connection between the McCoys and Starkweathers is unknown. It is possible Mary Ann and John Starkweather hired McCoy to harvest their orchards. It is possible that Edwin and Harriet deGarmo Fuller, living next door, facilitated the McCoy's move to Ypsilanti. The Fullers were cofounders of the reorganized Michigan Anti-Slavery Society in the 1850s.

George McCoy resumed the business of growing tobacco and making cigars. He also purchased tobacco and made regular trips to Wyandotte and Detroit. Daughter Anna began to suspect her parents were engaged in more than the cigar business. One time she spied a black family in her barn and wanted to play with the three little girls she had seen. Milly McCoy kept Anna away from the children lest she reveal their presence and jeopardize everyone's safety. Thinking she could find them the next day, "Anna hunted for them all through the hay and other places in the barn." She was sadly disappointed and unaware that her father had slipped them away during the night.

One of Anna's jobs was to retrieve letters from the post office. On the days a letter came from John Hatfield of Cincinnati, her mother baked a large batch of bread, cooked hams, made coffee, put the children to bed early, and saw her husband off on a trip in his wagon. These curious incidents led to Anna's awareness of her parents' participation in the Underground Railroad. Anna described Mr. Hatfield as "a colored man from Cincinnati." This was likely John Hatfield, African American Deacon in the Zion Baptist Church in Cincinnati and Underground Railroad associate of Levi Coffin. Deacon Hatfield aided the escape of the Fairfield group that stayed at the Asher and Catherine Aray farm in Pittsfield Township in 1853, as described in Chapter 14.[12]

Interestingly, another man named John Hatfield wrote of his experiences helping freedom seekers during his service as a barber on a steamboat from New Orleans to Cincinnati. In Cincinnati, he said he harbored as many as fifteen and twenty seven at a time.[13]

As she grew up, Anna learned that her father transported refugees from bondage in a covered wagon with a false floor. William Lambert described, from his days in Virginia, using false-bottomed wagons in the South. Quaker Levi Coffin's wagon had a hidden compartment in the front portion of the box, just behind the driver. Bags of grains or hay piled in front and atop the compartment provided cover. The tobacco wagon was very heavy and cumbersome, with a deep box, curving up at both ends and hauled by six horses. Both types of wagons required hidden freedom seekers to crouch or lie in a suffocatingly small space for a painful journey on pitted or 'corduroy' roads, made up of log planks that would have thrown a body against the wagon boards. George McCoy's cigars, shielding the human cargo, were unloaded after stops at Underground Railroad stations, including one overseen by a black man in Wyandotte. The unidentified helpers sometimes put the refugees on the *Pearl*, and they were carried to Canada.[14]

When Anna's brother George was of an age to assist, the McCoys used two wagons and two sets of horses. In Anna's words, "When the case was urgent the fast horses were always used."[15] From the Starkweather Farm, McCoy could travel on Leforge Road to Geddes Road. Traveling east on Geddes, he passed the farms of conductors Jotham Goodell and Fowler along the southern part of Superior Township, at the intersection of Ridge Road. The eastern and northern paths met where the road led to Wayne County, Detroit, the Detroit River, and Canada.

Anna McCoy's recollections indicate McCoy shared a link in Deacon Hatfield to the Wesleyan Methodist network of Ohio and Southeast Michigan. Clearly, Detroit was not the only terminal station in Michigan, as Trenton and Wyandotte were mentioned.[16] Wyandotte may have been an ideal crossing place where a large parcel was owned but not occupied by Detroiter Major John Biddle. Biddle sold the property in 1854 to Captain Eber Ward, wealthy abolitionist from St. Clair, Michigan. Anna McCoy recalled the Wyandotte agent was named Bush.

George and Milly likely met while living near each other in Taylor Port, Boone County, near Louisville, Kentucky. Families by the name of McCoy and Gaines, both black and white, were found there in 1860. According to Anna McCoy, her mother went back to her old home and met with Mrs. Gaines. Mrs. McCoy was invited to stay permanently, but graciously declined. She had her own home in Ypsilanti and many children to keep her company.[17]

Daughter Anna McCoy sometimes delivered letters from Deacon Hatfield to the Prescotts.[18] The Prescotts have not been identified, but their cabin was on, or near, the Starkweather property. Mrs. Prescott taught school for black children in her home, where Anna McCoy was a pupil.[19] John and Mary Ann Starkweather lived in a simple 1840 Greek Revival–style clapboard house on Huron River Drive from 1841 until 1875 (still extant). By the 1860s, the Starkweathers increased their original holding of 160 acres to 400 acres, including a Michigan award-winning orchard.[20]

The Starkweathers first appear in antislavery records in the 1850s, after the state antislavery society was reorganized by their neighbors Harriet deGarmo Fuller and her husband Edwin. In the surviving record books of the Michigan Anti-Slavery Society, Mary Jane [*sic*] Starkweather pledged a donation in 1854.[21]

It may be that the trend of relocation from Canada to Michigan began in the late 1840s. As mentioned earlier, farming conditions were not as favorable in some of the settlements. The David Gordon family that was nearly kidnapped moved to Ohio, Canada, then Michigan. This pattern is shown by the birthplaces of the children. In the late 1840s, when the Gordons moved to a farm in Augusta Township, south of Ypsilanti, they were not the only black family in the area. Albert Cummings, an African American farmer, followed a similar pattern of migration, moving from an unknown state of birth to Canada and then Michigan by 1850. Both men were heads of their households. William Jurst, born in 1812 in Virginia, moved to Ohio, Canada and then Michigan. There is no record of the Gordons or Jursts in Washtenaw County after the attempted kidnapping.[22]

Another person who moved from Canada to Michigan in the late 1850s was John White, formerly enslaved as Felix White, who had escaped with help from the Watkins family and Laura Haviland. After his unsuccessful attempt to rescue his wife and his subsequent kidnapping, White remained in Canada. He recovered from the death of his first wife, Jane, and started a new family. His wife Mary and two children accompanied him to Livonia in Wayne County, where he worked as a landowning farmer. In 1860, his daughter was in school, and his wife was home with a son born in Canada West and an infant born on American soil.[23]

Uncle Tom's Cabin

For decades, antislavery activists funded tracts and slave narratives in order to persuade people to join the cause. A strong anti-abolition sentiment existed in the Northwest Territory states, including Michigan, in the early 1850s. A March 17, 1853, article in Detroit's *Daily Free Press*, cited in the previous chapter, expressed some commonly held views. The newspaper claimed white and black people could not "mix on terms of equality," and the black settlers in Michigan could not overcome existing prejudices.[24]

Into this world of racial intolerance, a book of fiction, by a woman, astonished abolitionists by its popularity and effect. No previous work had mass appeal comparable to Harriet Beecher Stowe's work of fiction, *Uncle Tom's Cabin*. Published in 1852, the book focused on the breakup of slave families. Within a year, *Uncle Tom's Cabin* had sold 300,000 copies, breaking book sales records.[25]

A man named Barber described the reaction to *Uncle Tom's Cabin* in Vermontville, Michigan, in Eaton County. The town was settled by a colony of people united by a dislike of slavery and a commitment to the preservation of the Union, above all else. For decades, the two or three abolitionists in the place were political outcasts. Dr. Robert C. Kedzie arrived in the anti-abolition town of Vermontville voicing fiery antislavery opinions. Kedzie and his wife, Harriet Eliza Fairchild, were graduates of Oberlin College. Oberlin graduate Almon Thompson, who moved to Vermontville to partner in the medical practice of Dr. Kedzie, joined the Kedzies. Those three represented the abolitionists of Vermontville. At least, until the publication of *Uncle Tom's Cabin*.

After the townspeople shared a single copy of *Uncle Tom's Cabin*, a change came over the people. Barber, the writer, observed that no "other book of this century had so remark-

UNCLE TOM'S CABIN

or, Life Among the Lowly

BY

HARRIET BEECHER STOWE

AUTHOR OF

"The Minister's Wooing," Etc.

WITH FOUR ILLUSTRATIONS

NEW YORK

A. L. BURT COMPANY, PUBLISHERS

Uncle Tom's Cabin touched the hearts of Americans previously indifferent to the inhumanity of slavery. *Uncle Tom's Cabin*, Young People's Edition, undated.

able an influence in moulding public opinion and in controlling the thoughts and actions of all classes of people." From Lansing to Detroit, Barber witnessed an incredible transformation. "So rapid was the progress of events that, in 1856, Willard Davis, the despised abolitionist of 1852, was nominated for representative of the Western district of Eaton County and Henry A. Shaw of Eaton Rapids for the eastern district. Both were elected."[26]

Two years before *Uncle Tom's Cabin* was published, Sojourner Truth's narrative was released. Truth proved to be a popular speaker, touring New England states for several years. As a member of a Spiritualist Church, Truth met Henry Willis, Giles and Catherine Stebbins, and other prominent Michigan abolitionists who visited New York. Henry Willis invited Sojourner Truth to Battle Creek to speak at the October 1856 Michigan Friends of Human Progress meeting. Within a year, Truth moved to the Spiritualist community of Harmonia, near Battle Creek.

Garrison, October, 1853

On Oct. 3, 1853, William Lloyd Garrison left Boston to begin a tour of the west, with Michigan of special importance. Garrison arrived in Adrian and was met by Thomas Chandler, brother of Elizabeth Chandler, founder of Michigan's first antislavery society. National antislavery lecturers, Marius Robinson, Sallie Holley, and Caroline Putnam, called for a visit. In a letter to his wife, Garrison wrote that he spent an hour at the grave of Chandler's sis-

Left: Sketch of Eliza escaping on the frozen river (frontispiece. H.B.S., *Uncle Tom's Cabin* [1851]). *Right:* Sojourner Truth moved to Battle Creek, Michigan, in 1857 (Carte de visite [1864]. Library of Congress, LC-USZC4–6165 (3–11b)).

ter, Elizabeth. "To me it was hallowed ground, and while standing there, I renewed my pledge of fidelity to the causes of the enslaved while life continues."

Garrison left Adrian for Marshall, with a stop in Jonesville. He thought both places very attractive, and admired Marshall's "delightful promenade" of plank sidewalks. Garrison waited in the hotel from late afternoon until midnight for the train. He wrote, "There are no abolitionists in the place." Had the men and women who defended the Crosswhites just a few years earlier left town? Numerous blacks remained in the city. Charles Gorham and George Ingersoll, who participated in the Crosswhite escape, were still in Marshall. Garrison left for Battle Creek where he stayed with Chandler's wife's parents, Joseph and Phoebe Merritt who were Quakers.

The halls and churches in Battle Creek were closed to him except the Friend's meetinghouse. Garrison wrote, "There has been considerable antislavery work done here by Henry G. Wright, Parker Pillsbury, Stephen S. Foster, James W. Walker, and other efficient laborers; but not much impression has been made upon the place owing to the strength of religious bigotry...." The people he named had only recently lectured in Battle Creek, while Hussey, Beckley, and Bibb had paved the way years earlier. He dined with Henry Willis, "an outspoken abolitionist, but a man without any influence." Garrison gave two lectures to an overflowing and receptive crowd and later wrote that he "was listened to with profound attention for two hours. A very favorable impression appears to have been made."[27]

In a second letter from Michigan to his wife, Garrison described his experience in Detroit. The city of 30,000, then comparable to Cleveland, impressed him greatly. Garrison, traveling with Marius Robinson, expected a hall to be prepared for him by Stephen and Abby Kelley Foster who had lectured with Sallie Holley in Detroit just days before his arrival. But, no halls were available. In fact, Steven and Abby Foster had received bad reports in the Detroit newspapers. Garrison was peeved that no one met them at the depot or offered any hospitality. Neither Garrison nor Marius Robinson knew anyone in the city. The men stayed at Seymour Finney's Temperance Hotel and, on Sunday, crossed over to Windsor, Canada, to see Henry Bibb. Apparently, like many other visitors, Garrison was unaware that Seymour Finney was a pronounced abolitionist and may have had self-emancipators in his barn during Garrison's stay.

Garrison found the Canadian village rude and impoverished and Bibb's house "inferior" (Bibb's printing office had been completely destroyed the previous week) and observed the black French Canadians attending the Catholic Church. Garrison and Robinson walked to Sandwich where they viewed the barracks and settlement but had no time to converse with anyone. Upon returning to Detroit, Garrison was invited to lecture in the evening at an African American Methodist church.[28]

Garrison's lecturing in Ann Arbor and Ypsilanti appeared in the *Liberator* of December 2, 1853. He left Detroit with Marius Robinson traveling 40 miles to the thriving village of 3,000 souls in Ypsilanti. Garrison spoke for an hour and a half and was followed by Robinson's "well-timed remarks." The following morning the men went to Ann Arbor, which Garrison described as "a county seat, and full of sectarianism and pro-slavery." Garrison's impression improved after he was warmly received at a "crowded meeting in the Court House, where he spoke for two hours."[29]

Garrison's general observations were unfairly influenced by the treatment he received in Michigan, as only the Quaker contingent embraced him on his travel through the state. Michigan's antislavery leaders may have been away attending meetings in New York. Or, perhaps, they resented the appearance of the Bostonian on the scene decades after they had struggled to introduce abolitionism to the masses. The prominent antislavery men of Michigan supported ending slavery through the ballot box, a tactic Garrison continued to challenge.

Garrison professed the United States Constitution was pro-slavery, and before 1850 was supported by Frederick Douglass, one of the nation's foremost orators. But, soon after that year, Douglass modified his opinion and came to see the Constitution as an antislavery document. Douglass merged his newspaper, the *North Star* with Gerrit Smith's Liberty Party paper. The newspaper was in competition with Garrison's *National Anti-Slavery Standard* and the divide between the Utica, New York, antislavery group led by Gerrit Smith, with Weld and the Tappans in the background, and Garrison grew ever wider.[30]

Michigan Anti-Slavery Society, Adrian, October 1853

Following the lectures in Ann Arbor, Garrison returned to Adrian for the Michigan Anti-Slavery Society convention. It appears that Garrison and others stayed in the Illenden home in Adrian. Richard Illenden moved to Ypsilanti in 1844, but after marrying Mary Rulon, the couple relocated to Adrian Township in 1854. Illenden remained a member of the Methodist Episcopal church until the issue of slavery caused his switch to the Wesleyan Church. Richard Illenden's mother was disowned by her church upon becoming a convert of John Wesley. His radical views of slavery led to his giving up on all churches. He was the treasurer of the reorganized Michigan Anti-Slavery Society. William Lloyd Garrison and other prominent abolitionists stayed at his house in Adrian. His wife's parents, Sarah and Ephraim Rulon were Hicksite Quakers who "did all they could to help on the cause of freedom" from their home in Adrian Township.[31]

Though similar in name to the original antislavery society, this one was distinctly different. The new antislavery organization was founded on Garrisonian, non-violent, non-political radical abolition of slavery by social reform. Women and men were equal partners in the State Central Committee, the executive committee. Harriet DeGarmo Fuller (neighbor of the Starkweathers in Ypsilanti), Cynthia Walton, and Sophia Volland served as vice presidents. Most members were birthright Quakers, including the Chandlers, Glaziers, Waltons, Merritts, and Fullers.

Their convention assembled at the Old Fellows Hall in Adrian on October 22, 1853. Thomas Chandler was chosen president while Jacob Walton served on the business committee with William Lloyd Garrison, Marius Robinson, and Stephen Foster. Laura Haviland and Giles Stebbins attended the convention. Over the next several months, Stephen and Abby Kelly Foster and Sallie Holley lectured in Michigan and collected donations. The organization of radical abolitionists remained small but active for several years. The group refused affiliation with churches that accepted slaveholders and made increasingly strident resolutions, such as, declaring the American Union a total failure and calling for separation from slaveholding states.[32]

Society organizers collected significant donations and pledges in 1853 and 1854, however, by 1856, the expenses of sending out lecturers exhausted the available funds. The last recorded meeting, January 1857, was held at the home of Richard B. Glazier, son of Ann Arbor's pioneer Glazier and brother of Robert Glasier. The Glaziers, Fullers, Waltons, Vollands, Havilands, and Laphams, who supported the reorganized society, were linked by numerous marriages and the Quaker faith. The same families were allied through networks between Adrian, Ann Arbor, and Farmington to help those escaping to freedom.

Captain John Lowry spoke before the Michigan Anti-Slavery Society in 1854 on the subject of the United States Constitution and the fact that its provisions of justice, common defense, and general welfare were no longer being upheld because of antislavery laws. Captain Lowry must have made a strong impression for the committee passed a resolution stating "we do not rely on the government to abolish slavery." This was followed by another resolution to focus efforts to end slavery by changing public sentiment. Captain Lowry facilitated these efforts by making a very substantial contribution of $25.00. This was more than double the donation of committee members, such as Robert Glazier. Perry Sanford, formerly enslaved, pledged $5.00.[33] The pacifist Quakers would have been shocked to learn William Garrison was clandestinely meeting with and funding John Brown's army at the same time.

In January 1854, Senator Stephen Douglas of Illinois introduced a bill that divided the land west of Missouri into two territories, Kansas and Nebraska. Ignoring the terms of the 1820 Missouri Compromise outlawing slavery in that territory, the proposed bill would allow the settlers of the new territories to decide if slavery would be legal.

After months of debate, the Kansas-Nebraska Act passed on May 30, 1854. Pro-slavery and antislavery settlers rushed to Kansas, each side hoping to determine the results of the first election held after the law went into effect. Men from the south invaded the unorganized territories with their enslaved workers, while emigration societies were formed at the North to send free-state men into the same territory. Each side was determined to affect the results of the first election. The pro and antislavery factions fought by words and actions. A Chicago paper reported that the Underground Railroad made improvements after the Nebraska bill.[34]

Antislavery workers in Kansas and Nebraska called for Underground Railroad agents to move west. "Slaveholders have organized to stop its operations, and more Conductors should be put on — should be regularly employed and paid fair wages." Two months later another article appeared in Canada's *Provincial Freeman* describing the "steady stream" of freedom seekers not only from the south, but the north and west.[35]

Dred Scott

The Dred Scott case reached the United States Supreme Court in 1857, a full decade after a series of appeals and court reversals. Scott, enslaved in Missouri, was taken with his wife, Harriet, and two daughters, by his "master" into the free state of Illinois and territory of Wisconsin. Scott's suit argued that as a resident of free regions, he was free. Scott's first lawsuit for his freedom was filed in 1847.

In an 1850 retrial, Scott and his family were freed by the St. Louis Circuit Court; however, two years later, the Missouri Supreme Court reversed the decision. Scott brought the case to federal court. Michigan had a connection to the case before the landmark trial. An attorney named Lyman Decatur Norris, from Ypsilanti and the first graduate of the University of Michigan, opposed Scott in an early trial.[36] Norris sympathized with Scott's "pitiful condition," but expressed no opposition to slavery. In a letter to his mother in 1852, Norris wrote that he offered an arrangement to Scott, in which Norris would buy him and his family, and Scott could work off the debt in two years. Norris failed to grasp the misery of an existence as property, rather than a human being.

Norris wrote to his mother that Dred Scott had grown thin and anxious during the trial. Norris won the case and was pleased to see that after his return to slavery, Scott appeared well fed and happy. "I admit he is in a poor state of existence but that is not his fault or his Masters—There he must remain, a happy and contented slave, than a poor squalid, disturbed free negro...."[37] Norris' view was not atypical in America, though it would have been very unacceptable to his grandfather. Justus Norris was an early and influential pioneer in Ypsilanti who was strongly antislavery.

In 1857, the United States Supreme Court decided to settle the debate over slavery in the western territories. In a 7–2 vote, the court ruled that Congress had no power to keep slavery out of any territory. African Americans, whether they were enslaved or free, could not sue in federal courts because they were not citizens, but property. The court ruled that property rights of the slaveholder followed enslaved people no matter where they traveled or resided.[38]

The case dealt a severe blow to the abolitionist cause and to free African Americans. Black leaders, uncertain of their identity in America, debated whether to encourage emigration to foreign countries. Many were unwilling to abandon the millions still enslaved. Men like Asher Aray were born free of free men in Colonial America, and now their future was uncertain.[39]

It appeared to some that only a large slave rebellion or war would crush the institution of slavery. Slaveholders considered the Dred Scott court victory a catalyst to renew efforts to drive free blacks from the South. Free blacks undermined their arguments that black people were inferior. Free blacks, who attained an education, lived independently, and accumulated wealth, threatened the stability of the slave system. Debates about expulsion in Virginia, North Carolina and Missouri, impelled many free black people to move north. These immigrants mingled with the self-emancipators arriving in Michigan in droves.[40]

After the decision, Dred and Harriet Scott were returned to slavery but were soon freed by a new "owner." They lived in St. Louis, Missouri, where Dred Scott died "in dire poverty" in 1858. Harriet Scott died shortly before the Civil War. Lyman Decatur Norris settled in Ypsilanti and later moved to Grand Rapids, Michigan.

War of the Knights and Orders

As described in an earlier chapter, secret societies met in St. Louis, Detroit and other cities from the 1840s. The eleven men who led the Knights and Daughters of Liberty with Chairperson Moses Dickson worked in the South recruiting and stockpiling weapons. In Michigan, the Mysteries organization improved the road to freedom. William Lambert described sending white men to live in "convenient" places. he confirmed that many of the men in the order had wealth and influence, necessary for bail and legal representation.

It appears that John Brown's League of Gileadites was not part of the international Order of Knights and learned of the Orders in 1858. George R. Gill, a member of John Brown's inner circle, referred in his diary to a secret order after attending a meeting of the African-American Mysteries in Detroit. Afterwards, Gill met a black man named Reynolds in Sandusky City, Ohio, who showed him the secret society's meeting place. Gill viewed a "fine collection of 'arms.'" Reynolds then sent Gill through the "Order" in Ohio to J. J. Pierce at Milard, then E. Moore at Norwalk and on to Cleveland. The men of the Order at each of these locations paid all Gill's expenses. Gill told Realf that the Orders learned about John Brown's plans through Mr. Reynolds. For this reason, John Brown postponed his plans to attack Harpers Ferry.[41]

Moses Dickson published after the Civil War, a book called "A Manual of Tabor, and Daughters of the Tabernacle, Including the Ceremonies of the Order, Constitutions, Installations, Dedications, and Funerals, with Forms, and the Taborian Drill and Tactics." The lengthy book is filled with detailed illustrations and rules. According to Dickson, thousands of men and women memorized the words and histories to become initiated into the Order. "These men, with their aides, formed organizations in all the Slave States, except Missouri and Texas. Silently, like the falling of Autumn leaves, the organizations multiplied, until, in 1856, the army of true and trusty men numbered forty-seven thousand, two hundred and forty Knights of Liberty."[42] Moses Dickson hesitated. The war would result in terrible bloodshed and he prayed for guidance.

The call finally came in July 1857. By this time, the army had grown to "at least 150,000 well-armed men. As the men and women armed themselves to wreak havoc on the South in order to break slavery's shackles, Moses Dickson told his army to stand down." Dickson wrote that his decision involved divine intervention and his own sense of timing. Dickson's reasons may have involved the activities of John Brown. Reynolds told Gill that the military men were "waiting for Brown or someone else to make a successful initiative move when their forces would be put in motion."

Dickson wrote, "At the end of this time, however, owing to the change in conditions in the North and the South, it was decided to change the plan of operation. From that time on the Knights became actively connected with the Underground Railroad, and it was claimed that they assisted yearly thousands of slaves to escape." After the Civil War, Dickson changed the purpose of the organization to one of benevolence: Temple and Tabernacle of the Knights and Daughters of Tabor, established 1871. The group had over 50,000 members around 1900.[43]

John Brown did not envision a natural end of slavery as Dickson had, and pursued his secret plan to attack Harpers Ferry. Brown's men stated they resisted proslavery forces in Kansas, though it was reported that they instigated deadly exchanges. A Michigan man, the Rev. Paul Shepherd, befriended one of Brown's army, John Kagi, while Kagi was in jail. Shepherd wrote that he knew the proslavery forces in Kansas attempted to lynch Kagi in order to stop his writing articles for the press. the Reverend Shepherd learned of Brown's "enterprise" [attack on Harpers Ferry] in the summer of 1857 from Kagi, but none of the particulars.[44]

Steady Business

Underground Railroad diaries and records describe increased activity during the final years preceding the start of war. Self-emancipators arrived singly or in large groups. In a rare letter between Underground Railroad workers, Frederick Douglass wrote to Maria Porter of Rochester on October 13, 1857.

> Miss Porter, William Oborne came to us last night from slavery. He looks fully able to take care of himself, but being destitute, he needs for the present, a little assistance to get to Canada — $2.50 will be quite sufficient. Yours Truly, Frederick Douglass.[45]

In his diary, Dr. Nathan Thomas wrote that George McDeary escaped from bondage to William Bradley of Madison County, Kentucky in 1856. Seven young men left together and were joined by two others who had had a later start. McDeary, aged 21, led the group. Two of those from Bradley were captured in Kentucky, one was captured in Indiana, but the rest made it through to freedom in Michigan.[46]

Giles Stebbins, faithful antislavery agent, stayed at the home of Richard Glazier in 1858.

The Glazier farm lay two miles east of the city of Ann Arbor. Stebbins described the Quaker preacher as a man "of positive will, just and true, and of remarkable personal weight of character. He had a direct and searching way of appealing to the moral intuitions that disarmed all prejudice." Stebbins was impressed by Glazier's earnest appeals to merchants for money to help freedom seekers.

> He approached a man of well-known proslavery views, and said to him: "I have a black man at my house, who has fled from a bad master and wants his liberty. I am satisfied his case is genuine. In thy heart thee is not a man who wants any human being oppressed or badly treated. I want thee to help this poor man." The help was readily given, by him and others like him, whom no one else would have thought of asking.[47]

Elizabeth Rous married John T. Comstock in 1858, moving from a Quaker community in Ontario to Rollin, Michigan, where they created a new station on the Underground Railroad. The first person to seek refuge in her house was Lucy, a tall, light-skinned woman with an infant in her arms. The Comstocks then placed the mother and child in the care of an agent who could escort her by stage to Sandusky, Ohio. Upon arriving at the station, Lucy spied a posting offering $1,200 for her and her child. The agent hid her until they could take the train to Detroit.

At the depot, Lucy waited in the baggage car after they encountered the same reward poster and problem. The escort traveled into the city and found a helper who brought a carriage to transport Lucy to his house. After several days, Lucy agreed to cut her beautiful ringlets in order to disguise herself as a young porter. The couple protecting Lucy carried her baby aboard a steamer taking the four of them across the Detroit River to Canada. Incredibly, Lucy's former "master" watched from the wharf as they steamed to freedom. When she stepped onto Canadian soil, Lucy fell to the earth to kiss the ground and ask God to bless Queen Victoria.

This is not the end of Lucy's story. After three years, she returned to the Comstock's home asking for help. Over that short time, Lucy provided for herself and her daughter by doing laundry and sewing, and she managed to save $375 to purchase her husband's freedom. The Comstocks learned Lucy was short of the $600 she needed and a collection was taken at the Friends meeting and in the neighborhood until there was sufficient money reunite the family.[48]

Another woman named Lucy arrived in Michigan about the same time. Lucy Millard was white, but looking for the man she had fallen in love with who was black. Lucy Millard lived in Oakland County, Michigan, until 1853. At that time her mother died and her father took the family to Missouri. Lucy's father, Solomon Nelson Millard of Rhode Island, was an abolitionist and encouraged his daughters to be kind to the enslaved people working on the Missouri prairies. One such person was Isaac Berry, who drove a team of oxen as a sodbuster and could hire out to neighbors like Solomon Millard.

The Millard girls were allowed to attend dances where Isaac Berry played the fiddle. Isaac Berry, born into slavery in Garrard County, Kentucky, in 1811, was sent with his mother and siblings to Missouri in a property settlement. Berry was one of about 100,000 humans enslaved as chattel just before 1860 in Missouri.[49] And, like many others, Berry planned to escape. He arranged passage across the Mississippi River, but was foiled by high water. By chance, he was able to pay a family to cross him over to Quincy, Illinois. Berry followed railroad tracks on a three week journey to freedom. When he arrived in Ypsilanti, Michigan, a local black man offered help.

Berry spent the day in Ypsilanti, where he was provided clothing and money and connections to the Underground Railroad. Aware that a Missouri slaveholder named Pratt followed him, Berry passed through Detroit, to settle in Canada. Meanwhile Lucy Millard, Solomon Millard's daughter, devised a plan to see Berry. When sent east to go to school, Lucy took a detour to Michigan. In Detroit, while working in a shirt factory, Lucy learned that most freedom seekers were in Canada. The young woman moved across the Detroit River where she worked by day and searched for Berry at night. Eventually, she found him playing music in a dance hall and the couple reunited. After their marriage in August 1859, the newlyweds moved to Puce, Ontario to start a family.

Apparently, Lucy's family refused to accept the interracial marriage and at that time, many states had laws preventing interracial marriages. In 1877, the Berry family moved to a multi-racial settlement in Mecosta County, Michigan.[50] Berry's escape to Michigan was one of many originating in western states.

John Evans was the child of an interracial couple, a white planter and enslaved woman. When the state of Georgia enacted laws expelling free blacks, James Evans, his wife and four children moved to Indiana. John moved to Michigan after the death of his father, where he engaged in barbering for several decades in Battle Creek.[51]

A Virginian named C. W. Thompson escaped via the Underground Railroad from a cruel "master" in Richmond, Virginia. Thompson spent two years in Pittsburgh, before settling in Detroit in 1854.[52] A couple escaped from Kentucky to Saline, Washtenaw County, in 1858. Beverly Johnson and his wife changed their names to James and Mary Williams. James Williams took up cigar-making, as that was his expertise in Kentucky, and later became a farmer.[53] The increased migration of self-emancipators from western states and the continued flow of southerners resulted in Michigan's becoming a pivotal freedom frontier for settlement and passage to Canada.

Chapter Sixteen

The Year of John Brown

Escape of the Monroe Family

A woman in bondage dreaded the news that her children were about to be sold. They would be placed upon the auction block, inspected and put up for bidding. Young women often commanded a high price. Mrs. Monroe had 10 daughters, aged six to 19 and learned they were about to be sold. There was no time to plan. She would rely on her grown son's knowledge of a path through Boone County, Kentucky, to the Ohio River. She would have the girls ready to leave at nightfall. The harvest moon would light the way.

Over three nights they walked 40 miles and then found a boat for crossing the mighty Ohio. On the northern shore, the Monroe females hid in the forest while the young man ferreted out sympathizers in New Richmond. Fortunately, it was a place with a black population and Underground Railroad agents. A reward of $2,000 ignited slave-hunters to join the slave owner's search for the Monroes. Under the protection of Underground Railroad agents, the family was conveyed in wagons under a covering of straw from station to station. The slave-owner heard Ann Arbor was a known stop on the way to Detroit and traveled there in advance of the Monroes. There the man who claimed them as property lay in wait.

Ann Arbor friends must have been on the lookout, for they quickly put the Monroes on a train and escorted them to Detroit. The family arrived just in time to catch the steamboat "Argo." As the ferry set sail, the slave-owner raced down Jefferson Avenue calling "stop" to the amusement of passersby.

The Rev. William Troy met Mrs. Monroe in Windsor and helped secure a house and food for the family. Though landed safely on British soil, Mrs. Monroe mourned the loss of friends in Kentucky. She was a stranger in a foreign land. Her girls were safe. With the strength of will that brought them on this journey, Mrs. Monroe faced the daunting task of providing for her large family.[1]

The annual report of the American Anti-Slavery Society, for the year ending May 1, 1860, bore the unique title "The Anti-Slavery History of the John Brown Year." The events surrounding the Harpers Ferry Raid in West Virginia engrossed the attention of the country. Every national political and economic issue involved the question of slavery. The population of the United States surged to 31 million. That figure included nearly 4 million people enslaved by race. A fraction of that number escaping to freedom, kept the Underground Railroad operating at full capacity. This activity added to the growing tension over the instability of the nation. In 1860, Republican Abraham Lincoln won the presidential election, having stated an opposition to slavery but no plan to interfere with slavery in the southern states.[2]

In June 1859, the *Detroit (Mich.) Advertiser* reported, "seventy Fugitive Slaves arrived in Canada, by one train, from the interior of Tennessee. A week before, a company of twelve arrived. Nearly the same time, one of seven, and another of five, safely landed on the free soil of Canada, making ninety-four in all. The Underground Railroad was never before doing so flourishing a business."[3]

Some self-emancipators in 1859 were prevented from completing their journey to Michigan because of kidnappings in Illinois and Ohio. The first occurred on September 12, when a man was grabbed who was traveling on business while enslaved. The following day a lone man was taken to the Jonesboro jail until he could prove he was in Illinois with permission. Soon after, a porter on the Illinois Central Railroad was about to be taken when the conductor intervened. With his revolver as witness, the conductor assured the men that the porter was a free man. And, within two months, another man was chased and fired on until being captured eighteen miles away in Carbondale, Illinois.[4]

In Ohio, Oliver Anderson "was forcibly dragged from his home, at night, and carried off to Slavery." The kidnapping of a free, industrious man happened in Chillicothe, Ohio, on the 12th of October, 1859. The *Scioto Gazette,* reported the illegal event and meeting of the citizens to investigate the outrage. It was discovered later that Oliver Anderson left Kentucky the following January in the company of his brother and another man. The threesome connected with the Underground Railroad and took the "express train" to Canada."[5]

No kidnappings of this sort were reported in Michigan, however the antislavery society report included a notice that a black minister in Detroit was fined for "preaching." The notice was incorrect. Black minister, the Rev. William Berry, was fined fifty dollars based on an 1838 miscegenation statute for officiating at the marriage ceremony of a black man and a white woman. The interracial marriage of Isaac Berry and Lucy Millard took place in the fall of 1859, and the minister's fine was reported in the same city in December of the same year.[6]

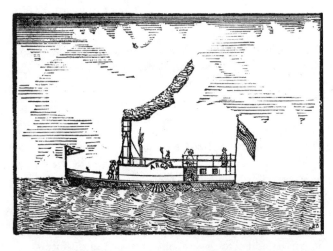

Mrs. Monroe and her children escaped capture when they boarded the *Argo* to cross the Detroit River to Canada (S.F. *History of Detroit* [1890]. Bentley Historical Library, University of Michigan).

An interracial marriage in Adrian, Michigan, did not draw the attention of officials. Levi Coffin and Laura Haviland helped in the escape of John Wilson, a white man, and Eliza, formerly enslaved, who married Wilson. The couple moved to Canada and back to Michigan. After the Civil War, the Wilsons found the daughter they were unable to rescue.[7]

John Brown's Trail to Michigan

John Brown's notoriety as a rabid abolitionist grew after the

1856 bloody massacres in Kansas. Few people knew Brown was secretly planning an armed uprising and had support from prominent antislavery men.

William Garrison was among six men who secretly met with and supported the militant actions of John Brown. After Brown and his men stole into Missouri late December 1858 to rescue 11 people, Samuel G. Howe was displeased. The other members of the Secret Six cheered the action as a precursor to Brown's Southern invasion. Incredibly, Brown and his men marched alongside the people they rescued in broad daylight.

North of Topeka Brown's band engaged in battle with federal forces who fled, were pursued, and five taken as prisoners. Brown released the federal agent when the group crossed into Nebraska and then Iowa. The Quakers in Tabor, Iowa, did not offer the welcome Brown expected and instead censured him for his use of violence. Brown's men passed through other towns, and were hailed as heroes in Grinnell.

By March, Brown and his four men, escorting eleven fugitives, reached Chicago. "Mr. Wagoner sheltered and fed these fugitives for three days, while an old time friend, John Jones, entertained the white men. For harboring fugitives, of course he was liable, under the then existing fugitive slave laws, to one thousand dollars fine and six months in prison." Wagoner bore the cost because he believed he was doing his duty and would account only to God. H. O. Wagoner, born in Maryland, regularly kept fugitives for Brown, according to a biography of prominent black men, written in 1885.[8]

From Chicago, Allan Pinkerton of the famous detective agency helped the escapees onto a boxcar to Detroit. Pinkerton wrote in later years of his opposition to the institution of slavery and secret work on the Underground Railroad. "Many times before the war, when I was associated with those philanthropic spirits who controlled the 'so-called' Underground Railroad, I have assisted in securing safety and freedom for the fugitive slave, no matter at what hour, under what circumstances, at what cost, the act was to be performed. John Brown, the white-haired abolitionist of Kansas fame, was my bosom friend, and more than one dark night has found us working earnestly together in behalf of the freedom of the fleeing bondman, who was striving for his liberty."[9]

There was no difficulty traveling through northern Illinois and Michigan. In Detroit, the former slaves crossed by ferry to freedom. John Brown sat down to do business with his friends in Michigan. The meeting took place March 12, 1859, at the home William Webb, 633 East Congress at St. Antoine, Detroit. Frederick Douglass happened to be in Detroit and joined the meeting. Reportedly, William Lambert, George DeBaptiste, Dr. Joseph Ferguson, Reverend William C. Monroe, Willis Wilson, John Jackson and William Webb were present. Here, John Brown revealed his plan for ending slavery with a planned attack at Harpers Ferry.[10]

John Brown laid out his plan to attack the Harpers Ferry federal arsenal to obtain weapons and then stage a series of guerilla attacks to free people from slavery. The freed slaves would be liberated in their own states by hiding in the mountains, where they would be protected. The Michigan men who shared Brown's inner circle were not all in favor of this plan. Apparently, Frederick Douglass was opposed to an attack and suggested they proceed with an earlier plan to "run off" slaves through the Underground Railroad.[11]

According to William Lambert, John Brown had been in the business of helping on the Underground Railroad for a long time. Lambert said he and John Brown were firm friends and his record books showed Brown brought to Detroit more than 200 fugitives. "He was always on time, and his personal courage tested a thousand times, was beyond dispute."[12]

In April 1859, John Brown spent several weeks in Canada trying to attract recruits. Dr. Martin R. Delany, who had broken with Garrison and other white abolitionists, offered to help plan a convention in Chatham. Advertisements promoted a rally on May 8th and May 10th to form a black Masonic Lodge. Of the 34 blacks and 12 whites attending, several of the blacks and nearly all the whites were part of Brown's band from Kansas. Brown invited Wagoner, the man who helped in Chicago, to attend a "secret convention in Chatham," but Wagoner declined.[13]

The Reverend William Monroe of Detroit presided over the convention and was elected as acting president of the new Provisional Government. Brown's plan was presented. George J. Reynolds, leader of Detroit's all-black League of Liberty Society, argued over an article of the constitution. There may have been many recruits from Canada West and Detroit, but Brown was forced to postpone the Virginia raid after the plans were made public.[14]

Up to this time, Michigan citizens appear to have thwarted every attempt to remove self-emancipators and free people of color from Michigan. In June 1859, Detroiters noticed a lame white man in the neighborhood, who seemed to be a peddler of some sort. Suddenly, five boys went missing. The lame man was suspected of enticing the black boys away. One of the boys was the son of city employee William Jones.[15]

John Brown did not linger in Detroit because he needed money to put his plan in action. He traveled through Cleveland to New York and on to Maryland. In July, Brown and some men viewed the confluence of the Shenandoah and Potomac Rivers at Harpers Ferry. The plan was to take over the arsenal, give the weapons to emancipated blacks and march into the Allegheny Mountains. From their stronghold, squads would raid plantations, arm more freed blacks and expect the surrender by slaveholders. He had only 21 recruits, and the well-known Harpers Ferry Raid ended disastrously for John Brown and his men.

John Brown met with Frederick Douglass and black leaders of Detroit to plan the attack on Harpers Ferry in the home of William Webb, 185 Congress Street, Detroit, Michigan (S.F. *History of Detroit* [1890]. Bentley Historical Library, University of Michigan).

However, the mission instigated by a white man, supported by black men, proved that armed incursions were possible. Southerners, unsure whether Brown's attack was a skirmish in a planned war on the slaveholders, considered the difficulty of preventing another sudden raid. Before his hanging, Brown addressed the court,

> "Now if it is deemed necessary that I should forfeit my life for the furtherance of the ends of justice, and mingle my blood further with the blood of my children and with the blood of millions in this slave country whose rights are disregarded by wicked, cruel, and unjust enactments — I submit; so let it be done!"
>
> Address of John Brown to the Virginia Court at Charles Town, Virginia on November 2, 1859.[16]

The cause of abolitionism had many martyrs, like Elijah Lovejoy and Jonathan Walker, but none who captured the nation's curiosity and attention like John Brown. The loss of his friend John Kagi and "those noble men, who sacrificed their lives in the cause of freedom," saddened the Rev. Paul Shepherd, returned from Kansas to Lenawee County, Michigan.[17]

Afterwards, the Secret Six, or seven, who helped finance John Brown's operations were identified as Gerrit Smith, Dr. Samuel Gridley Howe, George Luther Stearns, Frederick Douglass, Franklin Benjamin Sanborn and the Rev. Theodore Parker and the Rev. Thomas Wentworth Higginson.[18]

John Brown planned to escape to the hills above Harpers Ferry after the attack on the arsenal in West Virginia in 1859 (author photograph, overlooking the Potomac River, Maryland, 2007).

Most of these men denied involvement rather than face treason charges. In fact, if Douglass had not gone to Canada, he would likely have been arrested. A requisition for his arrest was made by Governor Wise of Virginia:

> [Confidential.] Richmond, Virginia, November 13, 1859. To His Excellency, James Buchanan, President of the United States, and to the Honorable Postmaster-General of the United States — Gentlemen: — I have information such as has caused me, upon proper affidavits, to make requisition upon the Executive of Michigan for the delivery up of the person of Frederick Douglass, a Negro man, supposed now to be in Michigan, charged with murder, robbery and inciting servile insurrection in the State of Virginia.[19]

Frederick Douglass moved to England. The Rev. William C. Monroe, leader of the Detroit black community since the time the Blackburns resided there in the 1830s, departed from Detroit for Liberia as a missionary.[20]

Prelude to War

John Brown's raid, coupled with the election of a Republican president, caused the persistent uneasiness to erupt into an attack against free blacks in the South. Missouri and Florida threatened free blacks in those states with enslavement, if they remained. Other slaveholding states began debates to accomplish the same goal. A tide of free men and women poured into northern states, Canada and abroad.

Of course, slaveholders were quick to complain when enslaved men and women joined the rush to liberty. "The negro exodus from Missouri continues" led an article published in pro-slavery newspapers in Missouri and Texas. The *St. Louis Evening News* in November 1859 announced the arrival of 26 Negroes in Detroit, Michigan. They were "carried through from Missouri by dirty agents of the Underground Railroad" to Canada. The slaves were 'decoyed' by agents, transported through Iowa, Illinois and Michigan and on to Canada. The pro-slavery faction expressed the plan to seek relief from the legislature as the exodus would soon 'destroy the last vestige of the Institution, and leave us entirely" without slaves.[21]

The Final Surge

The total population of Michigan nearly doubled in a single decade to reach nearly 750,000 in 1860, including 6,799 blacks. This data seems to controvert the idea of a mass exodus of blacks from Michigan to Canada after the passage of the Fugitive Slave Act, unless the loss of population was offset by new migration of free and self-emancipated black people.

Wayne County was home to the majority of black residents, but Cass County boasted over 1,000 as well. Fourteen counties in the northern parts of the state held not a single person of color, reportedly. Places that were too remote and unsettled earlier were populated with people who could offer rest to the freedom seeker. All along the western shore of Michigan ports provided possible landing sites. Grand Rapids, in Kent County, exploded with settlers to become a major center for western Michigan and link to new settlements in the northwestern area.

Remote black communities in Michigan continued to grow. In Mecosta and Isabella Counties a number of black settlers created havens that would grow primarily after the Civil War. The Wheatland Church of Christ, established in Remus, Mecosta County in 1869, was fully integrated.

A sampling of the black population in the 1860 federal census in one place, Washtenaw County, indicates that most of the men and women listed were new immigrants to the County. Men and women who owned property from a previous decade remained after 1850, however, the misspellings of names makes it challenging to find them. For instance, Underground Railroad helpers Nelson and Henry Ockrow are shown as Ockron and Ockro and Aray is listed properly, but shown as Ray in the 1850 census. At least two households of Days, Thomas Freeman, who was active in the Colored Conventions, Florilla Thompson, who helped found the Bethel A. M. E. Church and her husband remained in the county.

The most interesting data is the number of adults who claimed Canada as their birthplace. David Katzmann used census data to study population trends in Detroit, Michigan. He noted many pre-war Detroiters were from Kentucky and Virginia, and after 1870, around 15 percent were born in Canada. The percentages may translate for the rest of the state.

Following the birthplaces of children of some of these families offers a chance to study migration over a period of time. The McAlisters claimed Kent County, Canada, as their birthplace, their first three children were born in Indiana, and their baby was born in Canada. The family had moved from Canada to Michigan in 1859. Another family of eleven moved from North Carolina to Indiana, to Canada around 1855, and to Michigan around 1858. Two families were in Ohio in the 1840s, then Canada, then Michigan.

By the winter of 1860, unprecedented immigration and the instability of the Union caused friction between many groups on the basis of politics, religion, and race. The 'black codes,' restricting black citizens' rights, had been on the books for decades and, though rarely enforced, would not be lifted.

The election of Abraham Lincoln was not a display of majority support of abolition. As reported in the *Ann Arbor Journal,* the greatest share of Lincoln supporters favored protection of the Union and industry and no extension of slavery. Only in the states of Maine, New Hampshire, Michigan and Wisconsin were the majority of Republicans in favor of abolition. While it appeared that by Lincoln's inauguration, the Union would be dissolved, there was an appeal to consider that a natural decrease in slavery would occur until slavery was abolished by legislation.[22]

Wendell Phillips was due to speak in Detroit, but the "streets were full of threats" and the trustees of the Young Men's Hall refused to allow the lecture for fear the building would be destroyed. Eber B. Ward came forward to promise insurance against damages and a large audience heard the antislavery speech.[23]

In Lenawee County, Adrian College opened in 1859 with Weld agent, the Reverend Mahan as president. From its inception it was strongly antislavery. Adrian College absorbed a nearby Wesleyan Methodist college in its founding. In Lenawee County, the Reverend Mahan moved to a stronghold of abolitionist and Underground Railroad operators. The Rev. J. L. Tomlinson, Henry Tripp, and G. L. Crane were among those active in the antislavery society while the Comstock and Haviland families and Fitch Reed had stations on the Underground Railroad. Though welcomed, many freedom-seekers moved on.

Freedom Tracks

The number of people leaving the United States for Canada increased dramatically in 1860. In Ohio, Levi Coffin worked full time helping those arriving at his door. Though he was "heavily taxed," Coffin appreciated the outpouring of help from formerly indifferent neighbors. Donations of money allowed for transport by train. Coffin put most self-emancipators on trains for Detroit or Ohio ports, where he had friends who notified him of the "safe arrival of passengers by way of the Underground or Upperground Railways."[24]

William Mitchell's book about the Underground Railroad was published in 1860 in London. Mitchell had become a missionary in Toronto after years of helping freedom seekers in Ohio. He observed that 2,400 people passed through Detroit and Cleveland gateways annually.[25]

Laura Haviland returned to Adrian after three years teaching in Canada. Her home remained a beacon of hope for people on their way north and those settling in Michigan. Many times, separated family members found each other with her help. Mary Todd was forced to leave her husband behind when she escaped from Kentucky. He promised to follow but after three years, no news of him reached her.

As often happened, Mrs. Haviland discovered a light complexioned black man waiting on her porch. The stranger handed her a paper from another agent, directing her to help the six freedom seekers. There were three brothers, their mother and two small grandchildren. Mrs. Haviland, as usual, assigned the brothers new names, Benjamin, Richard and Daniel Ross. After several hours visiting, the men mentioned they were looking for a young woman named Mary Todd. One of the men was particularly excited to hear the woman lived nearby in the home of Fitch Reed. The Reverend Canfield carried the man to his wife and son he had never seen. Much of the neighborhood rejoiced over the reunion and legal wedding. Soon, Mary Todd had a home of her own with her husband, mother and three children.[26]

Soon after a man named Jim arrived from Tennessee. His journey to freedom took five weeks, during which he kept entirely to himself until reaching Michigan. Jim trusted no one since he was captured in Illinois months before when he attempted to escape. Slave hunters shot him during a bitter struggle and got him to a jail. His master saw the advertisement for him, went to Illinois, and brought Jim home. Jim's whipping was so severe, he lay on his stomach four weeks to recover. At the first opportunity he took off. His wife and children were sold away six years before and he could no longer tolerate life in bondage. Jim stayed only two days at the Havilands, leaving for the Queen's Dominion with warm clothes and a little money.

Laura Haviland wrote to Roswell Rexford, a wealthy farmer southeast of Jackson in Napoleon, for help. A self-freed man from Louisiana was a blacksmith in need of a business. Rexford replied that he was "glad to learn that another has escaped from the land of bondage, whips, and chains. In view of the wrongs and cruelty of slavery...."

Rexford left no doubt that he would willingly help fund an enterprise to help the blacksmith.

> I would rather enter the gloomy cell of your friend Fairbanks, [sic] and spend every hour of this brief existence in all the bitterness that the hand of tyrants can inflict, than live in all pomp and splendor that the unpaid toil of slaves could lavish upon man. Yours, etc.,.July 27th, 1860. R. R Rexford

As a self-freed resident of Michigan, Charles Williams "proved to be an honest and industrious man."[27]

Mrs. Haviland traveled to Arkansas on behalf of Charles McClain (a name given to him by Haviland) to rescue his sister. McClain attended the Raisin Institute where his light skin, blue eyes and auburn hair led many to believe it impossible he had spent his life enslaved. He was easily able to purchase a ticket to travel on public transportation for his escape.

Mrs. Haviland sent a letter to a black minister in Little Rock, asking that Ann be informed of her brother's safety. Then, Laura Haviland traveled to the deep south. Deeply troubled by beatings and torture, she dared not make even the mildest protest. Finally, the women met to make arrangements. Ann understood if anyone learned of her plans, she would have to wait to leave. Sadly, Ann was overheard asking a friend for a shawl for a journey. Mrs. Haviland took the first boat for home, alone. It would be two or three years and after her mother's death, before Ann could escape to freedom.[28]

West of Adrian, near a road leading directly north from the Indiana border to the tip of Michigan, the Comstocks were inundated with black and white visitors. Elizabeth Comstock's letter of August 2, 1860, reveals the regularity of freedom seekers passing through Southeast Michigan. She described one who visited with them and told the story of his life. His father was kidnapped in Africa and survived the harrowing Atlantic crossing in a slave ship. The son, a tall athletic man, had a terrible time enslaved in Virginia and fled to liberty. After encountering some difficulties, he arrived in Rollin, Lenawee County, where "our hearts, our hands, our houses, our purses, are freely opened."

Comstock was unable to finish letters because of the constant knockings on the door. When she resumed writing her letter seven months later, she named visitors William, Samuel, Joseph, Welcome, Pearce, Ira, Peleg, Addison, Martha, Charity and Hiram as the reason.[29]

Treason and Rebellion

"The year 1861 opened full of excitement. Both North and South assumed threatening attitudes," wrote Laura Haviland. In January of that year, the Michigan Legislature met in Lansing. From across the state, members traveled through the snow, for "every senator and representative felt the responsibility imposed upon him by the fact that treason and rebellion in the South were threatening the very existence of the Union." The Michigan men had polled their constituents before the meeting and must have feared that there would be conflicting views. Instead, "members found but one sentiment among the people; that secession is treason, and treason means war."[30]

Though citizens of Ann Arbor had listened to radical abolitionists for decades, the fear of disunion and war made this an inopportune time for a polarizing lecture. In January 1861, when abolitionist and Congregationalist minister Parker Pillsbury and Mrs. Josephine S. Griffing visited Ann Arbor to speak, a mob of students and residents opposed to the antislavery message stormed the Free Church. The building served as the Quaker Meeting House in the 1850s on land purchased by members of the Glazier family. Students from the University of Michigan walked from the south to north end of State Street for the lecture.[31]

Giles Stebbins recalled how Mrs. Griffing stood on the low platform, "a graceful beauty of person," "fearless, erect, radiant, speaking in clear tones." Mrs. Griffing spent her married life in Salem, Ohio, and traveled in that state and Michigan as an abolitionist speaker.[32]

Early shouts and threats disrupted the speakers as the level of anger escalated. When benches and windows were broken and stovepipes knocked down, the speakers were forced to escape through one of the church windows. Though the lecture was repeated peacefully the next day to full houses, the mob rioting was reported nationally and disgraced the city.[33]

South Carolinians believed Abraham Lincoln, the newly elected president, would abolish slavery and secede from the Union. During the month of January the states of Mississippi, Florida, Alabama, Georgia and Louisiana followed the lead of South Carolina in leaving the Union. On February 4, 1861, delegates from the seceding states, including Texas, met at Montgomery, Alabama, to organize the Southern Confederacy. Some northerners organized a 'Peace Congress,' but Michigan refused to endorse the plan or send delegates.[34]

Abraham Lincoln was inaugurated as president just one month before the attack on Fort Sumter (April 12, 1861). Across the nation, in towns, villages and cities, citizens gathered to learn the news. In Ann Arbor, Michigan, people filled the courthouse square, where prominent community leaders spoke. University of Michigan president, Dr. Henry Tappan, said, "Now an overt hostile act had been committed, and the government must respond or fall to pieces."

Even as Michigan prepared for war, the Underground Railroad funneled the masses of people escaping to Canada. Siebert believed the enslaved from the border states of Ohio were forwarded to ports on Lake Erie and sent to Detroit to cross to Canada. And, they poured in from the western states. The Elgin Settlement in Buxton, Canada, doubled in size every four years from 1852.

Few Underground Railroad workers wrote about this late period of the agency. Erastus Hussey and Pamela Thomas disclosed the lessening of passengers on the network crossing up to Schoolcraft and across to Battle Creek. The agents in the Wesleyan Methodist network recorded greater numbers after 1850. Mrs. Haviland and Comstock recorded dozens stopping for aid each year after 1860. If William Lambert's estimates can be believed, then thousands of enslaved people were led by members of the Knights of Liberty or Men of Oppression north, east, and west to freedom.

Levi Coffin forwarded freedom seekers without concern of slave hunters or public censure. The climate had changed in both the North and the South. In the north, Coffin wrote, "the early disgrace and danger were passed, "Much of my work for them [self-emancipators] was now done boldly and above board — or, I might say, above ground."[35]

The 1861 Wesleyan Methodist Michigan Conference reported increases in membership. One member wrote a letter about the change in public opinion in favor of helping the enslaved. The letter writer was slightly peeved that the early workers fought when other Christians would not, and now "they need not make any sacrifice."[36] Over the next few years, many Wesleyan Methodist Church members returned to their former Christian churches. In a matter of months, abolitionism had a new following.

President Abraham Lincoln, on the first day of January 1863, issued the Emancipation Proclamation, "I do order that all persons held as slaves," within the states in rebellion, "shall be, free." The declaration did not apply to Delaware, Maryland, or Kentucky, states not in secession from the Union, nor did it immediately free all slaves.

Essentially, the Underground Railroad after 1860 became less secretive and operated without the urgency of earlier times. The necessity of relieving the needs of self-emancipators was unchanged. Erastus Hussey was asked when the Underground Railroad ceased its operations. Hussey said it ended with the issuance of the Emancipation Proclamation.

Arnold Gragston was interviewed when he was 97 years old about his experiences on the Underground Railroad while enslaved by Jack Tabb in Mason County, Kentucky. For four years, he rowed people to freedom across the Ohio River, and then realized it was time to take his own freedom.

Conclusion

Arnold Gragston

[Interviewed in Jacksonville, Florida, 1930s, Slave Narrative Collection, Library of Congress].

"It was in 1863, and one night I carried across about twelve on the same night. Somebody must have seen us, because they set out after me as soon as I stepped out of the boat back on the Kentucky side; from that time on they were after me. Sometimes they would almost catch me; I had to run away from Mr. Tabb's plantation and live in the fields and in the woods...

"Finally, I saw that I could never do any more good in Mason County, so I decided to take my freedom, too. I had a wife by this time, and one night we quietly slipped across and headed for Mr. Rankin's bell and light. It looked like we had to go almost to China to get across that river: I could hear the bell and see the light on Mr. Rankin's place, but the harder I rowed, the farther away it got, and I knew if I didn't make it I'd get killed. But finally, I pulled up by the lighthouse, and went on to my freedom — just a few months before all of the slaves got their's. I didn't stay in Ripley, though; I wasn't taking no chances. I went on to Detroit and still live there with most of 10 children and 31 grandchildren."

The complexity of the Underground Railroad experience and scarce verifiable documentation do not allow for precise statistic-driven conclusions. However, this book is evidence that contemporaneous sources exist and, with scholarly rigor, illuminate the history of antislavery activism and the Underground Railroad in Michigan. Though the state of Michigan was comparatively unsettled, its geographic situation and antislavery activity thrust it onto the national stage of resistance to the system of slavery.

The Kentuckians who failed to recover their enslaved from Michigan seemed to grasp the enormity of that circumstance long before others. Michigan was the nearly indiscernible fissure in the wall of slavery. It provided a door to permanent escape in Canada with sentinels protecting the door throughout Michigan. Skirmishes in Ohio, Illinois and Indiana allowed capture of self-emancipators, who were returned to Southern soil and made an example for those contemplating escape. But, enslaved people noticed when the Kentuckians of Boone and Kenton Counties failed to bring home the formerly enslaved men and women from Michigan.

By this means, the illusion that the slave system was secure was unmasked. Self-emancipators returned south to carry their loved ones to freedom and spread the word about settlements in free states and Canada. The same Kentuckians provoked their legislators to draft and pass the 1850 Fugitive Slave Act. That law increased sectional strife and gave momentum to political action to defeat slavery. The trickling of freedom seekers escaping grew to a steady stream until the eve of the Civil War, when men and women poured into free states. The wall securing slavery was breaking apart when Southern states seceded from the Union.

This book provides profiles of individuals who contributed to the westward shift of both black and white political abolitionism. The detailed findings support the writings of revisionist historians like Dwight Dumond and John Myers, who identified an antislavery crusade in the Northwest Territory states led by Theodore Weld, the Tappan brothers, and Gerrit Smith. Henry Bibb and Frederick Douglass, notable abolitionist leaders, lived, respectively, in Michigan and Ontario, and western New York.

The reader may draw many conclusions from the stories and historical events described in this book. Primarily, historians need to recognize the significance of Michigan in the Underground Railroad experience. Secondly, it is time to take a fresh look at the various forms of resistance and apply scholarly rigor to a legitimate means of ending slavery, that of permanent escape. Contemporary documents can be found, as I experienced with letters and records privately held by descendants of the Beckley, Watkins, Harwood, Preston, Lowry, Benton and Aray families.

A few observations are worth noting, especially as they might help dispel misconceptions.

Escapes originated from several directions, and they changed with population shifts and new modes of transportation. Those fleeing slavery left in small groups or alone, suddenly or after much planning. Only rarely was assistance found in the southern states, where patrollers terrorized men and women of color, demanding passes or free papers, until just before the Civil War.

The geographical significance of Michigan, both as a place of refuge far north of slave catchers and as a gateway to Canada, made Detroit and other ports on Lake Erie critically important in the Underground Railroad. Self-emancipators moved to Canada both temporarily and permanently.

The first to prevent captures of freedom seekers in Michigan were free African Americans, soon supported by self-emancipators. They were not excluded from predominantly white antislavery societies in the 1840s. All the Underground Railroad networks investigated in Michigan were interracial.

Progressive Quakers and reformers from New York were among early settlers in all the Northwest Territory States. However, only Michigan and Wisconsin did not have a settlement of proslavery advocates as did southern Ohio, Indiana and Illinois.

Among reformers and missionaries in Michigan were Weld's men who shifted the antislavery movement to Ohio and other states in the Midwest. Michigan's antislavery society was in favor of abolition from the start. And, the prominent antislavery leaders helped on the Underground Railroad.

The Underground Railroad was an interstate network by the early 1840s. Set up by John Cross and run by a combination of every religious and racial group. The backbone was the radical Quakers, the Reverend Osborne's family and Laura Haviland, the Powers, Comstocks, Glaziers, and Fullers. Radical Underground Railroad workers like the Osborns in Cass County, Nathan and Pamela Thomas, the Husseys, Laura Haviland, John Lowry, and Guy Beckley, publicly promoted their stations.

The state of Michigan, from its territorial days, thwarted every known attempt at

Three generations of women descended from Asher and Catherine Aray represent family members who share an interest in their heritage. From left, Angela Billingslea, Dolores Burton, and DeLaurian Burton (author photograph, Ypsilanti, Michigan, 2009).

recovering slaves. The attempts to use the courts failed when they tried to take back Ben and Daniel and the Blackburns from Detroit. Sending in a small posse to grab John White in Jackson County and a large posse to the settlements in Cass and Berrien were unsuccessful.

Number of Self-Emancipators

As stated earlier, the actual number of people escaping was not as important as the fact that permanent escape from slavery was possible. Also, there is no mechanism for separating "fugitives" from free blacks in Michigan or Canada. Many free blacks moved from states that imposed restrictions and were hostile to them. The Pelhams were among a substantial number of free blacks from Virginia who moved to Michigan or other free states because of oppressive regulations. It is possible to measure the number of blacks settling in Michigan (in 1850 around 2,600; in 1860 around 6,800; and in 1870 nearly 12,000).

The number of people escaping through Michigan before 1850 was probably not more than a few thousand. The Hussey and Thomas families claimed to have helped up to 1,500. They were on the same network and gave assistance to many of the same people. The Southeast Michigan networks were equally as active. Additionally, the record of self-emancipators who did not use the Underground Railroad and those using maritime transportation are generally unknown.

After 1850, the organized Underground Railroad networks adapted to move more people directly to Canada. If half of Ohio's black population of 25,000 in 1850 crossed to Canada by way of Detroit, William Lambert's claim of tens of thousands on Canadian soil was not farfetched. Census data supports a range of blacks in Canada in 1860 of 15,000 to 25,000. Estimates of the number of blacks in Canada in 1860 range from 15,000 to 60,000. Of that number, an unknown percentage were free-born or manumitted. A study of Washtenaw County's census data, as a microcosm of statewide population trends, was attempted. Reporting of nativity was problematic; from one decennial census to the next, the same people gave different places of birth. The study was cancelled after a serious misreading of the data was found. In the 1860 federal census for the state of Michigan, in Washtenaw County, 58 adults listed Kent [Canada West (Ontario)] as their birthplace. The published aggregation interpreted Kent as Kentucky. This fact does support a trend of African American adults, who said they were natives of Canada, moving to Michigan in the antebellum period.

The Underground Railroad Agents

Underground Railroad agents in Michigan were not a homogeneous group connected by religion, race, gender or political affiliation. They were independent non-conformists who sought the adventure of taming the wild frontier, community-minded Puritans who traveled to Michigan in the safety of a social group, and a few sojourners. Some joined the antislavery society, Liberty Party or Wesleyan Methodist Church. The diversity of the Underground Railroad agency is clearly established in this book.

Their motivations for offering assistance are not always discernable. Missionaries like Elijah Pilcher and Henry Northrop, and Quakers like the Osborns, mentioned finding inspiration to care for their brothers and sisters in the Bible. Guy Beckley and Theodore Weld's recruits embraced the teachings of evangelical reformer Charles G. Finney. Laura Haviland's visions, she believed, were divinely inspired, and gave her courage to travel into the South and face armed men.

Some people were humanitarians that offered to someone in need what they themselves might need in return. Many Underground Railroad participants believed the founding fathers intended that institutionalized slavery not be allowed. Samuel Noble and John Lowry argued that slavery was not upheld by the Constitution. Jotham Goodell was not associated with any antislavery organizations and his participation is known only by his son's account.

Personal experiences motivated some to help. Capt. Lowry did not say he became a radical abolitionist because of his grandfather's kidnapping, but the story was imprinted in his conscience. John Critchett knew of a kidnapping in his family and Henry Willis experienced the loss of family as a child.

Within the Underground Railroad agency, there was disapproval of certain methods of releasing people from enslavement. Levi Coffin wrote that he opposed the violence of John Fairfield. The unspoken message was that helping self-emancipators was appropriate, but stealing them from within the South was not. Coffin said Fairfield emancipated not only hundreds, but thousands.

In 1855, Theodore Foster moved from Scio to Lansing to become Superintendent of the Boys Reform School. It appears he was not affiliated with the reorganized Michigan Anti-Slavery Society. However, he did dedicate time to organizing his lectures, essays, and historical materials into manuscripts. His manuscript entitled *The African Race* is a compendium of published histories reflecting racial biases prevalent among non–African observers. It is one of the interesting dichotomies in the study of the Underground Railroad, that many white men who made personal and financial sacrifices for the welfare of freedom seekers held racist views.[1]

Self-Emancipators

The accounts presented in this book are hardly sufficient to draw generalizations, but offer some interesting facts. A few of the earliest escapes with the least help covered the greatest distance. Nearly all the self-emancipators describe being pursued. Some were betrayed by black and white strangers and helped by the same. It was impossible to know whom to trust.

Every trip of this nature led to the passing of information about how to manage an escape. Underground Railroad agents went into the South to disseminate knowledge about the Underground Railroad and means of escape, as well. Laura Haviland, John Fairfield, Josiah Henson, and Harriet Tubman are well known as rescuers. It is curious that people like George and Martha Washington "heard" they were going to be taken back to slavery from Michigan. There seems to have been an informal system of communication that remains a mystery.

The motivation to leave slavery was not always to escape an intolerable situation. For some, it was based on a quest for freedom. Of those who landed in Michigan, individual accounts cite a desire to be with loved ones, to keep the money they earned, to legally marry or to receive an education and to escape abuse. In looking at the documented escapes in this book, we see the reasons are as diverse as the individuals who ran away. If any reason predominated, it was to escape being sold south.

In the 1830s, mostly men escaped, and they walked. It may be possible to learn of those who died on the journey, as stories come to light. As assistance was organized in places, self-emancipators were helped across major rivers and put on wagons, if needed. After the Fugitive Slave Act, Michigan workers got people through on trains

Citizens of Manchester dedicated a downtown street to the African-American Ockrow family (2009 author photograph, Manchester, Michigan).

and some self-emancipators paid for their own transportation. After 1860, people walked in daylight, and could follow roads and rail lines in Michigan.

Verification and Resources

Many other men and women might have been included in this book, but their histories did not include verifiable evidence of Underground Railroad participation. For instance, in Washtenaw County, Horace Carpenter was "a firm and uncompromising antislavery man." From the time he signed an Abolition Petition in 1837 until his death, Carpenter worked "in molding the minds of the people in favor of abolition of that cursed evil," and "proclaimed the right of the colored man to be free and independent."[2] Carpenter attended meetings of the Michigan State Anti-Slavery Society and the Liberty Party, and ran for office as Sheriff on the Free Soil ticket. But, it was not recorded that he helped freedom seekers in Michigan.

And, sometimes, there are stories about people who had no other involvement. According to an interview with Ernestine Flora Wilson Meenan, who grew up on the Langford Sutherland farm a century after it was built, there was a small door in the wall of an upstairs bedroom that led to a crawlspace. Ms. Meenan said, "I was told that my great-grandparents harbored the slaves who were escaping to Canada and when authorities came looking for them, they were told to hide in the "crawlspace" until the searchers left. I remember crawling in the dark, dusty, long space and trying to imagine how frightened they must have been."

On the western side of the state, passed down stories about the Bonine house are not yet verified.

In Manchester, Washtenaw County, Gamalia Bailey's house is listed as an Underground Railroad station in the papers of researcher Blanche Coggan. Chandler Carter's house was "an under-ground railway station," according to historian Annetta English. Carter was chosen chairman of the 1847 Liberty Party County Convention.[3]

William Moore founded a hamlet called Mooreville, and later York, near Monroe County.[4] In the 1860 census, there were 15 households with African Americans and seven were independent households.[5] The area had a long history as a place of safety and tolerance.

The practice of returning where one had assistance was not uncommon and is helpful in identifying areas of assistance. By the 1870 census, Michigan experienced a large population gain of African Americans (118,071 among 1,184,059 total). In 1860, there were 16,310 'free blacks' in Michigan. Most lived in Detroit, then Cass County and other places across the state. Aaron and Ellen Wilson moved to Farmington, where they stayed a short time during their escape, after the Civil War (see Chapter 8). The Crosswhites returned to Marshall.

Stories Are Linked

In examining the accounts of Underground Railroad helpers in Michigan and beyond, it is very clear that a network of escape including Ohio, Indiana, Michigan and Canada existed from the 1840s. There are many examples in separate accounts, referring to the same participants. Calvin Fairbank wrote in his memoir of visiting the Coleman family in Detroit in 1849. He knew them in 1841, when he led the family through the woods and across the Ohio River on a journey to freedom.[6]

John Hatfield, the barber, wrote later that he helped Joseph Sanford and his wife among the 13 who escaped through Cincinnati to Michigan and were caught but set free in the courts. Both Hatfield and Sanford settled in Amherstburg, Canada, where Benjamin Drew interviewed them.[7]

The attempted captures of escaped slaves from Cass County on the west side of Michigan and the White family from Adrian and Ypsilanti were linked. In early 1847 an association of slave owners from Bourbon County, Kentucky, sent a scout to learn the whereabouts of self-emancipated men, women and children they heard were settled in Michigan. The Cass County history states the man gave his name as Carpenter and said he was an abolitionist from Massachusetts in Kalamazoo to study law. In this guise he traveled to Quakers' homes and black settlements promoting abolition journals while discovering the identities of freedom seekers and their helpers.

In the fall of 1847, Laura Haviland, across the state in Adrian, was visited by a man selling subscriptions to an abolitionist newspaper in Cincinnati. The man was J. L. Smith, lawyer for G.W. Brazier. Two days later, the man attempted to capture John White. On August 1, 1847, a gang of Kentuckians raided homes of Underground Railroad agents and the settlement called Young's Prairie. Though they captured numerous blacks, they were stopped at the border. The affidavit for a claim was signed by several men, including G. W. Brazier, who claimed John White as his property, and the Rev. A. Stevens. Jane White escaped from Benjamin Stevens, her owner and father.[8]

Female members of the Ypsilanti Evangelical Friends Church, which Prince Bennett, Edwin Comstock, and David Gorton organized in 1835, held antislavery meetings. At the end of the Civil War, these women tried to aid the "colored refugees having come before this meeting" by appointing a committee to raise funds and collect clothing to provide for the freed people's relief locally and nationally. Women such as Cynthia Derbyshire expressed a desire to visit "in Gospel Love" their "Colored Brethren in their homes who are living in our vicinity as far away as may open." Like-minded congregations also weighed the assistance they could offer to their African American neighbors.[9]

From the start, Michigan's antislavery society favored (gradual) abolition, but a decade later, endorsed immediate abolition and spoke of secession from slaveholding states. Society leaders were generally intellectual elites, who chose a path of righteousness over wealth. The majority of officers, including the Executive Committee, of the Michigan State Anti-Slavery Society during the 1840s, were Underground Railroad agents.

For example, in 1844, Seymour Treadwell served as president, and the following were vice presidents: Nathan Thomas, Erastus Hussey, Chester Gurney, Martin Cowles, Roswell Rexford, C. S. Youngs, J. Morrison, G. Crane, C. Cowlam, William Canfield, Arthur Porter and John King of Genesee. The Executive Committee members were Sabin Felch, S. D. Noble, C. J. Garland, Guy Beckley and Theodore Foster. The four or five names that are not linked to the Underground Railroad represent men who publicly promoted abolition and very likely were involved in helping freedom seekers.

As many as 1,600 of the men who found freedom in Michigan fought in the Civil War (see Norman McRae, *Negroes in Michigan During the Civil War*, Lansing, 1966). They ranged in age from George York, 15, to Sampson Saunders, 40. Their sacrifice for the nation was a fitting tribute to an era of struggle and perseverance. Our understanding of the people and events in Michigan's Underground Railroad expands our historical perspective. The stories of personal loss and triumph, of sacrifice and freedoms are universal and timeless and part of our shared experience in becoming Americans.

Appendix 1: Formerly Enslaved People, Post–Civil War

Thornton and Ruthie Blackburn

The Blackburns settled in Toronto, where Thornton started a taxicab service and became quite wealthy. Reports indicate he returned to Louisville 10 years after his escape to rescue his mother. The full story of their lives is told in the book, *I've Got a Home in Glory Land.*

Rev. John W. Brooks

After years of bondage to Richard Jones of Maryland and Phineas Bates of New York, Brooks fought for his freedom and moved to Michigan. He was a first purchaser of land in Pittsfield Township and lived on his farm for the next 25 years. His neighbors William Harwood, Roswell Preston and Asher Aray participated in the Underground Railroad. The Reverend Brooks was involved in antislavery activities, and a leader in the black community, but no records of efforts to help others escape slavery have been found.

In the 1830s, he was ordained to preach by the Reverend Swift, pastor in the Methodist Episcopal Church in charge of the Plymouth Circuit. Ironically, it appears that the Reverend Swift brought Brooks into the M. E. Church, as he and his followers left it over the issue of slavery.[1] Though the Reverend Brooks conducted missionary work after his ordination, not until 1857 would his name be linked to a church. The Union Church, Ann Arbor's first African American house of worship, split into factions that formed the Bethel African American Church and the Second Baptist Church. The Reverend Brooks ministered to the AME group.[2]

The Reverend Brooks continued to serve the Bethel AME congregation and play a leadership role among blacks in Michigan. At a later Colored Men's State Convention (1865) Brooks was nominated president of the convention. The Reverend Brooks lived through the Civil War and the emancipation of enslaved people. When the county history was published in 1881, the Reverend Brooks, nearing the end of a long life, was described as one of the oldest settlers, and "one well respected by all classes of society."[3]

John Armstrong

A family is listed in the 1851 census of Canada East headed by John Armstrong, a Methodist farmer, born in the United States.

Caroline Quarrls

Caroline Quarrls, decades after her journey and after the abolition of slavery in the United States, remained in touch with the man who conducted her to safety and freedom. She wrote Goodnow from the Canadian town of Sandwich on April 18, 1880:

> "Dearest Friend,
>
> Pen and Ink could hardly express my joy when I heard from you once more. I am living and have to work very hard but have never forgotten you nor your kindness. I am still in Sandwich — the same place where you left me. Just as soon as the Postmaster read the name to me — your name — my heart filled with joy and gladness and I should like to see you once more before I die, to return thanks for your kindness toward me. Dearest friend, you don't know how I rejoiced since I heard from you. Answer as soon as you get this and let me know how you are and your address. Caroline Watkins."

Caroline married Allen Watkins, also self-emancipated, and remained in Sandwich where they raised a family and helped found a church for Africans. She is listed in the 1881 census as 53 years old, meaning she was 17 or 18 when she escaped. Online records show that Watkins descendants continue to live in Sandwich (now Windsor) and attend the First Baptist Church.

The Quarlls-Watkins Heritage Project is a family history organization started by Kimberly Simmons, a great-great-great-granddaughter of Caroline Quarlls Watkins. The Project is a National Program Partner with the U.S. National Park Service's Underground Railroad Network to Freedom.

John White

As stated in the book, John White married while in Canada and returned to Michigan with his wife and three children before 1860. He lived first in Livonia and then moved to Ann Arbor. According to Laura Haviland, White's eldest daughter, though forced to remain enslaved in Kentucky, married Solomon. Benjamin Stevens, "slave-owner" and father of Jane White, had formerly enslaved Solomon.[4]

Nelson Ockrow/Royal Watkins

The Watkins Farm is connected to the John White escape described by Laura Haviland. After the destruction of two log homes by fire, Royal Watkins built a large Italianate house of hand-pressed brick near Brooklyn in Jackson County. The house sits on a hill where wide vistas could be viewed from the belvedere atop the two story structure. Residents of nearby Brooklyn and family descendants share memories of the property serving as a station on the Underground Railroad. Both Royal and his son Lucius D. Watkins were known to offer assistance.[5]

Descendant Douglas Watkins of Brooklyn, Michigan, was born in the farmhouse and lived there until 1944. He regularly drives through the park created by his great-grandfather, L. D. Watkins, and remembers when everything for miles around was part of the 2,300 acre farm. And, he described the connection to the Ockrow family of Manchester, Washtenaw County.

Harry Ockrow's children were Nelson, Harriet and William. Nelson was credited with riding to the Watkins farm to warn John White of the approaching posse. Nelson and Ann Okrow

lived in a house behind the stores on the south side of Manchester's Main Street. The street was named Ockrow Street. Nelson worked as miller and later a barber.[6]

William Ockrow worked for Lucius D. Watkins as a farm laborer. In the 1860–70s, William and his sister Harriet, married to George Washington Hill, raised their families in houses on the Watkins' farm. When William Ockrow became infirm the family built a wing on the back of the house and cared for him. William Ockrow was buried with the Watkins family with a headstone acknowledging he was a "faithful servant."[7] By the time Nelson Ockrow died in 1893, his story of helping John White to freedom was legendary.

Martha (Grandma) Washington

Martha settled in Colchester, Canada when she was a girl of 12. She married at 16 and bore eleven children. She came to Ypsilanti around 1868 while in her late fifties to live out the rest of her long life. When interviewed by Ms. Goddard, Martha was living on First Avenue in Ypsilanti with a caretaker who seemed very proud of her. Not one of her eleven children survived. She was nearly 100 years old at the time of the interview.[8]

Caroline Hill

Mrs. Hill remained in Ypsilanti the rest of her life. She did washing for a woman named Mrs. Wallace, who was a "lady." At some point, Caroline visited her former home in Chatham but chose not to stay. In 1910, she resided at 21 Center Street in Ypsilanti, widowed and poor. Caroline Hill died just days after Ms. Goddard produced her paper in 1913.[9]

George and Milly McCoy

After living in a cabin on the Starkweather farm, George moved his family to a house on Congress Street. George McCoy died in 1870 in his 57th year. Milly became the head of the household with five children, aged from 10 to 23, under her care. In 1872 Milly returned to Kentucky to visit Mrs. Gaines. Anna said that Mrs. Gaines asked whether Milly had told her parents she planned to escape and she said they had not been told because they would have revealed the plans. Mrs. Gaines pleaded with

Milly to remain in Kentucky, but Milly would not be separated from her children. In 1883 Milly resided as a widow at 167 W. Congress (now Michigan Avenue).

The children attended school in Ypsilanti. Thomas Andrews' son said his father, from Scotland, helped Elijah study engineering in Edinburgh, Scotland. He returned to live and work near his parents in Ypsilanti, then moved to Detroit where he invented a lubricating device for locomotives in 1872. He would achieve fame, though little wealth, for a lifetime of inventions. Anna married a non-relation named Harvey McCoy. Anna McCoy told the family history to Goddard before 1913.

Henry Shephard and George McDeary

Nathan Thomas wrote in his diary that George McDeary [McGeary] visited him after the close of the Civil War. McDeary recalled stopping at Thomas' house when he and seven others were guided through Michigan by Henry Shephard. Of the self-emancipators, four enlisted and took part in the capture of Charleston. McDeary said they marched through the streets singing the John Brown song in celebration. McDeary told Dr. Thomas that through his efforts to put them on the path to freedom and fighting, Thomas helped take Charleston. McDeary settled in Brady, Michigan.

David Bristol

Changed his name to Anthony Philips. He was a friend of Lewis Hill. [Nathan Thomas diaries]

Malinda Robinson Paris

Malinda Paris lived out her life in St. Clair. She bore seven children, including Henry, who served over three years in the Civil War but died of illness soon after. Mrs. Paris continued to work after she was widowed in 1860. At her death on October 22, 1892, there was a community outpouring to honor her generosity in life: "The immense concourse of people present on the occasion was sufficient testimony that 'Aunt Malinda' will long be held in loving remembrance by the people of St. Clair."[10]

Mrs. Monroe Family

The family continued to live in Windsor, Ontario at least until 1860. In that year Fannie Ellen Troy wrote to her father that one of the daughters, Georgiana, passed away. The older girls worked as domestics and the younger ones attended school- a privilege denied them in slavery.[11] [*Hair-breadth Escapes from Slavery to Freedom*].

Willis and Elsie Hamilton

After their attempted capture around 1845, the Hamiltons, traveling as Bill and Jane Willis, moved to Canada with their two children. It is not known whether they were reunited with their children left behind in slavery.

C. W. Thompson

After arriving in Detroit in 1854, Thompson used his musical talents to form choirs, a school of music and the Detroit Philharmonic Society.[12] Thompson was born into slavery in Virginia, escaped via the Underground Railroad, and became an esteemed citizen of Michigan.

Mary Ann Shadd Cary

Many descendants of the Buxton settlement in Canada moved to Ypsilanti during and after the Civil War.

Ann Arborite Ruth Spann's great-aunt came from North Buxton, and Lydia Morton's great-grandfather lived in nearby Fletcher. Viola Henderson's great-aunt, Mary Ann Shadd Cary, ran a school in Windsor for black refugees. After the passage of the 1850 Fugitive Slave Act made life more dangerous near the border, she moved inland to North Buxton, where in 1853 she became the first black woman in North America to edit a weekly newspaper. After the war, Cary returned to the United States, where she was the first black woman to graduate from Howard University Law School.

John Freeman Walls

Dwight Walls, pastor of the Greater Shiloh Church of God in Christ in Ypsilanti, is descended from John Freeman Walls, a former slave from North Carolina, and Jane Walls, the white widow of his original master. The Walls escaped the South, reached Canada by boat from Toledo, and settled in Puce, Ontario. Dwight Walls' grandfather moved to Detroit to work after World War II, but his family still has many Canadian connections. He reports that a number of black Ypsilantians have Canadian roots, including the Bass, Perry, and Kersey families, as well as the Grayer family of his mother.[13]

Appendix 2:
Underground Railroad Participants*

Key: B = Blackburn Case; C = Coffin, Levi; CR = Crosswhite; D = DeLand, Charles; F = Foster, Theodore; G = Geddes, Norman; GO = Goddard, Mary; GR = Green, Liberetta; GS = Goodell, Solon; H = Hussey, Erastus; H1 = Hussey, Susan; HA = Haviland, Laura; L = Lambert, William; M = McCoy, Anna; MC = McGee, Melville; N = Noble, Pamela; NO = Northrop, H. H. ; P = Preston, Roswell; PO = Power, Nathan; R = Reed, Fitch; S = Sanford, Perry; S1 = Stebbins, Giles; SOL = *Signal of Liberty*; T = Thomas, Nathan; T1 = Thomas, Pamela; T2 = Thomas, Susan; » = Self emancipator; **Bold** = black American; Non-bold = white American

Berrien County

Alexander, Lorenzo P. = T
Bowles, Samuel [kidnapped] = SOL
Elliot, W. S. = T
McIlvain, Ebenezer = T
Orr, John = Bowles
Reese, William P. = Bowles

Branch County

»**Smith, Andrew** = S1
Zimmerman, John D. = [S1]

Calhoun County

Albion

Johnson, Edwin M. = H

Battle Creek City and Township

»**Agnes** =
Atlee, E.A. = H
Buckley, Lester = H
»**Casey, William** = S

Chadwick, Theron A. = H
»**Coleman, William** = H
Cowles, Charles = H
Cushman, Henry J. = H
Densmore, Abel = H, T
Dodge, Silas W. = H, T
Gore, Edwin = H
»**Hampton, Wade** = H
»**Henderson, Thomas** = H
Hussey, Erastus = T, H, S
Hussey, Sarah = H
Hussey, Susan = H1
»**Logan, Jim** = H
McCullum, William = H
Merritt, Joseph & Phoebe = T
Mott, Elijah T. = H
Mott, Isaac = H
Nichols, Samuel S. = H
»**Skipworth, Joseph** = S
»**Stevens, Nancy** = H [likely same as Cass Co. listing]
Strauther, Samuel = H
Thayer, Dr. S. B. = T, H
»**Truth, Sojourner**
Willis, Henry = T, H
»**Wood, Stephen** = H

Listed by geographical location and name. References are linked to primary sources shown in the key above. This list is not conclusive, as the names of self-emancipators, and some agents, were not recorded.

175

Marshall
»**Bergen, Charles** = CR
Comstock, Oliver C. =
»**Crosswhite, Adam** = T
»**Crosswhite, Sarah** = T
Fitch, Jabez S. = H
Gorham, Charles T. = T
Hackett, Calvin = CR
Hurd, Jarvis = CR
Marshall, **Morse [Moss], Planter** = CR
Patterson, Moses = CR
»**Smith, James** = CR
»**Parker, William** = CR

Cass County

Bogue, Stephen= T, H, S
Bonine, Isaac= H
»**Casey, William** = S [Note: Sanborn named oth-
ers who escaped in a group of 22 as, **George
Hamilton, Nelson Stephens, Mrs. Stephens**]
»**Bristow, Moses**
Duncan, William & Delamore = T
East, Joel = T, H
Jones, William = S
»**Layne, George** = T
Lee, Ishmael = T
Maudlin, Wright = H1, T
Nicholson, Thompson = T
Osborn, Charles = T
Osborn, Ellison & Jefferson & Josiah & Parker
= T
»**Powell, David and family**
»**Reynolds, Susan**
»**Sanford, Perry & others** = S
Shepherd, Henry
Shugart, Zachariah & John = T, H, S
»**Skipworth, Joseph** = S, H
»**Stanford, Joe** = S
»**Stephens, Reuben** = S
»**Walker, Dave** = S
Wheeler, William = T

Genesee County

»**Cromwell, Robert** = L [later in Wayne Co.]
Northrop, H. H. = NO

Hillsdale County

Adams, ____ = R
Backus, Anson = R
Streeter, Oliver = R

Jackson County

Brooklyn area
Rexford, Roswell = HA
Watkins, Royal & Lucius = HA

Concord area
McGee, Thomas & sons = M
Smalley, David = M

Leoni
Francisco, Henry = H

City of Jackson
Allen, Norman = H
DeLand, William = D
Sullivan, William M. = T
Treadwell, Seymour B. = T
Wilcox, Lonson = H

Michigan Centre area
Gurney, Chester = No
Fitch, Abel = H
Fitch, Abijah = H

City of Parma
Gidley, Townsend = H
Hoag, William & Samuel = D
Mott, Isaac & Uriah = D
Upton, Samuel & Edward = D

Kalamazoo County

Crooks, George W. = T
Montague, Henry = T
Royes, Rufus = T
Shafter, Hugh M. = T
Taylor, William = T
Woodruff, William = T

Climax
Gardner, Joel & William = T, H

Schoolcraft
Thomas, Nathan & Pamela = T

Lenawee County

Coe, John M. = R
Gilbert, Warren & Almira [R]

Hall, Reuben, Tecumseh
Parker, James H. = HA
Shepherd, Paul = letter

Adrian/ Raisin Valley

Beecher, Robert = HA
»**Hamilton, Willis & Elsie a.k.a. Bill and Jan Willis** = HA
Geddes, Norman = G
Haviland, Laura = HA, C
»**McClain, Charles** = HA
Martin, James = HA
»**Ross brothers, Benjamin, Richard & Daniel** = HA
Spofford, Sumner = HA
Stebbins, Giles = S1
»**Taylor, George** = HA
Tibbet, ___ = G
»**Todd, Mary** = HA
»**White, John** = HA
»**Williams, Charles** = HA

Cambridge Junction

Dolbeare, Jeremiah = R
Reed, Fitch & Almira = HA, R

Clinton

Wells, James B. [R]

Rollin Township

Comstock, John T. & Elizabeth = letter
»_____, **Lucy**

Macomb County

Canfield, ___ = HA

Shelby Township

Hixson, Richard, & Mary = GR
Lerich, Peter & Sarah = GR
Naramoor, John & Nancy = GR
Waters, John = GR

Monroe County

Adair, Samuel L. = letter
Critchett, John & Abigail
Monteith, John
»_____, **Saby& Isom and others**

Muskegon County

Walker, Jonathon

Oakland County

Farmington

Gilmour, William = marker
Power, Arthur & Nathan
Thayer, John

Shiawassee County

Barnes, John

St. Clair County

»**Lisette, Denison & siblings**
»**Paris, Melinda**
Sheley, Alanson
Thompson, Oren C.
Ward, Eber

St. Joseph County

Flowerfield

Bird, Friend C. = T
»**Hatchel, Nathaniel**
Wheeler, Joseph = T

Washtenaw County

Ann Arbor Area

Beckley, Guy = H, T
Brooks, John W. = Brooks
Cleaveland, John P. = NO
»**Coxe, Robert & brother** = SOL
Geddes, John = H
Glasier, Robert & Maria = S1
Glazier, Richard = S1
»**Lewis, George** = SOL
Noble, Sylvester = N
»**Quarrls, Caroline** = SOL
»_____, **Sylvester** =SOL
Volland, Jacob =
»**Washington, George & Martha** = N

Augusta Twp

Bennett, Prince & Esther = Bennett

Dexter

Clarke, Charles G. = NO
Dexter, Samuel W. = H
Foster, Samuel W. = F

Freedom Twp

Preston, Jacob [P]

Saline Area (Pittsfield & Lodi)

Aray, Asher & Catherine = B, P, R
Bartlett, Moses & Pebses = G
Benton, Eli = Benton
Harwood, William W. = R
Hull, Sylvanus = G
Hunt, Timothy = Hunt
Kanouse, John = N
Lowry, John & Sylvia = S1
Preston, Roswell & Mehitable = P
Mills, Louis = NO
Wood, Selleck = Cheever

Scio

Foster, Theodore = H, F

Sharon Twp

Gillet, Amasa = T
»**Hill, Lewis** = T
Ockrow, Henry & Nelson = HA

Superior Twp

Camp, Ira = G1
»**Davis, William** = G1
Goodell, Jotham = G1
»**Granger**, G1
Fowler, Joseph = G1

Ypsilanti Area

Bennett, Prince & Esther = Bennett
Chase, A. Leonard & Elizabeth = G
Gordon, David & family = Hav
Gorton, Job & Eliza = Gorton
»**Hill, Caroline** = G
Lay, Ezra & Zina = GS

McAndrew, Helen & Thomas = McAndrew
McCoy, George & George, Jr. = M
»**McCoy, Millie** = M
Morton, Maria = G
»**Washington, Martha** = G
Weed, Ira M. = N

Wayne County

Beecher, Luther = L

Detroit

»**Blackburn, Thornton & Rutha** = B
»**Brown, John**
»**Cooper, Edward**
»**Dade, Benjamin**
DeBaptiste, George = L
»**Denison, Lisette & Scipio**
Finney, Seymour = L
Foote, Charles C. = H, GR
French, George & Caroline = B
Gordon, Richard
»**Gragston, Arnold** = Gragston
Hallock, Horace = T, H
Hoag, _____
Holmes, Silas M. = H
Lambert, William = L
Lightfoot, Madison & Tabitha = B
Maten, James
Monroe, William C
Porter, Arthur L. = SOL
Reynolds, J.P. = L
»**Rose, Giles** = Am. Anti-Slavery Soc.
Schwarz, John
Underwood, Farmer = L
Walker, William
Watson, Walter = G1
Zug, Samuel = T, H

Livonia

Chubb, Glode = L
Trenton = M

Wyandotte

Bush ___ = M

Appendix 3: Michigan Underground Railroad Historic Sites

Places designated by the State of Michigan as Historic Sites,
though not always based on the Underground Railroad–related history.

De Baptiste, George, Home Informational Site
Southwest corner of East Larned and Beaubien streets, Detroit — Wayne County

Dexter, Judge Samuel W., House
8347 Island Lake Road, Dexter vicinity — Washtenaw County

Douglass, Frederick, and John Brown Meeting Informational Site
633 East Congress, at St. Antoine, Detroit — Wayne County

Elmwood Cemetery
1200 Elmwood Avenue, Detroit — Wayne County

Emmendorfer House [William Gilmour]
4121 Pontiac Trail, Orchard Lake — Oakland County

Evergreen Cemetery [Jonathan Walker]
Bounded by Grand, Wood, Pine, and Irvin streets, Muskegon — Muskegon County

Farmington Historic District [Arthur & Nathan Power]
Grand River Avenue and Shiawassee Avenue from Warner Street to junction of Grand River and Shiawassee, Farmington — Oakland County

Finney Hotel / Underground Railway Informational Site
46 State Street, northeast corner of State and Griswold streets, Detroit — Wayne County

First Michigan Colored Regiment Informational Site
Duffield School Ground, 2700 Clinton Street at Joseph Campau, Detroit — Wayne County

First Quaker Meeting Informational Designation
Farmington Municipal Building — Grand River, 1 block west of Farmington Road, Farmington — Oakland County

Fitch, Jabez S., House
310 North Kalamazoo Avenue, Marshall — Calhoun County

Forth, Elizabeth Denison, Home Site, Informational Site
328 Macomb, Detroit — Wayne County

Forth, Elizabeth Denison, Informational Site
Oak Hill Cemetery, 216 University Drive, Pontiac — Oakland County

Gorham, Charles T., Informational Designation
Michigan National Bank, 124 W. Michigan, Marshall — Calhoun County

Hussey, Erastus & Sarah, Res. & Store, Informational Site
Kellogg Foundation Headquarters, One Michigan Avenue, Battle Creek — Calhoun County

Lambert, William, Homesite Informational Site
1930 East Lafayette, Detroit — Wayne County

McCoy, Elijah, Commemorative Designation
229 Michigan Avenue, Ypsilanti — Washtenaw County

McCoy, Elijah, Home Informational Site
5730 Lincoln Avenue, Detroit — Wayne County

Marshall Informational Site
Town Square, West Michigan Ave. Marshall—
Calhoun County

Merritt, Charles, House
327 North Capital Avenue, Battle Creek — Calhoun County

Methodist Episcopal Church
302 Cedar Street, Niles — Berrien County

Michigan Central Railroad Detroit Station
2405 West Vernor Street, Detroit — Wayne County

Nankin Pioneer Informational Designation Marcus Swift
Warren Road and Sunset Drive, Garden City — Wayne County

Nankin Township School District No. 3 Commemorative (Designation) [Abel Patchen]
6420 Newburgh Road, Westland — Wayne County

Negro Settlers Informational Designation
School Section Lake Park, intersection of 9 Mile Road and 90th Avenue, Mecosta vicinity — Mecosta County

Newberry Hall [John S. Newberry, Mary Ann Theresa Newberry, Elihu Newberry]
434 South State Street, Ann Arbor — Washtenaw County

Newport Academy [Emily Ward, sister of Eber Ward]
405 South Main Street, Marine City — St. Clair County

Olivet College Informational Designation
Burrage Library, NE corner of College Avenue and Main Street, Olivet — Eaton County

Raisin Valley Friends Meetinghouse [Daniel Smith, Laura Smith Haviland, Elizabeth Margaret Chandler, Raisin Institute]
3552 North Adrian Highway, Adrian — Lenawee County

Resisting Slavery [Robert Cromwell] Informational Site
920 South Saginaw Flint, Genesee County

Richards, Fannie, Home Informational Site
1357 East Congress, Detroit — Wayne County

Starkweather Hall [Mary Ann Starkweather]
901 West Forest, Ypsilanti — Washtenaw County

Stowers, Walter
4180 Burns, Detroit — Wayne County

Straker, D. Augustus, Informational Site related
428 Temple, Detroit — Wayne County

Sutton House
3901 Sutton Road, Adrian — Lenawee County

Thomas, Dr. Nathan M., House
613 East Cass Street, Schoolcraft — Kalamazoo County

Tucker, William, House
29020 Riverbank, Harrison Township — Macomb County

Under the Oaks, Commemorative Designation
NW corner of Second and Franklin Streets, Jackson — Jackson County

Underground Railroad Informational Designation
Bonine Elk Park, M-60, 1/2 mile west of Vandalia, Vandalia — Cass County

Village of Romeo Informational Designation [Romeo Academy mentioned]
Corner of Main and Church streets, Romeo — Macomb County

Webster Presbyterian Church [Charles Clark, Moses Kingsley]
5484 Webster Church Road, SE of Farrell Road, Dexter vicinity — Washtenaw County

White Pigeon
White Pigeon Village, White Pigeon — St. Joseph County

Zimmerman, John D., House
119 East High Street, Union City — Branch County

Chapter Notes

Preface

1. Resources online include a website by historian Douglas Harper called "Slavery in the North" which includes states of New England and all the states of the Northwest Territory, except Michigan. http://www.slavenorth.com/author.htm.

2. *Hidden in Plain View* by Jacqueline L. Tobin and Raymond G. Dobard, Ph.D. (New York: Anchor Books, 2000) and *Sweet Clara and the Freedom Quilt* by Deborah Hopkinson and James Ransome (New York: Knopf Books for Young Readers, 2003) are among the most successful of many quilt-related books published since 2009.

3. The highly publicized book *Hidden in Plain View* (Tobin and Dobard) was based on the oral history of one person, decades removed from the time of historical significance. *The Trackless Trail Leads On* by Frances Cloud Taylor (Kennett Square, PA: F. C. Taylor, 1995) stated, without footnoted references, that many abolitionists used lawn jockeys to identify their Underground Railroad stations (p. 8). The use of quilts and lawn jockeys may not be apocryphal, but the fact of extreme rarity and lack of primary resources is misleading when they are referenced out of context.

4. Larry Gara, *The Liberty Line: the Legend of the Underground Railroad* (Lexington: University Press of Kentucky, 1961), 94.

5. Fergus M. Bordewich, *Bound for Canaan: The Underground Railroad and the War for the Soul of America* (New York: Amistad Books, 2005); Wilbur Siebert, *The Underground Railroad from Slavery to Freedom* (Mineola, NY: Dover, 2006).

6. Bruce Chadwick, *Traveling the Underground Railroad: A Visitor's Guide to More Than 300 Sites* (Secaucus, NJ: Carol, 1999).

Chapter One

1. Siebert, *Underground Railroad from Slavery to Freedom*, 39–40. Bert Joseph Griswold and Mrs. Samuel R. Taylor, *The Pictorial History of Fort Wayne, Indiana*, vol. 1 (Chicago: Robert O. Law, 1917).

2. *Ibid.*, Frederic Hoover, son of Andrew Hoover, was born in North Carolina, Sept. 24, 1783. The fam-ily settled on Middle Fork in 1806. He married Catharine Yount. The Frederick Hoover Collection and many other Quaker records can be found at Earlham College.

3. Thomas Gorton, *Samuel Gorton of Rhode Island and his Descendants* (Baltimore: Gateway Press, 1982); John Hope Franklin and Alfred A. Moss, Jr., *From Slavery to Freedom*, 6th ed. (New York: Alfred A. Knopf, 1988); Jonathan Earle, *The Routledge Atlas of African American History* (New York, Routledge, 2000).

4. Earle, *Routledge Atlas*, 26–27. A rebellion occurred in New York in 1712.

5. William Goodell, *The American Slave Code in Theory and Practice: Its Distinctive Features Shown by Its Statutes, Judicial Decisions, and Illustrative Facts* (New York: American and Foreign Anti-Slavery Society, 1853).

6. Revolutionary War papers, State Archives Collection of the Connecticut State Library. http://www.hartford-hwp.com/archives. The witness to the petition, Jonathan Sturges, is an ancestor of the author.

7. Taylor, *Trackless Trail*.

8. Earle, *Routledge Atlas*, 34.

9. Alan Brinkley, *The Unfinished Nation* (Davis: University of California, 1997), 148.

10. Brinkley, *Unfinished Nation*, 150–151; Miscellaneous Papers of the Continental Congress, 1774–1789; Northwest Ordinance, July 13, 1787 (National Archives Microfilm Publication M332, roll 9); Records of the Continental and Confederation Congresses and the Constitutional Convention, 1774–1789, Record Group 360, National Archives (U.S.); and United States, *National Archives Publication* (Washington: The Archives, 1900s).

11. Franklin and Moss, *Slavery to Freedom*, 81–95.

12. Acts of the Second Congress of the United States, Statute II, Library of Congress website: http://memory.loc.gov.

13. "Minutes of the proceedings of a convention of delegates from the abolition societies established in different parts of the United States," from the *Samuel J. May Anti-Slavery Collection* (Ithaca: Cornell University Library, Rare and Manuscript Collections), 2000s. <http://resolver.library.cornell.edu/misc/4270009>.

14. Henry Clay Fox, *Memoirs of Wayne County and*

the City of Richmond, Indiana: from the Earliest Historical Times Down to the Present, Including a Genealogical and Biographical Record of Representative Families in Wayne County (Madison, WI: Western Historical Association, 1912), 27–31, 147–50.

15. Charles Osborn, Journal of that Faithful Servant of Christ, Charles Osborn, Containing an Account of Many Travels and Labors in the Work of the Ministry, and His Trials and Exercises in the Service of the Lord, and in Defense of the Truth, as it is in Jesus, (Cincinnati: A. Pugh, 1854), xiii.

16. John Rankin and Thomas Rankin. Letters on American Slavery: Addressed to Mr. Thomas Rankin, Merchant at Middlebrook, Augusta Co., Va., (Boston: Garrison & Knapp, 1833). For a documented history of John Rankin, see Ann Hagedorn's Beyond the River: The Untold Story of the Heroes of the Underground Railroad (New York: Simon & Schuster, 2004).

17. Census data from the University of Virginia Library. Acts of the 32nd General Assembly of New Jersey, Chapter II, Section 1, 1807, (courtesy of the Special Collections/ University Archives, Rutgers University Libraries). In 1807, New Jersey passed an act granting the right to vote to "free, white males."

18. History of St. Clair County, Michigan, Containing an Account of its Settlement, Growth, Development and Resources, its War Record, Biographical Sketches, the Whole Preceded by a History of Michigan (Chicago: A.T. Andreas, 1883) 642–3.

19. Reports and Collections of the Michigan Pioneer and Historical Society 1–15 (1874–1890) vol. 6, 357–61.

20. Silas Farmer, History of Detroit and Wayne County and Early Michigan: 1839–1902 (Detroit: S. Farmer for Munsell, New York, 1890).

21. Robert F. Eldredge, Past and Present of Macomb County, Michigan (Chicago: S.J. Clarke, 1905), 625–8.

22. In one case, Richard Patterson of Sandwich, Ontario, Canada, tried to apprehend Joseph Quinn and Jane as slaves. Judge Woodward did not allow it on the grounds that they were not in Patterson's possession when the British ceded Michigan to the United States. See Edward Cahill, "Historical Lights from Judicial Decisions" Michigan Historical Collections (Michigan Historical Commission, 1912), 38.

Judge Woodward ruled in the Elliot/Heward case on October 23, 1807. See David G. Chardavoyne, "Michigan and the Fugitive Slave Acts" The Court Legacy, vol. 12, no. 3 (November 2004), 1–3. A marker honors Elizabeth Denison Forth (c. 1787–1866) at 328 Macomb Street in Detroit.

23. The William Tucker House is one of the oldest surviving houses in Michigan and is currently a private residence in Macomb County. See Appendix: Michigan's Historic Sites for further information.

24. Farmer, History of Detroit, 750–751. Lemuel Shattuck served as Superintendent at the time.

25. Siebert, Underground Railroad from Slavery to Freedom, 37–41.

26. Talcott Enoch Wing, History of Monroe County, Michigan (New York: Munsell, 1890), 138.

27. David M. Katzman, Before the Ghetto: Black Detroit in the 19th Century (Urbana: University of Illinois Press, 1975), 5–7.

28. Several names appear under different spellings, including Hudnall, McDonel, and Witherel. I used spellings found in Michigan documents, rather than those that appear on the affidavit. The affidavit from the "Territorial Papers of the United States," compiled and edited by Clarence Edwin Carter, vol. 11, is reproduced on the Central Michigan University website. http://clarke.cmich.edu.

Chapter Two

1. Paul R. Peck, Landsmen of Washtenaw County: An Atlas and Plat of the First Landowners of Washtenaw County, Michigan (Ann Arbor: P.R. Peck, 1986), 308. His purchase of 80 acres, E½-NE¼ of Sec. 36, was registered on December 12, 1826.

2. Portrait and Biographical Album of Washtenaw County, Michigan, Containing Biographical Sketches of Prominent and Representative Citizens, Together with Biographies of all the Governors of the State, and of the Presidents of the United States (Chicago: Biographical Publishing, 1891), 546–7. Ira Camp married Mary Godfrey and the couple had four children: Hiram, Mary, Elvira, and Joel. Hiram Camp married Frances Bacon and remained in Superior Township.

3. Wilbur Siebert papers, MSS116, Box 91, Ohio Historical Society Archive/Library (Ohio Historical Society, Columbus, OH). Dr. Wilbur Siebert interviewed Solon Goodell in Ypsilanti, Michigan, on July 28, 1895. The reference in which William Davis helped Henry Smith is found in the Coggan Collections, Charles Wright Museum Library. By 1856, most property on Geddes Road in the southeast corner of Superior Township was owned by a Fowler or Goodell. There was Fowler school, Fowler mill, and Fowler creek. George W. and Jacob Fowler were brothers who emigrated from Canada. Other members of the family settled in an area called Fowlerville.

4. Wolcott B. Williams, "New England Influence in Michigan," Reports and Collections of the Michigan Pioneer and Historical Society 17 (1892), 311. The Second Great Awakening is discussed in most American history books.

5. The pattern of population dispersion from specific cultural regions is explored by numerous settlement geographers including Henry Glassie and Fred Kniffen. The references in this chapter are drawn primarily from Pierce F. Lewis "The Northeast and the Making of American Geographical Habits" first published in 1990 by HarperCollinsAcademic and reprinted in The Making of the American Landscape edited by Michael P. Conzen (New York: Routledge, 1994).

6. In West to Far Michigan, Kenneth E. Lewis explores the formation of frontier communities and the concepts of social group identity (East Lansing: Michigan State University Press, 2002).

7. Anson DePuy Van Buren, "Michigan in Her

Party Politics" *Michigan Pioneer and Historical Society Collection,* vol. 17 (1892), 240.

8. The original interview of Erastus Hussey was printed May 3 and May 10, 1885 in the *Battle Creek Sunday Morning Call.* The interview was reprinted in other newspapers, including the *Ann Arbor Courier,* May 13, 1885. Charles E. Barnes reproduced the interview (without the questions of the interviewer) in the *Michigan Pioneer and Historical Society Collections,* vol. 38 (Lansing: Wynkoop Hallenbeck, 1912), under the title "Battle Creek as a Station on the Underground Railway." Quotes from the interview will cite Barnes for the benefit of researchers who wish to consult the publication at libraries or online.

9. Stephen D. Bingham, *Early History of Michigan: with Biographies of State Officers, Members of Congress, Judges and Legislators* (Lansing: Thorp & Godfrey, 1888).

10. Siebert, *Underground Railroad from Slavery to Freedom, 106.* Siebert cited an interview with Judge Finney of Detroit, Michigan.

11. L. H. Glover, *A Twentieth Century History of Cass County, Michigan* (Chicago: Lewis Publishing, 1906), 41.

12. Richard Illenden Bonner, *Memoirs of Lenawee County, Michigan* (Madison: Western Historical Association, 1909), 259–60. The road is located south of US 12 off Monagan Highway, east of Sand and Evans Lakes.

13. James E. Pilcher, ed., *Life and Labors of Elijah H. Pilcher of Michigan* (New York: Hunt & Eaton, 1892).

14. Glover, *Twentieth Century Cass County,* 381; Franklin Ellis and Crisfield Johnson, *History of Berrien and Van Buren Counties, Michigan: its Prominent Men and Pioneers* (Philadelphia: D.W. Ensign, 1880), 494.

15. Siebert papers, letter from H. H. Northrop.

16. Carlisle G. Davidson, "A Profile of Hicksite Quakerism in Michigan, 1830–1860," *Quaker History,* vol. 59, no. 2 (Autumn, 1970), 106–112.

17. Ann and Conrad Burton, *Michigan Quakers, Abstracts of Fifteen Meetings of the Society of Friends 1831–1960* (Decatur: Glyndwr Resources, 1989), 525.

18. Thomas D. Hamm, *The Transformation of American Quakerism: Orthodox Friends, 1800–1907* (Bloomington: Midland Books, 1988), xvi–xvii; Burton, *Michigan Quakers.*

19. Russell E. Bidlack, *John Allen and the Founding of Ann Arbor* (Ann Arbor: University of Michigan, 1962), 6.

20. Jonathan Marwill, *A History of Ann Arbor* (Ann Arbor: Ann Arbor Observer, 1987).

21. Nettie Schepeler-Van Der Werker, *History of Earliest Ann Arbor* (Ann Arbor: N. I. and E. B. Van Der Werker, 1919), 29–31.

22. Sources include Dexter's death announcement from the *Michigan Argus,* February 18, 1863; Norma McAllister, *Judge Samuel William Dexter* (Madison: University of Wisconsin, 1989); Louis W. Doll and Geneva Smithe, Pioneer Society of Washtenaw County, *History of Washtenaw County, Michigan To-gether with Sketches of its Cities, Villages and Townships and Biographies of Representative Citizens: History of Michigan* (Chicago: Chapman, 1881).

23. Brothers Eleazar and Nathaniel Millard in Oakland County, and David Millard with his wife Celia Hicks in Jackson; and Siebert papers, The Fourth Annual Report of the American Anti-Slavery Party.

24. Theodore Raeljeph [Ralljeph] Foster was born April 3, 1812, in Foster, RI, and died in 1865 in Lansing, MI. The Millard family was bound to the Fosters with the marriage of Theodore Foster (1752–1828) and Esther Bowen Millard (1785–1815). George Millard served as secretary of the Dexter branch of the Michigan Anti-Slavery Society in 1837. Siblings Dwight and Luzelia Foster migrated not long after and all four married members of the Seymour family. Family information is found in the Theodore Foster Papers and Pattengill Papers at the Bentley Historical Library.

25. Doll and Smithe, *History of Washtenaw County,* 997.

26. *Report of the Pioneer Society of the State of Michigan,* vol. 2 (1880).

27. The Friends Church was established at the township line on the farm of G. H. Alban. Ypsilanti Evangelical Friends Church Records, Bentley Historical Library.

28. Burton, *Michigan Quakers,* 24.

29. Prince Bennett file, Ypsilanti Historical Archives, Ypsilanti Press, includes a photocopy of an article, 1/19/1992.

30. Cathy Stromme Horste and Diane Follmer Wilson, *Water Under the Bridge: A History of Van Buren Township* (Belleville, MI: Van Buren Township Bicentennial Commission, 1977), 433–4; the *Ypsilanti Daily Press,* October 30, 1954. The original meeting house was built in 1842 at the corner of Bemis and Tuttle Hill Roads on land between the existing church and Youth House. Prince Bennett is buried in the Alban Cemetery; Ypsilanti Evangelical Friends Church Records.

31. The Rev. G. P. Tindall, *A Discourse on the Life and Character of the Late Rev. Ira M. Weed* (Ypsilanti: Pattison's Steam Printing House, 1872), 9.

32. Mrs. Mark (Rocenna) Norris wrote the comment, James Dubuar papers, 1834–1886; Records of the First Presbyterian Church in Ypsilanti, Michigan.

33. *Biographical Album of Washtenaw County,* 999. Richard was born in 1790 in Hudson, New York, to Goddard Glazier of Rhode Island and Lydia Bunker. Quaker records state that every male over 21 was taxed 25 cents for the military and that property was taken from the Friends when they refused to pay. Robert Glasier chose a traditional spelling of his name; however, in references to the entire family, the spelling of Glazier will be used.

34. Dubuar papers: Peter, Jacob, Rachel, Eve, Abraham, and Betsy Cook; David, Phoebe, Ira, and Sally Ann Hathaway; and John Kanouse, Jr. and Nelly Kanouse were named on the petition. John G. Kanouse, obituaries in *New York Evangelist and Peninsular Courier and Family Visitant,* Washtenaw County

Genealogy Society. J. G. Kanouse (parents: Jacob and Mary Kanouse) married Elizabeth Dodd on June 4, 1818.

35. Doll and Smithe, *History of Washtenaw County*, 1279. The church was built at 143 E. Michigan Avenue in Saline, on land donated by Orange Risdon. The church history states that at the christening of the church Ira Hathaway, John Kanouse and Abram Cook were elected and ordained; and History of the First Presbyterian Church Society of Saline, Michigan, 1899. In 1898 the Presbyterians built a new church in the Romanesque Revival style on the site of the old church at 143 E. Michigan Avenue. The elegant new church was built of brick on a cut stone foundation, with stained glass windows on the south and east elevations. It is listed on the National Register of Historic Places.

36. *Ann Arbor State Journal*, vol. 3 (1838); and John G. Kanouse Sermon 1842, Bentley Historical Library.

37. Amherst College Records online; and Dubuar papers.

38. James Baldwin Parker and John Pugh Gardner, *Treasure from Earthen Vessels: the History of Webster Church* (Dexter, MI: J. B. Parker, 1984).

39. *Michigan Pioneer and Historical Collections*, 1–15, vol. 11 (1874–1890), 279.

40. Anson DePuy VanBuren, "The Emigrant Family," *Michigan Pioneer and Historical Society,* vol. 14 (Lansing: Wynkoop Hallenbeck Crawford, 1908), 318–373.

41. Schepeler-Van Der Werker, *Earliest Ann Arbor,* 29–31.

Chapter Three

1. *Biographical Album of Washtenaw County, Michigan*; and McIntosh, W. H., "History of Ontario County, NY" (Ontario County: The American History and Genealogy Project, 1878).

2. David Walker, *Walker's Appeal, in Four Articles; Together with a Preamble, to the Coloured Citizens of the World, but in Particular, and Very Expressly, to Those of the United States of America, Written in Boston, State of Massachusetts, September 28, 1829* (Boston: David Walker, 1830), 79.

3. Charles Trabue, "The Voluntary Emancipation Of Slaves In Tennessee As Reflected In The State's Legislation And Judicial Decisions," *Tennessee Historical Magazine*, vol. 4.

4. Campbell Gibson and Kay Jung, *Historical Census Statistics on Population Totals By Race, 1790 to 1990, and by Hispanic Origin, 1970 to 1990, for the United States, Regions, Divisions, and States* (Washington, D.C.: U.S. Bureau of the Census, 2002).

5. Carter Godwin Woodson, *A Century of Negro Migration* (New York: AMS Press, 1970).

6. Henry Addison Nelson and Angelina Emily Grimké, "Report on the Condition of the People of Color in the State of Ohio: from the Proceedings of the Ohio Anti-Slavery Convention, Held at Putnam, on the 22d, 23d, and 24th of April, 1835" (Boston:

Isaac Knapp, 1835), *Samuel J. May Anti-Slavery Collection.*

7. Katzman, *Before the Ghetto*, 5–6.

8. Text of state marker read by the author in Louisville, Kentucky.

9. *Michigan Pioneer and Historical Collections,* 1–15 (1874–1890) vol. 12, 591–3; for a thorough investigation of the Blackburns, see *I've Got a Home in Glory Land* by Karolyn Smardz Frost.

10. Nathaniel Leach, *Reaching Out to Freedom, The Second Baptist Connection, History of Second Baptist Church, revised ed.* (Detroit: Second Baptist Church, 1988). Bethel AME Church is located at 5050 Saint Antoine, Detroit, history on state marker.

11. His house was located at 1930 East Lafayette, Detroit, per a State Historical Marker.

12. Levi Coffin, *Reminiscences of Levi Coffin* (New York: Arno Press and the New York Times, 1968), 139–42.

13. "Death of George DeBaptiste," *Detroit Daily Post* (February 23, 1875). DeBaptiste is honored with a State marker at the southwest corner of East Larned and Beaubien Streets, Detroit.

14. Julius Friedrich Sachse, *The German Pietists of Provincial Pennsylvania: 1694–1708* (Philadelphia: printed for the author, 1895), 323, 376–381. The Native American was enslaved by Peter Woglarn.

15. The DePuy and Aray families were linked in the eighteenth century when Cornelius Depuy attended the Reformed Dutch Church at Smithfield, PA, where Susannah, daughter of "Adam Aray (a Black man)" and "Caty Aray (a Black woman)" baptized their daughter, Susanna, on May 5, 1787; Nicholas Albertson, J.P., "Sussex County Marriages, 1773–1804" *The Genealogical Magazine of New Jersey* vol. 24, no. 1 (January, 1949), 3.

16. Henry H. Mitchell, *Black Church Beginnings: the Long-Hidden Realities of the First Years* (Grand Rapids: William B. Eerdmans, 2004), 70. The family name appears as Array, Aree, Aurray, and Ray in 300 years of records. A photocopy of the James Aray muster sheets shows him in the Capt. Helm's Company, 2nd New Jersey Regiment, Israel Shreve, Col. Aray Family Files, YHSA; also, see New Jersey Pensioners, 1835 Database at Ancestry.com.

17. Earle, *Routledge Atlas*, 38.

18. Aray and Ray descendants were numerous in New Jersey, where A. B. Ray led the Colored Newark Antislavery Society in 1836; U.S. Federal Census Records, 1850 (Pittsfield Township Roll 432, 1009) show Asher Aray's place of birth was New Jersey and Catherine's Pennsylvania; photocopy of original handwritten indenture of land purchase by Jacob Arree of Joseph Hall of Bridgewater Township, Somerset County, New Jersey, August 1805. A descendant of Jacob Aray stated he was born in Holland and this mistake is repeated in other records (Doll and Smithe, *History of Washtenaw County)*, Aray files, YHS.

19. In the same section of land with Aray, other purchasers were James Martin and his wife Letitia Depue, and Jacob Larzelere. Judge Jacob L. Larzelere from New Jersey, and later New York, purchased

land in Michigan but apparently did not move to the state.

20. *Combination Atlas Map of Washtenaw County* (Chicago: Everts & Stewart, 1874). Sharon Township residents, lacking a post office, collected their mail in Manchester.

21. The name is shown as Ockron and Ockro in the 1860 census; Ockry and Ockrow in Manchester accounts.

22. Glover, *Twentieth Century Cass County*, 287–30. A log building was erected about 1850. On the Michigan Historic State Marker description in 1848, Harrison Ash and Turner Byrd helped organize the Chain Lake Baptist Church in 1838, but Glover sets the date at January 4, 1848. The church is located at Chain Lake Road between Calvin Center and Union Roads. The cemetery has several hundred early graves with names of Black Americans: Allen, Artis, Evans, Sanders, and others.

23. Siebert papers, letter from John A. Marsh dated August 7, 1941.

24. Siebert papers, interview with the Rev. Anthony Bingey of Windsor, Ontario, Canada, Wednesday, July 31, 1895, by W. H. Siebert in MSS 116, Box 106.

25. Woodson, *Century of Negro Migration*, 36.

26. Siebert, The *Underground Railroad from Slavery to Freedom*, 150.

27. Josiah Henson, *The Life of Josiah Henson, Formerly a Slave, Now an Inhabitant of Canada, as Narrated by Himself* (Boston: Arthur D. Phelps, 1849), 70.

28. Henson, *Life of Josiah Henson*, 70–73.

29. John Lobb, ed., *An Autobiography of the Rev. Josiah Henson* (London: Christian Age Office, 1876); and www.archive.org/details/albertatest_01238, chapter 16.

Chapter Four

1. Henry Bibb, *Narrative of the Life and Adventures of Henry Bibb, an American Slave, Written by Himself* (New York: self-published, 1849), 46–47.

2. President Jackson enslaved up to 150 people at one time. Information and photographs of enslaved people at the Hermitage is found at The Hermitage website, http://www.thehermitage.com/index.

3. Earle, *Routledge Atlas*.

4. Edward Chambers Betts, *History of Huntsville, Alabama 1804 to 1870* (Huntsville: Brown, 1909, revised 1916), 61.

5. Samuel J. May, *Some Recollections of our Antislavery Conflict* (Boston: Fields, Osgood, 1869), 136–140; and Benjamin P. Thomas, *Theodore Weld: Crusader For Freedom* (New Brunswick: Rutgers University Press, 1950), chapter 3.

6. The Rev. Carroll Cutler, *A History of Western Reserve College: During Its First Half Century, 1826–1876* (Cleveland: Crocker's, 1876); President, Charles Backus-Storrs; and Professors Elizur Wright, Elizur Green, and Rufus Nutting.

7. Thomas, *Theodore Weld*, chapter 3; Hagedorn, *Beyond the River*, 65–89.

8. Dwight L. Dumond, *Antislavery Origins of the Civil War in the United States* (Ann Arbor: University of Michigan Press, 1939).

9. John L. Myers, "American Antislavery Society Agents and the Free Negro, 1833–1838," *Journal of Negro History*, vol. 52, no. 3 (July 1967), 200–201.

10. Thomas, *Theodore Weld*, 100; the history of antislavery societies is found in general history books, though there are some discrepancies in the founding dates. I consulted primarily Dumond, *Antislavery Origins*, and Otto J. Scott, *The Secret Six: John Brown and the Abolitionist Movement* (New York: New York Times Books, 1979), 88–91.

11. Dumond, *Antislavery Origins*, 88–9.

12. Thomas, *Theodore Weld*. Weld was born on November 23, 1803, in Hampton, Connecticut.

13. Dumond credited Weld with creating a crusade in the Midwest. See Dumond, *Antislavery Origins*.

14. *Signal of Liberty*.

15. On March 25, 1871, Catherine Stebbins, accompanied by her husband, attempted to register to vote in Michigan and was turned away; Giles Stebbins, *Upward Steps of Seventy Years* (New York: John W. Lovell, 1890), 90.

16. Myers, "Antislavery Society Agents." While Laura Haviland in Lenawee County and the Osborns in Cass County practiced a lease program in Michigan, the majority of farm communities were in Canada from Dawn to Sandwich to Buxton and more.

17. Siebert lists Monteith as an Underground Railroad agent in Ohio. Monteith's house in Ohio is a museum and registered site.

18. Sereno W. Streeter served as an agent in Ohio and then moved to Union City, Michigan, in 1857. John Clark settled in St. Clair, and Deodat Jeffers moved to Alamo Township, north of Kalamazoo. Jeffers is listed in the 1850 Census of Kalamazoo, living in a household with Amos Dean. Jeffers has not been linked to any church until 1883, when he was a Congregational minister in Silver Lake, Cass County, and living as a tenant in Comstock Village.

19. *Territorial Kansas Online, 1854–1861,* http://www.territorialkansasonline.org.Created and maintained by the Kansas State Historical Society and the Kansas Collection of the University of Kansas.

20. David S. Reynolds, *John Brown, Abolitionist: the Man Who Killed Slavery* (New York: Alfred A. Knopf, 2005).

21. *Territorial Kansas Online, 1854–1861.*

22. Edward W. Barber, *The Vermontville Colony, its Genesis and History, with Personal Sketches of the Colonists* (Lansing, MI: Robert Smith, 1897). Dr. Kedzie was born at Delhi, NY, January 28, 1823; he came to Michigan in 1826 with his father, William Kedzie, to Deerfield in Lenawee County.

23. Elizabeth Margaret Chandler papers; Laura S. Haviland, *A Woman's Life-Work: Labors and Experiences* (Cincinnati: Walden and Stowe for the author, 1882); Chandler was likely influenced by the writing of Elizabeth Heyrick, whose pamphlet was published in the *Genius*. See Elizabeth Heyrick, *Immediate, Not Gradual Abolition: or, An Inquiry into the Shortest,*

Safest, and Most Effectual Means of Getting Rid of West Indian Slavery (London: Sold by J. Hatchard, 1824). Benjamin Lundy published Chandler's works in 1845.

24. For further reading about Lenawee County's antislavery activity, see Charles Lindquist's *The Antislavery-Underground Railroad Movement: in Lenawee County, Michigan, 1830–1860* (Lenawee: Lenawee County Historical Society, 1999).

25. Foster papers, Bentley Historical Library.

26. The Aray name is written as Ray in the Michigan census and in Seibert, *Underground Railroad,* 36, 95, 99; "Report of the Third American Anti-Slavery Society Meeting," Samuel J. May Anti-Slavery Collections (2000s), <http://resolver.library.cornell.edu/misc/4270009>.

27. *Michigan Pioneer and Historical Society* , vol. 21; George H. Hazelton married the Reverend Beach's daughter Lucy B. Beach in 1838. The families moved to Flint, where the Reverend Beach preached. The Rev. John Beach was born in 1789 in Greene County, NY, and died in 1852 in Michigan. He married his cousin Lucy Beach, daughter of Jonathan (1761–1850) and Lucy Baldwin Beach.

28. See appendix: Michigan Historic Division, Registered State Site #488.

29. The committee of arrangements included Robert Stuart, Nathan Power, Elijah Bromer, Arthur L. Porter, and William Kirkland; the arrangements for the founding convention were made by Ezekiel Webb, Thomas Chandler, and Darius C. Jackson.

30. Robert H. Abzug, *Passionate Liberator: Theodore Dwight Weld and the Dilemma of Reform* (USA: Oxford University Press, 1982), 31.

31. *Report on the Proceedings of the Anti-Slavery Society State Convention Held at Ann Arbor, Michigan the 10th and 11th of November, 1836* (Detroit: Snow and Fisk, 1836).

32. *Michigan Argus,* February 16, 1837.

33. *Ibid.*, February 2, 1837.

34. W.A. Whitney and R.I. Bonner, *History and Biographical Record of Lenawee County, Michigan Containing a History of the Organization and Early Settlement of the County, Together with a Biographical Record ... Obtained from Personal Interviews* (Adrian, MI: W. Sterns, 1879), 143–44.

35. From the *Samuel J. May Anti-Slavery Collection.*

36. Bibb, *Narrative.* Henry, born in 1815, never knew his father, James Bibb.

Chapter Five

1. Nathan M. Thomas papers, Box 1, Bentley Historical Library. The Dr. Nathan Thomas House is listed in the National Park Service Network to Freedom. The house was moved to 613 East Cass Street, Schoolcraft, and is open for tours.

2. Betts, *Huntsville, Alabama,* 54.

3. Nathan Coggeshall, Thomas Baldwin, and John Shugart settled in Grant County, Indiana, after their Quaker families moved from southern states; and

Siebert, *Underground Railroad from Slavery to Freedom,* 407.

4. Siebert papers. In the Society of Friends organization, several quarterly meetings made up the yearly meeting, the highest authority for Friends. Decisions at the yearly meeting in matters of faith and practice were final. See Hamm, *Transformation of American Quakerism,* xvi–xvii.

5. Glover, *Twentieth Century Cass County,* 112.

6. Coffin, *Reminiscences,* 160–170. There is some discrepancy in Coffin's account as to whether Rachel was living in Detroit in 1844 or had crossed for a visit.

7. The writings of Nathan Thomas are found in two collections at the Bentley Historical Library. The Arthur R. Kooker Papers contain correspondence and three small diaries of miscellaneous notes related to farming, newspaper subscriptions, and voting records, as well as some recollections of people who escaped from slavery. The quote is from Folder "Autobiography" and the account is dated Sep 8, 1868.

8. Nathan M. Thomas papers, Box 1, folder "History of the Anti-Slavery Movement, 1839–42."

9. Nathan M. Thomas papers, Box 1.

10. A transcribed letter from descendants of Amasa Gillet, Elizabeth Heap Anderson and Richard Anderson, dated Dec. 5, 2002, used with permission. Sharon Mills, on Sharon Hollow Road, was purchased and restored by the Washtenaw County Parks and Recreation Commission in 2002 and is open to the public.

11. Gillet family members are buried in Sharon Township. *Signal of Liberty*, January 19, 1842.

12. *Signal of Liberty,* March 4, 1842.

13. *Ibid.*, November 18, 1844.

14. John Patchin, *Sketches of the Life of John Patchin,* from the National Society of the Daughters of the American Revolution. Also from the document of Claribel L. Bickford (Duarte, CA: April 1966). Cited with permission from Shel Michaels, www.shel.net/shel/genealogy/txt/jp.txt.

15. Haviland, *A Woman's Life-Work,* 57–58.

16. Haviland, *A Woman's Life-Work.* Charles Haviland, Laura's parents and one of her children died around the same time from a skin infection called Erysipelas.

17. Stephen Decatur Helms letter photocopy, Carol Mull papers. The Helms letter photocopy was sent to me by Gary McIntyre of Ft. Collins, Colorado, and donated by me to the Michigan Historical Library, Lansing, Michigan. Wystan Stevens contacted Mr. McIntyre to solicit a copy in May 2006. Mr. McIntyre described the letter as follows: an unstamped, folded letter, postmarked Raisin, MI, September 7, 1844, by Stephen Decatur Helms (b.1813 Walkill, Orange County, NY) to his brother Silas Y. Helms (b.1817 Walkill, Orange County, NY). Stephen sent it to Silas Helms in Galesburgh, Knox County, IL, from Raisin Township, Michigan. The parents of these brothers were born in Walkill, Orange County, NY, and were Reuben Helms (b. Oct. 27, 1785) and Sarah Coleman (b. about 1789). They had four children: Elmira, Stephen Decatur, Benjamin and Silas Youngs Helms.

18. Wing, *Monroe County,* 458–459.

19. James M. Thomas, *Kalamazoo County Directory: with a History of the County from Its Earliest Settlement* (Kalamazoo, MI: Stone Brothers, 1869). Henry Montague and Moses Kingsley moved from Webster Township, Washtenaw County, to Oshtemo, Kalamazoo County, in 1837.

20. Montague was nominated as a representative on the Liberty Party ticket in 1845 and listed at the 1846 Anti-Slavery Society meeting in Marshall.

21. Stebbins, *Upward Steps,* 86.

22. According to the History of Branch County, the four men who created the village were Richard L. Clark, Israel W. Clark, Lyman Gilbert, and Isaac Diamond. The previous description of Union City and the story that follows are from that account and Stebbins, *Upward Steps.*

23. The John Zimmerman House is recognized as a Michigan Historic Site for its significance as an Underground Railroad station. It is a private residence on High Street, Union City. See appendix.

Chapter Six

1. Burritt Hamilton, "The Underground Railroad" in Washington Gardner, *History of Calhoun County, Michigan: a Narrative Account of its Historical Progress, its People, and its Principle Interests* (Chicago: Lewis, 1913).

2. Raymond Bial, *Underground Railroad* (New York: Houghton Mifflin, 1995); original document in collections of Illinois Historical Society.

3. Historical Census Browser, University of Virginia Library, http://fisher.lib.virginia.edu/collections/stats/histcensus/php/state.php.

4. John L. Myers, "The Early Antislavery Agency System in Pennsylvania, 1833–1837," *Pennsylvania History,* vol. 31 (January 1964).

5. Siebert, *Underground Railroad from Slavery to Freedom,* 50–51.

6. *History of Page County, Iowa: Containing a History of the County, Its Cities, Towns, Etc.* (Des Moines: Historical Company, 1880), 622–623.

7. *Michigan Pioneer and Historical Society* , vol. 22 (1893), 526–541; and Wolcott B. Williams, *A History of Olivet College* (Olivet, MI: Olivet College, 1901).

8. Thomas papers, box 1; and Barnes, "Battle Creek," 279–285.

9. Thomas papers, box 1, folder "History of the Anti-Slavery Movement."

10. Barnes, "Battle Creek," 279–285.

11. Barnes "Battle Creek," 55; originally published in the *Sunday Morning Call,* May-August, 1885; reprinted "Stories of Slave Days," Jan. 20, 1889, *Chicago Daily Tribune.*

12. Barnes, "Battle Creek;" and Coffin, *Reminiscences,* 244–9.

13. *Ibid.*

14. Coffin, *Reminiscences,* 244–9.

15. McGee, Melville, "Early Days of Concord,

Jackson County, Michigan," *Michigan Pioneer and Historical Society,* vol. 21, 427.

16. Charles Victor DeLand, *DeLand's History of Jackson County, Michigan: Embracing a Concise Review of its Early Settlement, Industrial Development and Present Conditions, Together with Interesting Reminiscences* (Chicago: Bowen, 1903), 344. Smalley, a native of Vermont, moved to Hampton, Saratoga County, NY, in 1816 and then to Michigan. George L. Smalley was chosen sheriff in 1858, and again in 1860, and Jacob V. Smalley was elected sheriff in 1872.

17. DeLand, *DeLand's History of Jackson County,* 812–813. Thomas McGee was born in Coleraine, Franklin County, MA, on January 6, 1790. He married Polly Stowe, born September 2, 1791, in Granville, NY. Their home was located in Section 22, one and a half miles northwest of Concord.

18. *Signal of Liberty,* May 12, 1841, Bentley Historical Library.

19. *Ibid.,* May 12, 1841.

20. William J. Switala, *Underground Railroad in Delaware, Maryland and West Virginia and Underground Railroad in Pennsylvania* (Mechanicsburg, PA: Stackpole Books, 2004).

21. Siebert, *Underground Railroad from Slavery to Freedom,* 62.

22. Siebert papers, Northrop letter.

23. Barnes, "Battle Creek."

24. Foster papers.

25. *Colored American,* September 26, 1840.

26. Barnes, "Battle Creek."

27. McGee, "Early Days of Concord," 427.

28. Annetta English, *History of Manchester,* 1930; Bentley Historical Library, 102.

29. The Ann Arbor City Directory, 1860, shows he lived on the northwest corner of Division and Washington Streets; Volland attended Friends of Human Progress Meetings in Waterloo, NY, in 1854, 1855, and 1857, http://ublib.buffalo.edu/libraries. A later newspaper account (*Ypsilantian,* March 20, 1885) stated that older citizens knew Volland was a conductor on the Underground Railroad.

30. "Freedom's Railway: Reminiscences of the Brave Old Days of the Famous Underground Railroad Line," *Detroit Tribune,* January 17, 1886, 2.

31. Katherine Dupre Lumpkin, "'The General Plan was Freedom': A Negro Secret Order on the Underground Railroad," *Pylon: The Atlanta University Review of Race and Culture,* vol. 28, no. 1 (Spring 1967), 69.

32. William Walker and Thomas S. Gaines, *Buried Alive (Behind Prison Walls) for a Quarter of a Century: Life of William Walker* (Saginaw, MI: Friedman & Hynan, 1892), 54–55; and "Documenting the American South," National Endowment for the Humanities, http://docsouth.unc.edu/neh/gaines/summary.html.

33. Tom Dodd and James Mann, *Our Heritage: Down by the Depot in Ypsilanti* (Ypsilanti: Depot Town Association, 1999).

34. *Ibid.*

35. James Mann, "Tunnels Drained of Dramatic

Story More Prosaic," *Ypsilanti Community News* (November 7, 2005).

36. Grace Shackman, "The Underground Railroad in Ann Arbor," *Ann Arbor Observer* (December 1998).

37. Hamilton, "The Underground Railroad," in Gardner, *History of Calhoun County.*

38. Arthur R. Kooker Papers, Box 1, "Diaries."

39. Nathan Thomas papers. The listings that follow are taken from this source and the Erastus Hussey account previously cited as Barnes.

40. *The History of Cass County, Michigan* (Chicago: Waterman, Watkins, 1882), chapter 27, 109–110.

41. *Ibid.*, 261.

42. *Ibid.*, chapter 27, 109–110.

43. Chapman Brothers, *Portrait and Biographical Album of Jefferson and Van Buren Counties, Iowa* (Chicago: Lake City, 1890), 186.

44. Samuel W. Durant, *History of Kalamazoo County, Michigan: with Illustrations and Biographical Sketches of its Prominent Men and Pioneers* (Philadelphia: Everts and Abbot, 1880); Bird was settled by the first tax roll with 120 acres, valued at $360.

45. David Fisher and Frank Little, *Compendium of History and Biography of Kalamazoo County, Mich.* (Chicago: A. W. Bowen, 1906), 68.

46. *Biographical Review of Calhoun County, Michigan: Containing Historical, Biographical and Genealogical Sketches of Many of the Prominent Citizens of To-Day and Also of the Past* (Chicago: Hobart and Mather, 1904) 625.

47. *Michigan Pioneer and Historical Collection*, Pioneer Society of the State of Michigan, Michigan State Historical Society, vol. 5, Pen Pictures of Pioneers (Published by The Society, 1884), 271.

48. DeLand, *History of Jackson County,* 332–3.

49. *Ibid.*, 347.

50. *Ibid.*, 347; and Barnes, "Battle Creek."

51. DeLand, *History of Jackson County*, 269.

52. DeLand, *History of Jackson County*, 270.

53. *Signal of Liberty*, 1841 to 1844.

54. Hussey continued the list of agents: Francisco, Francisco; Dexter, Samuel W. Dexter; Scio, Theodore Foster; Ann Arbor, Guy Beckley; Geddes, John Geddes; Ypsilanti and Plymouth forgotten; Swartsburg, no name; Detroit, Horace Hallock, Silas M. Holmes, and Samuel Zug.

55. Seymour Boughton Treadwell papers. Treadwell's farm was in Section 20, Jackson County. Seymour B. Treadwell was born in 1792 in Connecticut.

56. Barnes, "Battle Creek;" Historic American Buildings Survey/Historic American Engineering Record, http://lcweb2.locgov. Gordon Hall (Judge Samuel W. Dexter House) is located at 8347 Island Lake Drive, Dexter, Washtenaw County; and Norma McAllister, *Judge Samuel William Dexter* (Dexter, MI: Thomson-Shore, 1989), 30.

57. *Michigan Argus*, February 18, 1863.

58. "Biographical Directory of the United States Congress, 1774-Present," http://bioguide.cogress.gov. Esther Bowen Millard's parents were Noah and Hannah Millard of Rehoboth, Massachusetts.

59. Pattengill papers, 1767–1963, Bentley Histor-

ical Library. The collection contains letters of Seymour Foster and writings of Theodore G. Foster related to the Underground Railroad. Samuel W. Foster was born November 30, 1806 in Foster, RI, and died in California.

60. Pattengill papers; the story has been recounted by Ted G. Foster in "Village of Scio was Stop on 'Underground Railroad,'" Lansing State Journal, May 15, 1955, and by Nicholas A. Marsh in "Scio's Lost Landmark," *Ann Arbor Observer*, May 1995. The original reference to the event is found in the Pattengill family papers; Theodore G. Foster compiled letters and articles by his father Seymour and grandfather T.R. Foster into an article about the Underground Railroad. In a reference to Erastus Hussey revealing the names of conductors to Charles Barnes, T.G. Foster writes that Samuel Foster and his sons, of Dexter, had a station, yet the article as printed states Samuel Dexter and his sons.

61. *State Journal*, July 12, 1838, AADL microfilm.

62. *Signal of Liberty*, August 19, 1844.

63. Barnes, "Battle Creek."

Chapter Seven

1. "Lyman Goodnow's Story," Wisconsin Historical Society Archives; and Lyman Goodnow, "Recollection 1880?" transcription, state of Wisconsin Digital Collection, http://digital.library.wisc.edu/1711.dl/WI.Goodnow2e. Information about Dyer is found at the Burlington Historical Society website, http://www.burlingtonhistory.org/.

2. Theodore Clarke Smith, *The Liberty and Free Soil Parties in the Northwest: Toppan Prize Essay of 1896* (New York: Longmans, Green, 1897), 43.

3. Dwight L. Dumond, ed. *Letters of James Gillespie Birney* (New York: Appleton-Century, 1938).

4. Treadwell papers, letter to Treadwell from A. L. Porter, Detroit, April 23, 1840.

5. William Birney, *James G. Birney and His Times: the Genesis of the Republican Party with Some Account of Abolition Movements in the South before 1828* (New York: D. Appleton-Century, 1890), 350.

6. Smith, *Liberty and Free Soil*, 52.

7. *Signal of Liberty*, February 20, 1843.

8. Thomas papers, letter dated November 21, 1841.

9. Guy Beckley's house at 1425, and Josiah Beckley's house at 1709 Pontiac Trail were still standing in 2009. They are private residences, not open to the public.

10. *Signal of Liberty*, December 1, 1841.

11. *Ibid.*, May 19, 1841.

12. *Ibid.*

13. *Ibid.*; and *Colored American*, June 5, 1841.

14. See Coffin House website for photograph of attic: http://www.waynet.org/levicoffin/default.htm. Stories have appeared in newspapers and local histories. The current owners of the house provided their passed down histories to the author and Marnie Paulus, who wrote a National Park Service "Network to Freedom" application in 2003. The house remains

a private residence on the Register. See the NPS website: http://www.nps.gov/history/nr/travel/underground/in2.htm.

15. The author visited the schoolhouse and viewed the cellar in 2007.

16. *Signal of Liberty*, 1840s issues.

17. Swift Family papers 1934–1921, Bentley Historical Society.

18. Swift papers, folder 1.

19. Melvin D. Osband, "My Recollections of Pioneers and Pioneer Life in Nankin," *Michigan Pioneer and Historical Society*, vol. 14, 431–483.

20. Wesleyan Methodist Church, Michigan Conference Records, 1852–1942, Bentley Historical Society.

21. *The Journal Newspapers*, February 17, 2005; the W.W. Harwood farmstead was registered by the National Park Service "Network to Freedom List" in 2005.

22. Other trustees were Samuel D. McDowell, Elihu Drury, Moses F. Collins, Horace Kellogg, and Exra Carpenter. E.W. Whitmore and Thomas Smith were members. The record is in the Pittsfield Township File, YHSA.

23. Wesleyan Methodist Church. Records.

24. *Signal of Liberty*, January 22, 1844. Throughout the years of publication, the newspaper listed agents who sold subscriptions to the newspaper, as well as meeting attendees.

Chapter Eight

1. Helen W. Farrand, "Memorial Report — St. Clair County," *Collections and Researches Made by the Michigan Pioneer and Historical Society*, vol. 22 (1893), 170–172. Malinda Robinson Paris died in St. Clair, October 22, 1892, aged 68 years. She was born at Paris, KY, December 24, 1824. Dates associated with where she lived were determined from census records of 1860 and 1870, St. Clair County, Michigan, M593, Roll 699, page 442.

2. Siebert, *Underground Railroad from Slavery to Freedom*, 80–83; Benjamin Drew, *A North-side View of Slavery* (Boston: Jewett, 1856).

3. Siebert, *Underground Railroad from Slavery to Freedom*, 147.

4. Eber M. Pettit and W. McKinstry, *Sketches in the History of the Underground Railroad: Comprising Many Thrilling Incidents of the Escape of Fugitives from Slavery, and the Perils of Those who Aided Them* (Fredonia, NY: McKinstry, 1879).

5. Siebert, *Underground Railroad from Slavery to Freedom*, 80.

6. *Detroit Daily Post*, February 23, 1875.

7. The First Congregational Church is located in its third building at 33 E. Forest at Woodward, Detroit. The church operates a "Flight to Freedom Tour" as part of the Underground Railroad Living History Museum.

8. Suzanne Wesbrook Frantz, *Whispers Along the River, The Underground Railroad in East China & St.*

Clair (St. Clair, MI: St. Clair Historical Commission, 2003), 4.

9. William Lee Jenks, *St. Clair County, its History and its People* (Chicago: Lewis, 1912), 821. For more information on the Underground Railroad in this area, see Frantz, *Whispers Along the River.*

10. The Lerich property was located on River Bends Drive in Shelby Township, Macomb County. The tree was cut down around 1888 after the Leriches moved from the farm. In the 1870 Macomb county census record, Peter and Sarah Lerich remain on the farm, with neighbors Mary Phillips and Nancy Naramoor nearby.

11. Eldredge, *Macomb County*, 514–516.

12. Chapman Brothers, *Portrait and Biographical Album of Oakland County, Michigan: Containing Full Page Portraits and Biographical Sketches of Prominent and Representative Citizens of the County, Together with Portraits and Biographies of All the Presidents of the United States and Governors of the State.*(Salem, MA: Higginson, 1998), 764.

13. *History of Lapeer County, Michigan: with Illustrations and Biographical Sketches of Some of its Prominent Men and Pioneers* (Chicago: Page, 1884).

14. Interview with Kel Keller, 7/30/08, current owner of the Nutting house. The Professor Rufus Nutting residence on Fremont was occupied from 1849–1851 by the Rev. Philo Ruggles Hurd, minister of the Congregational Church who regularly spoke out against slavery. Keller is researching Nutting's and Hurd's links to Underground Railroad activity in the area. Keller has heard that hiding places existed in the attic and a carriage house.

15. The first meeting house was near Seven Mile and Farmington Roads. In 1846, the Livonia Meeting House, about a quarter mile away, replaced the original and is currently the Livonia Historical Commission Museum according to the Carlisle Davidson histories in the Bentley Historical Library. Jean Fox identified Lapham's Corners at Eight Mile Road and Farmington in Livonia.

16. Siebert papers, Fourth Annual Report of the American Anti-Slavery Society, Box 48, OHSA.

17. George Franklin Wisner, *The Wisners in America and Their Kindred* (Baltimore: Wisner, 1918), 167–171.

18. Kooker papers, folder "Research notes and miscellanea."

19. Chapman Brothers, *Portrait and Biographical Album of Oakland Co.*, 634.

20. *Federal Censuses of Michigan, Wayne County,* 1, 870, Bentley Historical Library.

21. Samuel W. Durant, *History of Oakland County, Michigan* (Philadelphia: Everts, 1877), 314–316.

22. Siebert papers, census records. H. H. Northrop was born June 18, 1814, in Galway, New York. He lived at the northeast corner of East Court and Harrison Streets in Flint in his later years and is buried in Glenwood Cemetery.

23. *Signal of Liberty*, Oct. 31, 1846.

24. *History of Shiawasee and Clinton Counties, Michigan with Illustrations and Biographical Sketches of*

their Prominent Men and Pioneers (Philadelphia: Ensign, 1880), 135.

Chapter Nine

1. Mary A. Goddard, "The Underground Railroad," presented to the Ypsilanti Chapter of the Daughters of the American Revolution, April, 1913, McCoy File, Ypsilanti Historical Society. Professor Mary Goddard interviewed Anna McCoy, one of the eleven children born to the McCoys, before 1913.

2. Census of 1851 Canada West, Essex County, Enumeration District 1, Township 9, shows members of the family: George, Emillia, Aferd, Eloner, Elijah, Milton, Prockoy (listed as Roxy A in 1870), and boarder Henry Lee.

3. *Signal of Liberty*, April 28, 1841; February 10, 1843.

4. William J. Richardson. "The Life and Times of Samuel H. Davis: an Anti Slavery Activist," *Afro-Americans in New York Life and History,* vol. 33, no. 1 (January 2009). http://www.thefreelibrary.com/The life and times of Samuel H. Davis: an anti slavery activist.-a0192404032, 75, 112, 124, 279. Samuel McCarty's brother left home first and chose the name Davis. William left in 1799, chose a different name when he lived in New Hampshire, but after finding his brother in Boston chose the same surname.

5. Philip S. Foner, and George E. Walker, eds., *Proceedings of the Black State Conventions 1840–1865, vol. 1.* (Philadelphia: Temple University Press), 181–183.

6. Bonner. *Memoirs of Lenawee County*, 532. A Michigan Historical Marker honors the school once located at 18123 Greenleaf Road, Addison, Lenawee County.

7. *Signal of Liberty*, January 23, 1843; Ripley, *The Black Abolitionist Papers*, vol. 3 (Chapel Hill: University of North Carolina Press, 1985), 397–400..

8. *Signal of Liberty*, May 12 and May 19, 1841..

9. Charles Frederic Goss, *Cincinnati, the Queen City, 1788–1912* (Chicago: Clarke, 1912), 179–81.

10. Bibb, *Narrative*, 180–181.

11. *Signal of Liberty*, October 21, 1844; February 20, 1847.

12. Donald Riddering, *Salem, A Hot-Bed of Abolitionists* (Salem Area Historical Society, 2001).

13. Frederick Douglass, *Life of an American Slave* (Boston: Anti-Slavery Office, 1845), 100.

14. "St. Matthew's Episcopal Church, Detroit, Celebrates its Centennial, 1846–1946: 100 Years of Service to God and His People." (Detroit: St. Matthew's Episcopal Church, 1946), Bentley Historical Library.

15. *Signal of Liberty*, Dec. 8, 1845, and Jan. 5, 1846, identify John Wittenmyer as sheriff; R. W. Landon, treasurer, wrote the warrant issued by Jacob Statler, and John Defield helped Gunn take Bowles out of state.

16. Siebert, *Underground Railroad from Slavery to Freedom*, 70–74; F.B. Sanborn, *The Life and Letters of John Brown; Liberator of Kansas and Martyr of Virginia* (New York: Negro Universities Press, 1969), 124–127.

Sanborn refers to an original agreement written by John Brown.

17. Gary L. Collison, "The Boston Vigilance Committee: a Reconsideration," *Historical Journal of Massachusetts* vol. 12, no. 2 (June 1984), 104–116.

18. John Brown Collection, #299, box 1, folder 31, item #102706, Kansas State Historical Society, www.territorialkansasonline.org.

19. Lumpkin, "General Plan was Freedom," 71.

20. *Detroit Tribune*, January 17, 1886.

21. *Ibid.*

22. International Order of Twelve of Knights and Daughters of Tabor, and Moses Dickson, *A Manual of the Knights of Tabor, and Daughters of the Tabernacle, Including the Ceremonies of the Order, Constitutions, Installations, Dedications, and Funerals, with Forms, and the Taborian Drill and Tactics* (St. Louis: Jones, 1879).

23. Franklin, *Slavery to Freedom*, 152.

24. *The North Star*, January 21, 1848.

25. *Detroit Tribune*, January 17, 1886.

26. Siebert, *Underground Railroad from Slavery to Freedom*, 70.

27. *Detroit Tribune*, Dec. 27, 1889, obituary of Samuel Zug.

Chapter Ten

1. James K. Polk, *The Diary of James K. Polk* (Chicago: McClurg, 1910), 251. Polk brought slaves from his farm to the White House and continued to hold people in slavery until the Emancipation Act. http://www.whitehousehistory.org.

2. Siebert papers, box 48, letter from Alfred C. Lane, Lansing, Michigan, dated November 17, 1906.

3. Siebert papers, box 48, #28, reply of Norman Geddes of Adrian, Michigan.

4. The interview with Erastus Hussey was published in the *Detroit Daily Post,* March 1885. *Ypsilantian*, March 20, 1885.

5. *Saline Observer*, May 26, 1927, photocopy from R.W. Lane.

6. Foster papers; *Signal of Liberty*, May 15, 1847; *Portrait and Biographical Album of Ingham and Livingston County, Michigan,* 844–5. Hull was an anti-slavery man who subscribed to the *Signal of Liberty* newspaper, where his name was listed for public scrutiny as a donor to the State Liberty Fund in 1847. The county history states that Hull was born in Morris County, New Jersey, in 1796, lived in New York as a young man, and immigrated to Michigan in 1833. He farmed in Saline until 1863.

7. Lorenzo Davis papers, 1822–1899, Bentley Historical Library.

8. *Report and Collections of the Pioneer Society of the State of Michigan,* vol. 2 (1880).

9. Stebbins, *Upward Steps*, 90.

10. Capt. Lowry's house at 5650 Ann Arbor-Saline Road was destroyed by fire in February 1963, according to Robert Lowry.

11. Noah W. Cheever, *Pleasant Walks and Drives*

About Ann Arbor (Ann Arbor: University of Michigan, 1909).

12. E. P. Nutting papers. A record from a student in 1851 includes classmates with the familiar antislavery names of Bartlett, Benton, Lowry, and Bliss.

13. *Portrait and Biographical Album of Washtenaw County, Michigan,* 1279.

14. The church was built in 1837 (South Ann Arbor and East Henry Streets) and the parsonage two years later. A new church was built in 1904 and the parsonage moved to The Henry Ford Greenfield Village. The information is from the publication, "First Baptist Church, Saline, Michigan 1830–1956."

15. Norman Asa Wood Papers, Bentley Historical Library. Includes an article, "The Woods of Lodi Township," *Pioneers of Washtenaw County, Michigan.*

16. Cheever, *Drives About Ann Arbor.*

17. Mary Culver, "Fruit Cultivation in Early Washtenaw County," *Washtenaw Impressions,* April 1997. Ann Arbor District Library Clippings File: 1964–1972. The house was saved from demolition in 1962 and moved from 1701 Michigan Avenue to 3401 Berry Road in Superior Township.

18. *Portrait and Biographical Album Washtenaw,* 443; family records online at http://FamilySearch.org. Ezra D. Lay was born in Saybrook, CT, December 6, 1807, and died in Ypsilanti, April 28, 1890.

19. Siebert, "Michigan Records."

20. Earle, *Routledge Atlas,* 42–43.

21. Keen O'Hara is known for educating his son Theodore at his academy. Theodore (born February 11, 1820) gained national notoriety for his poetry and military service. Keen O'Hara was born in Ireland on September 24, 1768, and died in Frankfort, Kentucky, on December 22, 1851.

22. *Letters of James Gillespie Birney, 1831–1857,* Letter of Hiram Wilson, dated Sep. 3,1845, from Detroit River to James G. Birney, 966–7; Henson, *Life of Josiah Henson,* 73–75.

23. *Signal of Liberty,* August 26, 1844.

24. *Ibid.,* September 9, 1844.

25. The meeting was held at the Ann Arbor courthouse on September 25, 1845. Chandler Carter presided and J. Chandler, Jr., served as secretary. Darius S. Wood of Lodi, Daniel Pomeroy of Salem, Robert Powell of Bridgewater, Alvah Pratt of Pittsfield, Charles Tripp of Ann Arbor, and Samuel W. Foster of Scio were all nominated as representatives to the Legislature.

26. Foster papers.

27. *Signal of Liberty,* June 3, 1844.

28. *Detroit Free Press,* October 18, 1850; Katzman, *Before the Ghetto,* 36.

29. Siebert, *Underground Railroad from Slavery to Freedom,* 155–6.

30. Chas. C. Chapman, *History of Knox County, Illinois* (Chicago: Blakely, Brown & Marsh, 1878), 201–215.

31. *History of Muskegon County, Michigan: with Illustrations and Biographical Sketches of Some of its Prominent Men and Pioneers* (Chicago: H.R. Page, 1882), 39.

32. Siebert, *Underground Railroad from Slavery to Freedom,* 88.

33. *Signal of Liberty,* March 4, 1844.

34. *Ibid.,* February 20, 1843.

35. *Report on Proceedings of Anti-Slavery Society at Ann Arbor.*

36. James G. Birney, *The American Churches, the Bulwarks of American Slavery* (Newburyport, MA: Parker Pillsbury, 1892).

37. Thomas papers, letter from R. B. Bement, Battle Creek, December 16, 1843.

38. The Political Graveyard, http://politicalgraveyard.com/geo/MI/ofc/usrep.html.

39. *Reports and Collections of the Michigan Pioneer and Historical Society, Michigan Pioneer Historical Collections* 11, 279.

40. Siebert papers, box 48, letter from Northrop.

41. Congregational Churches of Michigan. *Minutes of the General Association of the Congregational Churches of Michigan: At Their Meeting in … with an Appendix,* S.l., The Association, 1873.

42. Dubuar papers, box 1, signers: F. M. Lansing, Caroline Lansing, Isaac Elliot, Sarah H. Elliott, Eli Benton, Ann Benton, Charlotte Benton, Austin S. Wood, Jesup S. Wood, Ann Elisa Wood, Geo. S. Wood, Amos Evans, Sarah A. Evans, and Sellick (Sillik) Wood.

43. *Signal of Liberty,* May 15, 1847; and Foster papers.

44. Foster papers, folder "Trial of Eli Benton, Member of the First Presbyterian Church of Lodi."

45. Family History Capers, Genealogical Society of Washtenaw County, vol. 8, No. 1. (1984), 14.

46. Pattengill papers.

47. *Ibid.*

48. *State Journal,* July 12, 1838. Other Executive Committee members: Luther W. Guitteau, W. A. Abel, Calvin Townson, Samuel B. Noble, Samuel W. Foster, and Theron Ford.

49. Pattengill papers describe an account of Seymour Foster visiting the homestead he left at the age of nine. The house stood vacant in the mid–1900s and was later torn down. The foundation remains.

Chapter Eleven

1. The story is arranged from facts in the Palmer papers and Haviland, *Life-Work.*

2. James Knox Polk and Allan Nevins, ed., *The Diary of a President, 1845–1849: Covering the Mexican War, the Acquisition of Oregon, and the Conquest of California and the Southwest* (London: Longmans, Green, 1929), 359.

3. Howard S. Rogers, *History of Cass County, from 1825 to 1875* (Cassopolis, MI: Mansfield, Vigilant Book and Job Print, 1875), 134–5.

4. Several sources were used to document this event. *Signal of Liberty,* April 10 and June 12, 1847, carried an article from the National Era; Giltner vs. Gorham et al., typescript of trial, Siebert papers; *History of Calhoun County; Detroit Advertiser and Tribune,* February 23, 1875. Calvin Hackett, a barber, was

elected a vice president at the 1843 Michigan Colored Convention. Transcriptions of trial testimonies are online at the Michigan History, Arts, Libraries website, http://www.michigan.gov/hal.

5. The Crosswhite cabin on the Ferguson Farm was located where East Mansion Street meets Michigan Avenue. A marker notes the site.

6. *Signal of Liberty*, Feb. 20, 1847.

7. *Ibid.*

8. Dumond, *James Gillespie Birney*, 1057–1061.

9. *Signal of Liberty*, April 3, 1847.

10. *Ibid.*, April 10, 1847.

11. Siebert, *Underground Railroad from Slavery to Freedom*, 262, 278, 282.

12. Glover, *Twentieth Century Cass County*, 285–290.

13. *Signal of Liberty*, April 24, 1847.

14. *Ibid.*, April 24, 1847; a "Robert Cromwell" was listed as a barber in Chatham, Ontario, in 1851 according to the marker recognizing him in Flint, Michigan. Michigan Historic Markers, www.michmarkers.com.

15. Mary G. Butler and Martin L. Ashley, ed., "Out of Bondage," *Heritage Battle Creek*, vol. 9 (Winter 1999), 78–81. Original interview of Perry Sanford printed in the *Sunday Morning Call*, August 3, 1884, 78–80.

16. Butler and Ashley, ed., "Out of Bondage."

17. *Ibid.*

18. *Signal of Liberty*, May 15, 1847.

19. Arthur T. Pierson, *Zachariah Chandler: An Outline Sketch of His Life and Public Services* (Detroit: Post and Tribune, 1880), 78.

20. Perry Sanford described the Cass County raid in detail in "Out of Bondage." Charles Osborn moved to Cass County, Michigan, in 1842, joining some of his sons and daughters who moved to the area in the 1830s. Several people have conducted intensive research in this area: Virginia Springsteen, Sondra Mose-Ursery, and Dr. Michelle Johnson. An archaeological dig found indications of many places of occupation from that era. Dr. Nazzaney of Western Michigan University conducted a survey of the area. The African American settlements were populated after 1840.

21. Rogers, *History of Cass County*, 134.

22. Glover, *Twentieth Century Cass County*, 287–90; Barnes, "Battle Creek."

23. Nothing is left of the log cabin meeting house, first built in 1837, and rebuilt in 1856.

24. Butler and Ashley, ed., "Out of Bondage."

25. Butler and Ashley, ed., "Out of Bondage;" Rogers' *History of Cass County* provides the Bristow account, 138.

26. Butler and Ashley, ed., "Out of Bondage;" Rogers's *History of Cass County*.

27. Glover, *Twentieth Century Cass County*, 289–90. The Kentuckians named in court records include Hubbard Buckner, the Reverend Stevens, C. B. Rust, Sheriff John L. Graves, James Scott, G. W. Brazier, Thornton Timberlake, and Messrs. Bristow and Lemon.

28. Thomas papers; Kooker papers, diaries.

29. Haviland, *A Woman's Life-Work*, 96–97.

30. Chardavoyne, "Michigan Fugitive Slave Acts 5, 7;" originally twelve were named in the lawsuit. George Ingersoll, Asa B. Cook, and John M. Easterly were among those who confronted David Giltner and Troutman.

Chapter Twelve

1. Mary Goddard, "The Underground Railroad."

2. The copy of "Sacred Memories" was donated by Marshall D. Hier, descendant of Guy Beckley's sister, Nancy Beckley Felch, to the African American Cultural and Historical Museum of Washtenaw County in 2003 and is stored in their library. The book was published by Beckley, Foster & Co. in Ann Arbor, Michigan, 1846. No records have been found concerning the number of volumes published, and no other copies have been located by the author.

3. John W. Quist, "'The Great Majority of Our Subscribers are Farmers: The Michigan Abolitionist Constituency of the 1840s," *Journal of the Early Republic* vol. 14, no. 3 (Autumn 1994), 325–358.

4. *Michigan Liberty Press*, June 30, 1848.

5. *Michigan Liberty Press*, August 25, 1848, lists the following State Central Committee appointees: William Finley, Emanuel Mann, C.N. Ormsby, C.J.F. Vail, William Kinsley, and Sabin Felch.

6. Barnes, "Battle Creek."

7. *Michigan Liberty Press,* June 9, 1849; and Thomas Papers.

8. Nancy Stevens, also known as Nancy Fowler, was one of the first group to travel from northern Kentucky to Cass County in 1847. See Chapter 11. After the raid, Nancy went to Battle Creek where the Hussey family heard her story. Hamilton, *History of Calhoun County*.

9. *Signal of Liberty*, April 24, 1847, and June 12, 1847; accounts and a photocopy of the court report (Michigan: Calhoun County, Gorham Case) in the Siebert papers; and *The North Star*, December 15, 1848.

10. *The North Star*, April 7, 1849.

11. Congressional Globe, 30th Congress, 1st Session, 1848. (bill S. No 239); U.S. Senate Report No. 143.

12. *The North Star*, December 29, 1848.

13. *The Chicago Tribune*, January 29, 1893, as cited by Siebert in *The Underground Railroad from Slavery to Freedom*, 236.

14. *Michigan Argus*, February 21, 1849.

15. Thomas Papers.

16. Jehu Z. Powell, ed., *History of Cass County Indiana: From its Earliest Settlement to the Present Time: with Biographical Sketches and Reference to Biographies Previously Compiled* (Chicago: Lewis, 1913). Original from the New York Public Library, digitized Feb 7, 2008. The Powell account shows the name as Morris; Chardavoyne, *Michigan Fugitive Slave Acts*, wrote about the case in "The Court Legacy" November

2004, and cited the case as Norris v. Newton, 18 F. Cas. 424 (C.C. Mich., 1848).

17. Chas. C. Chapman, *History of St. Joseph County, Indiana.* (Chicago: Chapman, 1880), 618–626.

18. United States, *Federal Censuses of Michigan,* 1850, 1860 and 1870, Bentley Historical Library.

Chapter Thirteen

1. The 1850 federal census report of Washington County, Tennessee, shows John P. Chester as a Tavern Keeper in a household with Thomas K. Chester, whose occupation was Trader. The town of Jonesborough has an historic inn on Main Street built in 1797 by Dr. William P. Chester.

2. Haviland, *Woman's Life-Work,* 89.

3. The 1850 census was conducted in July in Washtenaw County Michigan, ahead of the passage of the Fugitive Slave Law (September 18, 1850) and therefore not a useful statistical measure of black migration out of the area.

4. *The National Era,* November 21, 1850, written by S. B. Noble, dated November 7, 1850.

5. *The National Era,* November 21, 1850.

6. DeLand, *History of Jackson County,* 373–4.

7. *Voice of the Fugitive,* January 29, 1851. Notice submitted by Henry Montague.

8. Siebert, *Underground Railroad from Slavery to Freedom,* 246–50

9. *Ibid.,* 250.

10. *Liberator,* November 7, 1851.

11. Siebert, *Underground Railroad from Slavery to Freedom,* 82, 159.

12. Lewis Tappan, *The Fugitive Slave Bill* (New York: American and Foreign Anti-Slavery Society, 1850), 32.

13. Samuel May, *The Fugitive Slave Law, and Its Victims: Anti-Slavery Tracts, No. 18* (New York: American Antislavery Society, 1861).

14. May, *Fugitive Slave Law,* No. 18.

15. Coffin, *Reminiscences,* 546–7.

16. Clarence Monroe Burton, *Compendium of History and Biography of the City of Detroit and Wayne County, Michigan* (Chicago: Taylor, 1909), 119; Floyd Benjamin Streeter, *Political Parties in Michigan, 1837–1860: an Historical Study of Political Issues and Parties in Michigan from the Admission of the State to the Civil War* (Lansing: Michigan Historical Commission, 1918), 130–132.

17. Butler and Ashley, ed., "Out of Bondage."

18. Bonner, *Memoirs of Lenawee County,* 199, 597. In 1855, Beecher, a leading lawyer at Adrian, was a law partner of Judge Cooley and of Hon. F.C. Beaman. He held the office of judge of probate from 1861 until his death in 1871.

19. Whitney and Bonner, *History of Lenawee County,* 78–80. In 1855, Spofford moved to Des Moines, IA.

20. Goddard, "The Underground Railroad," includes an interview of Pamela Noble. Sylvester Drake

Noble was born in 1794 in Hoosick Falls, New York. His address from 1868 until his death is listed as 38 West Huron, which became 220 W. Huron. An antebellum Greek Revival house at 115 Chapin Street was shown to belong to E. A. Noble in 1874, per plat map, and was deeded to Pamela Noble from Europa Noble in 1883 per Liber 99, page 554, Ypsilanti Historical Society.

21. Goddard, "The Underground Railroad."

22. *Ibid.*

23. *Portrait and Biographical Album of Washtenaw County, Michigan,* 489. Noble died Jan. 28, 1879, aged 85 years.

24. *Ibid.,* 318–319. White was born in Schenectady, New York, in 1798. He arrived in Ann Arbor in 1824 and in 1840 built a frame house on the southeast corner of Eberwhite and Liberty Streets, Ann Arbor.

25. Barnes, "Battle Creek."

26. Siebert papers, Fitch Reed letter to Wilbur Siebert.

27. Siebert papers, interview with the Rev. Anthony Bingey. MSS 116, box 106.

28. The Liberator, July 29, 1852. Reprint from *Voice of the Fugitive.*

29. *Voice of the Fugitive,* February 26, 1851.

30. *Ibid.,* May 7, June 1, and November 5, 1851.

31. Siebert papers, interview with the Rev. Anthony Bingey of Windsor, Ont., Canada, July 31, 1895, by W. H. Siebert, mss 116, box 106.

32. Siebert, *Underground Railroad from Slavery to Freedom,* 253.

33. *Voice of the Fugitive,* February 26, 1852.

34. *Provincial Freeman,* July 1, 1852.

35. Ripley, *Black Abolitionist Papers,* 1.

Chapter Fourteen

1. *Detroit Daily Free Press,* March 17, 1853.

2. Coffin, *Reminiscences,* 445.

3. "'Freedom's Railway' Reminiscences Of The Brave Old Days Of The Famous Underground Line," *Detroit Tribune,* January 17, 1886.

4. Siebert, *Underground Railroad from Slavery to Freedom,* 32.

5. *Portrait and Biographical Album of Hillsdale County, Mich. Containing Full Page Portraits and Biographical Sketches of Prominent and Representative Citizens of the County, Together with Portraits and Biographies of All the Governors of the State, and of the Presidents of the United States* (Chicago: Chapman Bros, 1888), 517–518.

6. *Ibid.,* 778–779.

7. Siebert papers, "Reply of Fitch Reed of Lawrence Kansas, March 28, 1893." Reed Road intersects Gilbert Highway south of Loch Erin in Lenawee County.

8. John I. Knapp and R. I. Bonner, *Illustrated History and Biographical Record of Lenawee County, Mich* (Adrian, MI: Times Printing, 1903), 199–200. The purchased land was in the southwest quarter, Section 14.

9. Knapp and Bonner, *Lenawee County,* 224–5.

Gilbert was born in Richmond, Ontario County, NY, on April 3, 1822.

10. *Voice of the Fugitive*, February 26, 1851.

11. Siebert papers, Fitch Reed. In his letter of 1893, Reed uses the name 'Ray.' The name was misspelled in at least one census record, also. There were no families by the name of Ray, and other evidence indicated Reed was referring to Aray; and Knapp and Bonner, *Memoirs of Lenawee County*, 262. Charles Lindquist described the Wells property in Sections 11 and 12 in an article in *News from the Tower*, Lenawee Historical Society, 2004.

12. Emil Lorch File, Bentley Historical Library. The 1,000 acres was all of Section 27, Pittsfield Township; U.S. Federal Census, 1850.

13. Interview with Carol Mull, Willie Edwards, and Jerry Samons on September 9, 2003.

14. *Portrait and Biographical Album of Washtenaw County, Michigan*, 1256. The Wesleyan Methodist Church was built in 1846 in Section 27, and in 1860 service was stopped.

15. Roswell Preston, Jr. purchased 160 acres in the SE¼ of Section 3 on July 20, 1832. Captain Roswell Preston purchased 241 acres in W½-NE¼ and NW¼ of Section 8 on the same date. Captain Roswell's farm appears to be located on Waters Road, west of Rogers Corner. See Peck, *Landsmen,* for source.

16. Edward M. Preston, *A History of Captain Roswell Preston of Hampton, Connecticut, His Ancestry and Descendants, 1899,* from the Preston folder.

17. George and Quida Shire donated copies of Preston family history and other documents to the Ypsilanti Historical Museum Archives.

18. In 1852, members obtained a building at Ballard and Congress Streets; the church's current site, at South Adams and Buffalo Streets, was given to the church in 1858 by Mrs. Jesse Steward.

19. Record of Deeds, Liber T, p 76. Washtenaw County, Michigan.

20. Goddard File, Goddard interview with Anna McCoy, 1915. Eurotas Morton came with his wife, Maria White Morton, from Whately, Massachusetts, to Detroit and then Rawsonville, Michigan. In the 1840s, Eurotas worked as a merchant and was listed as Postmaster and Justice of the Peace in Van Buren Township. According to the *Ypsilanti Press*, January 4, 1965, the Eurotas Morton house, 214 N. River Street, was demolished the previous week. A photograph of the original house is in the collections of the Ypsilanti Historical Museum.

21. Hatch Family file, Ypsilanti.

22. Helen Walker's parents were Thomas Walker and Margaret Boyd of Dunbarton, Scotland. William McAndrew died in 1895 and Helen McAndrew on October 26, 1906.

23. William McAndrew, "The McAndrews," *Ypsilanti Business and Professional Women's Club* (1931), edited reprint in *Ypsilanti Gleanings*, Summer, 2004.

24. United States, *Federal Censuses of Michigan,* 1850, 1860 and 1870, Bentley Historical Library.

25. Siebert papers.

Chapter Fifteen

1. Goddard papers.

2. "Fugitive Slaves in Ohio," *New York Daily Times,* September 7, 1853.

3. *Frederick Douglass' Paper,* March 24, 1854.

4. *New York Daily Times,* June 14, 1854.

5. *Detroit Daily Free Press,* March 14, 1853.

6. Coffin, *Reminiscences,* 149–52

7. *Provincial Freeman,* November 24, 1855.

8. Drew, *North-side,* 358–360.

9. *Ibid.*

10. Walker and Gaines, *Buried Alive,* 54–55; William Walker's story was written as a narrative by himself and Thomas S. Gaines.

11. Federal census, 1860, Washtenaw County, Superior Township, M653, 563 p 710.

12. Goddard papers; Coffin, *Reminiscences.*

13. Benjamin Drew with introduction by George Elliott Clarke, *The Refugee: the Narratives of Fugitive Slaves in Canada* (Toronto: Dundurn, 2008), 326.

14. Perry Sanford described the tobacco wagon. Anna McCoy named Bush, but he remains unidentified. Census data from 1870, 4th Ward, Ypsilanti City, shows George and Milly of Kentucky with their younger children born in Canada. Milly could not read or write.

15. Goddard papers.

16. A man by the name of John Hatfield appears in the Ohio 1850 census record as a male, mulatto, barber from Pennsylvania, aged 44, married to Frances with two children.

17. U.S. Census, 1860, Kentucky, M653, Roll: 355, p 333; in 1870 the Gaines family was listed in same area.

18. Goddard, "Underground Railroad." Goddard personally interviewed Anna McCoy, Pamela Noble, Martha Washington, and Caroline Hill. See also Harvey C. Colburn, *The Story of Ypsilanti* (Ypsilanti, MI: Committee on History for the Centennial Celebration of the Founding of the City, 1923).

19. Goddard papers. It is possible that the Prescotts who helped on the Underground Railroad were Warren and Eliza Hilliard Prescott. Their place of residence is not shown in the 1840 record, but in 1850 the family is living in Sylvan Township. Interestingly, their daughter, born in 1840, was named Mary Ann. She would later marry Seth Field, and live in Livingston County with her children and father.

20. *Ypsilanti Heritage News,* November 2005. On May 3, 2005, the Ypsilanti City Council created the Starkweather Historic District, providing legal protection of the historic farmhouse. The house remains standing at 1226 Huron River Drive.

21. Harriet deGarmo Fuller papers.

22. Census records of Canada and the United States were searched for members of the Gordon family. It is possible they changed their names.

23. It is possible that this is another person of the same name; however, all the data of the 1860 Census report is consistent with the known facts of John White. Census series: M653 roll: 564 p 289.

24. *Detroit Daily Free Press*, March 17, 1853.

25. Two prominent apologists for the institution of slavery were George Fitzhugh and James Henry Hammond. Virginian Fitzhugh wrote *Sociology for the South* (1854) and *Cannibals All!* (1857).

26. Barber, *Vermontville Colony*, 44–5.

27. Letters from the manuscript collection at the Boston Public Library, Ms. A.1.1. v.4. 127. In the letter dated Oct. 15, 1853, Battle Creek, Garrison described Elizabeth Chandler's burial place as on a rising elevation in a large wheat field, with nothing to identify who was buried there.

28. Letters from the manuscript collection at the Boston Public Library, ms.A.1.1. v.4. 128. In the letter dated Oct. 17, 1853, from Detroit, to Mrs. Helen Eliza Garrison, Boston, MA.

29. Garrison, William Lloyd, Walter M. Merrill, Louis Ruchames, and Louis Ruchames, *The Letters of William Lloyd Garrison, Vol. 4, From Disunionism to the Brink of War, 1850–1860* (Cambridge: Harvard, 1975), 73–74.

30. Franklin, *Slavery to Freedom*, 150–152.

31. Knapp and Bonner, *Lenawee County*, 219–223.

32. Fuller papers.

33. *Ibid.*

34. *New York Daily Times*, June 14, 1854.

35. Provincial Freeman, June 30, 1855, and August 29, 1855, Library of Congress.

36. The family home of Mark and Roccena Norris is on North River Street, Ypsilanti, Michigan.

37. Norris Family Papers, Letter to Rocenna Norris, dated March 31, 1852.

38. Earle, *Routledge Atlas*, 58–9.

39. *New York Daily Times* (1851–1857), April 11, 1857, http://www.proquest.com/ (accessed August 14, 2009). "Massachusetts Legislature," *New York Daily Times* (1851–1857), March 11, 1857, http://www.proquest.com/ (accessed August 14, 2009).

40. Ira Berlin, *Slaves Without Masters: the Free Negro in the Antebellum South* (New York: New Press, 2007), 364–372; Franklin, *Slavery to Freedom*, 178.

41. Richard Realf., letter dated May 31, 1858, from Cleveland, Ohio, to "Dear Uncle" John Brown. Cited with permission from Territorial Kansas Online-Transcripts: www.territorialkansasonline.org; Lumpkin, "General Plan Was Freedom."

42. International Order of Twelve of Knights and Daughters of Tabor, and Moses Dickson, *Knights of Tabor*, 9.

43. Booker T. Washington, *The Story of the Negro: The Rise of the Race from Slavery* (New York: Doubleday, Page, 1909) item notes v. 2, 7–15.

44. *Territorial Kansas Online*, Letter from Paul Shepherd to James Redpath, dated Jan. 30, 1860, Dover, Lenawee Co. Michigan.

45. Rochester Ladies Anti-Slavery Society Collections.

46. Kooker papers, folder: diaries.

47. Stebbins, *Upward Steps*, 145.

48. Caroline Hare, *Life and Letters of Elizabeth L. Comstock, Compiled by Her Sister C. Hare* (Philadelphia: Winston, 1895), 61–65.

49. Missouri census records at Ancestry.com.

50. Stories told by Mary Berry Pointer are found on the Old Settlers Reunion website, http://www.oldsettlersreunion.com, which also includes "Negro Folktales in Michigan," edited by Richard M. Dorson; Millard family genealogy is from Adin Ballou, *An Elaborate History and Genealogy of the Ballous in America* (Providence, RI: Freeman and Son, 1888) and the Millard/Millerd website; also, 1880 U.S. Census data shows Solomon Millard, Jr. in Missouri, aged 71.

51. Francis H. Warren, *Michigan Manual of Freedmen's Progress* (Detroit: Secretary of Freedmen's Progress Commission, 1915), 117.

52. *Ibid.*, 296.

53. *Ibid.*, 50.

Chapter Sixteen

1. The Rev. William Troy, *Hair-Breadth Escapes from Slavery to Freedom* (Manchester: Bremner, 1861), 39–43.

2. American Anti-Slavery Society, *The Anti-Slavery History of the John Brown Year; Being the Twenty-Seventh Annual Report of the American Anti-Slavery Society* (New York: American Anti-Slavery Society, 1861); and May, *Anti-Slavery Collection* (Ithaca: Cornell University Library, Rare and Manuscript Collections), 2000s, <http://resolver.library.cornell.edu/misc/4270009>.

3. *Ibid.*, 49.

4. *Ibid.*, 40.

5. *Ibid.*, 39.

6. Katzmann, *Before the Ghetto*, 92; original source, *Detroit Free Press*, December 6, 1859.

7. Coffin, *Reminiscences*, 374–380.

8. William J. Simmons, *Men of Mark: Eminent, Progressive and Rising* (Cleveland: Rewell, 1887), 682.

9. Allan Pinkerton, *Spy of the Rebellion: Being a True History of the Spy System of the United States Army During the Late Rebellion, Revealing Many Secrets of the War Hitherto Not Made Public* (Hartford; Winter & Hatch, 1885), 25–27.

10. Michigan's Historic Sites Online, http://michsite.state.mi.us.

11. Simmons, *Men of Mark*, 70.

12. *Detroit Tribune*, January 17, 1886. Katherine Dupre Lumpkin searched for Lambert's records through family members but was unable to locate them [noted in the article cited].

13. *Ibid.*, 683.

14. Reynolds, *John Brown*.

15. May, *Fugitive Slave Law*, 120.

16. Franklin, *Slavery to Freedom*, 179.

17. Territorial Kansas Online, letter from Paul Shepherd.

18. Scott, *Secret Six*.

19. Simmons, *Men of Mark*, 20.

20. Katzmann, *Before the Ghetto*, 21.

21. "Things in Missouri," *Texas State Gazette*, vol. 11, is. 17, December 3, 1859, p 1. America's Historical Newspapers 12/3/1859.

22. *Ann Arbor Journal*, January 30, 1861.

23. Stebbins, *Upward Steps*, 171.
24. Coffin, *Reminiscences*, 595.
25. Siebert papers.
26. Haviland, *Woman's Life-Work*, 212–13.
27. *Ibid.*, 233–4.
28. *Ibid.*, 227.
29. Hare, *Life and Letters*, 76–86, letter from E. L. Comstock in Rollin, Michigan, dated August 2, 1860.
30. Charles Moore, *History of Michigan, vol. 1* (Chicago: Lewis, 1915), 411–416.
31. Marjorie Reade and Susan Wineberg, "Historic Buildings, Ann Arbor, Michigan" (Ann Arbor: Ann Arbor Historic District Commission, 1992), 119. The house at 410 N. State Street is currently divided into rental apartments. The house was sold by the Society of Friends in 1866.
32. *Ibid.*, 241.
33. Stebbins, *Upward Steps*, 115 and 214; Cheever, *Drives About Ann Arbor.*
34. Moore, *History of Michigan,* 416.
35. Coffin, *Reminiscences*, 596.
36. Wesleyan Methodist Church, microcopy, reel 1.

Conclusion

1. Foster papers, box 1 includes drafts and final manuscripts. Some of his writing is in Pitman shorthand that has not been transcribed.
2. *Michigan Argus*, March 2, 1837; and *Portrait and Biographical Album of Washtenaw County.*
3. The Sutherland farm is in Washtenaw County [http://pittsfieldhistory.org]; English, *History of Manchester*. Ms. English wrote that in 1930 the house was owned by Miss Flava Bailey, and the street name was changed to Railroad Street. The *Signal of Liberty* subscribers from Manchester were C. Carter, W. Pease, C.T. Lyon, C. Parsons, H. Holloway, H. Dodge, and Hugh Graham, 191.
4. Everts & Stewart, *Combination Atlas Map*, 22.
5. Per the 1860 census, other African American heads of household in York include Rhoda Barbs (NY), Joseph Beard (PA), John Briggs (MD), Henry Prater (OH), and John Thompson (KY).

6. Siebert, *Underground Railroad from Slavery to Freedom*, 236.
7. Drew, *North-side*, 348–365.
8. Glover, *History of Cass County*; Haviland, *Woman's Life-Work.*
9. Report of Monthly Meetings of the Women's Records, December 5, 1853, April 5, 1865, and January 2, 1867 in Ypsilanti Evangelical Friends Church Records, 1848–1987, Bentley Historical Library.

Appendix 1

1. Swift papers.
2. The Union Church today is a private residence at 504 High Street in Ann Arbor. The first Bethel AME church (1869) and a new building at the same location (1896) were built at 632 North Fourth Avenue per *Ann Arbor Observer*, April, 2000.
3. *Portrait and Biographical Album of Washtenaw County;* Federal Census of 1850 and 1880 of Washtenaw County, Michigan; and Grace Shackman, "Church and Community on North Fourth Avenue," *Ann Arbor Observer*, April, 2000.
4. Haviland, *Woman's Life-Work*, 110.
5. Files of Laura Watkins-Koelewijn. Article written by Mrs. Douglas A. Watkins, published in *The Exponent*, [Manchester] August 25, 1976.
6. Palmer papers, 83.
7. Koelewijn files, interview with Douglas Watkins and Laura Watkins, July 19, 2008.
8. Goddard papers.
9. Goddard papers.
10. Farrand, "Memorial Report," 170–172.
11. William Troy, *Hair-Breadth Escapes from Slavery to Freedom*. First published in Manchester, England in 1861. Found in Chapel Hill: Academic Affairs Library, 2000. http://docsouth.unc.edu/neh/troy/menu.html.
12. Warren, *Michigan Manual*, 296.
13. Shackman, "Underground Railroad in Ann Arbor."

Bibliography

Abzug, Robert H. *Passionate Liberator: Theodore Dwight Weld and the Dilemma of Reform.* USA: Oxford University Press, 1982.

Albertson, Nicholas. "Sussex County Marriages, 1773–1804." *The Genealogical Magazine of New Jersey.* Vol. 24, no. 1, January, 1949.

Aldrich, Robert D. Papers, 1783–1983. Bentley Historical Library, University of Michigan, Ann Arbor.

American Anti-Slavery Society. *The Anti-Slavery History of the John-Brown Year; Being the Twenty-Seventh Annual Report of the American Anti-Slavery Society.* New York: American Anti-Slavery Society, 1861.

American Anti-Slavery Society. *Third Annual Report of the American Anti-Slavery Society; with the Speeches Delivered at the Anniversary Meeting, Held in the City of New-York, on the 10th May, 1836, and the Minutes of the Meetings of the Society for Business.* New York: William S. Dorr, 1836, http://digital.library.cornell.edu.

Ann Arbor District Library Clippings File. 1964–1972. Ann Arbor, MI.

Ann Arbor State Journal.

Aray family files. Ypsilanti Historical Society. Fletcher White Archives, Ypsilanti, MI.

Ballou, Adin. *An Elaborate History and Genealogy of the Ballous in America.* Providence, RI: Freeman and Son, 1888.

Barber, Edward C. *The Vermontville Colony, its Genesis and History, with Personal Sketches of the Colonists.* Lansing, MI: Robert Smith, 1897.

Barnes, Charles E. "Battle Creek as a Station on the Underground Railway." *Michigan Pioneer and Historical Collections.* Vol. 38, 1912: 279–285.

Beakes, Samuel Willard. *Past and Present of Washtenaw County, Michigan: Together with Biographical Sketches of Many of its Prominent and Leading Citizens and Illustrious Dead.* Chicago: S. J. Clarke, 1906.

Bechler, G. R., and E. Wenig. *1856 Map of Washtenaw County, Michigan.* Philadelphia: Bechler, Wenig, & Co. Reproduced by the Genealogical Society of Washtenaw County, Michigan, Inc. August, 1997.

Beckley, Guy. Letters, 1839 and 1847. Bentley Historical Library, University of Michigan, Ann Arbor, MI.

Benjamin, Howard C. "Dred Scott v. Sanford." *Reports of Cases Argued and Adjudged in the Supreme Court of the United States, December Term, 1856.* Washington, D.C., 1857.

Bennett, Prince. Prince Bennett File. Ypsilanti Historical Society Fletcher White Archives, Ypsilanti, MI.

Berlin, Ira. *Slaves Without Masters: the Free Negro in the Antebellum South* New York: New Press, 2007.

Bert, Joseph Griswold, and Mrs. Samuel R. Taylor. *The Pictorial History of Fort Wayne, Indiana: A Review of Two Centuries of Occupation of the Region About the Head of the Maumee River.* Vol. 1. Chicago: Robert O. Law, 1917.

Betts, Edward Chambers. *Early History of Huntsville, Alabama 1804 to 1870.* Montgomery, AL: Brown Printing, 1916.

Bial, Raymond. *Underground Railroad.* New York: Houghton Mifflin, 1995.

Bibb, Henry. *Narrative of the Life and Adventures of Henry Bibb, an American Slave, Written by Himself.* New York: self-published, 1849.

Bidlack, Russell E. *John Allen and the Founding of Ann Arbor.* Ann Arbor, MI: University of Michigan, 1962.

Bingham, Stephen D. *Early History of Michigan: with Biographies of State Officers, Members of Congress, Judges and Legislators.* Lansing, MI: Thorp & Godfrey, 1888.

"Biographical Directory of the United States Congress, 1774-Present." http://bioguide.congress.gov.

Birney, James. *Letters of James Gillespie Birney, 1831–1857.* Edited by Dwight Lowell Dumond. New York, London: D. Appleton-Century, 1938.

Birney, James G. *The American Churches, The Bulwarks of American Slavery.* Newburyport, MA: 1892.

Birney, William. *James G. Birney and His Times: The Genesis of the Republican Party with Some Account of Abolition Movements in the South Before 1828.* D. Appleton, 1890.

Blockson, Charles L. *The Underground Railroad: Dramatic Firsthand Accounts of Daring Escapes to Freedom.* New York: Prentice-Hall, 1987.

Bonner, Richard Illenden, editor. *Memoirs of Lenawee County, Michigan.* Madison, Wisconsin: Western Historical Association, 1909.

Bordewich, Fergus. *Bound for Canaan: The Under-*

ground Railroad and the War for the Soul of America. New York: Amistad/HarperCollins, 2005.

"Born in Slavery: *Slave Narratives from the Federal Writers' Project, 1936–1938.*" American Memory Project, Library of Congress.

Brinkley, Alan. *The Unfinished Nation. Vol. One: To 1877.* New York: McGraw-Hill, 1993.

Brown, John. John Brown Collection, #299, Box 1, Folder 31, Item # 102706. Kansas State Historical Society. www.territorialkansasonline.org.

Brown, William Wells. *Narrative of William Wells Brown, a Fugitive Slave.* Boston: Bela Marsh, 1848.

Burton, Ann, and Conrad Burton, editors. *Michigan Quakers: Abstracts of Fifteen Meetings of the Society of Friends, 1831–1960.* Decatur, MI: Glyndwr Resources, 1989.

Burton, Clarence Monroe. *Compendium of History and Biography of the City of Detroit and Wayne County, Michigan.* Chicago: Henry Taylor, 1909.

Butler, Mary G., and Martin L. Ashley, editors. "Out of Bondage." *Heritage Battle Creek.* Vol. 9 (Winter 1999): 78–81. Original interview of Perry Sanford printed in the *Sunday Morning Call.* August 3, 1884: 78–80.

Cahill, Edward. "Historical Lights from Judicial Decisions." *Michigan Historical Collections.* Vol. 38. *Michigan Historical Commission,* 1912.

Catterall, Helen T. *Judicial Cases Concerning American Slavery and the Negro.* Washington DC: Carnegie Institution, 1926–29.

Chadwick, Bruce. *Traveling the Underground Railroad: A Visitor's Guide to More Than 300 Sites.* Secaucus, NJ: Carol Pub. Group, 1999.

Chandler, Elizabeth Margaret. Elizabeth Chandler Papers, 1793–1854. Bentley Historical Library. University of Michigan, Ann Arbor.

Chapman, Charles A. *Portrait and Biographical Album of Ingham and Livingston Counties, Michigan.* Chicago: Chapman Brothers, 1891.

Chapman, Chas. C. *History of Knox County, Illinois.* Chicago: Blakely, Brown & Marsh, 1878.

_____. *History of St. Joseph County, Indiana.* Chicago: Chas. C. Chapman, 1880.

Chapman Bros. Publishing Company. *Portrait and Biographical Album of Oakland County, Michigan: Containing Full Page Portraits and Biographical Sketches of Prominent and Representative Citizens of the County, Together with Portraits and Biographies of All the Presidents of the United States and Governors of the State.* Salem, MA: Higginson Book, 1998.

Chapman Brothers. *Portrait and Biographical Album of Calhoun County, Michigan: Containing Full Page Portraits and Biographical Sketches of Prominent and Representative Citizens of the County Together with Portraits and Biographies of All the Presidents of the United States and Governors of the State.* Chicago: Chapman Bros, 1891.

Chapman Brothers. *Portrait and Biographical Album of Jefferson and Van Buren Counties, Iowa.* Chicago: Lake City Pub., 1890.

Chardavoyne, David G. "Michigan and the Fugitive Slave Acts." *The Court Legacy.* Vol. XII, no. 7 (November, 2004).

Cheever, Noah W. *Pleasant Walks and Drives About Ann Arbor.* Bentley Historical Library. University of Michigan, Ann Arbor, 1909.

Coffin, Levi. *Reminiscences of Levi Coffin.* New York: Arno Press and the New York Times, 1968. Reprint of Cincinnati: Robert Clarke, 1898.

Coggan, Blanche. "The Underground Railroad in Michigan." *Negro History Bulletin* 27 (February 1964).

Coggan, Blanche B. Blanche Coggan Papers. Michigan Anti-Slavery Society 1852–1857, 1962–1982. Record Group 82–18. Archives of Michigan, Michigan Historical Center, Lansing, MI.

Colburn, Harvey C. *The Story of Ypsilanti.* Ypsilanti, MI: Committee on History for the Centennial Celebration of the Founding of the City, 1923.

Collison, Gary. "The Boston Vigilance Committee: A Reconsideration." *Historical Journal of Massachusetts.* Vol. 12, no. 2 (June 1984).

Colored American, Sep. 26, 1840.

Combination Atlas Map of Washtenaw County. Chicago: Everts & Stewart, 1874.

Congregational Churches of Michigan. *Minutes of the General Association of the Congregational Churches of Michigan: At Their Meeting in ... with an Appendix.* [S.l.]: The Association, 1873.

Conzen, Michael P. *The Making of the American Landscape.* Boston: Unwin Hyman, 1990.

Culver, Mary. "Fruit Cultivation in Early Washtenaw County." *Washtenaw Impressions.* (April 1997).

Cutler, Rev. Carroll. *A History of Western Reserve College, During Its First Half Century, 1826–1876.* Cleveland, OH: Crocker's Publishing House, 1876.

Davidson, Carlisle G. "A Profile of Hicksite Quakerism in Michigan, 1830–1860." *Quaker History.* Vol. 59, no. 2 (Autumn 1970).

Davidson, John Nelson. *Negro Slavery in Wisconsin and the Underground Railroad.* Milwaukee, WI: printed for the Parkman Club by E. Keogh, 1897.

Davis, Calvin Olin. *A History of the Congregational Church in Ann Arbor, 1847 to 1947.* Ann Arbor, MI: First Congregational Church, 1947.

Davis, Lorenzo. Lorenzo Davis Papers. 1822–1899. Bentley Historical Library. University of Michigan, Ann Arbor.

DeLand, Charles Victor. *DeLand's History of Jackson County, Michigan: Embracing a Concise Review of its Early Settlement, Industrial Development and Present Conditions, Together with Interesting Reminiscences.* Chicago: B. F. Bowen, 1903.

Detroit Advertiser and Tribune, February 23, 1875.

Detroit Daily Free Press.

Detroit Daily Post, February 23, 1875.

Detroit Tribune. "Freedom's Railway: Reminiscences of the Brave Old Days of the Famous Underground Railroad Line." January 17, 1886.

Dodd, Tom, and James Mann. *Our Heritage: Down by the Depot in Ypsilanti.* Ypsilanti, MI: Depot Town Association, 1999.

Doll, Louis W., Geneva Smithe, and Pioneer Society

of Washtenaw County. *History of Washtenaw County, Michigan, Together with Sketches of its Cities, Villages and Townships and Biographies of Representative Citizens: History of Michigan.* Chicago: Chas. C. Chapman, 1881.

Douglass, Frederick. *Life of an American Slave.* Boston: Anti-Slavery Office, 1845.

Drew, Benjamin. *A North-side View of Slavery.* Boston: Jewett, 1856.

_____, with introduction by George Elliott Clarke. *The Refugee: the Narratives of Fugitive Slaves in Canada.* Toronto: Dundurn Press, 2008.

Dubuar, James. James Dubuar Papers. 1834–1886. Bentley Historical Library. University of Michigan, Ann Arbor.

Dumond, Dwight L. *Antislavery Origins of the Civil War in the United States.* Ann Arbor: University of Michigan Press, 1939.

_____, ed. *Letters of James Gillespie Birney.* New York: Appleton-Century, 1938.

Durant, Samuel W. *History of Kalamazoo County, Michigan.* Philadelphia: L. H. Everts, 1880.

_____. *History of Oakland County, Michigan.* Philadelphia: L. H. Everts, 1877.

Earle, Jonathan. *The Routledge Atlas of African American History.* New York: Routledge, 2000.

1830–1877 History of Calhoun County, Michigan with Illustrations Descriptive of its Scenery, Palatial Residences, Public Buildings, Fine Blocks and Important Manufactories. Philadelphia: L. H. Everts, 1877.

Eldredge, Robert F. *Past and Present of Macomb County, Michigan.* Chicago: S.J. Clarke, 1905.

Ellis, Franklin, and Crisfield Johnson. *History of Berrien and Van Buren Counties, Michigan: its Prominent Men and Pioneers.* Philadelphia: D.W. Ensign, 1880.

English, Annetta. History of Manchester, 1930. Bentley Historical Library. University of Michigan, Ann Arbor.

Everts, L. H. *History of St. Joseph County, Michigan, with Illustrations Descriptive of its Scenery, Palatial Residences, Public Buildings, Fine Blocks and Important Manufactories, from Original Sketches by Artists of the Highest Ability.* Philadelphia: L. H. Everts, 1877.

Everts and Stewart. *Combination Atlas Map of Washtenaw County, Michigan; Standard Atlas of Washtenaw County, Michigan.* The Heritage Collection. Mt. Vernon, IN: Windmill Publications, 1991.

Family History Capers. Genealogical Society of Washtenaw County. Vol. 8, no. 1. 1984.

Farmer, Silas. *The History of Detroit and Michigan: Or, the Metropolis Illustrated, a Chronological Cyclopaedia of the Past and Present, Including a Full Record of Territorial Days in Michigan, and the Annals of Wayne County.* Detroit: Silas Farmer, 1884.

_____. *History of Detroit and Wayne County and Early Michigan: 1839–1902.* Detroit: S. Farmer for Munsell, New York, 1890.

Farrand, Mrs. Helen W. "Memorial Report — St. Clair County Historical Collections." *Michigan Pioneer and Historical Society Collections and Research.* Vol. XXII (1893), Lansing, MI: Robert Smith, 1894.

First Baptist Church (Saline, MI) Records. 1830–1920 and 1956. Bentley Historical Library. University of Michigan, Ann Arbor.

First Presbyterian Church (Saline, MI). *History of the First Presbyterian Church Society of Saline, Michigan, from its Organization in the State of New York, and Christening in the Village of Saline, in the Year 1831, with Names of its Pastors and Officers to the Present Time … with Extracts from a Peculiar Address Delivered by the Hon. Nehemiah P. Stanton … on the Subject of "Our New Church."* Detroit: Wolverine Printing, 1899.

_____. Records. 1831–1985. Bentley Historical Library. University of Michigan, Ann Arbor.

Fisher, David, and Frank Little. *Compendium of History and Biography of Kalamazoo County, Mich.* Chicago: A.W. Bowen, 1906.

Flower, Frank Abial. *History of Milwaukee, Wisconsin, From Pre–Historic Times to the Present Date, Embracing a Summary Sketch of the Native Tribes, and an Exhaustive Record of Men and Events for the Past Century; Describing the City, its Commercial, Religious, Educational and Benevolent Institutions, its Government, Courts, Press, and Public Affairs; and Including Nearly Four Thousand Biographical Sketches of Pioneers and Citizens.* Chicago: Western Historical, 1881.

Foner, Philip S., and George E. Walker, editors. *Proceedings of the Black State Conventions 1840– 1865. Vol. I.* Philadelphia: Temple University Press, 1979.

Foster, Mary E. Lowry, "Echoes of the Past." *Pioneer Society of the State of Michigan. Vol. II.* Detroit: Wm. Graham's Presses, 1880.

Foster, Theodore. Theodore Foster Papers. 1835– 1862. Bentley Historical Library, University of Michigan, Ann Arbor.

Fox, Henry Clay, editor. *Memoirs of Wayne County and the City of Richmond, Indiana: from the Earliest Historical Times Down to the Present, Including a Genealogical and Biographical Record of Representative Families in Wayne County.* Madison, WI: Western Historical Association, 1912.

Fox, Jean M. "Tracking the Underground Railroad." Monograph no. 3. The Farmington Hills Historical Commission, 1993.

Franklin, John Hope, and Alfred A. Moss, Jr. *From Slavery to Freedom: A History of Negro Americans.* 6th ed. New York: McGraw-Hill, 1988.

Frantz, Suzanne Westbrook. "Whispers Along the River, The Underground Railroad in East China & St. Clair." St. Clair, MI: St. Clair Historical Commission, 2003.

"Freedom's Railway: Reminiscences of the Brave Old Days of the Famous Underground Railroad Line." *Detroit Tribune,* January 17, 1886.

Frelinghuysen, Theodore Chambers. *The Early Germans of New Jersey: Their History, Churches and Genealogies.* Dover, NJ: Dover, 1895.

Frost, Karolyn Smardz. *I've Got a Home in Glory Land.* New York: Farrar, Straus and Giroux, 2008.

Fuller, Harriet deGarmo. Harriet Fuller Papers. 1852–

1857. Clements Library. University of Michigan, Ann Arbor.

Gara, Larry. *The Liberty Line: the Legend of the Underground Railroad.* Lexington, KY: University Press, 1961.

Gardner, Washington. *History of Calhoun County, Michigan; A Narrative Account of Its Historical Progress, Its People, and Its Principal Interests, by Hon Washington Gardner.* Chicago: Lewis Publishing, 1913.

Garrison, William Lloyd. William Lloyd Garrison Papers. Letters from the manuscript collection at the Boston Public Library, Ms. A.1.1. Vol. 4, 128. Anti-Slavery Manuscripts. Boston Public Library. Boston, MA.

_____. Walter M. Merrill and Louis Ruchames, editors. *The Letters of William Lloyd Garrison, Vol. 4, From Disunionism to the Brink of War, 1850–1860.* Cambridge, Mass: Belknap, 1975.

Gibson, Campbell, and Kay Jung. *Historical Census Statistics on Population Totals By Race, 1790 to 1990, and by Hispanic Origin, 1970 to 1990, for the United States, Regions, Divisions, and States.* Washington, D.C.: U. S. Bureau of the Census, 2002.

Glover, L. H. *A Twentieth Century History of Cass County, Michigan.* Chicago: Lewis Publishing, 1906.

Goddard, Mary A. Mary Goddard Papers. Ypsilanti Historical Society Fletcher White Archives. Ypsilanti, MI.

_____. "The Underground Railroad." Daughters of the American Revolution, 1913. Ypsilanti Historical Society Fletcher White Archives. Ypsilanti, MI.

Goodell, William. *The American Slave Code in Theory and Practice: Its Distinctive Features Shown by Its Statutes, Judicial Decisions, and Illustrative Facts.* New York: American and Foreign Anti-Slavery Society, 1853.

Goodnow, Lyman. "Recollection 1880?" Transcription. State of Wisconsin Digital Collection. http://digital.library.wisc.edu/1711.dl/WI.Goodnow2e.

Gorton, Thomas. *Samuel Gorton of Rhode Island and his Descendants.* Baltimore: Gateway Press, 1982.

Goss, Rev. Charles Frederic. *Cincinnati: The Queen City, 1788–1912.* Chicago: S. J. Clarke, 1912.

Hagedorn, Ann. *Beyond the River: The Untold Story of the Heroes of the Underground Railroad.* New York: Simon & Schuster, 2004.

Hamm, Thomas D. *The Transformation of American Quakerism: Orthodox Friends, 1800–1907.* Bloomington, IN, 1988).

Hare, Caroline. *Life and Letters of Elizabeth L. Comstock, Compiled by Her Sister C. Hare.* Philadelphia: John C. Winston, 1895.

Hatch Family File. Ypsilanti Historical Society Fletcher White Archives. Ypsilanti, MI.

Haviland, Laura S. Laura Haviland Papers. 1868–1933. Bentley Historical Library. University of Michigan, Ann Arbor.

_____. *A Woman's Life-Work: Labors and Experiences.* Cincinnati: Walden and Stowe for the author, 1882.

Henson, Josiah. *The Life of Josiah Henson, Formerly a Slave, Now an Inhabitant of Canada, as Narrated by Himself.* Boston: Arthur D. Phelps, 1849.

"Highlights of the Struggle: The Underground Railroad." Detroit Free Press (February 22, 1999).

Historical Census Browser. Geospatial and Statistical Data Center, University of Virginia. http://fisher.lib.virginia.edu/collections/_stats/histcensus/index.html.

History of Cass County, Michigan. Chicago: Waterman, Watkins, 1882.

History of Lapeer County, Michigan: with Illustrations and Biographical Sketches of Some of its Prominent Men and Pioneers. Chicago: H.R. Page, 1884.

History of Muskegon County, Michigan: with Illustrations and Biographical Sketches of Some of its Prominent Men and Pioneers. Chicago: H.R. Page, 1882.

History of Page County, Iowa: Containing a History of the County, Its Cities, Towns, Etc. Des Moines, IA: Iowa Historical, 1880.

History of St. Clair County, Michigan, Containing an Account of its Settlement, Growth, Development and Resources, its War Record, Biographical Sketches, the Whole Preceded by a History of Michigan. Chicago: A.T. Andreas, 1883.

Hobart and Mathers, *Biographical Review of Calhoun County, Michigan: Containing Historical, Biographical and Genealogical Sketches of Many of the Prominent Citizens of To-Day and also of the Past.* 1904. Index by Clyde E. Benson. Chicago: Bureau of Library Services, 1970.

Hopkinson, Deborah, and James Ransome. *Sweet Clara and the Freedom Quilt.* New York: Knopf Books for Young Readers, 2003.

Horste, Cathy Stromme, and Diane Follmer Wilson. *Water Under the Bridge: A History of Van Buren Township.* Belleville, MI: Van Buren Township Bicentennial Commission, 1977.

Howe, Samuel Gridley. "The Refugees from Slavery in Canada West." *Report to the American Freedman's Inquiry Commission.* Boston: Dana, Estes, 1906.

International Order of Twelve of Knights and Daughters of Tabor, and Moses Dickson. *A Manual of the Knights of Tabor, and Daughters of the Tabernacle, Including the Ceremonies of the Order, Constitutions, Installations, Dedications, and Funerals, with Forms, and the Taborian Drill and Tactics.* St. Louis: G.I. Jones, 1879.

Jenks, William Lee. *St. Clair County, its History and its People.* Chicago: Lewis, 1912.

Journal Newspaper.

Julian, George W. "Charles Osborn Anti-Slavery Pioneer." *Indiana Historical Society Publications.* Vol. 2, no. 6. Indianapolis: Bowen-Merrill, 1891.

Kanouse, John. "Early History of Montville Township." 1881. *Township of Montville, Morris County, New Jersey.* 2005–2009. http://www.montvillenj.org/index.

Kanouse, John G. sermon, 1842. Bentley Historical Library. University of Michigan, Ann Arbor.

Kansas State Historical Society and University of Kansas. Territorial Kansas Online. http://www.territorialkansasonline.org.

Katzman, David M. *Before the Ghetto.* Urbana, IL: University of Illinois Press, 1975.

Kephart, John E. "A Pioneer Michigan Abolitionist." *Michigan History* 45 (Mar 1961).

Kephart, John Edgar. "A Voice for Freedom: Signal of Liberty, 1841–1848." PhD diss., University of Michigan, Ann Arbor, 1960.

Kleber, John E. *The Kentucky Encyclopedia.* Lexington: University Press of Kentucky, 1992.

Knapp, John I., and R. I. Bonner. *Illustrated History and Biographical Record of Lenawee County, Mich.* Adrian, MI: Times Printing, 1903.

Kooker, Arthur. *The Anti-Slavery Movement in Michigan, 1796–1840: A Study in Humanitarianism on an American Frontier.* Ann Arbor: University of Michigan Press, 1941.

_____. Arthur Kooker Papers. 1850–1882. Bentley Historical Library. University of Michigan, Ann Arbor.

Leach, Nathaniel. *Reaching Out to Freedom, The Second Baptist Connection, History of Second Baptist Church,* revised ed. Detroit, Second Baptist Church, 1988.

Lemon, Rev. William Philip. "The History of the Presbyterian Church in Ann Arbor and Washtenaw County." *Washtenaw Impressions* (April 1946). Washtenaw County Historical Society, Ann Arbor, MI.

Lewis, Kenneth E. *West to Far Michigan.* East Lansing: Michigan State University Press, 2002.

Lewis, Pierce F. "The Northeast and the Making of American Geographical Habits" first published in 1990 by HarperCollinsAcademic and reprinted in *The Making of the American Landscape,* edited by Michael P. Conzen. New York: Routledge, 1994.

Libby, Mrs. Wilber E., and Franklin Ellis. *History of Shiawassee and Clinton Counties, Michigan, with Illustrations and Biographical Sketches of their Prominent Men and Pioneers.* Philadelphia: D.W. Ensign, 1880.

The Liberator.

Lindquist, Charles. *The Antislavery-Underground Railroad Movement: in Lenawee County, Michigan, 1830–1860.* Lenawee, MI: Lenawee County Historical Society, 1999.

Lobb, John, editor. *Uncle Tom's Story of His Life: An Autobiography of the Rev. Josiah Henson (Mrs. Harriet Beecher Stowe's "Uncle Tom") from 1789 to 1876.* London: "Christian Age" Office, 1876. www.archive.org/details/albertatest_01238.

Lorch, Emil. Emil Lorch Papers. Bentley Historical Library. University of Michigan, Ann Arbor.

Lumpkin, Katherine Dupre. "'The General Plan was Freedom': A Negro Secret Order on the Underground Railroad." *Phylon: The Atlanta University Review of Race and Culture.* Vol. 28, no. 1 (Spring 1967).

Mann, James. "Tunnels Drained of Dramatic Story More Prosaic." *Ypsilanti Community News.* November 7, 2005.

Marwil, Johnathan. *A History of Ann Arbor.* Ann Arbor, MI: Ann Arbor Observer, 1987.

Matlack, Lucius C. *The History of American Slavery and Methodism from 1780 to 1849 and History of the Wesleyan Methodist Connection of America.* New York: No. 5 Spruce Street, 1849.

May, George S. "Parker Pillsbury and Wendell Phillips in Ann Arbor." *Michigan History.* Vol. 33 (June 1949).

May, Samuel J. *Samuel J. May Anti-Slavery Collection.* Ithaca, N.Y.: Cornell University Library, Rare and Manuscript Collections, 2000s. http://resolver.library.cornell.edu/misc/4270009.

May, Samuel M. *The Fugitive Slave Law and Its Victims.* New York: American Antislavery Society, 1861.

_____. *Some Recollections of our AntiSlavery Conflict.* Boston: Fields, Osgood, 1869.

McAllister, Norma. *Judge Samuel William Dexter.* Dexter, MI: Thomson-Shore, 1989.

McAndrew, Helen. Helen McAndrew File. Ypsilanti Historical Society Fletcher White Archives. Ypsilanti, MI.

McAndrew, Thomas. Thomas McAndrew File. Ypsilanti Historical Society Fletcher White Archives. Ypsilanti, MI.

McAndrew, William. "The McAndrews." First published by the Ypsilanti Business and Professional Women's Club in 1931, edited reprint in *Ypsilanti Gleanings,* Summer, 2004. Ypsilanti Historical Society.

McCoy, George. George McCoy File. Ypsilanti Historical Society Fletcher White Archives. Ypsilanti, MI.

McGee, Melville. "Early Days of Concord, Jackson County, Michigan." *Michigan Pioneer Collections.* Vol. 21 (1892).

McIntosh, W. H. "History of Ontario County, NY." Ontario County, NY: The American History and Genealogy Project, 1878.

Michigan Argus.

Michigan Genealogical Council. *Index to the Federal Population Census of Michigan 1850.* Lansing, MI: Michigan Society Daughters of the American Revolution and the Michigan Genealogical Council, 1976.

Michigan Legislature Collection. Bentley Historical Library. University of Michigan, Ann Arbor.

Michigan Liberty Press. Bentley Historical Library. University of Michigan, Ann Arbor.

Minutes of the State Convention of the Colored Citizens of the State of Michigan, Held In the City of Detroit On the 26th And 27th of October, 1843, for the Purpose of Considering Their Moral & Political Condition, As Citizens of the State. Detroit: William Harsha, 1843.

Mitchell, Henry H. *Black Church Beginnings: the Long-Hidden Realities of the First Years.* Grand Rapids, MI: William B. Eerdmans, 2004.

Mitchell, William. The *Underground Railroad from Slavery to Free*dom. London: W. Tweedie, 1860.

Moore, Charles. Charles Moore File. Ypsilanti Historical Society Fletcher White Archives. Ypsilanti, MI.

_____. *History of Michigan. Vol. 1.* Chicago: Lewis, 1915.

Moore, Eli. Eli Moore Family File. Ypsilanti Historical Society Fletcher White Archives. Ypsilanti, MI.

Moore, James E. James Moore File. Ypsilanti Historical Society Fletcher White Archives. Ypsilanti, MI.

Morton, Eurotas. Eurotas Morton File. Ypsilanti Historical Society Fletcher White Archives. Ypsilanti, MI.

Muelder, Owen W. *The Underground Railroad in Western Illinois.* Jefferson, NC: McFarland, 2008.

Mull, Carol E., and Susan Kosky. "Crossroads of Freedom: the Underground Railroad in the Saline, Michigan Area." June, 2005.

Myers, John L. "American Antislavery Society Agents and the Free Negro, 1833–1838." *Journal of Negro History.* Vol. 52, no. 3 (July 1967).

_____. "The Early Antislavery Agency System in Pennsylvania, 1833–1837." *Pennsylvania History.* Vol. 31 (January 1964).

National Archives (U.S.), and United States. *National Archives Publication.* Washington: Archives, 1900s.

National Era.

New York Daily Times. ProQuest.

New York Evangelist. New York: N.C. Saxton, 1830.

Norris, Lyman Decatur. Lyman Decatur Norris File. Ypsilanti Historical Society Fletcher White Archives. Ypsilanti, MI.

Norris, Mark, and Rocenna Norris. Mark and Rocenna Norris File. Ypsilanti Historical Society Fletcher White Archives. Ypsilanti, MI.

North Star newspaper and *Frederick Douglass' Paper* newspaper.

Nutting, E.P. E.P. Nutting Papers. Bentley Historical Library. University of Michigan, Ann Arbor.

100 Dollars Reward: Ranaway From the Subscriber, On Thursday, 7th May, 1857, Negro Man Luke, Commonly Called Luke Williams ... [S.l.]. Printed at the office of the "Marlboro" Gazette, 1857. Clements Library, University of Michigan, Ann Arbor.

Osband, Melvin D. "My Recollections of Pioneers and Pioneer Life in Nankin." *Michigan Pioneer and Historical Collections.* Vol. 14.

Osborn, Charles. *Journal of that faithful servant of Christ, Charles Osborn, containing an account of many travels and labors in the work of the ministry, and his trials and exercises in the service of the Lord, and in defense of the truth, as it is in Jesus.* Cincinnati: A. Pugh, 1854.

Palmer, Jane. Jane Palmer Papers, ca. 1966. Bentley Historical Library. University of Michigan, Ann Arbor.

Parker, James Baldwin, and John Pugh Gardner. *Treasure from Earthen Vessels: the History of Webster Church.* Dexter, MI: J. B. Parker, 1984.

Patchin, John. *Sketches of the Life of John Patchin.* From the *National Society of the Daughters of the American Revolution.* From document of Claribel L. Bickford, Duarte, CA. April, 1966. Cited with permission from Shel Michaels, www.shel.net/shel/geneal ogy/txt/jp.txt.

Pattengill. Pattengill Family Papers. 1767–1963. Bentley Historical Library. University of Michigan, Ann Arbor.

Peck, Paul R. *Landsmen of Washtenaw County: An Atlas and Plat of the First Landowners of Washtenaw County, Michigan.* Ann Arbor, MI: P.R. Peck, c. 1986.

The Peninsular Courier, and Family Visitant. Ann Arbor, MI: A.W. Chase, M.D., 1866.

Pettit, Eber M., and W. McKinstry. *Sketches in the History of the Underground Railroad: Comprising Many Thrilling Incidents of the Escape of Fugitives from Slavery, and the Perils of Those who Aided Them.* Fredonia, NY: McKinstry, 1879.

Pierson, Arthur T. *Zachariah Chandler: An Outline Sketch of His Life and Public Services.* Detroit: Post and Tribune, 1880.

Pilcher, James E., M.D., editor. *Life and Labors of Elijah H. Pilcher of Michigan.* New York: Hunt & Eaton, 1892.

Pinkerton, Allan. *The Spy of the Rebellion; Being a True History of the Spy System of the United States Army During the Late Rebellion, Revealing Many Secrets of the War Hitherto Not Made Public.* Hartford, CT: M. A. Winter & Hatch, 1885.

Polk, James K. *The Diary of James K. Polk.* Chicago: A.C. McClurg, 1910.

_____. Allan Nevins, editor. *The Diary of a President, 1845–1849: Covering the Mexican War, the Acquisition of Oregon, and the Conquest of California and the Southwest.* London: Longmans, Green, 1929.

Portrait and Biographical Album of Hillsdale County, Mich. Containing Full Page Portraits and Biographical Sketches of Prominent and Representative Citizens of the County, Together with Portraits and Biographies of All the Governors of the State, and of the Presidents of the United States. Chicago: Chapman Bros, 1888.

Portrait and Biographical Album of Washtenaw County, Michigan, Containing Biographical Sketches of Prominent and Representative Citizens, Together with Biographies of all the Governors of the State, and of the Presidents of the United States. Chicago: Biographical Publishing, 1891.

Powell, Jehu Z., editor. *History of Cass County, Indiana: From its Earliest Settlement to the Present Time: with Biographical Sketches and Reference to Biographies Previously Compiled.* Chicago: Lewis, 1913.

Preston, Edward M. *A History of Captain Roswell Preston of Hampton, Connecticut, His Ancestry and Descendants, 1899.* Preston Family Folder. Ypsilanti Historical Society Fletcher White Archives. Ypsilanti, MI.

Priebe, Fred. "Abraham Lincoln and His Michigan Connections." *Michigan Humanities* (Summer, 2008).

The Provincial Freeman. Windsor, Canada West: Mary Ann Shadd Carey, 1853.

Quist, John W. "'The Great Majority of our Subscribers are Farmers': The Michigan Abolitionist Constituency of the 1840s." *Journal of the Early Republic.* Vol. 14, no. 3 (Autumn 1994).

Rankin, John, and Thomas Rankin. *Letters on American Slavery: Addressed to Mr. Thomas Rankin, Merchant at Middlebrook, Augusta Co., Va.* Boston: Garrison & Knapp, 1833.

Reade, Marjorie, and Susan Wineberg. *Historic Build-*

ings, Ann Arbor, Michigan. Ann Arbor: Ann Arbor Historic District Commission, 1992.

First United Presbyterian Church. Records. 1829–1979. Bentley Historical Library. University of Michigan, Ann Arbor.

Redpath, James. *The Public Life of Capt. John Brown, with an Auto-Biography of his Childhood and Youth*. Boston: Thayer and Eldridge, 1860.

Reports and Collections of the Michigan Pioneer and Historical Society. Vol. 1–15 (1874–1890). Lansing, MI: Robert Smith Printing, 1904.

Report of the Proceedings of the Anti-Slavery State Convention Held at Ann Arbor Michigan, the 10th and 11th of November, 1836. Detroit: Snow and Fisk, 1836. Burton Historical Collections. Detroit Public Library, Detroit, MI.

Revolutionary War Papers. State Archives Collection of the Connecticut State Library. http://www.hartford-hwp.com/archives.

Reynolds, David S. *John Brown, Abolitionist: the Man Who Killed Slavery, Sparked the Civil War, and Seeded Civil Rights*. New York: Alfred A. Knopf, 2005.

Richardson, William J. "The Life and Times of Samuel H. Davis: an Anti Slavery Activist." *Afro-Americans in New York Life and History*. Vol. 33, no. 1 (January 2009).

Riddering, Donald. *Salem, a Hot-Bed of Abolitionists*. Salem, MI: Salem Area Historical Society, 2001.

Ripley, Peter C., et al., editors. *The Black Abolitionist Papers*. 5 vols. Chapel Hill: University of North Carolina Press, 1985.

Rochester Ladies' Anti-Slavery Society Papers. Clements Library. University of Michigan, Ann Arbor.

Rogers, Howard S. *History of Cass County, from 1825 to 1875*. Cassopolis, MI: W. H. Mansfield, Vigilant Book and Job Print, 1875.

Sachse, Julius Friedrich. *The German Pietists of Provincial Pennsylvania: 1694–1708*. Philadelphia: printed for the author, 1895.

"St. Matthew's Episcopal Church, Detroit, Celebrates its Centennial, 1846–1946: 100 Years of Service to God and His People." Detroit: St. Matthew's Episcopal Church, 1946.

Saline Observer.

Sanborn, F. B. *The Life and Letters of John Brown; Liberator of Kansas and Martyr of Virginia*. New York: Negro Universities Press, 1969.

Scott, Otto J. *The Secret Six: John Brown and the Abolitionist Movement*. New York: New York Times Books, 1979.

Second Baptist Church Centennial, 1865–1965. Ann Arbor, MI: Second Baptist Church, 1965. Bentley Historical Library. University of Michigan, Ann Arbor.

Shackman, Grace. "The Underground Railroad in Ann Arbor." *Ann Arbor Observer* (December 1998).

Shepherd, William R. *Historical Atlas*. New York: Henry Holt, 1923.

Siebert, Wilbur. *The Underground Railroad from Slavery to Freedom*. New York: Macmillan, 1898; Mineola, NY: Dover Publications, 2006.

_____. Wilbur Siebert Papers. MSS116, Box 91. Ohio Historical Society Archive/Library. Ohio Historical Society. Columbus, OH.

Simmons, William J. *Men of Mark: Eminent, Progressive and Rising*. Cleveland: Geo. M. Rewell, 1887.

Smith, Theodore Clarke. *The Liberty and Free Soil Parties in the Northwest: Toppan Prize Essay of 1896*. New York: Longmans, Green, 1897.

State Journal. Ann Arbor District Library, microfilm.

Stebbins, Giles. *Upward Steps of Seventy Years*. New York: John W. Lovell, 1890.

Stowe, Harriet Beecher. *Uncle Tom's Cabin*. New York: A. L. Burt, 1851.

Streeter, Floyd Benjamin. *Political Parties in Michigan, 1837–1860: An Historical Study of Political Issues and Parties in Michigan from the Admission of the State to the Civil War*. Lansing: Michigan Historical Commission, 1918.

Sunday Morning Call [Battle Creek, MI].

Swayne, Norman Walton. *Byberry Waltons: Account of Four English Brothers, Nathaniel & Thomas & Daniel & William Walton*. Philadelphia: Stephenson Brothers, 1958.

Swift Family Papers. 1834–1921. Bentley Historical Library. University of Michigan, Ann Arbor.

Switala, William J. *Underground Railroad in Delaware, Maryland and West Virginia* and *Underground Railroad in Pennsylvania*. Mechanicsburg, PA: Stackpole Books, 2004.

Tappan, Lewis. *The Fugitive Slave Bill*. New York: American and Foreign Anti-Slavery Society, 1850.

Taylor, Frances Cloud. *The Trackless Trail Leads On*. Kennett Square, PA: F. C. Taylor, 1995.

Territorial Kansas Online. 1854–1861. http://www.territorialkansasonline.org. Created and maintained by the Kansas State Historical Society and the Kansas Collection of the University of Kansas.

Texas State Gazette. Vol. 11, issue 17, p. 1 (December 3, 1859). America's Historical Newspapers. http://infoweb.newsbank.com.

"Things in Missouri." *Texas State Gazette* (Dec. 3, 1859).

Thomas, Benjamin P. *Theodore Weld: Crusader for Freedom*. New Brunswick, NJ: Rutgers University Press, 1950.

Thomas, James M. *Kalamazoo County Directory: With a History of the County from Its Earliest Settlement*. Kalamazoo, MI: Stone Brothers, 1869.

Thomas, Nathan M. *Nathan M. Thomas: Birthright Member of the Society of Friends, Pioneer Physician, Early and Earnest Advocate of the Abolition Society, Friend and Helper of the Fugitive Slave*. Cassopolis, MI: S. B. Thomas, 1925.

_____. Nathan M. Thomas Papers. 1818–1889. Bentley Historical Library, University of Michigan, Ann Arbor, MI.

Tindall, Rev. G. P. *A Discourse on the Life and Character of the late Rev. Ira M. Weed*. Ypsilanti, MI: Pattison's Steam Printing House, 1872.

Tobin, Jacqueline L., and Raymond G. Dobard, Ph.D. *Hidden in Plain View*. New York: Anchor Books, 2000.

Trabue, Charles. "The Voluntary Emancipation Of Slaves In Tennessee As Reflected In The State's Legislation And Judicial Decisions." *Tennessee Historical Magazine*. Vol. 4.

Treadwell, Seymour Boughton. Seymour Boughton Treadwell Papers. Bentley Historical Library. University of Michigan, Ann Arbor.

Troy, William. *Hair-Breadth Escapes from Slavery to Freedom*. First published in Manchester, England: Bremner, 1861. Chapel Hill: Academic Affairs Library 2000. University of North Carolina at Chapel Hill. <http://docsouth.unc.edu/neh/troy/menu.html>.

Underground Railroad Folder. Ann Arbor District Library, Ann Arbor, MI.

"Underground Railroad." *Ypsilantian*. March 30, 1885.

"Underground Railway." *Saline Observer*. May 27, 1927.

United States. *Federal Censuses of Michigan, 1850, 1860 and 1870*. Bentley Historical Library. University of Michigan, Ann Arbor.

Van Buren, A.D.P. "Michigan in Her Party Politics." *Michigan Pioneer and Historical Society Collection*. Vol. 17 (1892).

Van Buren, Anson DePuy. "The Emigrant Family." *Michigan Pioneer and Historical Society Collections*. Vol. 14. Lansing, MI: Wynkoop Hallenbeck Crawford, 1908.

Voice of the Fugitive.

Walker, David. *Walker's Appeal, in Four Articles; Together with a Preamble, to the Coloured Citizens of the World, but in Particular, and Very Expressly, to Those of the United States of America, Written in Boston, State of Massachusetts, September 28, 1829*. Boston: David Walker, 1830.

Walker, William, and Thomas S. Gaines. *Buried Alive (Behind Prison Walls) for a Quarter of a Century: Life of William Walker*. Saginaw, MI: Friedman & Hynan, 1892. Documenting the American South. http://docsouth.unc.edu/neh/gaines/summary.html.

Warren, Francis H. *Michigan Manual of Freedmen's Progress*. Detroit: Secretary of Freedmen's Progress Commission, 1915.

Washington, Booker T. *The Story of the Negro: The Rise of the Race from Slavery*. New York: Doubleday, Page, 1909.

Washtenaw County Historical Society Records. 1827–2006. Bentley Historical Library. University of Michigan, Ann Arbor.

Wesleyan Methodist Church, Michigan Conference Records, 1852–1942. Bentley Historical Library. University of Michigan, Ann Arbor.

Whitney, W.A., and R.I. Bonner. *History and Biographical Record of Lenawee County, Michigan, Containing a History of the Organization and Early Settlement of the County, Together with a Biographical Record ... Obtained from Personal Interviews*. Adrian, MI: W. Sterns, 1879.

Williams, James B. *Life Adventures of James Williams, a Fugitive Slave, With a Full Description of the Underground Railroad*. San Francisco: Women's Union Print, 1873. Documenting the American South. http://docsouth.unc.edu/neh/williams/menu.html.

Williams, Wolcott B. *A History of Olivet College*. Olivet, MI: Olivet College, 1901.

_____. "New England Influence in Michigan." *Reports and Collections of the Michigan Pioneer and Historical Society*. Vol. 17 (1892).

Wilmot, Franklin A. *Disclosures and Confessions of Frank A. Wilmot, the Slave Thief and Negro Runner, with an Accurate Account of the Under-Ground Railroad! What It Is and Where Located!* Philadelphia: Barclay, 1860.

Wing, Talcott Enoch. *History of Monroe County, Michigan*. New York: Munsell, 1890.

Winks, Robin W. *The Blacks in Canada: A History*, 2nd edition. Montreal: McGill-Queen's University Press, 1997.

Wisner, George Franklin. *The Wisners in America and Their Kindred*. Baltimore: G. Franklin Wisner, 1918.

Woodson, Carter G. *A Century of Negro Migration*. New York: Russell & Russell, 1969.

_____. *Free Negro Heads of Families in the United States in 1830: Together with a Brief Treatment of the Free Negro*. Washington, D. C.: Association for the Study of Negro Life and History, 1925.

Ypsilanti Daily Press.

Ypsilanti Evangelical Friends Church Records. Bentley Historical Library. University of Michigan, Ann Arbor.

Ypsilanti Gleanings.

Ypsilanti Heritage News.

Ypsilanti Press.

Ypsilantian. Underground Railroad File. March 20, 1885. Ypsilanti Historical Society Fletcher White Archives. Ypsilanti, MI.

Interviews

Benton, James Smith. Telephone interview of Dr. Smith in DePere, WI, by Carol E. Mull, Ann Arbor, MI, 2005.

Harwood, Janice. Telephone interview of Ms. Harwood in Salinas, CA, by Carol E. Mull, Ann Arbor, MI, Jan. 4, 2005. Notes in the collection of Carol E. Mull, Ann Arbor.

Katz, Elizabeth Harwood. Interview by Carol E. Mull, Sep. 9, 2003, Ann Arbor, MI. Notes in collection of Carol E. Mull, Ann Arbor.

Keller, Kel. Interview by Carol E. Mull, July 30, 2008, in Romeo, MI.

Lowry, Robert. Interview by Carol E. Mull and Willie Edwards. Notes from the interview in the collection of Carol E. Mull, Ann Arbor, MI.

Watkins, Douglas, and Laura Watkins-Koelewijn. Interview by Carol E. Mull, July 19, 2008. Notes from the interview in the collection of Carol E. Mull, Ann Arbor, MI.

Index

Numbers in *bold italics* indicate pages with photographs.

Abolition Petition 168
Abolitionist ticket 66, 133
An Act to Regulate Blacks and Mulattoes, and to Punish the Kidnapping of Such Persons 14
Adair, Samuel Lyle 41
Adams, Mr. 132
Addison 161
Adrian College 41, 159
Affidavit of Francis Troutman 119
African-American Mysteries 87, 90, 149
African-American Mysteries: Order of the Men of Oppression 89
African-Americans, free 2, 5, 6, 10, 28, 32, 93, 120, 149, 152, 158, 165, 168
African Methodist Episcopal church *see* Bethel African Methodist Episcopal Church; Brown African Methodist Episcopal Church
The African Race 167
Agnew, Professor 26
Alabama 47, 52, 89, 97, 116, 161; Franklin County 116; Montgomery 162
Alexander, J.L. 87
Alexander, Lorenzo P. 63
The Algoma 87
Allegheny Mountains 40, 156
Allen, John 21, 22, 23, 26
Allen, Norman 65, 66
Allen, Richard 12
Allen, Stephen 66
Allen, William 103
Alton Observer fire 28
Ambler's 69
American Anti-Slavery Society 34, 37, 39, 40, 42, 43, 53, 98, 153
"The American Churches, the Bulwarks of American Slavery" 101
American Colonization Society 36
The American Freeman 49, 74
"American Liberties and American Slavery" 70
American Missionary Association 41
The American Mysteries 88
American Union 147
Amherst College 26

Amity College 56
Anderson, Elijah 128
Anderson, Oliver 154
Andover Theological Seminary 40, 123
Ann 161
The Ann Arbor Journal 159
Ann Arbor State Journal 25
anti-abolition 24, 28, 50, 99, 101, 143
The Anti-Slavery History of the John Brown Year 153
Anti-Slavery Missionary Society 74
Anti-slavery societies: American Anti-Slavery Society 34, 37, 39, 40, 42, 43, 53, 98, 153; American Colonization Society 36; American Missionary Association 41; Anti-Slavery Missionary Society 74; Detroit Anti-Slavery Society 45; Female Anti-Slavery Society of Grand Prairie 124; Female Anti-Slavery Society of Philadelphia 41; Free African Society 12; Home Missionary Society 25, 26; Kentucky Abolition Society 12; Ladies Anti-Slavery Society 43, 86; League of Liberty Society 156; Logan Female Anti-Slavery Society 41, 42; Michigan Anti-Slavery Society 141, 143, 147, 148; Michigan State Anti-Slavery Society 42, 68, 71, 85, 101, 102, 117, 183; Michigan Wesleyan Anti-Slavery Society 50; New England Anti-Slavery Society 37; New York Anti-Slavery Society 39; New York Manumission Society 27; Pennsylvania Society for Promoting the Abolition of Slavery, the Relief of Free Negroes Unlawfully Held in Bondage, and for Improving the Condition of the African Race 10, 12; Refugee Home Society 127, 140; Washtenaw County Anti-Slavery Society 68; Western Reserve Anti-Slavery Society 41
Anti-Slavery State Convention (MI) 42

Appalachian Mountains 18, 78, 116
"An Appeal in Four Articles" 27
Aray, Asher 23, 25, 32, 55, 71, 93, 130, *130*, 134, 135, 136, *136*, 142, 149, 159, 164, *165*
Aray, Catherine Watts 25, 32, 71, 93, 130, 134, 135, 142, *165*
Aray, Jacob 28–29, 31, 32, 135
Aray, James 32, 71
Aray, Jora 32
Arey, Adam 32
The Argo 153, *154*
Arizona 118
Arkansas 85, 160; Little Rock 161
Armstrong, James 114
Armstrong, John 171
Artis, Kinchen 109
Ash, Harrison 109
Atlee, Dr. E.A. 64
Atwood, Captain 78
Auburn Theological Seminary 20, 26, 81
Auray, Jacob *see* Aray, Jacob

Backus, Anson 132
Bagley, John J. 141
the Bahamas 99
Bailey, Gamalia 168
Baldwin, Francis 60
Banks, Robert 71, 90
Bansill, Captain George 132
Baptist churches: Emancipation Baptist Churches 12; First Baptist Amherstburg 33; First Baptist Church 30; First Baptist Church, Dresden 87; First Baptist Church of Saline 96; Michigan Street Baptist Church of Buffalo 84; Second Baptist Church 30; Second Baptist Church, Detroit 84, 85, 87, *89*; Zion Baptist Church 129
Baptists 12, 20, 58, 92, 96, 101, 122
Barber 143, 145
Barker, Capt. George J. 32, 60
Barnes, Dr. John B. 82
Bartlett, Enoch N. 41, 103
Bartlett, Mary *see* Hull, Mary Bartlett

Bartlett, Moses 93
Bartlett, Pebses 93
Bates, Phineas P. 27
Baumfree, Isabella *see* Truth, Sojourner
Bayliss, Deacon John 51
Beach, the Rev. John 42
"The Beacon Tree" 79
Beaman, Amos Q. 84
Beard, John 57
The Beautiful Girl 62
Bebbens, Samuel 74
Beckley, Abby 117
Beckley, Charles 117
Beckley, the Rev. Guy 40, 62, 72, 73, *73*, 97, 98, 117, 164; Caroline Quarrls 72; lecturer 40, 70, 146; Liberty Party 40, 98, 108–109; Michigan State Anti-Slavery Society 40, 75, 98, 108–109; New York convention 72; *The Signal of Liberty* 49, 58, *67*, 71, 97, 98, 117, 118; Treadwell 70, 72; Underground Railroad 65, 69, 72, 166, 169; Weld Agent 40, 103; Wesleyan Methodist church 40, 68, 74
Beckley, John 117
Beckley, Josiah 62, 71, 72, 73
Beckley, Luke 73
Beckley, Martha 117
Beckley, Nancy *see* Felch, Nancy
Beckley, Olive *see* Hicks, Olive
Beckley, Oramel 73
Beckley, Phyla 117
Beckley, Sarah 117
Beckley/Foster plan 109
Beecher, Harriet *see* Stowe, Harriet Beecher
Beecher, Luther 90
Beecher, Lyman 37
Beecher, Robert R. 122, 125
Begole, Josiah 20
Belle River 80
Bement, the Rev. Rufus Budd 101
Ben and Daniel 165; *see also* Daniel and Ben
Bennett, Esther McCloud 24, 25
Bennett, John D. 102
Bennett, Prince, II 24, 169
Bennett family 24
Benton, Eli 24, 95, 102, 164
Bergen, Charles 114
Berry, Isaac 151, 152
Berry, the Rev. William 154
Bethel African Methodist Episcopal Church 30, 150, 171
Bibb, Catherine 140
Bibb, Frances 35, 45
Bibb, Henry *33*, 84, 120, 140, 141, 164; Canada 127, 128, 131, 134, 140, 146; escape 35–36, 45; Laura Haviland 140; lecturer 85–86, 99, 146; Levi and Catharine Coffin 140; Michigan State Anti-Slavery Society 85–86; Voice of the Fugitive 127, 134, 146; William Lloyd Garrison 146
Bibb, Malinda 45, 85

Bibb, Mary Miles 127, 134, 140
Biddle, Maj. John 142
Billingslea, Angela *165*
Binga, the Rev. Anthony 33, 34, 127, 128
Bingey, Anthony *see* Binga, the Rev. Anthony
Birch Lake Meeting House 112
Bird, Friend C. 63
Birney, James G. 36, 37, 70, 71, 80, 82, 84, 97, 98, 101, 109, 118, 125
Black codes 14, 15, 159; *see also* Slave codes
Black Vigilance Committees 84
Blackburn, Rutha (Lucie) 29, 30, 62, 87, 158, 165, 171
Blackburn, Thornton 29, 30, 87, 158, 165, 171
Blackburn kidnapping 2
Blackburn Riots, 1833 *29*
Blanchard, Jonathan 103
Bogue, Stephen 111, 112
Bonine, Isaac A. 63
Bonine, Mrs. James E. 48
Bonine, Samuel 63
Bonine house 168
Bordewich, Fergus 2
Bowles, Samuel 87
Boys Reform School 167
Bradley, William 150
"The Branded Hand" 99
Brazier, George W. 105, 114, 169
Bretherton 105
Bristol, David *see* Philips, Anthony
Bristow, Moses 112
British and American Institute 97
British Emancipation Act 30
Brooks, Fanny Williams 27
Brooks, the Rev. John Wesley 27, 32, 71, 84, 171
Brooks, Louis 27
Brown, Esek 80
Brown, Florella 41
Brown, Jeremiah 114
Brown, John ("a fugitive slave") 128
Brown, John: 21, 88, 154, 155, 156, 157; Chatham Conference 155, 156; Detroit 41, 156; Harpers Ferry 30, 149, 150, 155, 156, *156*, 157, *157*; Kansas 155; League of Gileadites 87, 149; radicalized 41; Secret Six 155, 157; William Lloyd Garrison 148, 155
Brown, Mary 124
Brown, Owen 41
Brown, Pamela S. 56
Brown, General S.B. 76
Brown, William Wells 33, 78
Brown Chapel African Methodist Episcopal Church (Ypsilanti) 136
Brown University 66
Brush, Elijah 13, 14
Buchanan, Pres. James 158
Buckingham, Lewis 82
Burgess, Wash 34
Burned Over District 18
Burnell, J.C. 42
Burr, James E. 99

Burton, DeLaurian 165
Burton, Delores 165
Bush 142
Byrd family 109

Cady, David 114
California 109, 118, 121
Camp, Ira 16
Canada 2, 7, 8, 14, 16, 17, 28, 29, 30, 34, 40, 46, 49, 50, 51, 55, 57, 58, 59, 60, 62, 69, 72, 73, 74, 76, 77, 78, 79, 80, 83, 85, 89, 90, 91, 92, 93, 95, 96, 100, 101, 108, 109, 110, 111, 113, 114, 117, 120, 122, 123, 124, 125, 126, 127, 128, 130, 131, 133, 134, 135, 137, 138, 139, 140, 141, 142, 143, 149, 150, 151, 152, 154, 156, 158, 159, 160, 162, 163, 164, 165, 166; Amherstburg (Fort Maldin) 15, 32, 33, 34, 124, 128, 140, 169; Buxton 34, 127, 162; Canada Mission 97; Canada West 15, 124, 127, 128, 143, 156, 166; Carey Mission 47; Chatham 34, 76, 78, 87, 116, 127, 156; Colchester 127, 139; Colchester Township 83; Cuckston *see* Buxton; Dawn Settlement 34, 97, 128; Dresden 34, 78, 87, 127; Elgin Settlement 127, 162; Essex County 83; Hamilton 127; Kent 166; Kent County 159; Kitley 42; Malden 78, 126; New Canaan 127; Puce 152; St. Catherine's 34, 127; Sandwich 32, 33, 34, 69, 127, 146; Sandwich Settlement 131; Sarnia 33, 34; Toronto 127, 160; Upper Canada 14, 28, 40; Wallaceburg 78; Wilberforce 15, 28; Windsor 32, 34, 91, 116, 139, 140, 141, 146, 153
Canfield, the Rev. William 75, 160, 169
Carpenter (alias) 169
Carpenter, Ezra 75
Carpenter, Horace 168
Carpenter, Philo 77
Carpenter, Sally *see* Watkins, Sally Carpenter
Carter, Chandler 168
Cary, Mary Ann Shadd 173
Caseway, Pamella 139
Casey, Mary 112
Casey, William 109, 112, 114, 125
Cass, Gen. Lewis 15, 26, 30, 119
Cass County (MI) Raid 63, 64
Catholicism 146
Central Michigan Railroad 126
Chadwick, Theron H. 64
Chandler, Elizabeth Margaret 22, 41, 42, 145, 146
Chandler, Thomas 22, 41, 43, 45, 145, 147
Chandler, Zachariah 20, 119
Chapin, Mayor 30
Charity 161
Chase, Andrew Leonard *see* Chase, Leonard

Chase, Charles 136
Chase, Elizabeth Holright 136
Chase, Elizabeth Swift 136
Chase, James 136, 138
Chase, Leonard 61, 136, 138
Chase, Sophia 138
Chatham Convention 156
Chedsey, J. 119
Cheever, Noah 95, 96
Chesapeake Valley/PA region 7, 18
Chester, Dr. John P. 51, 122, 123
Chester, Thomas K. 122, 123, 125
Chicago Military Road *see* Chicago Turnpike
Chicago Road *see* Chicago Turnpike
Chicago Turnpike 19, 93, 96, 100, 132, 134, 136
Child, Lydia 86
Chippewa Indians 13, 25
The Christian Herald 96
Chubb, Glode 19, 61, 74, 75, 90, 91
Church of Christ *see* Wheatland Church of Christ of Remus
Civil War 1, 3, 16, 26, 30, 61, 80, 88, 89, 90, 126, 132, 149, 150, 154, 158, 164, 168, 169
Clara *see* George and Clara
Clark, the Rev. Charles G. 21, 26
Clark, John 78
Clarke, Hovey K. 118, 119
Clarke, Israel 53
Clarke, Lewis 86
Clarke, Richard 53
Clay, Henry 14, 97
Cleaveland, the Rev. John P. 21, 101
Clinton River 13, 79
Coe, John M. 130, 134, 133
Coffin, Catharine 114, 126, 130, 132, 140
Coffin, Levi 31, 47, 48, 57, 61, 72, 114, 125, 126, 129, 130, 131, 132, 139, 140, 142, 154, 159, 162, 166
Coggan, Blanche 168
Colclazer, the Rev. Henry 20
Cole, Sylvanus 43
Colebrook, Sir James 28
Coleman, William 57, 120, 168
Colonial Acts 8
Colonization 5, 36, 39, 37, 43, 91, 127, 139, 140
The Colored American 59, 70
Colored Conventions 84, 159
Colored People of Detroit 119
Colored Persons of Detroit 110
Colored Vigilant Committee of Detroit 84, 85
Compromise of 1850 98, 121
Comstock, Addison J. 19
Comstock, Darius 19, 42, 43, 45, 78
Comstock, Edwin 45, 169
Comstock, Elizabeth Rous 151, 159, 161, 162
Comstock, Oliver Cromwell, Jr. 108, 114
Comstock, Rhoda *see* Lowry, Rhoda Comstock
Comstocks 22, 164
Conant, Shubael 45

Congregational churches: First Congregational Church, Detroit 78; General Association of Congregational Ministers and Churches of Michigan 101; Osawatomie Congregational Church 41
Congregationalism 20, 21, 41, 53, 56, 65, 78, 81, 95, 96, 101, 134, 161
Connecticut 10, 12, 18, 24, 32, 36, 37, 41, 52, 135; Fairfield County 10; New Haven 64; Preston 26
"The Constitution Is Pro-Slavery, and Therefore Ought to Be Amended" 97
Continental Congress 10
Convention of the Friends of Immediate Abolition 42
Cook 134
Cooper, Edward J. 120
court cases/judicial decisions: Ben and Daniel/Daniel and Ben 15, 165; Crosswhite trial 114, 119–120; Denison 14; *Dred Scott v Sanford* 139, 148–149; John Cross 99; *Jones v VanZandt* 109; Robert Cromwell 122; Wright Maudlin 120–121
Cowlam, Charles 75, 169
Cowles, Dr. Charley 64, 68
Cowles, the Rev. John S. 40, 43, 45
Cowles, Martin 72, 75, 103, 169
Coxe, Robert 71, 92, 93, 97
Craft, Ellen 125
Craft, William 125
Crane, G.L. 75, 159, 169
Critchett, Abigail 52
Critchett, John 52, 166
Cromwell, Robert 110, 122
Cross, the Rev. John 118; arrest and imprisonment 99; challenges Illinois black laws 99; establishes networks to freedom 55–58, 64, 65, 99, 164; Theodore Weld 39, 55–58, 99
Cross, Robert 119
Crosswhite, Adam 107, 108, 114, 119, 120, 146, 168
Crosswhite, Sarah 108, 114, 119, 146, 168
Crosswhite kidnapping 108; *see also* court cases/judicial decisions
Cummings, Albert 143
Curtis, Major 77, 78
Cushman, Henry J. 64

Dade, Benjamin F. 120
The Daily Free Press 143
Daniel and Ben 15; *see also* Ben and Daniel
Daniels, Mrs. 138
Davis, the Rev. Samuel H. 84, 85, 87
Davis, Willard 145
Davis, William 16, 141
Day, Jora 32
Day, Sarah 32

Day, Silas Randall 32, 55, 159
DeBaptiste, George 60, 78; Chatham Convention 156; Detroit 88, 89, 108, 117, 120, 122, 140, 155; Indiana 30–31
Declaration of Independence 9, 84
DeGarmo, Harriet *see* Fuller, Harriet deGarmo
DeLand, Charles Victor 63, 65
DeLand, William R. 65
Delany, Dr. Martin R. 90, 156
Delany, Robert 90
Delaware 7, 18, 53, 162
Delon [Dellon], Adam 136
Democratic party 36, 66, 71, 93, 97, 98, 99, 109, 117
Denison, Elizabeth (Lisette) 13, 14, 29, 34
Denison, Hannah 13
Denison, Peter 13
Denison, Scipio 28
Densmore, Abel 64, 113
Depue family 32
Derbyshire, Cynthia 24, 169
The Detroit Advertiser 154
Detroit Anti-Slavery Society 45
Detroit River 13, 30, 33, 46, 59, 69, 72, 77, 90, 91, 95, 96, 110, 118, 127, 131, 132, 136, 142, 151, 152, 154
Dexter, Amelia 23
Dexter, James 12
Dexter, Samuel 66
Dexter, Judge Samuel William 22, 23, 65, 66, 68, 109, 126
Dickey, Charles 119
Dickson, the Rev. Moses 89, 90, 149, 150
Disenfranchisement 32
Dodge, Silas W. 64, 113
Dolarson, George 91
Dolbeare, the Rev. Jeremiah 50, 134
Donihoo, John 78–79
Donihoo, Martha Walker 78–79
Doremus, Jacob 26
Dougherty, Samuel 69
Douglas, Sen. Stephen 148
Douglass, Frederick 80, 84, 86, 98, 118, 147, 150, 155, *156*, 157, 158, 164; *see also* Chatham Convention
Dred Scott v Sanford 139, 148–149
Dresser, Amos 41, 103
Drew, Benjamin 140, 169
Dumond, Dwight 164
Duncan, Delamore 48, 64
Duncan, William 48
Dunn, David 110
Dunn, Esther *see* Gillet, Esther Dunn

East, Joel 63
East Indies 103
Edgerton, Joseph 114
Edgerton, Mary 114
1820 Missouri Compromise 148
elections 66, 93, 148; (1840) 71; (1844) 97, 98; (1848) 119; (1850) 123; (1860) 153, 158, 159

Elgin Association 127
Elliot, W.S. 63
Ellyson, Zachariah 63
Emancipation Proclamation 162
The Emancipator 40
England 20, 95, 125, 128, 132, 158;
   London 160; *see also* Great Britian
English, Annetta 168
English Barracks 131
The Erie 77
Erie Canal 18, 32, 105
Evans, James 109, 152
Evans, John 109, 152

Fairbank, the Rev. Calvin 120, 124,
   160, 168
Fairchild, Harriet Eliza *see* Kedzie,
   Harriet Eliza Fairchild
Fairfield, John 129, 130, 131, 132,
   134, 136, *137*, 139, 142, 166, 167
Farley family 80
Felch, Nancy Beckley 73
Felch, Sabin 73, 75, 118, 169
Female Anti-Slavery Society of
   Grand Prairie 124
Female Anti-Slavery Society of
   Philadelphia 41
Ferguson, Dr. Joseph 155
Ferguson family 107
Ferry, Col. Peter P. 14
Fillmore, Calvin T. 66
Fillmore, Pres. Millard 66, 68, 121
Finney, Charles Grandison 18, 36,
   39, 40, 166; disciples of 18, 36
Finney, Seymour 79, *88*, 90, 91, 146
Fish, Catherine A. 40
Fitch, Abel 66
Fitch, Abijah 66
Fitch, Jabez S. 64, 65, 68
Florida 10, 99, 158, 161, 163
Foote, the Rev. Charles C. 68, 79,
   80, 91, 118, 119, 127
Foote, Dr. Henry K. 80
Foote, Minerva Henderson 80
Forth, Scipio 14, 29
Foster, Abby Kelley 99, 146, 147
Foster, Dwight 66
Foster, the Rev. Gustavus Lemuel
   123, 124
Foster, Joseph 84
Foster, Mary E. Lowry 94
Foster, Prior 84
Foster, Samuel 23, 66, 68, 97, 103,
   123
Foster, Seymour 103
Foster, Stephen S. 146, 147
Foster, Theodore Raeljeph 12, 22,
   23, 58, 68, 103, 123, 166–167;
   Judge Dexter 23, 66, 68; Liberty
   Party 98, 103; Michigan State
   Anti-Slavery Society 42, 75, 98,
   103, 169; Presbyterianism 26,
   102, 103; *The Signal of Liberty* 49,
   58, 59, *67*, 71, 97, 103, 117–118;
   Underground Railroad 23, 24,
   65, 72; *see also* Signal of Liberty
Fowler 142
Fowler, Deacon 69

Fowler, Joseph 16
Francisco, Henry 65, 66, 118
Free African Society 12
Free Soil party 117, 118, 119, 123,
   139, 159, 168
The Freedom's Journal 14
Freeman 69
Freeman, Thomas 159
French, Caroline 29, 30, 85
French, George 29, 30, 85
Friends of Human Progress 60
"Friends of Humanity in Michigan"
   127
From Slavery to Freedom 1
Frost, Karolyn Smardz 2
Fugitive Slave Act/Law: of 1850 3,
   12, 34, 121, 122, 123, 124, 125,
   126, 128, 129, 140, 141, 158, 164,
   167; Michigan reactions 122, 123,
   124, 125, 126, 128, 129; of 1793 12
Fugitive Slave Law and Its Victims
   124
Fuller, Edwin 74, 79, 141, 143, 164
Fuller, Harriet deGarmo 74, 79,
   141, 143, 147, 164

Gag rule 50
Gaines, Mr. and Mrs. 83, 142
Gallup, Dr. John C. 74, 82, 98
Galpin, Emily 51
Gara, Larry 1
Gardner, Joel 64
Gardner, William 64
Garland, C.J. 75, 169
Garnet, H.H. 84
Garrison, William Lloyd 25, 36,
   37, 39, 47; Chatham Convention
   156; John Brown 148, 155; *Libera-
   tor* 36, 37; Michigan 66, 145, 147;
   morals vs. politics 70, 73, 98,
   139, 146
Geddes, Albert H. 68
Geddes, John 22, 24, 65, 68
Geddes, Judge Norman 93, 95
*The Genius of Universal Emancipa-
   tion* 36, 42
George and Clara 77, 78
Georgia 124, 152, 161; Augusta 46,
   50; Decatur 128
Gidley, Townsend E. 65
Gilbert, Almira Reed 133
Gilbert, Warren 93, 133, 149
Gill, George R. 149, 150
Gillet, Amasa 46, *46*, 48, 49, 50
Gillet, Esther Dunn 49
Gilmour, William 81
Giltner, Francis 107, 114, 119
Giltner v Gorham see Crosswhite
   trial
Glasier, Robert Barclay 25, 147, 148
Glazier, Anna Hutchings 25
Glazier, Elizabeth C. 25
Glazier, Mary 25
Glazier, Richard Bunker 25, 40,
   147, 150
Glazier, Richard, Jr. 25
Glazier family 21, 151, 161, 164
Goodell, Jotham 16, 141, 142, 166

Goodell, Mary Jane 141
Goodell, Sarah Jane 141
Goodell, Solon 16, 96
Goodell, William 9, 70, 98
Goodnow, Lyman 69, 171
Gordon, David 122, 125, 126, 143
Gordon, Mrs. David 122
Gordon, J. Wright 119
Gordon, Margaret 123
Gordon, Richard 120
Gordon Hall 66
Gorham, Charles T. 65, 108, 114, 146
Gorton, David 24, 169
Gorton, Eliza Comstock 24
Gorton, Job 24
Gorton, Samuel 9, 24
Gradual Abolition Law 27
Gragston, Arnold 162, 163
Granger, Mr. 16
Graves, Jack 112
Graves, John 112, 120
Graves, Joseph 112
Graves, Milton W. 110, 112, 120
Great Britain 10, 17, 40, 109; *see also*
   England
The Great Compromise 10
Great Sauk Trail *see* Chicago Turn-
   pike
Green, Liberetta Lerich *see* Lerich,
   Liberetta
Griffing, Josephine S. 161
Grimké, Angelina 39
Grimké, Sarah 39
Guinea 31, 39
Gunn, Samuel S. 87
Gurney, Chester 21, 59, 75, 98,
   100, 169

Hackett, Calvin 108
Hackett, Nelson 85
Hale, John P. 117
Hall, Charles R. 69
Hall, Reuben L. 93
Hallock, Horace 65, 91, 110, 117
Hamilton, Elsie *see* Willis, Jane
Hamilton, George 109
Hamilton, Willis *see* Willis, Bill
Hamilton College 43
Hamlet, James 124
Harpers Ferry Raid 21, 87, 153; *see
   also* Brown, John
Harris, John 61, 141
Harris, Susanna 63
Harrison, Pres. William Henry 31,
   71
Hart, A.W. 82
Harwood, Janice 134
Harwood, William Webb 22, 23,
   66, 74, 75, 130, *130*, 134, *135*,
   164
Haskell, Rev. 69
Hastings, Charles 80
Hastings, Eurotas P. 42
Hatch, Eunice Morton Lambie 136
Hatfield, Deacon John 129, 132, 141,
   142, 169
Haviland, Charles 22, 42, 43, 51, 159
Haviland, Laura Smith 22, 41, 51

52, 114, *106*, 122–123, 125, 129, 131, 132, 147, 154, 160, 161; Canada 128, 131, 134, 160; Elsie and Willis Hamilton 50, 51; Henry Bibb 128, 140; James Martin 50, 51; John Chester 51, 122–123; kidnapping attempt of John White 105, 114, 143, 169; Logan Female Anti-Slavery Society 42; Quakerism 42, 164; Raisin Institute 24, 42, 43, 50, 51, 134, 160, 162; Underground Railroad 52, 61, 126, 159, 160, 164, 166, 167; Wesleyan Methodism 74

Haviland, Martha 24
Hawkins, Horace 33, 34
Helms, Stephen Decatur 51
Henderson, Thomas 114
Henson, Josiah 34, 97, 167
Hewitt, Joseph 84
Hicks, Elias 21
Hicks, Olive Beckley 73
Hicks, Sumner 73
Higginson, the Rev. Thomas Wentworth 157
Hill, Caroline 116, 117, 121, 172
Hill, Lewis *44*, 46, 47, 48, 49, *49*, 50, 56, 60, 61, 65
Hiram 161
Hiram Wilson School 34
Historic American Buildings Survey (HABS) 61, 66
Hoag, George 65
Hoag, H.P. 85
Hoag, William 65
Hobart, Justice Randall 108
Holley, Sallie 145, 146, 147
Holmes, Silas M. 65, 74, 91
Holright, Elizabeth *see* Chase, Elizabeth Holright
Home Missionary Society 25, 26
Howard, Edward 7
Howard, Jacob Merritt 20
Howe, Dr. Samuel Gridley 34, 155, 157
Hudnell, Ezekiel K. 15
Hull, John Wesley 93, 94
Hull, Mary Bartlett 93, 94
Hull, Sylvanus 93, 94
Hull, Gen. William 41
Humphrey, the Rev. Luther 20, 21
Hunt, Deacon Timothy 24, 96
Hunt, Mrs. Timothy 96
The Huntsville Advocate 125
Hurd, Jarvis 114
Huron River 16, 23, 25, 61, 69, 72, 141
Hussey, Erastus 19, 25, *57*, *60*, 118, 146; the "Beautiful Girl" 62; John Cross 57; Kentucky raid 112–113; Liberty Press 118; Michigan State Anti-Slavery Society 75; personal liberty laws 124; Underground Railroad activities 19, 21, 57, 58, 59, 61, 63, 64, 65, 66, 68, 118, 126, 162, 169
Hussey, Sarah 60, 62, 64

Hussey, Susan *53*, 55, *60*, 62, 64
Husting (office of) 60

Illenden, Mary Rulon 147
Illenden, Richard 147
Illinois 2, 10, 18, 19, 28, 47, 55, 56, 57, 60, 76, 84, 99, 103, 124, 128, 131, 140, 141, 148, 154, 155, 160, 163; Alton 28, 69; Carbondale 154; Chicago 19, 47, 55, 77, 98, 105, 140, 148, 155, 156; Knox County 99; Naperville 69; Quincy 99, 151; Shawneetown 124; *see also Alton Observer* fire
Illinois Central Railroad 154
Indiana 2, 7, 10, 12, 18, 28, 31, 32, 46, 47, 48, 51, 55, 56, 57, 58, 60, 62, 100, 103, 105, 110, 114, 121, 126, 130, 131, 132, 150, 152, 159, 161, 163, 164, 168; Bristol 112; Brookville 7; Cass County 62; Cassopolis 100, 111, 112, 120; Door Village 87; Economy 47; Fort Wayne 7, 126; Fountain City 72; Grant County 46; Jonesborough 110, 122; Kenton County 112; LaGrange 53, 100; LaPorte 69, 87; Lawrenceburg 120; Madison 30, 31, 114, 124, 128; Newport (Fountain City) 130; Richmond 7, 34; South Bend 120; Terre Haute 76, 128; Territory 13; Three Rivers 100; Turkey Prairie 111; Vincennes 76; Wayne County 47, 63
Ingersoll, George 65, 108, 146
International Order of Twelve of the Knights and Daughters of Tabor *see* Knights and Daughters of Tabor
Iowa 155; Farma County 63; Grinnell 155; Tabor 155
Ira 161
Isom *see* Saby and Isom
I've Got a Home in Glory Land 2

Jackson, Pres. Andrew 15, 36
Jackson, John 155
Jackson, Milldred 35
Jackson, William W. 84
James 77
Jaxon, Peter 80
Jeffers, Deodat 103
Jefferson, Pres. Thomas 14
Jefferson Circuit 132
Jenkins, William Baldwin 20, 47
Jim 31, 160
Johnson, Beverly *see* Williams, James
Johnson, Edwin 65
Johnson, Matthew 138
Johnson, Nathan 136, 138
Johnson, Col. Oliver 8
Johnson family 120
Jones, Absalom 12
Jones, Bill 116
Jones, John 155
Jones, Richard 27

Jones, Wharton 109
Jones, William 63, 156
Jonesboro, IL 154
Joseph 161
Joy, James F. 141
Jurst, William 143

Kagi, John 150, 157
Kanouse, the Rev. John George 25, 25, 96
Kanouse, the Rev. Peter 25
Kansas 41, 140, 148, 150, 155, 156, 157; Territory 140; Topeka 155
Kansas-Nebraska Act 148
Katz, Elizabeth Harwood 134
Katzmann, David 159
Kedzie, Harriet Eliza Fairchild 143
Kedzie, Dr. Robert C. 143
Kelley, Abby *see* Foster, Abby Kelley
Kenny, Munnis 26
Kentucky 7, 12, 15, 34, 36, 45, 47, 48, 57, 62, 64, 69, 86, 107, 109, 111, 112, 113, 114, 119, 124, 126, 128, 129, 152, 154, 159, 160, 152, 153; Bedford 35; Boone County 110, 142, 153, 163; Bourbon County 34, 107, 169; Carlisle 12; Carroll County 108; Covington 110; Danville 93; Frankfort 78, 92; Gerrard County 151; Greenup County 110; Harrisons County 15; Kenton County 110, 163; Louisville 29, 83; Madison 36; Madison County 150; Mason County 162, 163; Maysville 34; Newport 33; Paris 76; Rising Sun 114; Shelby County 35; Taylor Port 142; Trimball County 108
Kentucky Abolition Society 12
Kentucky Raid of 1847 111, 112
Keys 48
Kightlinger, Jacob 99
King, Jane 139
King, John W. 75, 82, 169
King, the Rev. William 127
Kinne, Malinda 97
Kirkland, Caroline 19, 20, 43
Kirkland, William 19, 20, 43
Knights and Daughters of Liberty 149
Knights and Daughters of Tabor 89
Knights of Liberty 150, 162

Ladies Anti-Slavery Society 43, 86
The Lady of the Lake 24
Lake Erie 2, 16, 40, 18, 24, 76, 77, 78, 162, 164
Lake Huron 2, 76
Lake Michigan 2, 76
Lake Ontario 34, 132
Lambert, William 85, 87, 120, 131; Convention of Colored Citizens 30, 84; Detroit 30, 60, 91; John Brown 30, 155; John Fairfield 131–132; Michigan State Anti-Slavery Society 71; secret societies and rituals 88, 89, 90, 162;

Underground Railroad 30, 60, 90, 91, 142, 149, 166;
Lane Agency Scheme 39
Lane Debates 40, 50
Lane Rebels 39
Lane Theological Seminary 37, 39, 40, 41, 45
Lansing, F.M. 102
Lapham, Ethan 21, 25, 80, 147
Larned, General 26
Larzelere, Elizabeth 32, 94
Law to Regulate Blacks and Mulattoes 27
Lawson 32
Lay, Ezra Dennison 96, 97
Lay, Malinda Kinne 97
Lay, William H. 97
Lay, Zina 96
Layne, George 48
League of Gileadites 87, 149
League of Liberty Society 156
Lee, Ishmael 63, 113
Lerich, Liberetta 79, 80
Lerich, Peter 79, 80
Lerich, Sarah Fishbaugh 79, 80
Lerich, Will 79
Lewis 36
Lewis, George 71, 72
Lewis, Pierce 18
The Liberator 36, 37, 99, 146
Liberia 120, 158
the *Liberty Line* 1
Liberty party 40, 45, 66, 68, 70, 71, 74, 75, 82, 84, 86, 97, 98, 101, 103, 105, 108, 109, 117, 118, 119, 147, 166, 168
Life and Letters of John Brown 88
Life of an American Slave 86
Lightfoot, James 34
Lightfoot, Madison J. 29, 30, 34, 71, 87, 120
Lightfoot, Tabitha 29, 30
Lincoln, Pres. Abraham 153, 159, 161, 162
Lodi Academy 95
Logan Female Anti-Slavery Society 41, 42
Loomis, Albert 136
Louisiana 12, 45, 86, 97, 160, 161; New Orleans 51, 103, 142; Purgoo plantation 141
Lovejoy, Elijah 28, 157
Lowry, Captain John 24, 79, 94, *94*, 96, 126, 148, 164, 166
Lowry, John Peter 56, 93, 95
Lowry, Mary E. *see* Foster, Mary E. Lowry
Lowry, Peter 95
Lowry, Rhoda Comstock 95
Lowry, Robert James 95
Lowry, Sylvia 94
Lowy, John *see* Lowry, John
Lucy 151
Lundy, Benjamin 36, 42, 47
Lutheran churches: Zion Lutheran Church 32
Lutheranism 31, 32; German Lutherans 32

Lyons, William 140

Mackenzie 131
Mahan, the Rev. Asa 39, 41, 103, 159
Maine 53, 159
Mallory, Joseph *see* Hill, Lewis
Mandlin, Wright *see* Maudlin, Wright
A Manual of the Knights of Tabor, and Daughters of the Tabernacle, Including the Ceremonies of the Order, Constitutions, Installations, Dedications, and Funerals, with Forms, and the Taborian Drill and Tactics 90, 150
Marithew, William 80
Markwood 125
Marsh, the Rev. Justin 102
Marshall College 101
Martha 161
Martin, James 51
Maryland 7, 18, 32, 34, 100, 128, 139, 155, 156, 162; Baltimore 59, 124, 137
Mason, Sen. James 123
Masonic Lodge 26, 156
Massachusetts 18, 23, 37, 56, 66, 169; Boston 24, 36, 37, 39, 86, 105, 127, 145; Brookfield 66; Hadley 52; Richmond 60; Springfield 87
Master Tom 118, 119
Maten, James 120
Maudlin, Wright 62, 63, 68, 120, 121
Maumee River 7
Maumee Valley 7
May, Samuel J. 37, 124, 125
McAlister family 159
McAndrew, Dr. Helen 137, 138
McAndrew, William 137, 138
McArthur tavern 65, 66
McCarty, Samuel *see* Davis, the Rev. Samuel H.
McClain, Charles 160
McCoy, Anna 141, 142
McCoy, Emillia *see* McCoy, Milly
McCoy, George 61, 83, 141, 142, 172
McCoy, Henry 83
McCoy, Milly 61, 83, 141, 142, 172
McDeary [McGeary], George 150, 173
McDonnell, John 15
McGee, Judge Melville 58, 59
McGee, Thomas 58, 118
McIlvain, Ebenezer 63, 112, 113
McKinseyites 131
McKnight, Virgil 29
McQuerry, Washington 125
McRae, Norman 169
Meenan, Ernestine Flora Wilson 168
Men of Mysteries 91
Men of Oppression 83, 89, 162
Merritt, Charles 21, 64
Merritt, Joseph 21, 64, 146, 147
Merritt, Phoebe 64, 146
Methodism 126

Methodist churches: African American Methodist church 146; Colored Methodist Church 119; Colored Methodist Society 30; Methodist Episcopal 124; Methodist Episcopal Annual Conference 74; Methodist Episcopal Church 20, 49, 50, 74, 147; Plymouth Circuit (Methodist Episcopal Church) 74
Mexican-American War 117
Mexico 98, 118, 120
Michigan 1, 2, 3, 4, 8, 10, 12, 13, 15, 17, 18, 27, 28, 29, 31, 39, 40, 41, 42, 45, 47, 48, 49, 54, 55, 56, 58, 62, 64, 66, 68, 70, 71, 74, 79, 80, 81, 82, 83, 84, 85, 89, 91, 96, 98, 99, 100, 101, 103, 107, 108, 109, 111, 114, 118, 121, 122, 124, 125, 126, 127, 128, 131, 134, 139, 140, 141, 143, 145, 146, 147, 149, 150, 154, 155, 156, 159, 160, 161, 162, 163, 164, 165, 166, 167, 168, 169; Adams 132; Addison 84; Adrian 16, 19, 22, 24, 40, 41, 51, 52, 66, 74, 86, 92, 93, 95, 105, 114, 122, 125, 126, 128, 131, 133, 134, 145, 146, 147, 152, 154, 160, 161, 169; Alamo 40, Albion 58, 65; Allegan County 41; Anchor Bay 13; Ann Arbor 22, 23, 24, 25, 32, 40, 45, 49, 52, 59, 60, 61, 65, *67*, 68, 69, 70, 71, 72, 73, *73*, 74, 78, 79, 81, 86, 95, 102, 109, 117, 118, 123, 125, 126, 146, 147, 151, 153, 161, 162; Augusta 24, 122, 143; Battle Creek 19, 21, 53, 55, 57, 58, *60*, 62, 64, 65, 68, 101, 112, 113, 114, 118, 124, 125, 126, 145, 146, 152, 162; Bay City 71, 77; Beardsley's Prairie 20; Belle Arbor 80; Berrien 87; Berrien County 20, 42, 55, 56, 63, 77, 87, 112, 121, 165; Blackman 65; Bloomfield 80; Bois Blanc Island 33; Brady 64; Branch County 42, 75; Bridgewater 134; Brooklyn 134; Calhoun County 46, 48, 74, 121; Calvin 32, 47, 63, 110; Cambridge 130, 133; Cambridge Station 132; Canton 16; Cass 20, 32, 46, 47, 57, 58, 63, 77, 98, 110, 111, 112, 120, 121, 125, 158, 164, 168, 169; Cassopolis 57; Centreville 59, 100, 101; China 78; Chippewa County 28; Climax 64; Clinton 49, 93, 130; Clinton Station 138; Coldwater 53, 100, 132; Concord 58; Cooper's Corners 20; Crawford County 28; Detroit 2, 8, 13, 14, 15, 17, 18, 19, 22, 24, 25, 26, 28, 29, 30, 31, 32, 34, 37, 40, 42, 47, 55, 56, 57, 58, 60, 52, 65, 68, 70, 71, 76, 78, 79, 83, 84, 85, 86, 87, 89, 90, 91, 93, 96, 100, 108, 110, 116, 117, 120, 121, 123, 125, 126, 127, 128, 130, 131, 132, 135,

137, 139, 140, 141, 145, 146, 149, 151, 152, 154, 155, 156, 158, 159, 160, 152, 164, 166 168; Dexter 22, 23, 49, 65, 66, 68, 82, 103, 126; Diamond Lake 112; Dundee 41; East Bloomfield 80; Eaton County 108, 145; Eaton Rapids 145; Farmington 147, 168; Farmington (Quakertown) 24, 45, 80, 81, 93; Flint 59, 75, 81, 82, 86, 110; Flowerfield 63, 64, 113; Fort Gratiot 30, 78; Foster's Station (Washtenaw County) 68; Francisco 65, 66; Freedom 135; Galesburg 53; Garden City 19; Geddesburg (Ann Arbor) 22, 24, 65; Genesee 75, 169; Genesee County 74, 75, 78, 81, 82, 98; Gibraltar 33; Grand Rapids 118, 149, 158; Grand River/Ionia 75; Grass Lake 65; Grosse Ile 15, 93; Harmonia (Calhoun County) 145; Harrison 14; Hillsdale County 74, 126, 132; Homer 82, 101; Houghton 128; Hudson 51; Isabella County 158; Jackson 46, 48, 49, 58, 60, 65, 70, 71, 72, 74, 75, 84, 118, 123, 126; Jackson County 32, 46, 48, 58, 74, 105, 165; Jonesville 126, 132, 146; Kalamazoo 48, 52, 64, 108, 169; Kalamazoo County 42, 46, 48, 64, 98; Lake Harbor 99; Lansing 145, 166; Lapeer County 80; Lapham's Corners (Farmington) 80; Lawrence 20; legislature 120; Lenawee County 20, 41, 42, 45, 74, 75, 93, 105, 127, 132, 157, 159; Leoni 66, 74; Livingston County 19, 42; Livonia 143; Lockport 69; Lodi 25, 94, 96, 102, 126; Lodi Plains 93, 95; Logan (Adrian) 41; London 52; Macomb County 45, 78, 79, 80; Madison 66; Manchester 32, 60, 71, 74, 134, 168; Marine City 78; Marshall 26, 59, 64, 65, 84, 98, 101, 107, 111, 114, 119, 128, 146, 168; Mecosta County 152, 158; Milford 80; Monroe (Frenchtown) 8, 14, 19, 28, 40, 51, 55, 82, 100, 126; Monroe County 42, 52, 55, 93; Mooreville (Washtenaw County) 168; Moscow 32; Mt. Clemens 49, 78, 79; Nankin (Plymouth) 19, 21, 74; Nankin Mills (Livonia) 19; Napoleon 160; New Buffalo 77; Newport 111; Niles 42, 63, 87; North Adams 132; Nutting's Corner (Lodi) 24, 95; Oakland 98; Oakland County 28, 42, 45, 55, 78, 80, 81, 151; Oshtemo 52; Owosso 82; Paint Creek 24; Palmyra 40; Parma 65; Penn 63; Pinckney 20; Pittsfield 71, 74, 75, 126, 132, 134, 135; Plainfield 26; Plymouth 19, 65, 68, 74, 75, 93; Pokagon Prairie

20, 47; Pontiac 14, 43, 79, 98, 126; Port Huron 33, 77, 78, 79; Porter 112; Prairie Ronde 53; Quaker County 45; Quincy 132; Raisin 51; Ramptown 112; Rawsonville 137; Remus 158; Rochester 150; Rollin 151, 161; Rome 93, 132, 133; Romulus 74; Saginaw 82; Saginaw County 82; St. Clair 45, 76, 78, 79, 142; St. Clair County 28, 42; St. Joseph 77; St. Joseph County 42, 63, 98; Salem 25, 86; Saline 61, 86, 93, 94, 134, 152; Schoolcraft 46, 47, 56, 58, 63, 64, *67*, 113, 126, 162; Schwarzburg 19, 65, 68; Scio 22, 23, 42, 65, 66, 68, 103, 166; Sharon *46*, 49; Sharon Hollow 49, 50; Shelby 89; Shiawassee County 82, 95; Spring Arbor 58; statehood 28; Stockbridge 65; Stoney Creek 25; Superior 16, 97, 141, 142; Sylvan 94; Tecumseh 19, 93, 125; Trenton 16, 33, 93, 138, 142; Troy 80; Unadilla 26; Union City 40, 53, 100; Van Buren 21; Van Buren County 98; Vandalia 48, 111; Vermontville 143; Vicksburg 64; Washtenaw County 2, 3, 17, 21, 22, 23, 24, 26, 29, 31, 32, 42, 45, 46, 50, 55, 66, 68, 84, 93, 96, 100, 105, 121, 127, 130, 132, 136, 143, 149, 166, 168; Waterloo 14; Wayne County 14, 19, 28, 29, 42, 45, 55, 61, 75, 77, 121, 138, 158; Webster 23, 42, 66, 68, 103; Wheatland 51, 132, 133; White Pigeon 59, 82, 100; Williamsburg 62; Wolf Creek 74; Wright 133; Wyandotte 33, 141, 142; York 168; York 16; Young's Prairie 48, 109, 111, 169; Ypsilanti 22, 23, 24, 25, 51, 61, 65, 68, 74, 93, 96, 117, 122, 130, 132, 134, 136, 137, 139, 141, 142, 146, 147, 148, 149, 151, 152, 169; Zug Island 91

The Michigan 34
Michigan Anti-Slavery Society 141, 143, 147, 148, 167
The Michigan Argus 45, 120
Michigan Central Railroad 60, 61, 89
The Michigan Freeman 70
Michigan Friends of Human Progress 145
The Michigan Liberty Press 118
Michigan Southern Railway 53
Michigan State Anti-Slavery Society 40, 42, 43, 45, 53, 68, 70, 71, 75, 81, 83, 84, 85, 93, 98, 73, 101, 102, 103, 108, 117, 169, 183
Michigan State Liberty Convention 118
Michigan State Pioneer Society 94
Michigan Territory 8, 13, 14, 25, 31, 40, 68
Michigan Union College 74

Michigan Wesleyan Anti-Slavery Society 50
Middle Rouge River 19
Midnight (Detroit, MI) *17*, 129, 130
Miles, Mary *see* Bibb, Mary Miles
Millard, Esther Bowen 68, 103
Millard, Isaac 154
Millard, Lucy 151, 152, 154
Millard, Solomon Nelson 151, 152
Mills, Asa 23
Mills, Daniel A. 60
Mills, Loren 23
Mills, the Rev. Louis 21
Mills Brothers Band 26
Mission Institute 99
Mississippi 97, 110, 116, 128, 161
Mississippi River 28, 151, 72, 89, 99
Mississippi Valley 97, 139
Missouri 47, 53, 55, 56, 72, 99, 109, 139, 141, 148, 149, 150, 151, 152, 155, 158; St. Louis 69, 72, 73, 87, 88, 90, 110, 141, 149; Supreme Court 148
Missouri River 141
Mitchell, William 160
Mitchum 124, 125
Miter, John 103
Modlin, Wright *see* Maudlin, Wright
Monroe, Mrs. 153, *154,* 173
Monroe, the Rev. William Charles 30, 71, 84, 85, 87, 90, 155, 156, 158
Montague, Henry M. 52, 53
Montieth, the Rev. John 8, 19, 40
Moore, E. 149
Moore, William 24, 168
Morris, Jonathan 133
Morris, Sophia 133
Morrison, J. 169
Morse, Planter 114
Morton, Maria 136
Mott, Abigail 64
Mott, Elijah 113
Mott, Isaac 59,
Mott, Lucretia Coffin 41, 118
Mott, Lydia 64
Mott, Uriah 65
Myers, John 164
the Mystery 90, 149

Nancy 7, 8
Naramoor, John 79
National Anti-Slavery Standard 147
National Convention of Colored Citizens 84
The National Era 123
Nebraska 148, 155; Nebraska Territory 140
Negroes in Michigan During the Civil War 169
New England 2, 10, 17, 18, 27, 37, 39, 84, 86, 98, 124, 127, 145
New England Anti-Slavery Society 37
New Hampshire 24, 159; Keene 105
A New Home—Who'll Follow? 20

New Jersey 13, 18, 30, 32, 36, 80, 131; Oldwick 32; Perth Amboy 137; Raritan Valley 32; Rockaway 25; Somerset County 32
New Mexico 109, 118, 121
New York 2, 10, 13, 18, 23, 24, 27, 31, 32, 36, 39, 40, 42, 55, 56, 66, 81, 84, 96, 98, 136, 137, 140, 145, 146, 156; Albany 70; Buffalo 18, 77, 78, 84, 87, 118, 124, 128; Canandaigua 27, 133; Cayuga County 19; Dunkirk 77; Genesee County 18; Jefferson County 16, 132; New York City 70; Newark 25; Onondaga County 95; Ontario 49; Ontario County 27, 134; Otsego County 24; Ovid 96; Palmyra 19; Rochester 124, 128; Utica 36, 39, 70, 74, 147
New York Anti-Slavery Society 39
New York Committee of Vigilance 84
New York Liberty Party 117
New York Manumission Society 27
The New York Observer 92
Niagara Falls 34, 127
Nichols, Samuel S. 64, 68
Nicholson, Thompson 63
Noble, Nathaniel 23
Noble, Pamela 95, 126
Noble, Samuel Burrell 74, 109, 123, 126, 166
Noble, Sylvanus 23
Noble, Sylvester D. 23, 75, 125, 126, 169
Non-denominational or unspecified churches: Free Church 161; Protestant churches 101; Protestant Society 19; Spiritualist Church 145; Union Church 171; Vine Street Church 84
Norris, John 120, 121
Norris, Justus 149
Norris, Lyman Decatur 148, 149
North Carolina 12, 32, 54, 63, 123, 149, 159
The North Star 90, 119, 147
Northrop, the Rev. Henry Horatio 1, 21, 59, 81, 82, 100, 101, 166
Northwest Ordinance of 1787 10, 13, 28
Northwest Territory 7, 12, 13, 27, 28, 85, 143, 164
Nubia 32
Nutting, Prof. Rufus 80, 81, 96
Nutting Academy 95

The Oakland Gazette 80
Oberlin College 39, 41, 50, 84, 124, 143; Theological Seminary 41
Observer and Telegraph 37
Ockro see Ockrow
Ockron see Ockrow
Ockrow, Henry (Harry) 32, 71, 159, 167
Ockrow, Jane 32, 167
Ockrow, Nelson 105, 159, 172
O'Hara, (O'Harra) Keen 92, 93

Ohio 2, 10, 12, 15, 17, 18, 20, 37, 39, 40, 41, 42, 43, 57, 61, 71, 84, 88, 92, 98, 105, 124, 125, 126, 129, 130, 133, 140, 142, 143, 154, 159, 160, 162, 163, 164, 166, 169; Brown County 40; Chillicothe 154; Cincinnati 13, 28, 33, 34, 37, 45, 83, 85, 89, 110, 114, 116, 126, 129, 132, 141, 142, 169; Cleveland 78, 146, 149, 156, 160; Columbiana County 133; Columbus 34, 128; Dayton 85; Defiance 7; Elyria 40; Erie County 37; Hamilton 110; Hamilton County 109; Hudson 37, 41; Huron County 37; Lake Erie 40; Logan County 109; Milard 149; Mount Pleasant 47, 48; New Richmond 153; Norwalk 149; Oberlin 78; Perrysburg 45; Putnam 50; Ripley 12, 39, 40, 78, 124, 163; Salem 161; Sandusky 34, 49, 78, 93, 116, 125, 126, 139, 151; Sandusky City 149; Springfield 34, 116; Stark County 40; Toledo 34, 52, 93, 108, 126
Ohio River 7, 12, 29, 30, 33, 35, 45, 46, 78, 83, 89, 93, 100, 110, 116, 129, 153, 162, 168
Ohio University 20
Old Agnes 55
Old Slave Mart, Charleston (SC) 11
Olivet College 41
Oneida Institute 56
Order of Emigration 89
Order of Knights 149
Orders of Mystery 90
Oregon 120
Orr, John 87
Osband family 74
Osborn, Charles 63, 112
Osborn, the Rev. Charles W. 12, 47, 164, 166
Osborn, Ellison 63
Osborn, Jefferson 47, 63
Osborn, Jordan 62
Osborn, Josiah 46, 47, 48, 57, 63, 112
Osborn, Leander 47
Osborn, Parker 63
Osborne, William 150
Ottawa Indians 7, 41
Owen, John 79

Paris, Jane 76
Paris, Malinda Robinson 76, 78, 173
Paris, William 76
Parker, James H. 133
Parker, Mrs. 133
Parker, S. Lucius 103
Parker, the Rev. Theodore 157
Parker, William 114
Patchin, John 50, 51
Patterson, Moses 108
Peace Congress 162
Pearce 161
The Pearl 142
Peleg 161

Pelham 165
Pennsylvania 10, 13, 18, 24, 32, 36, 39, 55, 56, 95, 99, 124, 133; Beaver County 133; Brownsville 87; Harrisburg 99; Philadelphia 12, 37, 41, 128; Pittsburgh 90, 152; Randolph 41; Wilkes-Barre 56
The Pennsylvania Freeman 86
Pennsylvania Society for Promoting the Abolition of Slavery, the Relief of Free Negroes Unlawfully Held in Bondage, and for Improving the Condition of the African Race 10, 12
People of Color in Philadelphia 84
Perry, William 61, 62
Personal Liberty Law 124
The Philanthropist 47, 85
Philips, Anthony 50, 60, 173
Phillips, Jay 79
Phillips, Wendell 31, 159
The Phoebus 34
The Phoenix 132
Pierce, J.J. 149
Pilcher, the Rev. Elijah 20, 123, 166
Pillsbury, Parker 146, 161
Pinkerton, Allan 155
Polk, Pres. James K. 95, 97, 105, 107, 111, 117
population 1, 14, 18, 28, 79, 118, 121, 124, 128, 158, 164 ; African-American 14, 28, 55, 121, 124, 128, 136, 140, 165, 158, 159, 166, 168
Porter, Dr. Arthur 70, 75, 85, 118, 169
Porter, George F. 45, 119
Porter, Maria 150
Potomac River 156
Pottawatomie Indians 41
Powell, David 120
Powell, George 120
Powell, James 120
Powell, Lewis 120
Powell, Lucy 120
Power, Arthur 21, 80, 140, 164
Power, Nathan 21, 43, 80, 164
Pratt 152
Pratt, Judge Abner 26, 101
Presbyterian churches: Ann Arbor First Presbyterian Church 42; First Presbyterian Church of Detroit 101; First Presbyterian Church of Lodi 102; First Presbyterian Church of Monroe 8; First Presbyterian Church of Webster 26, 103; First Presbyterian Church of Ypsilanti 123; Lodi Presbyterian Church 96; Presbyterian Church in Dexter 26; Presbyterian Church in White Pigeon 101; Presbyterian Church of New England 20; Presbyterian Church of Saline 25; Presbyterian Church Session of Lodi 102; Saline Presbyterian Church 96; Session of the Presbyterian Church 102;

Washtenaw Presbytery 42; Ypsilanti Presbyterian Church 25
Presbyterianism 19, 21, 26, 96, 99, 101, 134
Prescott family 142
Preston, Ann Eliza Morris 133
Preston, the Rev. Caleb M. 133
Preston, Jacob 135
Preston, Mehitable 134
Preston, Roswell, Jr. 126, 130, 134, 135, 164
Preston, William 133
Price and Allen 14
Prier, William E. 42
The Provincial Freeman 128, 140, 148
Provisional Government 156
Puritans 166
Putman, John W. 136
Putnam, Caroline 145

Quaker churches: Adrian Monthly Meeting 24; Evangelical Quakers 21, 22; Genesee Yearly Meeting 22; Hicksite Nankin Meeting 21; Hicksite Quakers 21, 22, 24, 42, 64, 147; Hicksites of Battle Creek (Milton Preparative Meeting), Plymouth Monthly Meeting 21; Hooker Friends 65; Nantucket Friends 25; North Carolina Quakers 47; Quarterly Meetings of the New York State, Upper, Canada, and Michigan 22; Raisin Valley Friends Meeting House 22; Society of Friends 21, 47; Yearly Meetings Indiana 22; Yearly Meetings Ohio 22; Ypsilanti Evangelical Friends Church 169; Ypsilanti Friends Church 24
Quakerism 2, 3, 7, 12, 17, 21, 22, 24, 25, 32, 34, 42, 43, 46, 47, 48, 51, 56, 57, 59, 61, 62, 63, 64, 65, 68, 74, 80, 93, 109, 110, 111, 112, 113, 114, 126, 128, 129, 131, 132, 133, 142, 146, 147, 148, 151, 155, 161, 164, 166, 169
Quarrls, Caroline 69, 71, 72, *73*
Quarrls, Robert Prior 69
Queen's Dominion *see* Canada
Quist, John W. 118

Rachel, Aunt 48
Raisin Institute 41, 43, 50, 51, 105, 134, 160
Rankin, the Rev. John 12, 39, 40, 79, 163
Rankin's Letters on Slavery 13
Raphael (poem) 95
Ray *see* Aray
Ray, Wright 114
Realf, Richard 88, 149
Reed, Almira *see* Gilbert, Almira Reed
Reed, Benjamin 26
Reed, Fitch 127, 130, 131, 132, 133, 134, 138, 159, 160
Reese, William P. 87

Refugee Home Society 127, 140
Refugees of Canada 59
Reign of Terror 37
Religious Society of Friends *see* Quakerism
Remond, Charles L. 84
Republican party 13, 66, 80, 119, 133, 153, 158, 159
Revolutionary War 8, 10, 27, 32, 37
Rexford, Roswell 75, 118, 160, 169
Reynolds 88, 149, 150
Reynolds, George J. 156
Reynolds, J.C. 60, 89
Reynolds, Susan 110
Rhode Island 9, 12, 23, 66, 151; Foster 68, 103; Providence 12; Providence Plantation 9
Rhode Island College 68
The Richmond Enquirer 140
Risdon, Orange 23
River Raisin 32, 49
Robinson, Marius 145, 146, 147
Robison, James 49
Romeo Academy 80
Roots, P.P. 50
Rose, Giles 125, 126
Ross, Amasa 80
Ross, Benjamin 160
Ross, Daniel 160
Ross, Richard 160
Rouge River 16, 61, 68, 91
Rous, Elizabeth *see* Comstock, Elizabeth Rous
Royce, Rufus *see* Royes, Rufus
Royes, Rufus 64
Roys, Rufus *see* Royes, Rufus
Ruggles, David 84
Ruggles, the Rev. Isaac W. 81
Rulon, Ephraim 147
Rulon, Mary *see* Illenden, Mary Rulon
Rulon, Sarah 147
Russell, William P. 84

Saby and Isom 7, 8, 14, 19, 28
Saginaw Bay (MI) 77
St. Clair, Arthur 13
St. Clair Academy 79
St. Clair River 33, 77
St. Joseph River 53
St. Louis Evening News 158
St. Matthew's Mission (Episcopal Church), Detroit 87
Samuel 161
Sanborn, Franklin Benjamin 87, 157
Sanders, Henry 28
Sanders, Sampson 109
Sandwich Islands 136
Sanford, Joseph 112, 169
Sanford, Perry 110, *111*, 112, 114, 125, 148
Schoolcraft 48
Schwarz, General John E. 19, 26, 75, 125
Scioto Gazette 154
Scotland 137
Scott, Dred 148, 149

Scott, Harriet 148, 149
Second Great Awakening 18, 36, 40
Secret Six, the 155, 157
the Seventy *see* Weld's Seventy
Seymour, Delia 103
Shafter, Hugh Morris 53
Shaw, Henry A. 145
Shaw, the Rev. Luther 80
Shea, Bill 78
Sheldon, Thomas 15
Sheley, Alanson 91
Shenandoah River 156
Shephard, Henry 63, 173
Shepherd, the Rev. Paul 41, 150, 157
Shipherd, John J. 41
Shugart, John 111, 112, 113
Shugart, Zachariah 51, 57, 63
Siebert, Dr. Wilbur 1, 19, 33, 59, 65, 76, 87, 140, 132, 162
The Signal of Liberty 50, 58, 59, 62, 63, 64, *67*, 68, 70, 71, 75, 82, 85, 86, 87, 92, 94, 97, 98, 99, 100, 103, 108, 109, 111, 117, 118, 126
Sinclair, the Rev. 102
S.J. 127
Skipworth, Joseph 114
slave codes 114
slave hunters (catchers) 15, 17, 24, 28, 46, 47, 62, 69, 72, 78, 79, 83, 88, 100, 125, 126, 129, 131, 135, 162
slave population 12, 120, 123, 149, 152, 162
"The Slave Ship" 42
Sloane, R. 125
Smalley, David 58
Smith, Andrew 53, 54
Smith, Daniel 22, 43
Smith, Gerrit 39, 66, 70, 92, 111, 118, 119, 147, 157, 164
Smith, Harvey 16, 41, 43
Smith, J.L. 105, 114, 169
Smith, James 114
Smith, Laura *see* Haviland, Laura Smith
Smith, Seth 102
Smith, Stephen 28
Solomon 114
South Carolina 9, 47; Charleston 9
Southern Confederacy 162
Southern Michigan Railroad 126
Spencer, John C. 27
Spofford, Sheriff Sumner F. 122, 125
Stanford, Joe 112
Stanton, Henry B. 39
Starkweather, John 141, 142, 147
Starkweather, Mary Ann 141, 142, 143, 147
Starkweather, Mary Jane *see* Starkweather, Mary Ann
State Anti-Slavery Convention 81
State Liberty Fund 94
Stearns, George Luther 157
Stebbins, Catherine 145
Stebbins, Francis R. 40
Stebbins, Giles B. 25, 40, 53, 94, 95, 103, 145, 147, 150, 151, 161
Stephens, Nelson 109

Stephens, Rube 112
Stevens, the Rev. A. 112, 169
Stevens, Benjamin 114, 169, 172
Stevens, Joe 118
Stevens, Nancy 57, 118
Stevens, Reuben 112
Stevens, Thomas, J. 128
Stewart, Charles Henry 45, 70, 98
Stewart family 120
Still, William 128
Stone, Nathan 80
Stone, Ned 107
Stono Rebellion 9
Stowe, Harriet Beecher 37, 143, 144
Straits of Mackinac 76
Strauther, Samuel 64, 68, 113
Streeter, Oliver 132
Streeter, Sereno 103
Stuart, Charles 37, 40, 70, 103
Sullivan, Nicholas 49, 68
Sullivan, the Rev. William 46, 48, 49, 65, 68, 74
The Sun 80
Sunday School Association (Detroit) 14
Sutherland, Langford farm 168
Swain brothers 12
Swift, Elizabeth *see* Chase, Elizabeth Swift Chase
Swift, George 74
Swift, the Rev. Marcus 19, 22, 74, 91, 136, 138
Switala, William J. 58
Sydenham River 97
Sylvester 72

T. Whitney 78
Tabb, Jack 162, 163
Tappan, Arthur 36, 147, 164
Tappan, Dr. Henry 162
Tappan, Lewis 36, 37, 39, 124, 147, 164
Taylor, Elder William 46, 48
Taylor, General 33
Taylor, Pres. Zachary 119, 121
Temperance 58, 65, 66, 72, 73, 74, 80, 85, 133, 138, 146
Temple and Tabernacle of the Knights and Daughters of Tabor 150
Tennessee 12, 28, 32, 36, 51, 122, 123, 154, 160; Fayette County 111; Jonesborough 51; Memphis 61
Tennessee Manumission Society 12, 47
Texas 89, 98, 118, 150, 158, 162
Thayer, John 80
Thayer, Dr. Stephen B. 48, 64, 68, 74
Thomas, Ella 59
Thomas, Dr. Jesse 48, 64
Thomas, Joseph S. 64
Thomas, Dr. Nathan Macy 46, 47, 48, 50, 53, 56, 57, 58, 62, 63, 64, 65, *67*, 68, 70, 71, 75, 98, 101, 113, 118, 150, 164, 165, 169
Thomas, Pamela 57, 64, *67*, 113, 120, 126, 162, 164

Thomas, Robert 28
Thomas, Susan 64
Thompson, Almon 143
Thompson, C.W. 152, 173
Thompson, Flora 136
Thompson, Florilla 159
Thompson, George 99
Thompson, the Rev. Oren Cook 45, 78, 79, 103
Titball 69
Titus, Captain T.J. 77
Todd, Mary 160
Tomlinson, the Rev. J.L. 159
Torrey, the Rev. Charles T. 100
Trall Institute 137
Treadwell, Seymour Boughton 45, 66, 70, 75, 98, 118, 169
Tripp, Henry 20, 159
Troutman, Francis 107, 108, 111, 114
Troy, the Rev. William 153
Truth, Sojourner 27, 61, 80, 145, *145*
Tubman, Harriet 167
Tucker, Catherine 13, 14
Tucker, George W. 90
Tucker, William 13, 14
Turner, Nat 28
Turner Rebellion 37
Tyler, Pres. John 71, 97

Uncle Tom's Cabin 37, 143, *144*, 145, *145*
Unconstitutionality of Slavery and the Fugitive Slave Law 123
Underground Railroad networks: Adrian-Tecumseh network 20; Central network 58; Cross network 68; Eastern network 58; Illinois network 58, 99; Indiana network 58; Indiana-Michigan network 57; Oberlin network 40; Port Huron-Pontiac-Detroit network 76–82; Wesleyan Methodist Network 93, 132, 162; Western network 58
United States Congress 13, 43, 50, 80, 98, 108, 109, 111, 140, 149
United States Constitution 10, 37, 97, 98, 99, 147, 148, 156, 166
United States League of Gileadites 87; *see also* League of Gileadites
United States Supreme Court 148, 149
University of Michigan 26, 148
Upton, Edward 65
Upton, Samuel 65
Utah 121

Van Buren, Pres. Martin 36, 119
Van Guinea, Aree 31
Van Guinea, Aree, Jr. 32
Van Guinea, Jora 31
Van Zandt, John 109
Vermont 10, 40, 53, 117, 124, 134; Vergennes 65
Vigilance Committees 87, 114
Virginia 7, 9, 12, 13, 22, 28, 49, 76, 79, 81, 100, 122, 123, 133, 136, 139, 142, 143, 149, 156, 158, 159,

161, 165; Charles Town 157; Fredericksburg 30; Richmond 152; Southampton County 28
Virginia Reserve 28
The Voice of the Fugitive 127, 128, 134
Volland, Jacob 60, 147
Volland, Sophia 147

Wade, Harvey 109
Wagoner, H.O. 155, 156
The Walk-in-the-Water 18
Walker, David 27, 37, 110
Walker, James W. 146
Walker, Jonathan 99, 100, 157
Walker, Martha *see* Donihoo, Martha
Walker, William 141
Walls, John Freeman 173
Walton, Cynthia 21, 25, 147
Walton, Jacob 21, 25, 147
War of 1812 14, 34, 41
Ward, Captain Eber 79, 142, 159
Washington, Booker T. 88
Washington, George 95, 125, 126, 167
Washington, Lewis 128
Washington, Martha 95, 125, 126, 167
Washington, Martha "Grandma" 131, 139, 172
Washington, DC 95, 107, 123
Washtenaw County Anti-Slavery Society 68
Washtenaw County Liberty Party 98, 117
Waters, John 79
Waters Road Cemetery 135
Watkins, Royal 32, 105, *107*, 114, 143, 163, 172
Watkins, Sally Carpenter 32, 105, 143
Watson, Walter 16
Wattles, Augustus 40, 103
Wattles, John 103
Watts, Catherine *see* Aray, Catherine Watts
Way 32
Wayne County (MI) Anti-Slavery Society 56
Wayne County (MI) Liberty Party 91
Webb, Dr. Ezekiel 80
Webb, William 155, *156*
Weed, the Rev. Ira Mason 21, 24, 25, 95, 100, 124
Welcome 161
Weld, Theodore 36, 37, 39, 40, 43, 56, 103, 147, 167, 166; disciples of 40, 41, 45, 166; Weld's Seventy 39, 40, 41, 43, 53, 55, 69, 99, 103
Wells, Deacon James B. 93, 133, 134
Wesley, John 147
Wesleyan Methodism 22, 40, 42, 74, 75, 101, 131, 132, 133, 134, 136, 138, 142, 147, 162, 166

Wesleyan Methodist churches: Ann Arbor District Wesleyan Methodist Conference 74; First and Second Wesleyan Society of the Township of Pittsfield 75; First Wesleyan Methodist Society 75; Wesleyan Church, Wright Township 133; Wesleyan Methodist Church of Pittsford 132; Wesleyan Methodist college 159; Wesleyan Methodist Michigan Conference 162; Wesleyan Methodist Society 74; Wesleyan Society and Church 133
West, Berthena 32
West Virginia 153, 157; Parkersburg 78
The Western Citizen 55
Western Reserve 28, 37
Western Reserve Anti-Slavery Society 41
Western Reserve College and Seminary 37, 41, 78, 80
Western Territories 139
westward expansion 17, 18, 22, 77
Wheatland Church of Christ of Remus 158
Whedon, Professor 26
Wheeler, William 63, 64, 113
Wheelwright, Miss. 39
Whig convention 25
Whig party 71, 80, 97, 98, 109, 117, 123, 133

Whipple, George 40, 40
White, Eber 126
White, Felix 143
White, Jane 114, 143, 169
White, John 32, 105, *107*, 114, 141, 143, 165, 169
White, Mary 143
Whitewater River 7
Whittier, John Greenleaf 95, 99
Wickham, Sylvia 95
Wilcox, Lonson 65
Wilkins, Judge Ross 122, 123
William 161
Williams, Charles 160
Williams, James 33, 152
Williams, Luke *38*
Williams, Mary 152
Williams, the Rev. Wolcott B. 56
Willibur, Captain 34
Willis, Bill 51, 61, 118, 122, 125
Willis, Henry 51, 64, 122, 145, 146, 166
Willis, Jane 51, 61, 122, 123, 125
Willis, Phoebe 64
Wilmot, David 98
Wilmot Proviso 98, 120, 121
Wilson, Aaron 80, 81, 168
Wilson, Eliza 154
Wilson, Ellen 80, 168
Wilson, the Rev. Hiram 34, 40, 97, 127; *see also* Hiram Wilson Institute 92
Wilson, John 154

Wilson, Sheriff 29
Wilson, William 155
Wisconsin 2, 10, 65, 69, 76, 80, 148, 159, 164; Pewaukee 69
Wise, Governor 158
Wisner, George W. 42, 80
Wisner, Moses 80
Witherell, James 15, 26
A Woman's Life-Work 50
Wood, Abijah 96
Wood, Darius S. 102
Wood, the Rev. Ira 96
Wood, Maryette 81, 82
Wood, Selleck 24, 95, 96
Wood, Stephen 57
Woodruff, William 64
Woodstock Manual Labor Institute 84
Woodward, Augustus B. 14
Work, Alanson 99
Wright, Elizur 37
Wright, Henry G. 146
Wright, Theodore S. 84

Young Men's Hall 159
Young Men's Liberty Association 74
Youngs, C.S. 75, 169

Zimmerman, John D. 40, 53, 54
Zug, Samuel 65, 91

4